Cambridge Series on Judgment and Decision Making

Decision Making in Health Care

WITHDRAWN

Decision making is a crucial element in the field of medicine. The physician has to determine what is wrong with the patient and recommend treatment, while the patient has to decide whether or not to seek medical care and whether to go along with the treatment recommended by the physician. Health policy makers and health insurers have to decide what to promote, what to discourage, and what to pay for. Together, these decisions determine the quality of health care that is provided. *Decision Making in Health Care* is an up-to-date, comprehensive overview of the field of medical decision making – a rapidly expanding field that includes quantitative theoretical tools for modeling decisions, psychological research on how decisions are actually made, and applied research on how physician and patient decision making can be improved.

Gretchen B. Chapman is Assistant Professor of Psychology at Rutgers University, where she is a member of the Health Psychology area.

Frank A. Sonnenberg is Associate Professor of Medicine at the Robert Wood Johnson Medical School of the University of Medicine and Dentistry of New Jersey and Medical Director of Clinical Information Systems of the Robert Wood Johnson University Medical Group.

Cambridge Series on Judgment and Decision Making

The purpose of the series is to convey the general principles of and findings about judgment and decision making to the many academic and professional fields to which these apply. The contributions are written by authorities in the field and supervised by highly qualified editors and the Publications Board. The series will attract readers from many different disciplines, largely among academics, advanced undergraduates, graduate students, and practicing professionals.

Decision Making in Health Care

Theory, Psychology, and Applications

Edited by

Gretchen B. Chapman
Rutgers University

Frank A. Sonnenberg
University of Medicine and Dentistry of New Jersey
Robert Wood Johnson Medical School

CAMBRIDGE
UNIVERSITY PRESS

PUBLISHED BY THE PRESS SYNDICATE OF THE UNIVERSITY OF CAMBRIDGE
The Pitt Building, Trumpington Street, Cambridge, United Kingdom

CAMBRIDGE UNIVERSITY PRESS
The Edinburgh Building, Cambridge CB2 2RU, UK
40 West 20th Street, New York, NY 10011-4211, USA
10 Stamford Road, Oakleigh, Melbourne 3166, Australia
Ruiz de Alarcón 13, 28014 Madrid, Spain
Dock House, The Waterfront, Cape Town 8001, South Africa

http://www.cambridge.org

First published 2000
First paperback edition 2003

Printed in the United States of America

Typeface Palatino 10/13 pt.   System LaTeX 2_ε [TB]

A catalog record for this book is available from the British Library

Library of Congress Cataloging in Publication data is available

ISBN 0 521 64159 4 hardback
ISBN 0 521 54124 7 paperback

Contents

Contributors

Ann S. Abbott, BA   *University of Hartford, Department of Psychology, 200 Bloomfield Ave., West Hartford, CT 06117*

David Asch, MD   *University of Pennsylvania, Department of Medicine, 317 Ralston, 3615 Chestnut St., Philadelphia, PA 19104*

Gretchen B. Chapman, PhD   *Rutgers University, Psychology Department, Busch Campus, 152 Frelinghuysen Rd., Piscataway, NJ 08854-8020*

Caryn Christensen, PhD   *University of Hartford, Department of Psychology, 200 Bloomfield Ave., West Hartford, CT 06117*

Joshua Cohen, PhD   *Philadelphia Medical Center, Department of Veterans Affairs, Health Services Research, Woodlawn and University Aves., Philadelphia, PA 19104*

Neal V. Dawson, MD   *Case Western Reserve University, Metro Health Medical Center, 2500 Metro Health Dr., Room 222A, Cleveland, OH 44109-1998*

Arthur S. Elstein, PhD   *University of Illinois, Department of Medical Education (M/C 591), 808 S. Wood St., Suite 986, Chicago, IL 60612-7309*

Antoine Geissbuhler, MD   *Vanderbilt University Medical Center, Division of Biomedical Informatics, 412 Eskind Biomedical Library, 2209 Garland Ave., Nashville, TN 37232-8349*

Mary Kane Goldstein, MD   *Palo Alto Health Care System, Grecc 182B, 3801 Miranda Ave., Palo Alto, CA 94304*

Robert M. Hamm, PhD   *University of Oklahoma Health Sciences Center, Clinical Decision Making Program, Department of Family and Preventive Medicine, 900 NE 10th St., Oklahoma City, OK 73104*

John P. A. Ioannidis, MD   *Therapeutics Research Program, DAIDS, National Institute of Allergy and Infectious Disease, Solar Building 2C15, 6003 Executive Blvd., Bethesda, MD 20892*

Holly Brügge Jimison, PhD   *Oregon Health Sciences University, Department of Public Health and Preventive Medicine, Division of Medical Informatics and Outcomes Research, School of Medicine, BICC-504, 3181 SW Sam Jackson Park Rd., Portland, OR 97201-3098*

Joseph Lau, MD   *New England Medical Center and Tufts University School of Medicine #63, Division of Clinical Care Research, 750 Washington St., Boston, MA 02111-1526*

David B. Matchar, MD   *Duke University Center for Clinical Health Policy Research, First Union Tower, Suite 230, 2200 West Main St., Durham, NC 27705*

Randolph A. Miller, MD   *Vanderbilt University Medical Center, Division of Biomedical Informatics, Eskind Biomedical Library, 2209 Garland Ave., Nashville, TN 37232-8340*

John M. Miyamoto, PhD   *University of Washington, Department of Psychology NI-25, Seattle, WA 98195*

Mark S. Roberts, MD, MPP   *Center for Research on Health Care, University of Pittsburgh School of Medicine, Montifiore University Hospital, Suite E-820, 200 Lothrop St., Pittsburgh, PA 15213*

Louise B. Russell, PhD   *Rutgers University, Institute for Health, Health Care Policy, and Aging Research, 30 College Ave., Room 201, New Brunswick, NJ 08903*

Greg P. Samsa, PhD   *Duke University Center for Clinical Health Policy Research, First Union Tower, Suite 230, 2200 West Main St., Durham, NC 27705*

Dewey C. Scheid, MD   *University of Oklahoma Health Sciences Center, Department of Family and Preventive Medicine, 900 NE 10th St., Oklahoma City, OK 73104*

Paul Phillip Sher, MD   *Oregon Health Sciences University, Division of Medical Informatics and Outcomes Research, School of Medicine, BICC-504, 3181 SW Sam Jackson Park Rd., Portland, OR 97201-3098*

Wally R. Smith, MD   *Virginia Commonwealth University, Medical College of Virginia Campus, Division of Quality Health Care, 1101 East Marshall St., Richmond, VA 23298*

Frank A. Sonnenberg, MD   *University of Medicine and Dentistry of New Jersey, Robert Wood Johnson Medical School, Department of Medicine, 97 Patterson St., New Brunswick, NJ 08903*

Anne M. Stiggelbout, PhD   *Medical Decision Making Unit, Leiden University Medical Center K6-R, Box 9600, 2300 RC, Leiden, the Netherlands*

Thomas G. Tape, MD   *University of Nebraska Medical Center, Department of Internal Medicine, 600 South 42nd St., Omaha, NE 68198-3331*

Joel Tsevat, MD   *University of Cincinnati Medical Center, Division of General Internal Medicine, Section of Outcomes Research, 231 Bethesda Ave., Cincinnati, OH 45267-0535*

Peter Ubel, MD   *University of Pennsylvania, Center for Clinical Ethics and Division of General Internal Medicine, 1223 Blockley Hall, 423 Guardian Dr., Philadelphia, PA 19104*

Acknowledgments

The editors gratefully acknowledge the invaluable assistance of many people. Thanks are due to the past and present members of the Society for Judgment and Decision Making Publications Committee, including Hal Arkes, Jonathan Baron, and Michael Birnbaum, who contributed to the development of this volume. Two anonymous reviewers provided helpful comments on the book prospectus. Jonathan Baron, Deborah Cook, David Hickam, Murray Krahn, Casimir Kulikowski, Karen Kuntz, Hillary Llewelyn-Thomas, Timothy Murphy, Craig Parks, Roy Poses, Jonathan Treadwell, and Peter Wakker provided reviews of the chapters, and Hal Arkes provided a review of the entire book. Julia Hough of Cambridge University Press dispensed valuable advice. Gretchen Chapman thanks her spouse, Paul Breslin, for his encouragement. Frank Sonnenberg thanks his wife, Kathleen, and his two sons, Daniel and Jonathan, whose love and support make all things possible.

Part I

Introduction and Theory

1   Introduction

*Gretchen B. Chapman, PhD, and Frank A.
Sonnenberg, MD*

Decision making is an essential part of health care. The physician has to
determine what is wrong with the patient and recommend a treatment.
The patient has to decide whether to seek medical care and whether to
go along with the treatment the physician recommends. Health policy
makers and health insurers have to decide what to promote, what to
discourage, and what to pay for. All of these decisions determine the
quality of health care that is provided and its financial cost. Increasingly,
decision makers at all levels are under pressure to practice medicine cost
effectively. This volume provides a comprehensive review of research
in medical decision making.

Normative, Descriptive, and Prescriptive Models

Decision research has traditionally explored three research questions.
The first question is the normative issue (addressed in Part I of this book):
how can decisions best be made? The second is the descriptive question
(addressed in Part III): how are decisions actually made? Finally, there is
the prescriptive question (addressed in Parts II and IV): how can decision
theory be used to improve decision making?

The normative model of medical decision making is decision theory. Expected utility theory is the normative theory of choice under
uncertainty, and multiattribute utility theory is the normative theory
of decision with multiple goals. Decision analysis is the direct implementation of these theories to specific decisions. Chapter 2 (Roberts
& Sonnenberg) introduces decision analysis and presents a number of
the techniques used, such as decision trees, Markov models, and influence diagrams. Chapter 6 (Russell) presents cost-effectiveness analysis,
a particular type of decision analysis in which economic outcomes are

3

analyzed in addition to health outcomes and the costs of achieving additional health benefits are determined. Russell presents the argument for using quality-adjusted life years (QALYs) as a universal metric of health outcome, thus permitting comparison of the cost-effectiveness of interventions that address different health conditions.

The application of decision theory to specific clinical problems introduces a host of modeling and measurement issues. Utilities and probabilities must be assessed or estimated. Chapter 3 (Miyamoto) presents utility assessment techniques under both normative and descriptive assumptions. Estimates of probabilities of health outcomes and the effectiveness of interventions are derived from a variety of sources, including "expert opinion," local or national databases, and published research in the medical literature. Over the past few years, increasing attention has been paid to the scientific quality of research that provides the evidence used to support clinical practices. The term *evidence-based medicine*, discussed in Chapter 4 (Ioannidis & Lau), refers to the application of evidence of the highest possible quality to clinical practice. The gold standard for quality of evidence has been the prospective, randomized clinical trial. More recently, meta-analysis of clinical trials (evidence synthesis) has been proposed as an even higher level of evidence than any single randomized trial (Cook, Guyatt, Laupacis, Sackett, & Goldberg, 1995).

However, high-quality research and well-supported numbers alone are not sufficient for good decisions. The numbers must be incorporated into a process that considers the likelihood of outcomes resulting from various options and the values of those outcomes. Decision analysis is a formal process in which these various elements may be combined to guide decision making. Thus, the first part of this book concerns the quantitative techniques that have been developed to address the modeling questions introduced by decision analysis, such as how utilities should be measured, how sequences of health states can be summarized into one measure of effectiveness, how the available medical evidence can be translated into numerical values that can be entered into a decision analysis, and what algorithm should be used to combine all of the components of a decision to produce a single choice.

In addition to identifying optimal decisions and developing normative decision algorithms, decision research has also sought to understand how clinicians, patients, health policy makers, and others actually do make decisions. This descriptive question about decision making is explored in psychological research and is the topic of the third part of this book. Much of this research has mirrored the heuristics and biases approach pursued in decision research outside of health (Kahneman, Slovic, & Tverksy, 1982). In this approach, descriptive decision making is contrasted with normative principles, and discrepancies or biases are identified. Chapter 7 (Chapman & Elstein) reviews some of the more recent medical decision-making research in this vein. Because judgments of uncertainty are a critical part of medical decision making, research has assessed the accuracy of these judgments via comparison to the normative standard of probability theory. Chapter 8 (Dawson) reviews techniques for evaluating probability judgments and research that has assessed physicians' judgments.

Some other aspects of psychological research on medical decision making explore topics somewhat unique to medicine. Ethically difficult decisions, for example, are perhaps more common in medicine than in other decision research application areas. This has led to a dialogue between bioethics and decision research, as exemplified by Chapter 9 (Cohen, Asch, & Ubel). Although many decisions can be made by a single individual, medical decisions are very often made by a group. Patients make decisions in consultation with their families, and clinicians make decisions as part of a medical team. This latter topic is explored in Chapter 10 (Christensen & Abbott).

Prescriptive models of decision making concern how decisions can be improved. One of the primary reasons for decision research in health is to improve decision making, with the goal of leading to better patient care and outcomes. Often efforts to improve decision making are directed at policy makers, the topic of Part 2 of this book. One important policy question is the cost-effectiveness of health interventions, as discussed in Chapter 6 (Russell). Translating a decision analysis or cost-effectiveness analysis into a health policy is not always an automatic process, as reviewed in Chapter 5 (Matchar & Samsa). This process depends on the scope of the policy (micro-, meso-, or macropolicies corresponding to decisions by individual practitioners, small groups of providers, or large societal or government entities). For certain policy efforts, a formal analysis is *free-standing*, meaning that it is created as a separate effort from the policy-making activity. In others, the model is *facilitative* and is used only to inform the policy makers. In some cases, exemplified by the Stroke Policy Prevention Model of Matchar et al. (1997), the analytic model is said to be *embedded* and becomes the centerpiece of a program of practice improvement.

Attempts to improve decision making are also directed at individual patients. The patients' rights movement has sought to increase involvement of patients in decisions about their care. There are many health problems for which the correct decision depends entirely on how patients value the relevant health states. The prototypical example is the work of Mulley, Barry, and colleagues on shared decision making in patients with benign prostatic hypertrophy (Barry, Fowler, Mulley, Henderson, & Wennberg, 1995). Since treatment has no effect on mortality, the recommended treatment depends entirely on how much patients are bothered by their symptoms. Patient preferences can be assessed and incorporated into a group-level decision analysis (Chapter 11, Stigglebout). Alternatively, patient utility can be assessed "at the bedside" and used as the basis for a customized treatment decision for the individual patient (Chapter 12, Goldstein & Tsevat). In both of these cases, a clinician or decision analyst combines the patient's preferences with other information to yield a decision. Yet another method is to present all the information to the patient and allow her or him to incorporate personal preferences and reach a final decision. This approach depends on finding the best way to present quantitative data to patients so that they can participate in the decision-making process, the topic of Chapter 13 (Jimison & Sher).

Finally, medical decision making can be improved by supporting or altering physician decision making. One approach is computerized decision support for physicians, as reviewed in Chapter 14 (Geissbuhler & Miller). These authors discuss the history and current state of the art in computer-based decision support. They explain why, at least for the forseeable future, computers will serve only as an adjunct to human decision making rather than as a substitute. Computers are most helpful when they address issues that are difficult for humans, such as providing exhaustive lists of diagnostic possibilities and performing correct updating of probabilities in response to diagnostic information. Perhaps the most important and most immediately apparent benefit of computer-based systems is that they bring the results of other decision support activities (such as policies and guidelines) directly to the point of care. Gaining full benefit from this approach will require linking such systems with computer-based patient records so that important input variables can be obtained directly from the record rather than needing to be entered by the clinician.

A second, more psychological approach is to identify the errors in the physician's decision process that lead to poor decisions and introduce an intervention to correct the errors. As reviewed in Chapter 15 (Hamm, Scheid, Smith, & Tape), such efforts are not always successful, and more work is needed on improving medical decision making.

A Two-Way Street

Ideally, the study of medical decision making should be a two-way street: decision theory should benefit medical practice, and medicine should advance the study of decision making. Decision theory can benefit medical practice because the quality of medical decisions is determined not only by specific clinical information but also by general principles of good decision making. For example, when making a risky decision, physicians and patients have to balance the severity of a possible bad outcome with its low probability. Or, when considering several differential diagnoses, the physician must use the available data, such as patient history and laboratory results, to update the likelihood of each diagnosis appropriately. Decision theory addresses these issues. Medicine can contribute to decision theory because medical decisions sometimes pose unique challenges that spur advances in both decision analyses and descriptive decision theories.

What Decision Theory Can Offer Health Care

One issue addressed in this book is what decision theory can offer to the practice of medicine. How can the principles that constitute decision theory explain or improve health care? At the most general level, decision theory provides a comprehensive framework within which all of the various elements (probability judgments, sources of data, evidence-based practice, utility assessment, economic evaluation, and principled handling of probabilistic information) can be studied, with the goal to understanding them and finding ways of improving them. Decision analysis provides a quantitative synthesis of all these elements so that all inputs into the decision can be considered according to both their probability and their importance. Standardization of outcomes as QALYs provides a unifying basis for comparing the results of one analysis with those of another even when they address different health problems. Utilities in decision models also provide a way in which decisions that affect quality of life can take into account the differences in preferences among patients.

The structure of decision models provides a framework for discussing a health care decision. By making choices, assumptions, and input parameters explicit, decision makers who come to differing conclusions can focus on the source of their disagreements. It is much easier, for example, to deal with a criticism such as "I disagree with your estimate of the prevalence of disease in the population" than it is to deal with the less specific "I don't agree with your conclusion." Decision models also provide a basis for performing sensitivity analyses. These analyses provide several benefits to decision makers. First is the ability to determine the parameters on which an analysis is most dependent. Further research to better define the values of such critical values may be deemed worthwhile. Second is the ability to determine a range of conditions under which a given clinical strategy may be worthwhile. For example, a screening program may be seen to be useful only when the prevalence of disease in a given population exceeds a certain threshold value (Pauker & Kassirer, 1980). Another important function of decision models is that they permit the optimal decision or cost-effectiveness analysis to be determined with a set of values specific to a given setting or patient population, and they allow the results of an analysis to be adapted to an individual patient. For example, a provider organization can modify a cost-effectiveness model to reflect local costs. A cancer treatment center can modify a model to reflect a differing distribution of disease stage in its population or differing local complication rates.

One of the most important advantages of decision models is that they provided the ability to analyze the effects of applying clinical elements (tests and treatments) in specific sequences known as *clinical strategies*, which have never been evaluated in precisely the same combination. This can help guide the optimal application of tests and treatments that have been evaluated individually in clinical trials but whose impact on the costs and outcomes of clinical care has not been determined. Increasingly, decision models are being used to inform the clinical guideline development process. This is in keeping with the idea of *explicit guideline development* proposed by Eddy (1990), which provides an explicit accounting of the trade-offs involved in application of a guideline, thus allowing informed and rational discussion. One must be very cautious when extending the analysis beyond directly obtained data, but in some situations, modeling provides the only means of evaluating a complex strategy.

What Medicine Can Offer Decision Theory

A second question addressed in this book is what medicine can offer decision theory. Medicine provides an ideal arena for the study of decision making because most decisions involve a fairly small set of options (e.g., diagnoses or treatments), uncertainty about outcomes, and multiple attributes on which to compare options. Medicine highlights particular decision principles that are not as salient in other application areas. For example, the trade-off between quality of life and length of life is unlike many of the trade-offs encountered in nonmedical decisions. Medical applications have in some cases inspired the development of new decision modeling techniques, such as the QALY model. In addition, the ability to measure directly and incorporate into analyses the individual preferences of patients supports the growing movement toward increased patient involvement in health care decisions. Concern for incorporating patient preferences has also led to advances in utility assessment techniques (such as the time trade-off). The measurement of health-related quality of life poses unique challenges and is an area of active research in its own right. Finally, as mentioned earlier, medical decision making suggests psychological issues not always addressed in other application areas, such as the role of ethics (Chapter 9) and processes of team decision making (Chapter 10).

Perspectives

A topic usually discussed in relation to cost-effectiveness analysis but relevant to all decision-making activities is the *perspective* of the decision. That is, whose costs and outcomes should be measured? In terms of health outcomes, it seems obvious that the perspective should be that of the person who will be affected by the decision. However, in many situations the patient is not the only one who is affected. For example, treatment for prostate cancer or breast cancer may affect sexual relations with the patient's partner. Complications of pregnancy may affect the health of the unborn child. A vaccination strategy, by affecting herd immunity, may prevent illness in people who are not vaccinated.

It is less obvious whose utilities should be measured when assessing quality of life. Two possibilities are (a) the patient who is currently experiencing the health state and (b) those who have not experienced the health state (but may do so at some future date). Some studies have shown that patients who have firsthand experience with an adverse health state assign a higher (more desirable) value to it than patients who have not experienced it (Boyd, Sutherland, Heasman, Tritchler, & Cummings, 1990). Thus, measuring utilities from patients who are contemplating a decision is likely to result in a more negative estimate of the adverse health effects from complications of therapy relative to later judgments when the therapy has been experienced. In a similar vein, studies have shown that proxies for the patient (family members and clinicians) provide lower estimates of the quality of life experienced by seriously ill patients than do the patients themselves (Tsevat, Cook, Green, Matchar, Dawson, Broste, Wu, Phillips, Oye, & Goldman, 1995; Tsevat, Dawson, Wu, Lynn, Soukup, Cook, Vidaillet, & Phillips, 1998). Again those who are experiencing the health state rate it more highly than those who are not.

The Panel on Cost-Effectiveness in Health and Medicine (Gold, Siegel, Russell, & Weinstein, 1996) recommended that cost-effectiveness analyses use community-based preferences because community preferences represent an extension of the societal perspective and are the best articulation of society's preferences. Also, the community is composed of individuals who have chronic illnesses and disabilities in proportion to their prevalence. Thus, according to the Panel's recommendation, many of those providing utility assessments would be people who have never experienced the health state in question. Because the general public values adverse health states as worse than do the patients who experience them, the Panel's recommendation has two related results. First, according to community judgments, saving the lives of those with disabilities would result in fewer QALY gains than if patients themselves provided the utility judgments. Second, however, use of community preferences also results in higher valuation of interventions to prevent or reverse disabilities, possibly leading to discrimination in favor of those with disabilities (see Chapter 6).

The perspective on costs is even more complex. In our rapidly changing health care delivery system, the parties bearing the costs and the arrangements by which those costs are borne change continually. For example, under a fee-for-service arrangement, health services rendered are costs only to patients and insurers and are a net benefit to the provider. However, under capitation (a fixed monthly fee paid to the provider for the care of each patient), resources expended on health care are costs from the perspective of the provider but not from the perspective of the insurer. Realistically, few patients have ever borne a significant portion of the cost of their own health care. Indigent patients cannot afford it and the care they receive is subsidized, usually by government programs. None but the wealthiest members of society are able to pay out of pocket for even routine hospital services, and that group tends to be well insured. Thus, the patient perspective on costs is not very useful.

Given the limits of most forms of health insurance, a substantial amount of care is provided outside the limits of an insurance policy;

thus the insurer's perspective is quite limited. For example, physician visits may be covered, but prescription drugs are not. Another issue is that much care is provided completely outside the limits of the health care system. For example, substantial time and effort may be required to care for a chronically ill or disabled patient at home. Much of this care is not reimbursable by health insurance and therefore does not appear on the balance sheet.

Because of the limits of individual perspectives on costs, Russell (in Chapter 6 and in the report of the Panel) argues in favor of the *societal perspective* in which all costs incurred in the process of patient care (regardless of who pays for them and whether they fall within the health system or not) should be included. This viewpoint is not without controversy, and methods for assessing nonmedical costs are not well developed. Perhaps the strongest argument in favor of the societal perspective is that it provides a unifying basis, the *reference case* for comparing cost-effectiveness results, which come from different studies. Although it would be unrealistic to argue that the more limited perspectives of special-interest groups such as health insurers are not important, the best option is to include the reference case in addition to the more limited perspective so as to provide a basis for comparison.

An Overview of Medical Decision Making

Figure 1.1 shows an overview of the different elements of medical decision making. The large rounded rectangle at the bottom represents decisions; the output of a decision is an action: a test, a treatment, or a strategy consisting of a combination of tests and treatments. There are a number of processes that may produce a decision. The most common is ad hoc decision making. This represents global judgments by a clinician about the appropriate course of action. It may be based on what the clinician was taught, his or her own interpretation of the evidence supporting each course of action, or the prevailing practice in a given institution. Because the decision-making process is unspecified, it is subject to biases, as discussed by Chapman and Elstein in Chapter 7. Other processes that produce decisions (arrows pointing to the "Decision" box) are knowledge-based systems, patient-centered approaches, decision models, clinical guidelines, and policies. Decision models and cost-effectiveness analyses may, in turn, influence knowledge-based systems, guidelines, and policies.

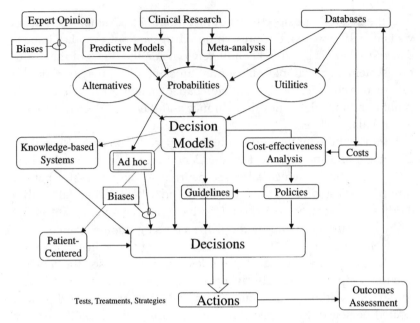

Figure 1.1. Overall scheme of medical decision making. Various activities (e.g., clinical research) and products (e.g., guidelines) are shown as rounded rectangles and inputs as ellipses. Arrows leading away from an activity indicate an output of that activity (e.g., decision models have decisions as an output), and arrows leading into an activity indicate a contribution to that activity (e.g., decision analysis contributes to cost-effectiveness analysis, which, in turn, contributes to policy formulation). Arrows drawn as dotted lines indicate potential relationships that are not currently implemented in clinical care.

The inputs to decision models are alternatives (the actions selected for comparison), probabilities, and utilities. Utilities are usually elicited from patients or other relevant decision makers, but they may also come from databases of past preference-elicitation studies. Probabilities may be obtained directly from expert opinion, also subject to biases (Chapter 8, Dawson), directly from clinical research, or from clinical research after refinement by predictive models or meta-analysis. Probabilities, utilities (particularly the life-expectancy component), and costs may be obtained from databases of outcomes measures that are part of ongoing clinical care rather than research efforts. A closed loop including outcomes, databases, and decisions can be used to inform clinical practice improvement efforts.

The dotted lines in Figure 1.1 indicate pathways that may exist in the future. Specifically, decision models may guide knowledge-based systems and patient-centered decision making.

A Detailed Example

To illustrate the various elements in a real-world clinical application, consider the decision on whether to prescribe anticoagulant therapy in patients with atrial fibrillation (AF). During AF, blood tends to pool in the heart, increasing the risk of a clot, which could cause a stroke. To decrease the risk of clotting, anticoagulant medication may be given; however, this medication raises the risk of bleeding. Sudlow and colleagues (Sudlow, Thomson, Thwaites, Rodgers, & Kenny, 1998) recently performed a study to determine the prevalence of AF in a population and the number of patients who were candidates for anticoagulant therapy who were receiving it. They studied the results of ad hoc decision making by practitioners in a community. Such decisions are subject to many biases (or uninformed opinion) including faulty assessment of the risk of stroke in AF, the risk of serious bleeding from anticoagulant therapy, and the clinical factors that modify these risks. For example, a practitioner may greatly overestimate the impact of advanced age on the risk of bleeding from anticoagulant therapy. In fact, Sudlow et al. found that anticoagulants were least likely to be used in elderly women, the group who may be most likely to benefit.

In order to assess the expected risk of stroke in their study population, Sudlow et al. referred to a number of clinical trials of anticoagulant therapy in AF. In addition to using these trials individually to determine the risk of stroke in patients with untreated AF, the authors performed a meta-analysis of five of the randomized, controlled trials to assess the risk of stroke (see the clinical research probabilities and meta-analysis probabilities paths in Figure 1.1). The authors used these data to derive three potential sets of criteria that could be used to determine which of the patients in the population-based study should be on anticoagulant therapy. They also determined the usefulness of echocardiography in various subgroups and found that it could have been omitted in many patients without affecting decision making. Although not done in this study, it would certainly be possible, given the data from these trials, to develop predictive models of stroke risk that could, in turn, be used as inputs into a decision model.

The decision to prescribe anticoagulant therapy in AF has been the subject of numerous guidelines (Matchar, McCrory, Barnett, & Feussner, 1994). However, these guidelines leave many situations uncovered, and these situations can be addressed by decision modeling. Decision modeling can also be used to individualize the decision to a specific patient by including an estimate of the risk of bleeding complications in that patient. Cost-effectiveness analysis can be used to address additional issues, such as whether specific anticoagulant therapy management services are cost-effective in a patient population, the financial impact of ordering echocardiograms more selectively, or the cost-effectiveness of efforts to improve compliance with the AF guidelines. The study of Sudlow et al. could be thought of as the creation of an outcomes database, such as those shown in the upper right corner of Figure 1.1, that provides a valuable component of a practice improvement effort. In the future, it is likely that knowledge-based systems will be deployed to provide advice that is individualized to specific patients.

What the Future Holds

The health care system will be shaped in the foreseeable future by the maturation of managed care, which will evolve from primarily a cost-containment vehicle into a more comprehensive effort to improve the quality of health care delivery while keeping costs under control. The importance of evidence-based medicine will grow as quality improvement efforts seek to bring the best possible evidence to bear on health care activities. It is not certain that the number of randomized clinical trials will increase, but it is certain that practice improvement efforts will make better use of the ones that have been performed and published. Evidence synthesis efforts such as the Cochrane collaboration (See Chapter 4) will facilitate the performance and dissemination of high-quality systematic reviews. In turn, the demand for high-quality evidence syntheses will encourage continued improvement in the quality of clinical trials. This will likely include prospective meta-analysis in which clinical trials that address the same clinical question will be designed collaboratively to facilitate meta-analyses involving combined databases from multiple clinical trials (see Chapter 4). It is to be hoped that educational efforts will increase so that clinicians will be exposed to the principles of evidence-based medicine during their schooling and clinical training.

Decision Models

No matter how many new clinical trials are performed and no matter how high their quality is, they will never address more than a small fraction of the knowledge needed for clinical practice. Even in areas well covered by clinical trials, care settings, individual patients, or populations may differ sufficiently from the conditions in the trial such that the correct decision will not be clear. Moreover, few health interventions are applied in isolation. They are generally combined into sequences comprising complete clinical strategies, which may never have been evaluated in trials. For these reasons, decision modeling will be increasingly important. The needs of modeling can be addressed in the design of clinical trials that are, with increasing frequency, incorporating utility-based measures of quality of life (Feeny & Torrance, 1989) and economic measures for use in cost-effectiveness analyses (Jonsson & Weinstein, 1997). We believe these trends will accelerate.

Decision modeling itself is in constant evolution. Over the past twenty years, models have evolved from simple trees with "arbitrary" (nonutility-based) outcome measures to increasingly sophisticated models including Markov cohort simulations and more sophisticated evaluation methodology such as Monte Carlo analysis. This has been made possible largely through the development of sophisticated microcomputer software that facilitates model construction, permits spreading of modeling efforts over multiple work sessions, saving differing versions of models, and automating evaluations. Enhanced computing power has made complex simulations possible, and advances such as parallel computing will provide even greater computational speed in the future. Innovations that permit application of models by nonexperts and interaction with decision models over the Internet are already beginning to appear (Sanders, Hagerty, Sonnenberg, Hlatky, & Owens, 1997) and will continue to evolve.

Decision-making research and work from the artificial intelligence research community have focused attention on the role of uncertainty in health care. More efficient methods of computing probabilities, such as Bayesian inference, and increasing computing power will make possible the application of these methods to increasingly complex (and therefore more realistic) scenarios. The ability to perform Monte Carlo simulations has provided a means for exploring more comprehensively the implications of uncertainty in the estimation of parameters of decision models and an appreciation for uncertainty in the results of analyses.

The relative paucity of clinical trial data also is accelerating the trend toward development of large-scale databases of clinical outcomes. There are many potential problems with these databases, including inadequate control of confounding factors and inadequate statistical power for infrequent events. However, such databases will provide the only way of answering certain questions and will provide a means for assessing the effectiveness of clinical strategies in individual practices, which will be an important component of efforts to improve practice.

Practice Guidelines

Managed care and quality improvement work have sparked an enormous effort to develop and implement guidelines. However, the track record to date has been decidedly mixed. Guidelines are seldom deployed successfully. This occurs for several reasons. First, clinicians may not be aware of guidelines, or there may be competing guidelines that create confusion. Second, even clinicians who are aware of a guideline may forget to apply it when it is relevant. Third, even if clinicians remember to apply the guideline, it may not be accessible where they are seeing patients (e.g., it might be on a bookshelf on another floor of the building). Fourth, implementing the guideline may be too time-consuming because it requires the clinician to consider a large number of clinical data, which may not be readily available. Fifth, guidelines may become obsolete if a new treatment appears or if the results of a clinical trial are published. Sixth, clinicians often do not understand the reasons why a guideline makes a specific recommendation. In addition to all these obstacles is the fact that each managed care plan may have a different preferred set of guidelines and may even create its own.

The only way this situation can be resolved is to implement computer-based patient records (CPRs). Guidelines embedded in CPRs can retrieve relevant patient data to determine whether a guideline should be triggered, can automatically present the guideline to the clinician, can provide all the data from the record needed to implement it and request any additional data, and can even carry out some of the implementation, for example by entering an order for a necessary test or treatment. Such guidelines, maintained in central locations and distributed via computer networks, can be updated periodically, avoiding the delay, expense, and inefficiency of disseminating the updates through printed media. Computer-based patient records will also provide an infrastructure by which large-scale clinical outcomes databases can be developed. In fact, the clinical guidelines can be used to guide the clinical details that need to be recorded in the CPR. Computer-based presentation of guidelines also can enable direct links to the literature supporting the guidelines and may, in the future, provide explanations of guideline advice to increase clinicians' comfort in carrying it out.

Cost-Effectiveness

Cost-effectiveness analysis, widely misunderstood and misapplied in the past (Doubilet, Weinstein, & McNiel, 1986; Udvarhelyi, Colditz, Rai, & Epstein, 1992), will continue to be an important part of health policy development. Efforts such as those by the Panel on Cost-Effectiveness in Health and Medicine (Gold et al., 1996) will help to ensure that future analyses are performed and reported correctly. In particular, advocating the reference case, based on the societal perspective, will facilitate comparisons across studies. Cost-accounting systems will increasingly be used by provider organizations to manage their own costs. Such systems will permit far more accurate microcosting efforts than are currently possible. A number of issues in cost-effectiveness analysis remain unresolved. One is the Panel's recommendation that the costs of nonmedical resources be included in analyses. Although included for good reasons, this recommendation is difficult to follow, and it is uncertain whether analysts will adopt it. Another controversial area is the inclusion of the future costs of illnesses that occur because patients live longer as a result of current medical treatment.

Psychological Questions

Despite our predictions about the increased relevance of outcomes databases, decision models, and cost-effectiveness analyses, these techniques will never address all health care decisions. The number of potential decisions is ever-increasing as more diagnostic tests and therapeutic strategies are developed. Consequently, some decisions will always be based on clinical intuition (ad hoc strategies). For this reason, research on the psychology of decision processes will continue to be important. If physician decision making is to be improved, it must first be understood (Hamm et al., Chapter 15). Although a large number of decision biases have been identified (Chapters 7 and 8) and although psychological explanations have been provided for some biases, more work is needed on techniques for eliminating or counteracting decision biases. If physicians come to rely more on practice guidelines and decision support for making clinical decisions, more of their time may become available for the less clinical, more psychosocial aspects of patient care. Such a change would introduce a new area of psychological research, that of physician decision making and patient evaluation of these psychosocial aspects of care.

Some decisions are essentially utility-based, meaning that the optimal decision is a function of the preferences of the particular patient (or other relevant decision makers) and cannot be globally determined by a practice guideline. Thus, research on patient preferences and perspectives is likely to increase. Assessment of patient utilities must balance the axiomatic basis for the method (e.g., whether the method yields true utilities), the feasibility of the method (e.g., whether the patient understands the questions posed), and the empirical validity of the methods (e.g., whether different methods agree with one another or with other criteria). As exemplified by Chapters 3, 11, and 12, these issues have spawned a lively research area. As health information becomes more accessible to patients and laypeople (Chapter 13), more research will be needed on how patients select and integrate information to form an evaluation or decision. We believe that there will be an increasing trend toward patient-focused decision making. At the simplest level, this involves sharing data and descriptions of outcomes with patients while arriving at a decision. More sophisticated techniques for presenting this information are now available, such as multimedia presentations of patients experiencing adverse health states. The ability to evaluate decision models with patient-specific data has the potential to permit the generation of precisely tailored advice.

Conclusion

The health care landscape of the twenty-first century promises to be much more influenced by the principles of decision making discussed in this volume than has been the case in the past. We have presented the successes, some of the unsolved problems, and a framework within which these principles can be applied to patient care and used to improve health care decision making.

References

Barry, M.J., Fowler, F.J. Jr., Mulley, A.G. Jr., Henderson, J.V. Jr., and Wennberg, J.E. (1995). Patient reactions to a program designed to facilitate patient participation in treatment decisions for benign prostatic hyperplasia. *Medical Care*, 33(8), 771–82.

Boyd, N.J., Sutherland, H.J., Heasman, K.Z., Tritchler, D.L., and Cummings, B.J. (1990). Whose utilities for decision analysis? *Medical Decision Making*, 10, 58–67.

Cook, D.J., Guyatt, G.H., Laupacis, A., Sackett, D.L., and Goldberg, R.J. (1995). Clinical recommendations using levels of evidence for antithrombotic agents. *Chest*, 108(4 Suppl), 227S–230S.

Doubilet, P., Weinstein, M.C., and McNeil, B.J. (1986). Use and misuse of the term "cost-effective" in medicine. *New England Journal of Medicine*, 296, 253–6.

Eddy, D.M. (1990). Guidelines for policy statements: the explicit approach. *Journal of the American Medical Association*, 263, 2239–43.

Feeny, D.H., and Torrnace, G.W. (1989). Incorporating utility-based quality-of-life assessment measures in clinical trials: two examples. *Medical Care*, 27, S190–S204.

Gold, M.R., Siegel, J.E., Russell, L.B., and Weinstein, M.C., Eds. (1996). *Cost-Effectiveness in Health and Medicine*. New York: Oxford University Press.

Jonsson, B., and Weinstein, M.C. (1997). Economic evaluation alongside multinational clinical trials. Study considerations for GUSTO IIb. *International Journal of Technology Assessment in Health Care*, 13(1), 49–58.

Kahneman, D., Slovic, P., and Tversky, A. (1982). *Judgment Under Uncertainty: Heuristics and Biases*. New York: Cambridge University Press.

Matchar, D.B., McCrory, D.C., Barnett, H.J.M., and Feussner, J.R. (1994). Guidelines for medical treatment for stroke prevention. *Annals of Internal Medicine*, 121, 54–5.

Matchar, D.B., Samsa, G.P., Matthews, J.R., Ancukiewicz, M., Parmigiani, G., Hassellad, V., Wolf, P.A., D'Agostino, R.B., and Lipscomb, J. (1997). The stroke prevention policy model: Linking evidence and clinical decisions. *Annals of Internal Medicine*, 127, 704–11.

Pauker, S.G., and Kassirer, J.P. (1980). The threshold approach to clinical decision making. *New England Journal of Medicine*, 302, 1109.

Sanders, G.D., Hagerty, C.G., Sonnenberg, F.A., Hlatky, M.A., and Owens, D.K. (1999). Distributed decision support for guideline development using a Web-based interface: Prevention of sudden cardiac death. *Medical Decision Making*, 19, 157–166.

Sudlow, M., Thomson, R., Thwaites, B., Rodgers, H., and Kenny, R.A. (1998). Prevalence of atrial fibrillation and eligibility for anticoagulants in the community. *Lancet*, 352, 1167–71.

Tsevat, J., Cook, E.F., Green, M.L., Matchar, D.B., Dawson, N.V., Broste, S.K., Wu, A.W., Phillips, R.S., Oye, R.K., and Goldman, L. (1995). Health values of the seriously ill. *Annals of Internal Medicine*, 122(7), 514–20.

Tsevat, J., Dawson., N.V., Wu, A.W., Lynn, J., Soukup, J.R., Cook, E.F., Vidaillet, H., and Phillips, R.S. (1998). Health values of hospitalized patients 80 years or older. HELP investigators. Hospitalized Elderly Longitudinal Project. *Journal of the American Medical Association*, 279(5), 371–5.

Udvarhelyi, I.S., Colditz, G.A., Rai, A., and Epstein, A.M. (1992). Cost-effectiveness and cost-benefit analyses in the medical literature. Are the methods being used correctly? *Annals of Internal Medicine*, 116, 238.

2   Decision Modeling Techniques

Mark S. Roberts, MD, MPP,
and Frank A. Sonnenberg, MD

The fundamental purpose of decision modeling in medicine is to create a quantitative representation of a set of clinical choices. Decision analysis provides a methodology for comparing those choices or strategies by calculating the expected value of the outcomes that result from the possible choices. This quantitative representation allows for the incorporation of choices, uncertainty (probabilities), and several measures of the decision maker's preferences for various outcomes. By requiring an explicit description of the possible events and their likelihood, decision analysis can focus discussion regarding clinical decisions, quantitatively compare choices, allow for the rapid assessment of the effect of variations in basic assumptions on the optimal choice, and provide a mechanism for evaluating the same clinical decision along multiple outcome dimensions, such as life expectancy, quality of life, and costs.

This chapter presents a concise review of various methods used to model clinical situations. Although tutorial in nature, it is not designed to be a complete course or introduction to decision analysis. For a more detailed exposition of the methods described in this chapter, the reader is directed to the list of references at the end of the chapter.

1.   Background to Decision Modeling

This chapter will provide an introduction to various techniques used to represent clinical decision problems. The actual mathematical representation of a decision analysis problem is termed a *decision model*, and there are many different methodologies that can be used to construct a model appropriate for a given problem. Through the context of an increasingly complex problem, this chapter will present standard decision trees, Markov processes, and simulation modeling. Where appropriate, other techniques useful in evaluating clinical problems such as sensitivity analysis and cost-effectiveness analysis will be described. Other methods, such as influence diagrams, discrete event simulation, and semi-Markov models, will be presented briefly.

1.1. Types of Problems Relevant to Decision Analysis

The most fundamental requirement for the construction of a decision analysis problem is that a choice needs to be made. Furthermore, there should be some uncertainty as to the possible outcomes or the optimal strategy. It is unlikely, for example, that a decision analysis that exactly replicates the strategies tested in a specific randomized clinical trial would be useful: the answer would be known from the results of the trial itself. However, decision analysis may still be useful to explore the consequences of altered clinical circumstances such as different local complication rates or costs. Decision analysis is helpful as an integrative methodology used to combine data from several sources into a single description of a clinical situation. Decision analysis may combine treatments in new ways to evaluate more complete clinical strategies that represent a sequence of clinical decisions. The power of the technique to integrate data from several different sources related to different parts of the problem is well illustrated in the work of Col regarding the use of hormone replacement therapy in postmenopausal women (Col et al., 1997) or the work of Krahn on the effects of screening for prostate cancer (Krahn et al., 1993).

1.2. Matching Methodology to the Specific Problem

The mathematical representation of a clinical situation needs to capture several different characteristics of the underlying problem. In addition to representing the various diagnostic and therapeutic choices that are available, the model must depict the potential consequences implied by those choices, assign likelihoods that the various outcomes will occur, and assign values (in a common metric) to those outcomes. When developing useful models, adequately addressing these concerns requires viewing the problem from the correct *perspective*, modeling the problem in a specific *context* at the appropriate level of detail or *complexity*, and modeling the problem over the relevant *time horizon*.

Perspective. The perspective of the model indicates for whom the model is being constructed, as different stakeholders may have different values for various outcomes. Commonly, problems are constructed from the perspective of the patient, a third-party payer, health policy makers, or society in general. Optimal strategies may depend entirely on the values placed on the outcome states, which may look quite different from the various perspectives.

Context and Complexity. By *context*, we mean the definition of the specific problem and the population of interest in the decision problem. Choosing a context is equivalent to developing the inclusion criteria for a randomized clinical trial: it defines the study population, the underlying disease, and the interventions that are to be studied. Context also encompasses the portion of the problem included in the analysis. For example, in conducting a cost-effectiveness analysis on the usefulness of ultrasound to screen for abdominal aortic aneurysms, should the costs and benefits of the detection of asymptomatic other diseases (e.g., gallbladder disease and renal disease) be included in the analysis? Determining the appropriate level of *complexity* (or *granularity*) is equally difficult. In creating a decision analysis of cardiac catheterization to define those patients with coronary disease who would benefit from bypass surgery, should each possible complication from the surgery be modeled, or should the complications be grouped into categories such as those that affect future mortality and those that do not? The proper choice of scope and detail depends on the purpose of the analysis, the data available to calibrate the model, and the time allotted for design and development. For example, a model examining different therapies for the treatment of coronary artery disease may stratify people based on the number of diseased vessels or the ejection fraction, replicating how the clinical stratification occurs.

Time Horizon. The time horizon of the model describes the period of time over which relevant intervention and outcome events are accounted for. For interventions or diseases that have immediate consequences, the time horizon may include only those immediate events. However, many diseases and interventions do not have an immediate effect but may carry with them or impart a *risk* of an event that persists over time. Patients with high cholesterol have an increased risk of developing cardiovascular conditions; patients who take a cholesterol-lowering agent may decrease that risk. However, the actual events of interest to the investigator (the development of coronary artery disease, stroke, etc.) do not occur immediately after the decision. If they occur at all, they take place in the future, according to specific risks. For some of these outcomes (and especially the cost outcomes), the value of the events varies, depending on the time of occurrence: future costs may be discounted with respect to current costs. If these effects are important in a real problem, the modeling system must have the ability to incorporate them. Similarly, many diseases are chronic, and interventions only alter the pace of decline (diabetes) or the level of symptoms (arthritis). Other diseases are characterized by recurrent episodes interspersed with periods of wellness (e.g., depression, stable angina). A model that represents a disease process must describe the disease or condition over a time frame that matches the actual pace of disease. A decision analysis of the effect of cholesterol-lowering drugs on 1-month mortality would be inappropriate, as might be a 10-year time horizon on the difference between multiple treatment regimens for treating acute dysuria in young women. The fundamental principle is that the time horizon of the model should match the natural history of the disease.

1.3. Sample Problem: Screening for HIV Infection

This chapter will explore the various techniques for developing analytic models using a clinical example that will be carried throughout the entire chapter. Starting with a simple model of the problem, increasing clinical realism will motivate the need for more complex modeling techniques. The fundamental issue in the example involves evaluating a screening program for the presence of human immunodeficiency virus (HIV). The basic assumption is that given the improvements in care for asymptomatic, HIV-infected individuals, HIV should be detected as early as possible. The problem is that the cost is high, and decision analysis can help provide estimates of the cost-effectiveness of different screening strategies. This example will be based on work by McCarthy et al. (1993). The description is not designed to be a realistic clinical representation of the general problem of screening for HIV disease; rather, it is designed to illustrate the manner in which different methods can be used to model different components of a problem.

As one might expect, there are many ways to describe a clinical problem. In this example, framing a problem as a decision analysis places the emphasis on the initial decision: whether or not to screen a particular population. This explicit choice characterizes a decision model. From that decision point, most decision analysis problems will follow logical, temporally appropriate descriptions of events that occur as a result of making each choice.

2.   Basic Decision Trees

The following section describes the components necessary to construct a standard decision model and illustrates several conventions and construction techniques that make the development, testing, and analysis of models more straightforward. The descriptions are generic, and the reader is encouraged to work with these structures either with pen and paper or in a software system designed to perform decision analyses.

2.1.   General Structure and Definitions

There are three major components of decision analysis problems: the structure of the model itself, the likelihoods (probabilities) of the various events that are being modeled, and the values (utilities) of the various outcomes that exist at the end of a particular path. The structure of a decision tree is composed of *nodes* (which describe decision points and the time at which chance events occur) and *branches* (which represent choices and specific events). Figure 2.1 depicts the elements of a standard decision model in the context of a hypothetical decision between two choices. The *decision node* (represented by the square) indicates the

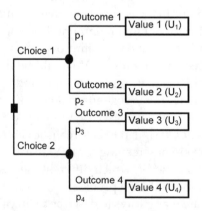

Figure 2.1. Structure of a decision model. A basic decision model is created from a *decision node* (square) which represents a decision point, *chance nodes* (circles) which represent occurrence of chance events given the choices made, and values for each *terminal node* or outcome (boxes) representing the utilities of ending up in each particular outcome state.

fundamental decision to be made. Examples of decision nodes include the decision between medical or surgical therapy, treatment versus watchful waiting, or any other set of choices to be made in a clinical situation. A decision node may have an arbitrary number of branches representing all of the possible choices involved. The decision node is followed by *chance nodes* (represented by the circles) that describe the various events that are subject to chance and are not under the control of the decision maker. Each possible outcome is associated with the probability that it will occur (represented by p_1 through p_4). The terminal end of the branch represents the value of the particular outcome state: for example, if Outcome 1 represents death and the problem measures outcome in life expectancy, then Value 1 would be equal to zero.

Several conventions allow for the standardization of models. In general, the logical sequence of temporal events flows from left to right, starting with the decision that is to be made. Events earlier in time are termed *proximal* or *upstream* events; those that occur later (to the right) are called *distal* or *downstream* events. The branches of the tree set internal contexts for the model, just as selecting a particular problem and population set external contexts. For example, in a choice between surgery and medical therapy, all events and parameters described distal (or downstream) from the surgery arm *must* relate only to that portion of the population that has had surgery. At each decision or chance node, the characteristics of the portion of the population beyond that point are defined by the combination of events that have taken place upstream in the tree.

By both convention and the need to model reality, all of the probabilities at a chance node must sum to 1 (e.g., the probability that *something* happens is always 1). This is an analytic expression of the condition that branches at a chance node be "mutually exclusive and collectively exhaustive," which indicates that all possible outcomes must be included but that only one branch at each node is possible for any given individual.

Consequences (usually out of the control of the decision maker) occur after each decision. In clinical problems, there is often a series of decisions to be made. A common scenario is the decision to perform a diagnostic test and then act according to the result of the test (e.g., obtain a throat culture and prescribe antibiotics if positive but withhold antibiotics if negative). Rarely are these implicit decisions modeled as actual decision nodes. For example, Figure 2.2 depicts two different representations of the information regarding a diagnostic test. In the panel on the left (the *embedded decision form*), the full array of possible

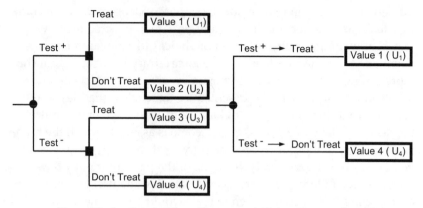

Figure 2.2. Implicit decisions. The tree on the left represents all possibilities in a simple test/treat decision. However, because the test is being performed to allow for changes in treatment, it is expected that one would treat a positive test and not treat a negative one. If this is not the case, the test is not useful. Therefore, these *implicit decisions* are modeled simply as a consequence of the result of the test, as in the tree on the right.

downstream events is described. However, if the purpose of the test is to guide therapeutic decisions, the depiction of a decision node after the test result is redundant: the assumption is that treatment will be initiated if the test is positive and will be withheld if the test is negative. Therefore the downstream decision is traditionally drawn as shown on the right side of the figure (called the *normal form*), eliminating the dominated or irrelevant decisions. The formulations are equivalent; there is no additional information contained in the embedded formulation. In fact, the embedded form represents the irrational assumption that the result of a test may not motivate or specify the treatment decision (Wellman et al., 1986). If the positive–treat and negative–no treatment action pairs do not dominate the positive–no treatment and negative–treat action pairs, then the test is not useful. It is better to determine the value of the diagnostic test by including "no test, no treatment" and empirical treatment strategies in the model. The other disadvantage of the embedded formulation is that when the model is evaluated, it is not possible to determine the optimal decision at the embedded decision node.

2.2.   *Method of Analysis: "Averaging Out and Folding Back"*

The analysis of a standard decision tree provides the expected value of the outcome for each modeled strategy. For example, in a decision problem modeling the choice between a medical treatment and a surgical treatment, it might be reasonable to measure the outcome in terms of average survival or life expectancy. In essence, the solution to this decision analysis problem asks, "*What is the average duration of survival of a cohort of identical individuals who are treated with medicine, compared to the average duration of survival of an identical cohort of patients treated with surgery?*"

To illustrate, consider the simple problem described in Figure 2.1 between two choices, each with two possible outcomes. The expected value of CHOICE 1 is simply the sum of the possible outcomes of that choice weighted by the probabilities of each outcome:

$$p_1 U_1 + p_2 U_2$$

Similarly, the *expected value* of CHOICE 2 is:

$$p_3 U_3 + p_4 U_4$$

Or, for an arbitrary number (*n*) of choices and outcomes:

$$\sum_{i=1}^{n} p_i U_i$$

As decision trees become larger, the process becomes quantitatively more complex but qualitatively equivalent. Starting with the terminal node, each chance node is replaced with its expected value, the simple sum of the terminal values weighted by their probability of occurrence. Figure 2.3 illustrates this process (*averaging out and folding back*), representing the averaging that occurs at each chance node and the folding together of successive branches until the final comparison is between the choices at the original decision node.

2.3. Clinical Example

Consider the problem mentioned at the beginning of the chapter: Should an HIV screening program be implemented in a particular population? For the purpose of this illustration, we assume that testing is not perfect. Therefore, some people with HIV infection may test falsely negative and some people without HIV infection may test falsely positive. We assume that all persons testing positive will be given treatment that will prolong their survival if they are truly HIV infected. We assume that

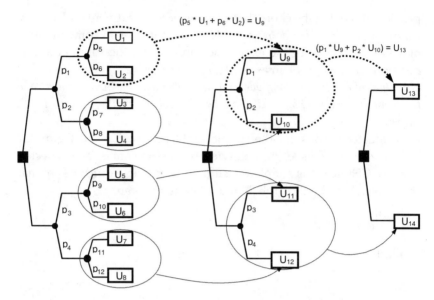

Figure 2.3. Averaging out and folding back. Starting from the terminal nodes, each chance node is replaced with its expected value until a decision node is encountered. At the decision node, the branch with the highest value is chosen.

persons testing negative will not undergo immediate treatment. Patients who are HIV infected but who are not treated (either because they were not tested or because they were tested and the result was a false negative) we assume will be treated only after they develop symptoms of HIV disease (which we term *late treatment*). We assume that treatment carries some toxicity (so there is a small penalty to the false positive, treated individual) and that treatment given early improves survival more than treatment given late. Table 2.1 identifies the basic parameters necessary to evaluate this problem, defines the variable names to be used in the analysis, and provides the baseline values for these variables.[1] The baseline analysis is provided for a population of 37-year-old males.

The structure of the decision model (Figure 2.4) begins with the choice of whether to screen or not. If screening is chosen (Screen), the test will either be positive (Test$^+$) or negative (Test$^-$). As described in the assumptions, all patients with positive results will be started on prophylactic treatment, and those who are HIV infected (HIV$^+$)[2] will receive

[1]These numbers are for illustrative purposes only and may not be clinically accurate.
[2]For notational convenience, HIV$^+$ means HIV infected.

Table 2.1. *Variable Definitions and Values, HIV Screening Problem*

Variable	Variable name	Value
Life expectancy of healthy 37-year old	LE	40.3 QALYs[a]
Life expectancy with early treatment	LERx	3.5 QALYs
Life expectancy with late treatment	LELateRx	2.75 QALYs
Life expectancy of healthy patient taking HIV treatment	LETox	39.4 QALYs
Sensitivity of HIV test	SENS	0.9700
Specificity of HIV test	SPEC	0.9988
Baseline prevalence of HIV	pHIV	0.5

[a] Quality-adjusted life years.

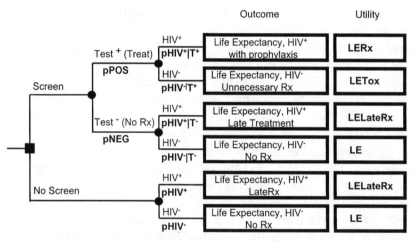

Figure 2.4. Decision tree for the HIV screening problem. The initial decision is to screen or not. The consequences of screening are that the test can be positive or negative; these results can be either true or false. The life expectancy associated with each branch is described in the outcome box. See text for details.

the benefit of early treatment. For these individuals, their life expectancy (LERx) will be 3.5 years. Because the test is not perfect, there are some uninfected individuals who will have a false positive test and will be treated. As we assumed a small toxicity to therapy, these individuals will have a quality-adjusted life expectancy (LETox) that is slightly lower than the average life expectancy of a 37-year-old male (LE). Similarly, some individuals who are infected will initially test falsely negative and will receive treatment only later, when symptoms develop (LELateRx).

If the choice is made not to implement a screening program (No-Screen), then none of the infected individuals will have the benefit of early antiretroviral and appropriate prophylactic treatment. These individuals will have a life expectancy of LELateRx. Individuals who are uninfected if not screened will have the life expectancy of a healthy 37-year-old male (LE).

The next step is to populate the tree with the various probabilities and outcomes (life expectancies) that apply to this problem. The outcomes (in terms of life expectancy) are entered at the end of each path through the tree. A brief examination of the tree structure indicates that the information as presented in the table cannot be applied to the decision problem directly. The baseline data provide characteristics of test performance (sensitivity and specificity), as well as information regarding the population (age, life expectancy, and HIV prevalence). The logical structure described in the tree requires that the information be represented differently: it requires the probability that a given test in the population will be positive and the probability of disease given a positive or negative test (predictive value positive and predictive value negative). The updating of probabilities given the result of a test (the clinical application of Bayes' Theorem) is such a common structure in decision analysis that it will be described in more detail. Figure 2.5 graphically describes the two methods for detailing the probabilities relevant to the use of diagnostic test information. In the top panel, the structure is drawn indicating the proportion of positive tests that would be expected to result from a population with a given prevalence and a test with a given sensitivity and specificity. However, the clinically more useful order is shown in the lower half of the figure, where the test *result* is followed by whether the patient has the disease or not. Although equivalent in information content, the latter formulation represents the order in which a clinician receives the data, and therefore represents the situation faced by clinicians treating patients with a given test result. Both trees provide identical path probabilities for the end results: true positive, false positive, true negative, and false negative. The tree is a graphical representation of Bayes' Theorem, which relates the prior probability of disease before the test result is known to the posterior probability of disease after the test result is known. For a more complete exposition of the use of Bayes' Theorem in medical decision making, the reader is referred to Weinstein et al. (1980).

Because it matches the logical temporal flow of events as they would occur clinically, the structure of the tree designed to answer the HIV

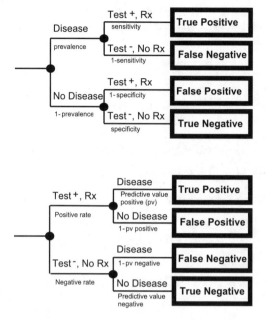

Figure 2.5. Decision tree description of Bayes' Theorem. The upper panel describes the order of information useful for the description of the characteristics of a test. The *sensitivity* of a test is the probability of a positive test in patients with disease; the *specificity* is the probability of a negative test in patients without disease. The bottom panel illustrates the clinical view of the problem: one is faced with a positive or negative test result and must determine the likelihood that the patient has the disease (*positive and negative predictive value*).

screening problem requires a Bayesian updating of the prior probability of disease. Figure 2.6 illustrates the appropriate Bayesian updating for the specific test results relevant to the HIV screening example; the resulting values (with their corresponding formulae) are presented in Table 2.2.

Once the probabilities are calculated, the analysis of the tree follows the standard averaging out/folding back procedure described earlier. For the HIV screening problem, this is shown in Figure 2.7. Each chance node is replaced with its expected value (sum of probabilities times the outcome or value), and the process is repeated until the expected values of the branches on the primary chance node are calculated. The branch with the highest expected value is the optimal choice. Given the probabilities assumed for this example, the value of the Screen strategy is 21.89 years and the value of the No Screen strategy is 21.53 years. This basic analysis would indicate that for these sets of initial conditions,

Table 2.2. *Revised Probabilities for HIV Screening Problem*

Probability of	Variable	Formula[a]	Value
Positive test	pPOS	pHIV * SENS + (1 − pHIV) * (1 − SPEC)	0.4856
Negative test	pNEG	1 − pPOS	0.5144
HIV+ given positive test	pHIV+|T+	$\dfrac{pHIV * SENS}{pHIV * SENS + (1 - pHIV) * (1 - SPEC)}$	0.9988
HIV+ given negative test	pHIV+|T−	1 − pHIV−|T−	0.0292
HIV− given positive test	pHIV−|T+	1 − pHIV+|T+	0.0012
HIV− given negative test	pHIV−|T−	$\dfrac{(1 - pHIV) * SPEC}{SPEC * (1 - pHIV) + (1 - SENS) * pHIV}$	0.9708

[a] SENS, sensitivity of test; SPEC, specificity of test; pHIV, prevalence of HIV.

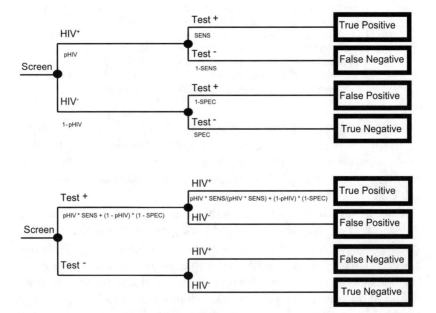

Figure 2.6. Tree structures for the Bayesian revision of HIV test results. Identical to Figure 2.5 in structure, this figure depicts the relevant outcomes and probabilities for the HIV screening problem.

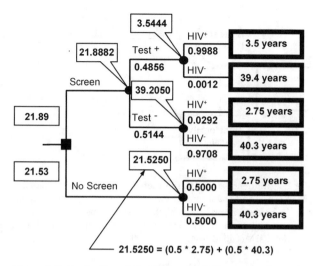

Figure 2.7. Evaluation of the HIV screening example. Averaging each chance node and replacing it with the expected value of the branches results in an expected value of 21.89 years of life expectancy for the Screen branch and 21.53 for the No Screen branch.

screening provides the longest life expectancy for a cohort of identical 37-year-old men at high risk for HIV infection.

3.   Influence Diagrams

As can be seen in many of the examples of decision trees provided in this chapter, the branch and node description of clinical problems often becomes very complicated and at times difficult to draw in a manner that preserves the relationships that actually drive the decision. The need to maintain symmetry across the branches for ease of model construction and validation, and the rapid increase in complexity that often arises from the liberal use of recursive structures, render the decision modeling process difficult to describe to others. The reason for this complexity is that the actual computational mechanism used to analyze the tree is embodied directly in the structure of the trees and branches. The average out/fold back approach flows directly from the structure of the tree. The probabilities and values necessary to calculate the expected value of the next branch are explicitly defined at each node.

Influence diagrams, first described by Miller et al. (1976), are being increasingly used for the development of decision models and are an alternate graphical representation of decision models (Howard & Matheson,

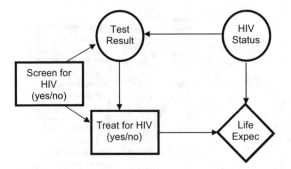

Figure 2.8. Influence diagram representation of the HIV screening example. Decision nodes and chance nodes are represented similarly as squares and circles. Arcs (arrows) imply probabilistic relationships between two events (i.e., HIV status may affect life expectancy and may affect the result of a test). See text for details. Modified from Owens, 1997.

1984). An influence diagram depicting the same HIV screening model shown in Figure 2.4 is shown in Figure 2.8. A detailed description of influence diagrams is beyond the scope of this chapter, and the reader is referred to a pair of papers by Owens and Nease for a more complete primer on the topic (Nease & Owens, 1997; Owens, Schachter, & Nease, 1997). Influence diagrams contain decision nodes (represented by rectangles) and chance nodes (represented as circles or ellipses), as in decision trees. However, there are no branches; alternate events are represented as a joint probability distribution associated with each chance node that specifies every possible combination of events represented by the node and its predecessors. These joint probability distributions are represented in influence diagrams by tables (see Table 2.3).

For chance nodes, the name of each outcome of the node is associated with the probability of that outcome. For nodes without predecessors called *marginal nodes*, a single row contains the probabilities for each possible state of the node (Tables 2.3A and 2.3C). For chance nodes and decision nodes with predecessors, the table has a column for each predecessor node and a separate row for each unique combination of the predecessor nodes (Tables 2.3B and 2.3D). Each row has the probability of each outcome of the chance node given the combination of values of predecessor nodes. In place of multiple terminal nodes found in decision trees, there is a single *value* node (the diamond in Figure 2.8)[3] associated with a table that specifies its value (utility) for every combination of

---

[3]Some authors represent the value node as a rounded rectangle (Shachter, 1986).

Table 2.3. *Influence Diagram Joint Distributions*

A. Decision node SCREEN FOR HIV		B. Decision node TREAT FOR HIV		
TEST	NO TEST	SCREEN	RESULT	TREAT
		Yes	Positive	Yes
		Yes	Negative	No
		No	Negative	\<computed\>

C. Chance node DISEASE PRESENCE[a]	
PRESENT	ABSENT
0.5	0.5

D. Chance Node TEST RESULT[a]				
TEST DECISION	HIV STATUS	POSITIVE RESULT	NEGATIVE RESULT	NO RESULT
TEST	PRESENT	0.97	0.03	0
TEST	ABSENT	0.0012	0.9988	0
NO TEST	PRESENT	0	0	1
NO TEST	ABSENT	0	0	1

E. Value node EXPECTED UTILITY		
TREATMENT DECISION	HIV STATUS	VALUE
TREAT	PRESENT	3.5 QALYs
TREAT	ABSENT	39.4 QALYs
NO TREATMENT	PRESENT	2.75 QALYs
NO TREATMENT	ABSENT	40.3 QALYs

[a] Numbers are the probability of the corresponding outcome.

its predecessors (Table 2.3E). Taken together, these tables specify all of the information contained in the structure of Figure 2.4 and Table 2.1. Taken together with the influence diagram itself, they provide sufficient information to do all the Bayesian calculations illustrated in Table 2.2. Thus, Table 2.2 is not necessary for the influence diagram representation.

Arcs connecting nodes specify the flow of information in the model. Arcs leading into a decision node indicate information that is available at the time the decision is made. For example, in the diagram shown in Figure 2.8, arcs into the decision node "Treat for HIV" indicate that the test decision and the test result are known at the time the treatment decision is made. Arcs leading into chance nodes are influences on the probabilities of events represented by those nodes. In this case, the test decision and the presence of disease influence the probability of each test result. The treatment decision and HIV status influence the value node since the disease and the treatment may be associated with morbidity. If cost is considered, the test decision may influence the value node directly.

It is important to realize that influence diagrams are semantically equivalent to decision trees (Shachter, 1986). A decision tree and the corresponding influence diagram will result in identical expected utilities; they are merely different representations. The advantages of influence diagrams are a more compact graphical representation, a more explicit representation of probabilistic dependencies, and freedom for the analyst to assess conditional probabilities in the most intuitive direction (Shachter & Heckerman, 1987). For example, in an influence diagram, one can assess the probability of a given test result given the presence of disease, whereas in a decision tree the analyst may have to specify directly the probability of disease given the test result, which may be less intuitive or require calculations to apply Bayes' Theorem (McNeill, Keeler & Adelstein, 1975). Evaluation of influence diagrams may be carried out using a number of computer-based algorithms (Shachter, 1986; Rege & Agogino, 1988) that automatically determine the Bayesian inference required to convert probabilities into the form needed for the analysis. The major limitation of influence diagrams is the lack of a direct equivalent of Markov models (see later). They are thus best suited to models that can be represented as simple trees.

4. Sensitivity Analysis

One of the most powerful attributes of decision analysis is the ability to assess rapidly the effect of uncertainty or variations in assumptions. Parameters needed to evaluate a decision model are not all known with the same certainty, and errors in those assumptions may have dramatic results on the optimal outcome. In our example, a variable that has an obvious impact on the outcome is the probability of HIV infection

Table 2.4. *Sensitivity Analysis*

pHIV	SCREEN	NO SCREEN
0.0	40.300	40.300
0.1	36.618	36.545
0.2	32.935	32.790
0.3	29.253	29.035
0.4	25.571	25.280
0.5	21.889	21.525
0.6	18.207	17.770
0.7	14.524	14.015
0.8	10.842	10.260
0.9	7.160	6.505
1.0	3.478	2.750

(pHIV). Initially assumed to be 50% (the prevalence in inner-city intravenous drug users), the probability of HIV infection is quite variable in different populations, and an analysis of this problem at different prevalence levels might be important. Decision analysis makes this task quite straightforward, as the entire evaluation process (average out/folding back) is easy to perform, especially if performed by a computer program with which the repetitive calculations can be done quickly.

Table 2.4 represents the values of the life expectancy of each strategy under different assumed probabilities of HIV disease. The same information is shown graphically in Figure 2.9. This *one-way sensitivity analysis* calculates the value of each branch of the decision node for different values for the probability of HIV disease. Several points regarding the value of sensitivity analyses can be derived from this analysis. First, as the probability of HIV disease rises, the life expectancy of both arms falls, as would be expected. Furthermore, at the extremes (pHIV = 0 and pHIV = 1), the calculations make sense and return the life expectancies of a healthy individual (40.3 years) and an HIV$^+$, untreated individual (2.75 years) for the NO SCREEN arm. The use of sensitivity analysis to check the performance of the model at the extremes where the actual answer to the problem is intuitively obvious is a useful method by which the structure and calibration of a decision model can be tested.

In addition, sensitivity analysis is useful for describing the performance of the model under different sets of initial conditions, which

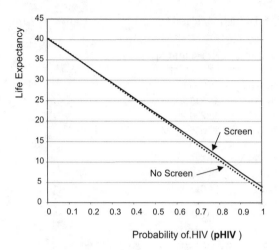

Figure 2.9. Sensitivity analysis across the probability of HIV disease. The threshold value of pHIV (0.0015) is not easily appreciated given the scale of the graph, but it can be calculated directly.

might represent different settings or classes of patients to which the model could be applied. For example, the model could be analyzed for high-risk (high probability of HIV) and low-risk (low probability of HIV) populations.

An examination of a complete one-way sensitivity analysis illustrates the important concept of the *threshold*, the value of a variable at which the value of two decisions is identical. For a probability of HIV disease less than 0.0015, No Screen is the optimal decision; for a probability greater than 0.0015, the Screen strategy is preferred. The crossover point is difficult to see in Figure 2.9, but it can be calculated directly (Pauker 1980). It is important to note that not all variables in a model will have a decision threshold: for some situations, no level of a given variable will alter the optimal strategy.

A straightforward extension of the one-way sensitivity analysis described earlier is to examine the optimal strategy when two variables are varied simultaneously. For example, returning to our problem, one would expect that the efficacy of prophylactic treatment would have an impact on whether screening is a preferred strategy: the more effective the prophylactic treatment, the greater the benefit in finding occult disease. The effect of varying both the probability of HIV disease and the efficacy of prophylactic treatment could be examined by finding the threshold probability of HIV disease for several different values of the effectiveness of prophylactic treatment. Plotting these thresholds produces a two-way sensitivity analysis that describes the ranges of the combination of the two variables for which each strategy is preferred.

5. Cost-Effectiveness Analysis

One of the significant advantages of constructing a decision model of a particular problem is the ability to compare the effect of various choices on many different outcomes simultaneously. Since the methodology provides an estimate of the expected value of the *outcome*, the outcome can be measured in life expectancy, quality-adjusted life expectancy, or costs. For example, in Figure 2.1, if the values of the outcomes (U_1 through U_4) are replaced with the cost of each path to that outcome, the evaluation of the tree will produce the expected cost of each strategy. This can be coupled with the expected value of the outcome to form cost-effectiveness measures for a given decision model. A more detailed explanation of cost-effectiveness methods appears in Chapter 6.

6. Markov Processes

In the previous section, the outcome variables assigned to the end of the decision tree were provided as life expectancies. In reality, the underlying process that a life expectancy represents is substantially more complicated than a single number can adequately describe. The terminal node represents the remaining lifetime of the individual. Many of the actions represented by the decision tree affect the value of that remaining life expectancy. Similarly, many decisions that we wish to analyze may contain events that can recur over time or may affect the probability of a future event (e.g., the development of acquired immunodeficiency syndrome [AIDS] in someone who is HIV infected). These types of extensions to the description of a clinical problem may be necessary to create a realistic model, but they are often difficult to accomplish in a standard branch and node structure. For example, in the HIV screening problem, suppose that you wanted to model a repetitive screening strategy in a high-risk population, perhaps for the purpose of evaluating the proper screening interval as a function of HIV risk. Constructing this scenario with standard tree and node methods rapidly becomes complex. For example, Figure 2.10 illustrates the addition of a second screening of all individuals who initially tested negative. These group includes people who are HIV$^+$ but tested falsely negative (perhaps they were in the

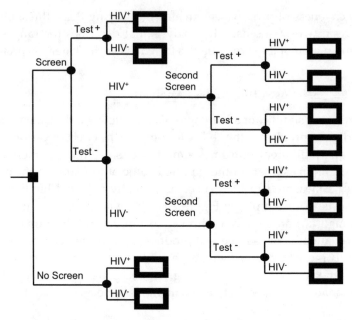

Figure 2.10. Sequential screening strategy. This figure represents the scenario of rescreening all of the initially HIV⁻ individuals. Note that even the single added screening adds significant complexity to the tree structure.

several-week-long "window" period shortly after exposure/infection in which there is viremia but no antibody response), as well as those who are true negatives. A second screening might pick up some of those HIV⁺ individuals. Furthermore, the truly HIV⁻ negative population is not necessarily static, and many HIV⁻ individuals may become HIV⁺ over time. Although one could account for this change by incrementally changing the probability of HIV between sequential branches, that adds complexity. Furthermore, extending the analysis to a series of sequential screenings at a given interval multiplies the complexity of the tree structure exponentially.

An equally difficult task would be to create a branch and node description that more realistically models what happens after the screening process takes place. In the SCREEN branch of Figure 2.7, the life expectancies at the ends of the branches are represented as single numbers but are in fact more complex. For example, the major consequence of not screening is that many people with occult infection have their diagnosis delayed to a future time. The stream of future events that results from each decision not only produces different consequences (life expectancies, utilities, and costs), but these events occur at different times. For many of these (costs and utilities), the value may change over time through discounting (Weinstein et al., 1987). The standard branch and node structure has no explicit method for keeping track of the time that events occur, and therefore discounting must be "hidden" in the determination of the particular outcome value. Although discounting of future consequences is described in more detail in Chapter 6, it is important to note that the particular structure used to represent a clinical situation can impede or facilitate the investigator's ability to include the discounting of future events.

One of the major advantages of screening is the early detection of asymptomatic, HIV-infected individuals so that they may benefit from early antiretroviral therapy. This therapy may slow the progression to symptomatic HIV disease or AIDS. Since this progression is dependent on the efficacy of drug therapy, an explicit description of the rate of progression from asymptomatic, HIV infected to AIDS would allow for an analysis of regimens with different efficacy, quality of life, and/or costs. Figure 2.11 represents expanding the model to the postscreening transitions between HIV^+, AIDS, and DEATH for several time periods after the screening takes place. Similar trees would be constructed at the end of each of the other initial screening branches (represented by $\cdots$ in the figure). The effect of drug therapy in the screened versus the nonscreened population would be modeled by changing the probability of developing AIDS if HIV infected. The tree structure presents models at only four time periods and is already quite complicated.

The difficulties encountered in modeling clinical events over time in standard tree and branch constructions are partially eliminated by another type of model called a *Markov process*. The structure illustrated in Figure 2.12 describes such a process, which is a mathematical construct for modeling events over time. Notice that in the tree solution to modeling postscreening events, there are really only three different states: ASYMPTOMATIC HIV^+, AIDS, and DEAD. The fundamental idea behind Markov processes is that conditions in the particular model are represented as a set of mutually exclusive states, the entire set of which describes all possible conditions in which an individual may be found for a particular problem. This structure models the same set of events depicted in the complex tree of Figure 2.11. Patients can initially be found in the ASYMPTOMATIC HIV^+ state, and in the next time period they either remain in that state (with probability p_1), progress to AIDS (with probability p_3), or die (and end up in the DEAD state, with

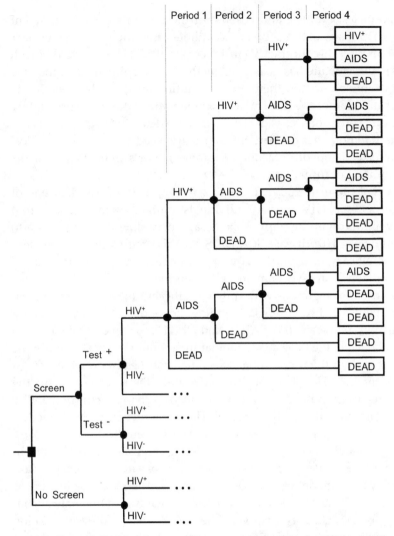

Figure 2.11. Modeling posttest events and outcomes. See text for details.

probability p_2). Once in the AIDS state, a patient may die (with probability p_6) or remain in the AIDS state (with probability p_5). This structure, while much simpler than the branch and node version, fully represents the possible events and paths that exist in the complex tree.

6.1.   Markov Process Definitions

Only a few definitions are required to understand the construction and evaluation of Markov processes. First, as shown previously, the

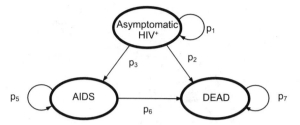

Figure 2.12. Simple Markov process. A Markov process describes the world as a series of independent states and the likelihood (probability) that a member of one state will transition to another state in the next time period. State membership is exclusive, i.e., an individual can be in only one state at a time.

world being modeled must be broken up into a series of *states*, defined so that an individual may be in one and only one of the states at a given time. Second, Markov processes assume that time is broken into discrete intervals (*cycles*) and that transitions between states occur only once during each cycle. Events generally are modeled as transitions between states. These transitions are governed by a set of *transition probabilities*, which are the probabilities of being in a given state in the next cycle conditional on membership in a particular state in this cycle. For example, for individuals in the ASYMPTOMATIC HIV$^+$ state, p_2 represents the probability that they will be in the DEAD state in the next cycle, and p_3 represents the probability that they will be in the AIDS state. When transition probabilities are constant over time, the process is defined as a *Markov chain*.

Figure 2.13 illustrates the state-transition diagram of several different types of states from which complex models can be constructed. The various types of states are designed to represent different clinical conditions that may be encountered. Judicious use of these components can model a large variety of clinical situations.

Recurrent State. Any state for which there is a nonzero probability of revisiting (either remaining in or returning to) is a recurrent state. This is the most common state used in standard modeling situations.

Transient State. A transient (or temporary) state is one for which the probability of leaving in the next time period is 1 (i.e., the patient may remain in the state for only one cycle). It is important to note that transient states can also be recurrent ones.

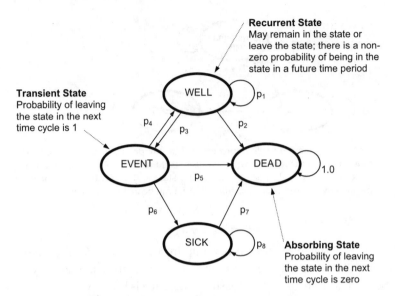

Figure 2.13. Types of Markov states. A complex clinical process can be modeled with the combination of various different types of states. Note that in addition to transient or absorbing states, entire sections or groups of states can be transient or absorbing as well. For example, once a person is HIV$^+$ even though there may be a large number of states describing event for HIV$^+$ individuals, transitions back to the part of the model in which patients are HIV$^-$ would not be allowed.

Absorbing State. An absorbing state is one for which the probability of leaving is 0. The most common absorbing state in medical decision analysis is DEATH. By extension, *groups of states* can be absorbing, meaning that once that portion of the model is entered, other states or sets of states become unobtainable. For example, in a more complicated model of HIV screening that included initially HIV$^-$ individuals, the transition between HIV$^-$ and HIV$^+$ involves a transition to an absorbing segment of the model: once HIV$^+$, an individual cannot become HIV$^-$ again.

    A defining characteristic of Markov processes is the "Markovian assumption" that transition probabilities are *path-independent*, meaning that the probability of moving between state A and state B is dependent only on being in state A; it does not depend on the state the individual occupied prior to being in state A. In other words, all individuals in state A are considered identical. This condition is sometimes referred to as *lack of memory* for the history of an individual prior to entering a given health state.

These individual elements can be combined to create complex models that represent clinical situations with varying levels of detail. The structure of the model describes the relationships that the investigator believes to be important; in fact, the structure of the model defines what assumptions regarding the real world will be incorporated into the model. A model that does not allow for a particular transition between state i and state j (probability of $state_j | state_i = 0$) mandates that, for the purpose of that model, this transition never occurs. We would urge substantial care in creating the structure of a model: the structure embodies the basic relationships that one assumes are operating in a particular clinical situation.

6.2. Representation

When transitions are modeled only as arrows in a state transition diagram or as a matrix (a single probability for each state-to-state transition), the details of the transitions are hidden within a single number and are lost to the analysis. For example, many compound events may happen between one state and another that the investigator desires to keep track of. In any transition between an alive state and death, the mechanism of death (myocardial infarction [MI], stroke, complication, etc.) may have importance in the analysis. By representing the transition probabilities as single numbers, standard Markov processes require the addition of multiple different states (Dead from MI, Dead from Stroke, Dead from Complication, etc.) to keep track of these outcome events. A more useful representation is a tree-based representation (*Markov cycle trees* [Hollenberg 1984]) of all the intermediate events that lead to a transition from one state to another.

For example, as noted earlier, instead of modeling the transition between SICK and DEAD as a single step in the state transition diagram (Figure 2.14), the cycle tree can describe the intermediate events that precede the patient's death, perhaps by several different paths. The majority of Markov processes described in the medical literature today are represented this way. Figure 2.14 illustrates the representation of a Markov process in a cycle-tree format. The branches of the *Markov node* represent all of the possible states in the model (in this case, HIV+, AIDS, and DEAD). The chance node following each branch represents the transitions between various states during the cycle. For the portion of the cohort in the HIV+ state, a fraction (p_1) will remain HIV+, a fraction (p_2) will progress to AIDS, and a fraction (p_3) will die (proceed to

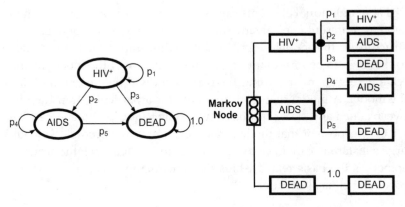

Figure 2.14. Comparison of the state transition diagram and Markov cycle trees. Branches arising from a Markov node are the possible states of the Markov process. The node and branch structure after each state represents the probability structure that determines transitions between states in the next time period.

the DEAD state) without progressing to AIDS. The terminal node no longer contains a value or utility but instead indicates the state that the portion of the cohort arriving at that terminal node will start in during the next cycle. The transition probability from state A to state B is the sum of path probabilities for all paths leading from state A to state B in the cycle tree (Figure 2.14).

6.3.   Evaluation of Markov Processes

The evaluation of a Markov process is more complex than the evaluation of a simple branch and node tree structure. As noted in the previous example, one use of a Markov process is to provide the value of a complex life history that forms the value of the terminal node of a tree. Conceptually, however, the expected value of a Markov process can be stated similarly to the expected value of a decision tree. For most decision analyses, the expected value of a Markov process represents the average life expectancy of a hypothetical cohort of individuals placed in that process. There are several methods for arriving at that value.

Matrix Algebra. As a purely mathematical construct, the simplest (and most restrictive) type of Markov process is the *Markov chain*, which assumes that transition probabilities are constant over time. Table 2.5

Table 2.5. *Transition Probabilities Necessary for Mathematical Matrix Solution to the Markov Chain*

	Period T + 1		
Period T	*HIV+*	*AIDS*	*DEAD*
HIV+	P(HIV+ given HIV+)	P(AIDS given HIV+)	P(DEAD given HIV+)
AIDS	P(AIDS given HIV+)	P(AIDS given AIDS)	P(DEAD given AIDS)
DEAD	0	0	1

presents the information required to represent the simple three-state example in a Markov chain. It lists the probabilities of moving from every state to every other state in one time period. All of the information one might want to know about such a process can be algebraically calculated from the set of known transition probabilities. These processes are directly solved using matrix algebra. The reader is referred to Beck or Sonnenberg (Beck & Pauker, 1983; Sonnenberg & Beck, 1993) for a detailed description of that methodology. The major advantage of Markov chains is that they can be solved analytically using straightforward matrix algebra. This provides not only a quick solution but also an exact solution, whereas the other methods are simulations. The disadvantage is that most medical processes do not fit the assumption of constant transition probabilities.

Evaluation by Cohort Simulation. Relaxing the requirement that probabilities be constant over time greatly expands the applicability of Markov models to medical decision making. However, time-varying probabilities make it impossible to use algebra to evaluate the process numerically, and other methods (cohort simulation, Monte Carlo simulation) must be used to calculate the expected value.

In *cohort simulation* a hypothetical cohort is assumed to start the process in a particular state or states at time 0, and portions of the cohort will make transitions to other states in the process for the next cycle according to the transition probabilities between the states or paths in a cycle tree. This will determine, for each time period or cycle, the portion of the cohort that inhabits each state. Typically, the entire cohort starts in one state (in this case, HIV+, but the cohort may be distributed among the different states). The expected utility of a Markov process is the sum over all time of the portion of the cohort in each state times the value of being in that state:

$$Cumulative\ utility = \sum_{t=1}^{T} \sum_{i=1}^{n} f_{i,t} q_i$$

where $f_{i,t}$ is the portion of the cohort in state i, at time t, q_i is the quality adjustment for life in state i, and T is the number of cycles the model runs. For models concerned only with life expectancy, the quality weights are either 1 (alive) or 0 (dead). However, the value of being in a state can be modified by the utility of being in that state to allow the model to accumulate quality-adjusted life years (QALYs) rather than life expectancy alone. These values are summed over time periods until a stopping rule is reached. The cycle-specific value that contributes to the overall sum is termed the *incremental utility* of membership in a given state for a given time period. The discrete time nature of the evaluation allows the incremental utility to be adjusted as a function of elapsed time in the model, similar to the manner in which probabilities can be time-varying. Typically, the analysis of a process stops when a certain number of cycles have been reached or when the cycle-by-cycle change in cumulative utility reaches an arbitrarily small number. This is synonymous with everyone in the cohort reaching an absorbing state such as death. The cohort simulation methodology produces cycle-specific output (Table 2.6), illustrating the remaining membership

Table 2.6. *Markov State Membership*

Cycle number	HIV$^+$	AIDS	DEAD	Cycle-specific value	Cumulative value
Start	1.000	.0000	.0000	0.5	0.50
1	.9552	.0398	.0050	.9950	1.50
2	.9122	.0762	.0115	.9885	2.48
3	.8714	.1090	.0194	.9806	3.46
4	.8323	.1391	.0286	.9714	4.44
5	.7950	.1661	.0389	.9611	5.40
6	.7593	.1905	.0502	.9498	6.35
7	.7253	.2124	.0623	.9377	7.28
8	.6927	.2319	.0753	.9247	8.21
$\vdots$					$\vdots$
~300	0	0	1	0	42.00

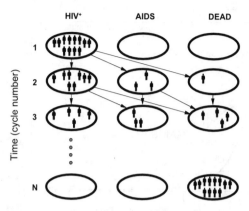

Figure 2.15. Cohort solution to the Markov process. In a cohort simulation, portions of the cohort start in a given distribution (in this example, all start in the HIV$^+$ state). As time progresses, members of the cohort move between states: patients who are HIV$^+$ develop AIDS; both patients who are HIV$^+$ and those who have AIDS will die. Eventually, the entire cohort will be found in the DEAD state.

in each state, and the cycle-specific (incremental) utility and cumulative utility.

Table 2.6 demonstrates state membership over time as the model progresses. In this example, only life expectancy is considered, and there is no quality of life penalty for the AIDS state. Therefore, the cycle-specific value of the process is simply the portion of the cohort in the HIV$^+$ state plus the portion of the cohort in the AIDS state (the value of being in the DEAD state is 0). The cumulative value is the running sum of the individual cycle-specific values. The value of 0.5 for cycle zero is known as the *half-cycle correction* and is described in Sonnenberg and Beck (1993).

The process is illustrated graphically in Figure 2.15. Membership in each of the three states (HIV$^+$, AIDS, and DEAD) is shown for each cycle. Members of the cohort move between various states (arrows) according to the probabilities defined by p_1 through p_6. Transitions from AIDS to HIV$^+$ are not allowed in this particular model, and DEAD is an absorbing state. Figure 2.16 describes the membership (portion of the cohort) in each state over time as the model progresses. In this particular case, the transition probabilities are constant over time, which produces an exponentially declining curve representing those individuals who remain HIV$^+$ (Beck, Kassirer, & Pauker, 1982; Beck, Pauker, Gottlieb, Klein, & Kassirer, 1982). The shape of the portion of the cohort who are defined as having AIDS is a combination of individuals entering the state (from

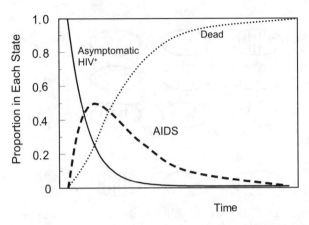

Figure 2.16. Plot of state membership over time. As the process moves forward cycle by cycle, individuals who are asymptomatic and HIV$^+$ develop AIDS, the incidence of which rises. However, as the cohort progresses, the influx of patients developing AIDS is matched by patients dying from complications of the disease, and the proportion of the initial cohort who are dead increases.

HIV$^+$) and those leaving the state through death. Models constructed as Markov cycle trees are quite flexible and allow for the creation of models that are reasonable representations of specific clinical situations. Because cycle trees are not required to have transition probabilities that are constant over time, they can use data directly from survival or cohort studies to calibrate the transition probabilities that flow between states. Further, it is clear from this example how one might model the effect of prophylactic therapy, which decreases the probability that a patient will progress from HIV$^+$ to AIDS. In Figure 2.14, p_2 represents the probability of progressing to AIDS. The effect of therapy can be modeled by modifying that probability (say, by multiplying it by a factor of less than 1 that represents the efficacy of therapy). Recalculating the probability as

$$p_2 = p_2 * \text{efficacy}$$

allows for the modeling of the effect of therapies with different abilities to slow the progression of the disease.[4]

[4]Technically, one should not multiply probabilities in this manner. To be mathematically correct, the probability should be converted into odds, the odds multiplied by a factor, and then the new odds reconverted into a probability. The reader is referred to Weinstein et al. (1980) for a more complete review of odds ratios and probabilities.

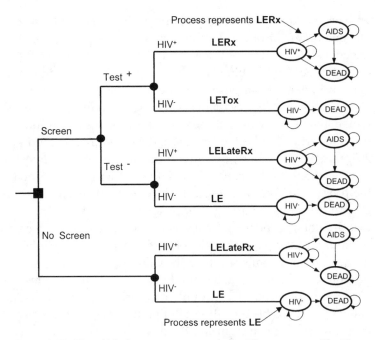

Figure 2.17. Use of Markov processes to estimate life expectancy. The life expectancy of each terminal node can be replaced by a Markov process that more realistically represents the transitions that occur for individuals in those situations.

The use of Markov processes to describe complex clinical situations is represented in Figure 2.17. This figure, which is an expansion of Figure 2.4, illustrates how the life expectancies at the terminal nodes of each of the branches in the tree can be replaced with a Markov process that represents the particular situation relevant to that branch. The value of the terminal node would first be determined by analyzing the Markov process and then folding back the tree in the standard manner described earlier. This method is very powerful in describing events that occur over time.

6.4. Complexity in Markov Processes

As useful as Markov cycle trees are, they have several limitations that arise as the clinical situation being modeled becomes more complex. For example, a logical extension of the model being used in this example is that the progression of HIV would be modeled in more detail, consistent with what is known about the pathophysiology of the disease. For example, one predictor of the development of complications (opportunistic infections, etc.) and progression is the absolute number of CD4 lymphocytes, a type of white blood cell involved in the body's immunological defense system. A simplistic but useful classification places individuals into three categories. Patients with CD4 counts of over $500/mm^3$ remain relatively healthy, those with counts between 200 and $500/mm^3$ develop certain kinds of infections, and those with CD4 counts less than $200/mm^3$ develop these infections plus a series of other infections and complications. Since many of the antiviral therapies designed to slow the progression of AIDS affect the level of CD4 cells, and since many clinical decisions regarding therapy are based on these levels, a model that did not incorporate CD4 levels would not be clinically credible.

Figure 2.18 expands the detail given in the prior Markov process to incorporate varying levels of the CD4 count. In this representation, portions of the cohort can be found in any one of three states, each representing a particular CD4 count. The various probabilities indicated allow for all possible transitions: individuals may either increase or decrease their CD4 count during the next cycle. This illustrates another important modeling point: it is the combination of the states and the transitions between them that provides a description of a clinical process. For example, if one wanted to make the progression of HIV disease monotonic and only allow for the continual decline in CD4 cells, the states would remain the same but certain transitions (those represented

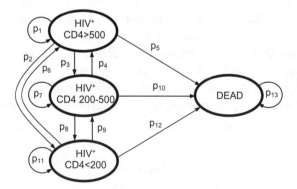

Figure 2.18. Markov process with inclusion of various CD4 counts. The HIV$^+$ and AIDS states of Figure 2.11 have been replaced by a series of states representing levels of immune functioning, proxied by the number of CD4 cells.

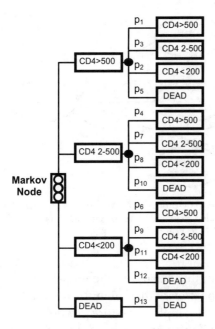

Figure 2.19. Markov cycle tree for the HIV example extended by the CD4 count. The number of branches has increased from 6 to 13, with a corresponding number of probabilities to estimate.

by p_4, p_6, and p_9) would be eliminated or set equal to 0. The cycle tree format for this extension to the problem is shown in Figure 2.19. Note that the number of branches required has increased, and the tree begins to become relatively complicated.

Models of clinical situations can rapidly become substantially more complicated. Another predictor of the rate of progression of HIV disease is the level of viral mRNA (nucleic acids found only in the HIV virus). The higher the RNA level (also called the *viral load*), the worse the prognosis and, on average, the faster the CD4 count falls. Therefore, for any level of CD4, knowing whether the viral load is high or low may make a difference in the particular prophylactic therapy used. Figure 2.20 illustrates the addition of viral loads to the Markov process describing HIV progression. As is demonstrated in the figure, the number of states increases quite rapidly with the number of different parameters modeled. In general, the number of states increases geometrically with the number of characteristics or variables that define the different states. A cycle tree version of this process is not shown, but it would contain

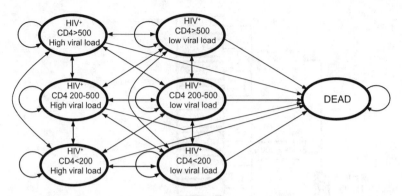

Figure 2.20. Complex Markov process. The Markov process depicted in Figure 2.18 has been expanded to include level of viral RNA (a measure of viral replication), as well as the CD4 count.

over 40 branches. Even with this extension, the model only scratches the surface of the clinical complexity that might be required to model a given clinical situation. For example, the entire process in Figure 2.20 would need to be replicated if the model accounted for changes in prophylactic therapy brought about by specific CD4 count levels. These extensions can lead to technically intractable models. Complex models are becoming more common in medical evaluations and provide more clinical realism. One of the first large, detailed models of a disease process was the Coronary Heart Disease Policy Model (Weinstein et al., 1987), which described the flow of the U.S. population throughout life under various interventions designed to alter cardiovascular risk factors. More recently, the Stroke Patient Outcomes Research Team (PORT) at Duke University has developed a complex model of cerebrovascular disease to predict the natural history of the disease and the effect of various interventions on morbidity and mortality (Matchar et al., 1997). However, this complexity comes with a price: these models are more difficult to develop, evaluate, and debug; they are harder to understand for a non-quantitative content expert; and they become very difficult to interpret for the nonquantitative clinical reader.

7.   Alternatives to Markov Models

The fundamental characteristic of a Markov process is the Markov property, the assumption that transition probabilities depend only on the current state of membership. Called the *no-memory* property, the path by

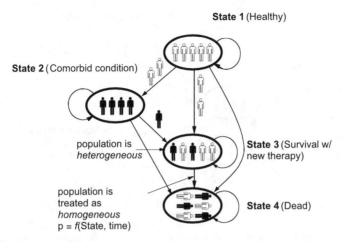

Figure 2.21. Markovian lack of memory assumption.

which portions of the cohort arrive in different states is not available for calculating transition probabilities for the next cycle. Therefore, a true Markov process requires significant complexity to represent a patient's history: different states are needed to represent different sets of prior events or paths through the model. All members of a state are treated the same way (have the same transition probability) whether they arrived in a given state in the previous cycle or whether they had been in that state for many cycles. Similarly, the portion of a cohort that arrives in a state cannot be treated differently in a standard Markov process even if that portion of the cohort arrived at that state along a different path than other portions. Figure 2.21 illustrates the problem graphically. The figure describes a four-state Markov process representing a hypothetical situation in which patients develop a medical condition (State 3) either before or after they develop a comorbidity (State 2). The problem is that if the particular condition is modeled only as a single state, all individuals in that state are treated the same way for the purpose of determining transition probabilities. In other words, in a standard Markov process or cycle tree, the population of patients in State 3 must be treated as *homogeneous*, but in fact, the population is quite *heterogeneous*. One portion of the cohort arrived in State 3 directly from State 1, whereas another portion of the cohort arrived after having been through State 2. This is what is meant by no memory: the process has no knowledge of state membership in the prior cycle or of the path by which the members of a cohort arrive in a particular state. Since past history is often crucial

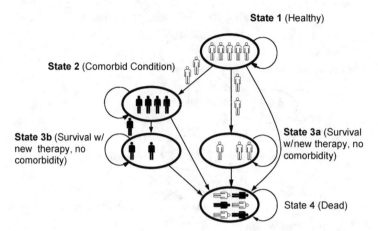

Figure 2.22.   Cohort simulation solution to the lack of memory problem.

in medical prognosis, this assumption is not appropriate for modeling many disease states.

The standard Markovian solution to this problem is to simply increase the number of states, as shown in Figure 2.22. In this solution, State 3 is divided into two separate states: State 3a, representing the path directly from State 1, and State 3b, representing the path through State 2. Now the transition probabilities from the two versions of State 3 can be different, as would be expected with the presence of a comorbidity. The problem is that this multiplication of states can become truly intractable, considering the potential number of factors that may need to be modeled. In fact, the number of states in a model will grow geometrically with the number of variables that affect transition probabilities from a given state. Problems can quickly become massive, requiring thousands of discrete states to model completely.

7.1.   Semi-Markov Processes

Analytically, a Markov process or Markov cycle tree breaks up a time span into intervals (cycles) and models the discrete motions of individuals through different states of the model during each time period. In essence, the model becomes a longitudinal series of static snapshots of an underlying dynamic process. An alternative approach is to consider time continuously and calculate transition rates and *holding times* for states rather than transition probabilities in a fixed time period. Relaxing the requirement of a fixed time interval defines a *semi-Markov* process

(Howard, 1971) of which Markov processes are a special case. Stochastic trees (Hazen, 1992) represent one solution method for this formalism.

7.2. Individual Simulations as a Solution

The crux of the no-memory problem is that in standard cohort analysis, each state is occupied by a fraction of the cohort, and the paths and histories of the different components of the cohort are not maintained. One pragmatic solution is to simulate the members of the cohort *individually* rather than as a group. By allowing only one member of the cohort into the model at a time, one can keep track of the complete history of state membership as the individual moves through the process. This process is depicted in Figure 2.23, where the same Markov process illustrated in Figure 2.21 is reproduced. To analyze the process, one individual at a time is placed into the process, and that person is followed from state to state until a terminal state is reached. The process is repeated for a large number of iterations, and the life expectancies of the individuals moving through the cohort is summed. The number of iterations must be large enough so that the average LE converges. The exact number depends on the complexity of the model and the variability in parameters but typically is between 10,000 and 100,000.

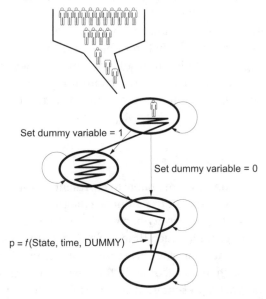

Figure 2.23. Individual simulation solution to the lack of memory problem.

The advantage arises from the ability to alter transition probabilities based on the history of the individual moving through the process. For example, in Figure 2.23, a variable representing comorbidity can be initially set to 0; it is changed to 1 only if the specific individual moving through the process arrives at State 2. Then, in State 3, the transition probability can be a function of the variable representing the presence or absence of the comorbidity. This Monte Carlo evaluation method reaches the same answer as the traditional expanded-state Markov process but does so with fewer states. The increased complexity is embodied in the functional definitions of the transition probabilities (Roberts, 1989).

The construction of a problem as an individual simulation allows the analyst to track many other parameters in the model that are generally unavailable in a model evaluated by cohort simulation. Counts of specific events (number of times hospitalized, number of episodes of an illness, acquisition of multiple risk factors, length of time in a certain state) are readily calculated from the individual simulation. Furthermore, the individual simulation methodology can provide distributions surrounding these estimates. Although statistical interpretation is not always clear-cut, given uncertainties in the definition of underlying distributions, the individual simulation approach can also provide estimates of the uncertainty of the outcome results, as well as estimates of the effect of uncertainty in a parameter on a specific outcome, as standard sensitivity analysis provides. However, Monte Carlo simulation can provide multiway sensitivity analysis in which all parameters in the model are varied simultaneously throughout their defined ranges.

Major disadvantages of individual simulations are that they are computationally intensive and require powerful computing technology and long evaluation times. Parallel computing architectures promise to make simulations more practical.

7.3.   Dynamic Influence Diagrams

Ordinary influence diagrams are unable to represent a prognosis that extends over time. An extension of the influence diagram referred to as a *dynamic influence diagram* (Tatman & Shachter, 1990) essentially creates a separate influence diagram for each time cycle. A decision made and the values of chance variables in one cycle influence the decision made and the probabilities of chance outcomes in the next cycle. This formulation has a more compact representation and more explicitly represents decisions that are sequential in nature. Dynamic influence diagrams are limited by computational complexity when the number of cycles is large and by the lack of software for evaluating them.

8.   Discrete Event Simulation

The models that we have described in this chapter provide answers to an optimization problem essentially in the absence of resource constraints. For example, the HIV screening example can answer the question *"For a population with a given risk of HIV disease, does screening make sense?"* It cannot, however, answer the question *"Is screening of that population possible?"* given the availability of testing machines, the infrastructure needed to draw blood tests, and so on. This dichotomy between what should be done and what is possible is common in other questions for which decision analysis is useful, such as *"Should women between 35 and 40 have annual mammograms?"* or *"Should diabetics with asymptomatic gallstones undergo prophylactic cholecystectomy?"* Standard decision analysis cannot answer several of the related questions that result from the answers to the question in an individual patient. For example, even if a decision analysis demonstrated that all women between 35 and 40 should have mammography, it is not clear that there are sufficient mammography machines to scan all women in the United States.

Another example is the optimal timing of liver transplantation in end-stage liver disease. Although the task is complicated, one could imagine developing a Markov model of the natural history of disease that compared expected survival with transplantation to expected survival without transplantation throughout the entire course of disease. The optimal time to transplant, based on clinical factors, would be the time that maximized life expectancy. However, organs are not immediately available; furthermore, the size of the waiting list is related to the types of patients listed and the time in their disease at which they are placed on the list. The dynamic interplay between the optimal decision rule *in a specific individual* and how that rule translates to its application to *a population* is not well modeled in standard decision analysis.

A methodology that has been in widespread use in other fields for a long time is *Discrete Event Simulation*. Developed as a tool for industrial engineering and management sciences, discrete event simulation incorporates many of the attributes of standard decision modeling with the ability to model queues and competition for various resources.

The application of discrete event modeling in health care has concentrated on physical relationships, such as the optimal location of helicopters for rural emergency transportation (Clark et al., 1994), the optimal allocation of resources in the intensive care unit (Lowery & Martin, 1992) and several other problems of resource or staffing allocation. However, given the increasing importance of resource constraints in the evaluation of health services, the use of this methodology is expected to increase. Klein et al. (1993) provides an excellent review of the application of these models to health care.

9. Summary

The purpose of this chapter was to provide a synopsis of the various common modeling tools and to describe their use in a progressively more complex clinical problem. All models are to some extent abstractions of the real world, and matching the appropriate modeling technique to a particular problem is one of the most important tasks in modeling. The purpose of using more sophisticated modeling techniques is to make the model as realistic a reflection of the real world as possible, within the constraints of available data, time available to the analyst, computational resources needed to evaluate the model, and the complexity that can be explained to consumers of the model.

The techniques described in this chapter address three dimensions of modeling. One is model type (simple model, Markov models, semi-Markov models, simulations). The second dimension is *model representation* (simple tree vs. influence diagram, probability matrix, Markov cycle tree, stochastic tree, dynamic influence diagram). The third dimension is *evaluation method* (foldback, Monte Carlo simulation, matrix algebra, cohort simulation, discrete event simulation, rollback of a stochastic tree). For example, Monte Carlo simulation is not a type of model but rather an evaluation method. Simple trees, influence diagrams, and Markov models can all be evaluated by Monte Carlo simulation. Monte Carlo evaluation incorporates statistical measures of uncertainty in model parameters, provides measures of uncertainty in the results, and provides multiway or all-way sensitivity analyses. Table 2.7 summarizes the advantages and disadvantages of each model type.

Decision trees have the advantage of simplicity in construction and evaluation but are limited by a fixed time horizon. Influence diagrams have the same limitation but have the advantages of a more compact representation and explicit representation of probabilistic relationships. Some authors believe that influence diagrams provide a representation

Table 2.7. *Advantages and Disadvantages of Decision Model Types*

Model type	Fidelity	Difficulty of construction	Time horizon	Computational demands	Availability of software
Standard decision trees	Low	Low	Fixed	Low	Many options
Markov processes	High	Moderate	Unlimited	Moderate	A few options
Stochastic trees	High	Low	Unlimited	Low	No
Monte Carlo Markov (individual simulations)	High	High	Not specified	High	A few options
Influence diagrams	Low	Low	Fixed	Moderate	A few options
Dynamic influence diagrams	High	High	Not fixed but limited	High	No
Discrete event simulation	High	High	Unlimited	High	A few options

of the problem domain that is more natural for a domain expert to specify and understand. However, for practical purposes, simple trees and simple influence diagrams are equivalent and are rarely useful in providing complex medical decision analyses. Simple trees and influence diagrams may be evaluated either deterministically or by Monte Carlo simulation. The latter method provides a multiway sensitivity analysis and quantifies the uncertainties in the results.

Decision models that represent time explicitly are needed to represent situations for which the timing of events is uncertain, risk is continuous over time, the utilities or risks of events vary over time, or events may occur more than once. Markov chains are the simplest to represent and the fastest to evaluate, but they require the usually unrealistic assumption that transition probabilities are constant over time. The more general Markov process, which may be represented in a variety of ways, permits changing transition probabilities but requires that the evaluation take place either by simulation of a cohort or by Monte Carlo simulation of individuals. The Markov cycle tree is a convenient representation of a Markov model that specifies the details of transitions from one state to another as branches of chance nodes. Cycle trees may be evaluated either by cohort simulation or by Monte Carlo simulation using readily available computer software.

The Markov property (according to which all members of a given Markov state are indistinguishable) prevents the consideration of prior history in determining the utility or prognosis of a state. The Markov property requires the addition of states to a model when the prior history is important. In certain situations, this can result in a very large number of states that may be unmanageable. The alternative method, Monte Carlo simulation, in which the prior history of individuals is explicitly represented, can avoid this problem, but at the expense of an evaluation process that is computationally more intensive and more time-consuming. Discrete event simulation can help to model situations in which the availability of resources to carry out a strategy cannot be controlled by the decision maker.

Other modeling methods are useful in certain situations. Stochastic trees are a more compact and more rapidly evaluated method of representing Markov models, but they are limited by the requirement of constant transition probabilities and a lack of available software to build and evaluate them. Dynamic influence diagrams are an extension of influence diagrams to a multiple-cycle time horizon, but they are limited in the number of cycles that can be represented and by a lack of software.

The analyst must match the modeling technique to the requirements of the clinical problem but must also be careful not to use a more complex modeling method that can be supported by available data. The techniques presented here represent a palette from which the analyst may choose the most appropriate tool for a given analysis.

References

Beck JR, Kassirer JP, Pauker SG. A convenient approximation of life expectancy (the "DEALE"). I. Validation of the method. *American Journal of Medicine.* 73(6):883–8, 1982.

Beck JR, Pauker SG, Gottlieb JE, Klein K, Kassirer JP. A convenient approximation of life expectancy (the "DEALE"). II. Use in medical decision-making. *American Journal of Medicine.* 73(6):889–97, 1982.

Beck RJ, Pauker SG. The Markov process in medical prognosis. *Medical Decision Making.* 3:419–58, 1983.

Brewer TF, Heymann SJ, Colditz GA, Wilson ME, Auerbach K, Kane D, Fineberg HV. Evaluation of tuberculosis control policies using computer simulation. *Journal of the American Medical Association.* 276(23):1898–903, 1996.

Clark DE, Hahn DR, Hall RW, Quaker RE. Optimal location for a helicopter in a rural trauma system: prediction using discrete-event computer simulation. *Proceedings of the Annual Symposium on Computer Applications in Medical Care.* 888–92, 1994.

Col NF, Eckman MH, Karas RH, Pauker SG, Goldberg RJ, Ross EM, Orr RK, Wong JB. Patient-specific decisions about hormone replacement therapy in postmenopausal women. *Journal of the American Medical Association.* 277(14):1140–7, 1997.

Hazen GB. Stochastic trees: a new technique for temporal medical decision modeling. *Medical Decision Making.* 12(3):163–78, 1992.

Hollenberg J. Markov cycle trees: a new representation for complex Markov processes. *Medical Decision Making.* 4:529, 1984.

The discrete time semi-Markov process. In Howard R, *Dynamic Probabilistic Systems.* Vols. I and II. New York: John Wiley and Sons, 1971.

Howard RA, Matheson JE. Influence diagrams. In Howard RA, Matheson JE, eds. *The Principles and Applications of Decision Analysis, Volume II: Professional Collection.* Menlo Park, CA: Strategic Decisions Group, 1984.

Klein RW, Dittus RS, Roberts SD, Wilson JR. Simulation modeling and health-care decision making. *Medical Decision Making.* 13(4):347–54, 1993.

Krahn MD, Mahoney JE, Eckman MH, Trachtenberg J, Pauker SG, Desky AS. A decision analysis of alternative treatment strategies for clinically localized prostate cancer. Prostate Patient Outcomes Research Team. *Journal of the American Medical Association.* 269(20):2650–8, 1993.

Leong TY. Dynamic decision modeling in medicine: a critique of existing formalisms. *Proceedings of the Annual Symposium on Computer Applications in Medical Care.* 478–84, 1993.

Lowery JC, Martin JB. Design and validation of a critical care simulation model. Review. *Journal of the Society for Health Systems.* 3(3):15–36, 1992.

Matchar DB, Samsa GP, Matthews JR, Ancukiewicz M, Parmigiani G, Hasselblad V, Wolf PA, D'Agostino RB, Lipscomb J. The Stroke Prevention Policy Model: linking evidence and clinical decisions. *Annals of Internal Medicine.* 127(8 Pt 2):704–11, 1997.

McCarthy BD, Wong JB, Munoz A, Sonnenberg FA. Who should be screened for HIV infection? A cost-effectiveness analysis. *Archives of Internal Medicine.* 153(9):1107–16, 1993.

McNeil BJ, Keeler E, Adelstein SJ. Primer on certain elements of medical decision making. *New England Journal of Medicine.* 293:211–15, 1975.

Miller AC, Merkofer NM, Howard RA, Matheson JE, Rice TR. Development of automated aids for decision analysis. Menlo Park, CA: Stanford Research Institute, 1976.

Nease RF, Owens DK. Use of influence diagrams to structure medical decisions. *Medical Decision Making.* 17(3):263–75, 1997.

Owens DK, Shachter RD, Nease RF. Representation and analysis of medical decision problems with influence diagrams *Medical Decision Making.* 17(3):241–62, 1997.

Pauker SG, Kassirer JP. The threshold approach to clinical decision making. *New England Journal of Medicine.* 302:1109, 1980.

Rege A, Agogino AM. Topological framework for representing and solving probabilistic inference problems in expert systems. *IEEE Transactions on Systems, Man and Cybernetics.* 18(3):402–14, 1988.

Roberts, MS. Simulating complex disease: Monte-Carlo models with memory. *Medical Decision Making.* 9(4):325, 1989.

Shachter RD. Evaluating influence diagrams. *Operations Research.* 34:871–82, 1986.

Shachter RD, Heckerman D. Thinking backward for knowledge acquisition. *AI Magazine.* 8:55–62, 1987.

Sonnenberg FA, Beck RJ. Markov models in medical decision making: a practical guide. *Medical Decision Making.* 13(4):322–8, 1993.

Tatman JA, Shachter RD. Dynamic programming and influence diagrams. *IEEE Transactions on Systems, Man and Cybernetics.* 20(2):365–79, 1990.

Weinstein MC, Fineberg HV, et al. *Clinical Decision Analysis.* Philadelphia: W. B. Saunders Co., 1980.

Weinstein MC, Coxson PG. Williams LW, Pass TM, Stason WB, Goldman L. Forecasting coronary heart disease incidence, mortality, and cost: the Coronary Heart Disease Policy Model. *American Journal of Public Health.* 77(11):1417–26, 1987.

Wellman MP, Eckman MH, Fleming C, Marshall SL, Sonnenberg FA, Pauker SG. Automated critiquing of medical decision trees. *Medical Decision Making.* 9:272–84, 1989.

3 Utility Assessment under Expected Utility and Rank-Dependent Utility Assumptions

John M. Miyamoto, PhD

Utilities have become a standard measure of value in the analysis of health decisions (Drummond, O'Brien, Stoddart, & Torrance, 1997; Gold, Siegel, Russell, & Weinstein, 1996). For purposes of decision analysis, utilities have a number of highly desirable properties. They are grounded in a normative theory of preference whose mathematical and theoretical foundations are well understood (Edwards, 1992; Fishburn, 1982, 1989; von Neumann & Morgenstern, 1944); they allow the construction of preference models that are adapted to the structure of specific decisions and outcome domains (Keeney & Raiffa, 1976; Sox, Blatt, Higgins, & Marton, 1988; von Winterfeldt & Edwards, 1986); and they possess a well-developed methodology for measuring the utilities of health outcomes as perceived by relevant populations of individuals (Keeney & Raiffa, 1976; Weinstein et al., 1980). It would seem that the stage is set for the unfettered application of utility theory to the task of assessing the value of health. There is, however, a serious obstacle to proceeding down this path. Extensive empirical research has demonstrated a variety of ways in which preferences are inconsistent with the assumptions of expected utility theory (Kahneman & Tversky, 1979, 1984; Slovic, Lichtenstein, & Fischhoff, 1988). If the methodology of utility assessment is largely based on expected utility theory, a theory that can be rejected as a descriptive theory of preference, how are utilities to be measured?

This is a big question, and its answer is still very much under development. What I hope to do here is to present one line of attack

I would like to thank Richard Gonzalez, Jonathan Treadwell, and Peter Wakker for helpful discussions of issues in utility theory and utility assessment and Han Bleichrodt for commenting on an earlier version of this manuscript.

on the assessment of utilities that is based on rank-dependent utility theory. Rank-dependent utility theory postulates that the probabilities as stated in lotteries do not directly determine the utility of lotteries. Rather, the probabilities are first transformed nonlinearly to decision weights, which are then combined with outcome utilities to determine the utility of lotteries (Karni & Safra, 1990; Quiggin, 1982). The nonlinear transformation of probabilities introduces fundamental changes in the methodology of utility assessment (Wakker & Stiggelbout, 1995). This chapter presents the Wakker–Stiggelbout analysis of the standard gamble method under rank-dependent utility assumptions and extends their analysis to problems in quality-adjusted life years (QALY) measurement and the characterization of risk posture. The chapter also describes the implications of nonlinear probability perception for the interpretation of certainty equivalents and time trade-offs. Many utility assessment procedures that are standard in medical decision making assume the validity of expected utility theory, and hence, they assume that the perception of probability is linear. What I hope to do is to describe how the nonlinear perception of probability distorts utilities that are assessed by standard methods and to present methods for removing the effects of these distortions.

Before undertaking this discussion, I should try to be clear about the perspective on utility analysis taken in this chapter. The focus of this chapter is on the theory that underlies *utility assessment procedures*, in other words, procedures by which numbers representing values are assigned to health outcomes. Of course, I do not have in mind just any procedures, but rather those that can be justified from the standpoint of a theory of preference under risk. I assume the normative validity of expected utility theory (henceforth, EU theory), and assume that the goal of utility assessment is to provide a quantitative measure of preference that can be combined with probabilities in a utility analysis of health decisions or policies (Gold et al., 1996; Weinstein et al., 1980). Because the descriptive validity of EU theory is no longer tenable, a need has arisen for utility assessment procedures that take violations of EU theory into account.

There are four major findings in the psychology of preference that must be taken into account in the theory of utility assessment. The first has already been mentioned, namely, the nonlinear perception of probability. Second, it has been argued that people represent outcomes as gains or losses relative to a neutral reference level rather than as absolute states of wealth (Kahneman & Tversky, 1979; Tversky &

Kahneman, 1992). The categorization of outcomes as gains or losses has predictable effects on risk posture and on the rate at which utility changes as a function of objective changes (so-called loss aversion). Third, preferences are affected by the way in which choices are framed (Kahneman & Tversky, 1984). Finally, preferences as inferred from choices are not identical to preferences as inferred from matching tasks like judgments of selling prices or certainty equivalents (Bostic, Herrnstein, & Luce, 1990; Fischer & Hawkins, 1983; Slovic & Lichtenstein, 1968; Tversky, Sattath, & Slovic, 1988). This chapter is primarily an attempt to incorporate nonlinear probability perception into the methodology of utility assessment. The other issues will not be addressed.

For simplicity, this chapter will focus on the problem of assessing the utility of health states that are better than death. A better-than-death health state is a state in which longer survival is preferred to shorter survival. Not all health states are better than death. Some health states are worse than death (shorter survival in these states is preferred to longer survival), and some health states are regarded as having a maximum endurable survival (longer survival is preferred to shorter survival up to the point of maximum endurable survival, and then shorter survival is preferred to longer survival beyond this point). Such health states give rise to important and interesting assessment issues, but a discussion of these issues would digress from the central questions of this chapter. Patrick, Starks, Cain, Uhlmann, and Pearlman (1994) and Drummond et al. (1997) discuss the problem of assessing worse-than-death health states. Sutherland, Llewelynn-Thomas, Boyd, and Till (1982) pointed out the occurrence of maximum endurable survivals, and Stalmeier, Bezembinder, and Unic (1996) noticed some problematic inconsistencies in judgments involving maximum endurable survival.

This chapter has the following organization. The first section describes four basic problems in utility assessment: the assessment of holistic outcomes, the assessment of a utility function for survival duration, the assessment of a linear QALY model, and the assessment of a power QALY model. The second section reviews how EU theory solves these assessment problems by means of standard gambles, certainty equivalents, and time trade-offs. Although this material is well known, the discussion will emphasize those features of assessment procedures that must be revised when nonlinear probability weighting is taken into account. The third section presents solutions to the utility assessment problems under the assumptions of rank-dependent utility theory. The goal of this section is to show how standard utility assessments must be reinterpreted in a framework that allows for the nonlinear weighting of probability. The fourth section presents some preference data and compares an analysis from the EU standpoint to an analysis from the rank-dependent utility standpoint. The section shows concretely how nonlinear probability weighting affects the interpretation of health preference data. The results presented in the third and fourth sections are the main contribution of this chapter. The final section reviews the problem of utility assessment from a perspective that takes violations of EU theory into account.

Four Problems in Utility Assessment

Before discussing the theory of utility assessment, I will list the types of assessment problems that this theory is intended to solve. As I describe these assessment problems, I will assume that we are trying to determine the utilities of a specific person, who I will refer to as the *client*. Depending on the research problem, the client may be a patient, a health professional, or a person drawn from the general public.

Conceptually, the simplest problem is one in which one has a short list of distinct health outcomes whose utility is to be assessed. For example, Sox et al. (1988) discuss a decision between surgical and medical treatment of a herniated intervertebral disc that is causing severe back pain. The potential outcomes in this decision are complete recovery, residual back pain, perioperative death, and residual back pain with foot drop. In this case, the utility assessment problem is to determine utilities that represent the relative worth for the client of each of these outcomes.

Utility Analysis (UA) Problem 1: Given a finite list of health outcomes, $A, B, C, \ldots$, determine utilities. $U(A), U(B), U(C), \ldots$ for the outcomes on this list.

This type of utility assessment problem is sometimes called an assessment of *holistic* outcomes because the analysis does not attempt to decompose the outcomes into attributes whose separate utilities are assessed and then combined by a composition rule.

Consider, next, the case in which duration of survival is a component of the possible health outcomes. In this case, one usually attempts to represent the utility of survival duration by means of a smooth curve that represents the increase in utility as a function of duration.

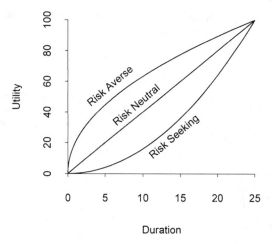

Figure 3.1. Risk-averse, risk-neutral, and risk-seeking utilities functions for survival duration.

UA Problem 2: Given that health outcomes lie on a continuum like survival duration, construct a curve that approximates the growth in utility along this continuum for a particular client.

Before proceeding to other assessment problems, it is worthwhile to digress briefly to the issue of risk posture. *Risk posture* or *risk attitude* refers to the curvature of a utility function over a continuum like survival duration or money. Technically, when talking about risk posture, one must specify the continuum in question, for it is perfectly reasonable (logically consistent) to have different risk postures with respect to survival duration, money, number of lives saved, and so on. Figure 3.1 displays utility functions for survival duration that exhibit different risk postures with respect to survival duration. A utility function is *risk averse* if it is concave downward over the continuum in question; it is *risk seeking* if it is concave upward over the continuum; and it is *risk neutral* if it is linear over the continuum. Risk posture is important in medical decision making because therapies can differ in their trade-offs between short- and long-term survival (Cher, Miyamoto, & Lenert, 1997; McNeil & Pauker, 1982; McNeil, Weichselbaum, & Pauker, 1978). In general, risk-averse utility functions are more favorable toward therapies that confer greater chances for short-term survival because such therapies provide higher probabilities of survival during the period in which risk-averse utilities increase most rapidly. One of the primary reasons why UA Problem 2 is important is that a solution to this problem yields

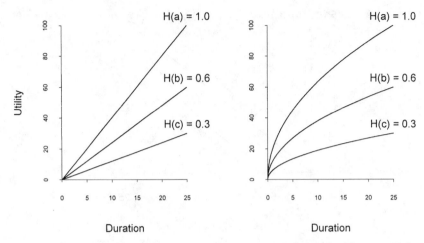

Figure 3.2. Left panel: The linear QALY model with three health states. Right panel: Power QALY model with three health states (power parameter $r = .5$).

a characterization of the risk posture of the client with respect to the continuum in question.

Next, we will consider assessment problems that arise when utility is based on a QALY model. The *linear QALY model* assumes that the utility of survival in any fixed health state is risk neutral. Furthermore, it represents the utility of alternative health states as factors that multiply the duration of survival. In other words, let a pair, (b, x), represent a survival of x years in health state b. The linear QALY model asserts that

$$U(b, x) = k \cdot H(b) \cdot x. \tag{1}$$

The left panel of Figure 3.2 shows the linear QALY model with three health states: a, b, and c. The function H maps health states to health state utilities. It is standard practice to assign the value $H(\text{full health}) = 1$. Thus, state a represents full health in Figure 3.2. All other better-than-death health states are assigned utilities between 1 and 0. The constant k is an arbitrary constant chosen so that the utilities range over a convenient interval of numbers. For example, if the longest survival to be considered in the decision analysis is 25 years, one can set $k = 4$. Under this choice, $U(\text{full health, 25 years}) = 4 \cdot H(\text{full health}) \cdot 25 = 100$. Since the utility of 0 years is 0, this choice of k yields utilities that range between 0 and 100.

Equation (1) describes the utility of a survival of x years in a constant (chronic) health state b. To apply the linear QALY model to a sequence of health states that change over time, one assumes that different time periods contribute additively to the overall utility. In other words, let $(b_1, x_1; \ldots ; b_n, x_n)$ stand for a health sequence where health state b_1 lasts for x_1 years, ..., and health state b_n lasts for x_n years, followed by death (any of the durations x_i can be a fraction of a year, if necessary). The linear QALY model applied to this health sequence asserts that

$$U(b_1, x_1; \ldots ; b_n, x_n) = \sum k \cdot H(b_i) \cdot x_i. \tag{2}$$

To illustrate this equation, suppose that we wish to calculate the utility of a sequence $(b_3, 3 \text{ years}; b_1, 12 \text{ years}; b_2, 5 \text{ years}; b_3, 5 \text{ years})$. Equation (2) states that

$$U(b_3, 3 \text{ years}; b_1, 12 \text{ years}; b_2, 5 \text{ years}; b_3, 5 \text{ years})$$
$$= k \cdot H(b_3) \cdot 3 + k \cdot H(b_1) \cdot 12 + k \cdot H(b_2) \cdot 5 + k \cdot H(b_3) \cdot 5. \tag{3}$$

The left panel of Figure 3.3 shows the implications of the additivity assumption (2) for the hypothetical case (3). The bottom left graph shows linear utility functions for survival in health states b_1, b_2, and b_3, assuming these health states to be constant. The upper left graph shows how the segments of the constant health state utility functions are combined according to Equation (2) to yield the utility of the sequence. The total utility of the sequence is indicated by the height of the point labeled U.

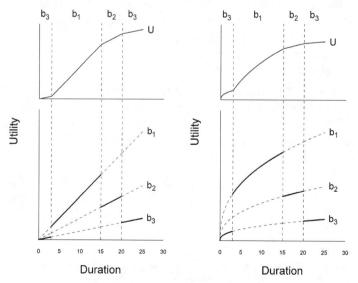

Figure 3.3. Left panel: Additivity across time periods in a linear QALY model. Right panel: Additivity across time periods in a power QALY model.

The key assessment problem for the linear QALY model is the determination of the health state utilities, $H(a)$, $H(b)$, $H(c)$, ...

UA Problem 3: Assuming the validity of the linear QALY model (1), determine the health state utilities, $H(b)$, for the various health states b in the decision analysis.

Given the health state utilities of a client, Equation (1) can be used to calculate utilities for chronic health states, and Equation (2) can be used to calculate utilities for sequences of health states. Most discussions of health utility analysis refer to the linear QALY model as simply the *QALY model*. In other words, when publications refer to *the* QALY model, it is assumed that Equations (1) and (2) describe the calculation of utility. This chapter uses the nonstandard term *linear QALY model* because an alternative, power QALY model will also be discussed.

One limitation of the linear QALY model is that it assumes that individuals are risk neutral with respect to survival duration. The following *power QALY model*[1] allows for risk aversion or risk seeking.

$$U(b, x) = k \cdot H(b) \cdot x^r. \tag{4}$$

The power QALY model implies that a utility function for survival duration is risk averse if $r < 1$, it is risk neutral if $r = 1$, and it is risk seeking if $r > 1$. The three utility functions shown in Figure 3.1 are power utility functions with r set at .5, 1, and 2, respectively. The right panel of Figure 3.2 shows the power QALY model with three health states, a, b, and c, for the specific power $r = .5$. As before, k is an arbitrary constant. If H(full health) is set equal to 1 and if 25 years is the longest duration in the decision analysis, then choosing $k = 100/25^r$ causes the utilities to range between 0 and 100.

The power QALY Model (4) describes the utility of a survival of x years in a constant health state b. To calculate the utility of a sequence of health states, one assumes that different time periods contribute additively to the overall utility. For any sequence, $(b_1, x_1; \ldots; b_n, x_n)$, let $x_0 = 0$. Then,

$$U[(b_1, x_1), \ldots, (b_n, x_n)] = \sum_{i=1}^{n} k \cdot H(b_i) \cdot \left[\left(\sum_{k=0}^{i} x_k \right)^r - \left(\sum_{m=0}^{i-1} x_m \right)^r \right]. \tag{5}$$

---

[1] More precisely, one might call Model (4) the multiplicative power model. Miyamoto (1999) discusses more general versions of the power model.

Although Equation (5) may look complicated, the intuition behind it is identical to the additivity assumption for the linear QALY model. The lower right panel of Figure 3.3 shows power utility functions for survival duration in constant health states b_1, b_2, and b_3. To compute the utility of the sequence (b_3, 3 years; b_1, 12 years; b_2, 5 years; b_3, 5 years), one takes the corresponding segments from the lower right panel and pieces them together to form the utility function in the upper right panel. The total utility of the sequence is indicated by the height of the point labeled U. Equation (5) is simply an algebraic description of this construction.

The main assessment problem for the power QALY model is the assessment of r and the values of H.

UA Problem 4: Assuming the validity of the power QALY model (4), determine the value of the power parameter, r, and the health state utilities, $H(b)$, for the various health states b in the decision analysis.

Given estimates of r and the values of H for a particular client, one can use Equation (4) to model utility in constant or chronic health states and Equation (5) to model the utility of sequences of health states.[2]

A brief word on the history of these models. The linear QALY model has a lengthy history that is recounted in Fryback (1999) and Drummond et al. (1997). Axiomatic work on QALY models began with Pliskin, Shepard, and Weinstein (1980). They published a set of axioms for the linear QALY model (1) and for the more general power QALY model (4) under EU assumptions. They showed that the linear QALY model is valid if preferences satisfy four properties: (i) survival duration is utility independent of health quality; (ii) health quality is utility independent of survival duration; (iii) proportional time trade-offs are constant; and (iv) preferences for lotteries over survival duration are risk neutral. They further showed that the power QALY model is valid if assumptions (i), (ii), and (iii) are satisfied and if assumption (iv) is replaced with the assumption that marginality is violated. Bleichrodt, Wakker, and Johannesson (1997) pointed out that the axioms for the linear QALY model can be substantially simplified if one assumes that different health

---

[2] Cher et al. (1997) explain an alternative way to compute the utility of a health sequence for a power QALY model. Their method uses derivatives of the utility function and yields an approximation to the utility of the sequence. Equation (5) yields an exact value, assuming the validity of a power QALY model.

states are equally preferred when the survival duration is zero. This assumption was called the *zero condition* by Miyamoto, Wakker, Bleichrodt, and Peters (1998), who reviewed its history and derived further implications from it. Bleichrodt, Wakker, and Johannesson showed that the zero condition and risk neutrality are jointly sufficient for the linear QALY model (1). Miyamoto (1999) showed that the zero condition, the constant proportional risk posture, and the utility independence of survival duration are jointly sufficient for the power QALY model (4). Both results are special cases of a general theorem in Miyamoto (1992) that showed that the zero condition and the utility independence of survival duration are jointly sufficient for a model in which the utility of duration and health quality combine multiplicatively and converge at zero duration. Miyamoto and Eraker (1988) investigated the empirical validity of the utility independence of survival duration, and Miyamoto and Eraker (1989) investigated the empirical validity of risk neutrality and constant proportional risk posture (a necessary condition for a power QALY model).

Utility Assessment under Expected Utility (EU) Assumptions

Basic Notation

To discuss utility assessments, we will need some notations for lotteries and preferences.

Notation	What it stands for:
$A, B, C, \ldots$	Health outcomes
$(A, p; B, 1 - p)$	A lottery in which one has a p- chance of receiving health outcome A and a $1 - p$ chance of receiving health outcome B
$(A, p; B, 1 - p) >_{\text{pr}} (C, q; D, 1 - q)$	$(A, p; B, 1 - p)$ is preferred to $(C, q; D, 1 - q)$
$(A, p; B, 1 - p) \sim_{\text{pr}} (C, q; D, 1 - q)$	$(A, p; B, 1 - p)$ and $(C, q; D, 1 - q)$ are equally preferred
$(A, p; B, 1 - p) \geq_{\text{pr}} (C, q; D, 1 - q)$	$(A, p; B, 1 - p)$ is equally or more preferred than $(C, q; D, 1 - q)$

For example, if A represents full health and B represents a specific inferior health state, then $(A, .75; B, .25)$ represents a lottery in which one has a 75% chance of full health and a 25% chance of the inferior health state.

Basic EU Theory

EU theory is a theory of preference under risk. When applied in a health domain, the basic objects of EU theory are lotteries for health outcomes and the fundamental empirical relation is the preference relation among such lotteries. Although health outcomes can be complex sequences of health states unfolding over time, and although lotteries can also be complex, the outcomes and lotteries that are used in utility assessment are only the most elementary types. The only options required for utility assessment are simple outcomes (riskless outcomes) and binary lotteries (lotteries with two outcomes). The basic claim of EU theory is that the preference ordering among lotteries is the same as the ordering of the lotteries by their expected utilities. This claim can be stated in terms of binary lotteries as follows:

$$(A, p; B, 1 - p) >_{pr} (C, q; D, 1 - q) \quad \text{iff}$$
$$pU(A) + (1 - p)U(b) > qU(C) + (1 - q)U(D) \tag{6}$$

and

$$(A, p; B, 1 - p) \sim_{pr} (C, q; D, 1 - q) \quad \text{iff}$$
$$pU(A) + (1 - p)U(b) = qU(C) + (1 - q)U(D). \tag{7}$$

(The expression "iff" is an abbreviation for "if and only if.") Condition (6) states that one gamble is preferred to another if and only if its expected utility is greater. Condition (7) states that equivalence in preference maps onto equality of expected utility. Conditions (6) and (7) represent the hypothesis of EU maximization for the special case of binary lotteries. For lotteries with more than two outcomes, one postulates that the EU of a lottery equals $\sum p_i U(x_i)$, where p_i represents the probability of receiving outcome x_i. More complicated notations such as this one will not be required in this chapter.

One special case of Condition (7) is especially useful in utility assessments, namely, the case where one observes an equivalence between a certain outcome C and a gamble $(A, p; B, 1 - p)$. From Condition (7), we may infer that

$$C;(A, p; B, 1 - p) \quad \text{iff} \quad U(C) = pU(A) + (1 - p)U(b). \tag{8}$$

Many utility assessment procedures require that one observe equivalences like the left side of (8), and then utilities are inferred from numerical relationships that are implied by the right side of (8).

For purposes of utility assessment, it is also important that if a utility function U satisfies the EU assumptions, then U is a *cardinal utility* or, equivalently, U is an *interval scale*. A precise definition of these terms requires the use of set theory (see Krantz, Luce, Suppes, & Tversky, 1971, or Roberts, 1979), but the essential idea is that in measuring a utility function, one is allowed two arbitrary assignments of utility. To give an analogy, if one were asked to assign coordinates to the points on an infinite straight line (infinite in both directions), one could pick any point and call it zero, and pick any other point and call it a unit distance from zero. After these two arbitrary choices, the coordinates of all other points would have definite values. In the context of utility assessment, researchers usually choose to assign 0 to the utility of death and 100 to the utility of full health. The logic of utility assessment and the empirically determined preferences of an individual then force all other outcomes to be assigned specific numerical utilities.

Conditions (6)–(8) exhibit a key property of EU theory. According to EU theory, utility is linear in probability. In other words, the probabilities by which the lotteries are defined, e.g., p and q on the left side of (6) or (7), are used directly in the calculation of the expected utility, e.g., p and q also appear on the right side of (6) or (7). Contrast this with the hypothesis that the probabilities are transformed nonlinearly in the cognitive process by which a risky option is evaluated. For example, suppose that in place of Condition (6), we had the condition

$$(A, p; B, 1 - p)B(C, q; D, 1 - q) \quad \text{iff}$$
$$w(p)U(A) + (1 - w(p))U(b) > w(q)U(C) + (1 - w(q))U(D) \tag{9}$$

In Condition (9), a nonlinear function w transforms the probabilities, p and q, into decision weights (psychological weights). In later sections, we will explore the implications of nonlinear probability weighting for the methodology of utility assessment. For now, I want to draw attention to the fact that EU theory implies that utility is linear in probability.

This assumption plays a central role in the EU theory of utility assessment.

Conditions (6)–(8) express all of the formal part of EU theory that is needed to discuss utility assessment procedures, but there is, of course, a great deal more that is relevant to the validity of utility assessments. Underlying EU theory is a set of preference assumptions, known as *EU axioms*, from which Conditions (6)–(8) and other related conditions can be derived. It should be noted that calling an assumption an axiom does not imply the empirical validity of the assumption. An axiom is simply one of a set of assumptions that are jointly sufficient to imply the validity of a theory, in this case, EU theory. The assumption that preferences are transitive, or the betweenness assumption (if $A >_{pr} B$ and $1 > p > 0$, then $A >_{pr} (A, p; B, 1 - p) >_{pr} B$), are examples of EU axioms. It can then be proved that if preferences are consistent with the EU axioms,[3] then there exists a utility function U that satisfies Conditions (6)–(8) and other related conditions. In this chapter, I will use the expression *EU assumptions* to refer to preference assumptions that are either EU axioms or are implied by the EU axioms. To assert that EU theory is descriptively valid is to assert that all EU assumptions are empirically valid properties of preference behavior. Conversely, when researchers claim that EU theory is descriptively invalid, they mean that at least some of the EU assumptions are violated by actual preference data. In fact, there is a great deal of evidence that preferences are inconsistent with the assumptions of EU theory. I will not attempt to review empirical tests of EU assumptions (see Camerer, 1989; Kahneman & Tversky, 1979, 1984; Luce, 1992; Slovic et al., 1988) and will assume that the evidence against the descriptive validity of EU assumptions is quite strong.

The EU Theory of Assessment Procedures

Most of the methods presented in this section are well known, but they are reviewed here in order to provide an explicit point of comparison with the non-EU approach discussed in the next section. More thorough descriptions of these methods are available in Sox et al. (1988), Froberg and Kane (1989b), and Drummond et al. (1997). The emphasis

---

[3] To be precise, there is not one unique set of EU axioms. Rather, theoretical analyses have uncovered a variety of alternative sets of assumptions, any one of which is sufficient to imply the validity of EU theory. Any of these sets of assumptions can be called *a* set of axioms for EU theory. Fishburn (1982) reviews alternative EU axiomatizations.

here will be on the logic by which utilities are inferred from preferences and the role of linearity in drawing these inferences. For the sake of brevity, I will not address statistical issues that arise in utility assessment beyond what is necessary to explain the specific examples in this chapter. The utility assessment methods described in this section all assume the descriptive validity of EU theory. This assumption will be dropped in the subsequent section on utility assessment under rank-dependent utility assumptions.

In the *standard gamble method*, a best outcome and a worst outcome are identified for the given health domain. Let A designate the best outcome, and let Z designate the worst outcome. As noted earlier, we are free to assign the utilities $U(A) = 100$ and $U(Z) = 0$. To assess the utility of any other outcome, B, the client is asked to judge the probability p^* that satisfies the relation

$$B \sim_{pr} (A, p^*; Z, 1 - p^*). \tag{10}$$

If p^* is the probability that creates the equivalence (10), then p^* will be called the *probability equivalent* of B with respect to the endpoints A and Z.[4] By Condition (8), we infer that

$$U(B) = p^* U(A) + (1 - p^*) U(Z) = p^*(100). \tag{11}$$

For example, if the client says that a *.8* chance of A and a *.2* chance of Z are equal in preference to B, then $U(B) = 80$. Clearly, the standard gamble method provides a straightforward solution to UA Problem 1.

The standard gamble method also provides solutions to the remaining three assessment problems. To solve UA Problem 2, let Z denote 0 years and let A denote the longest survival duration in the assessment problem. Assume that health state is fixed at some better-than-death health state. One then applies (10) and (11) to determine the utilities of a series of intermediate points, $X_1, \ldots, X_n$. Linear interpolation between these points provides a piecewise linear utility function that approximates the utility function for survival duration. To illustrate this procedure, the second column of Table 3.1 shows hypothetical probability equivalents for the durations 5, 10, 15, and 20 years with respect to the endpoints 0 and 25 years. Multiplying these probability equivalents by 100 yields utilities for the durations scaled from 0 to 100. The solid lines

---

[4] Some authors refer to p^* as the *indifference probability* of B (cf. Sox et al., 1988).

Table 3.1. *Hypothetical Probability Equivalents*

Duration	EU assessments		RDU assessments	
	p^*	$(23.8)X^{.446}$	$w(p^*)$	$(13.67)X^{.618}$
0	0.00	0.0	0.000	0.0
5	0.45	48.8	0.395	37.0
10	0.65	66.5	0.503	56.8
15	0.85	79.6	0.654	72.9
20	0.99	90.5	0.912	87.1
25	1.00	100.0	1.000	100.0

in the left panel of Figure 3.4 show the piecewise linear utility function for the data in the second column of Table 3.1.

As an alternative to the piecewise linear utility function, one could fit a parametric utility function like a power or exponential utility function to the pairs $[X_1, U(X_1)], \ldots, [X_n, U(X_n)]$ by means of a nonlinear regression procedure. Such procedures are available, for example, in the S-Plus, SPSS, and SAS statistical packages. To illustrate this approach, let $X_1, \ldots, X_n$ be a list of survival durations, and let $Z = 0$ and A denote the

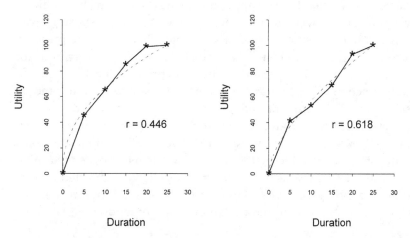

Figure 3.4. Left panel: Utilities assessed by the method of standard gambles under EU assumptions. The solid line is the piecewise linear approximation to the utility function; the dotted line is the power function approximation. Right panel: Utilities assessed by transforming probability equivalences to probability weights under RDU assumptions. The solid line is the piecewise linear approximation to the utility function; the dotted line is the power function approximation.

worst and the best survival durations. Let $p_1^*, \ldots, p_n^*$ denote the probability equivalents of $X_1, \ldots, X_n$ with respect to the endpoints, Z and A, and let $U(X_1), \ldots, U(X_n)$ be the corresponding utilities inferred by means of the standard gamble method. According to the power QALY model, $U(X_i) = k \cdot X_i^r$ for every i. Because utilities were assigned under the specification $U(A) = 100$, we must have $100 = U(A) = k \cdot A^r$, or $k = 100/A^r$. By Equation (11), $U(X_i) = p_i^*(100)$, where p_i^* is the ith probability equivalent. Therefore $p_i^*(100) = U(X_i) = (100/A^r) \cdot X_i^r$; that is,

$$p_i^* = X_i^r / A^r = (X_i/A)^r. \tag{12}$$

To fit a power function to utility data that were assessed by means of standard gambles, one lets the values of p_i^* serve as the dependent variable and the values of (X_i/A) serve as the predictor variable in a nonlinear regression[5] that solves for the value of r. Applying the nls procedure of S-Plus to the data[6] in the first and second columns of Table 3.1 yielded a fit of the power utility function, $U(X) = (23.8) X^{.446}$. The dotted line in the left panel of Figure 3.4 shows the fitted power model.

If one assumes that EU theory is descriptively valid and that the responses to the standard gamble questions are free from random variation, then the standard gamble method yields exact values of the utility function. In a sense, then, to approximate the standard gamble utilities by means of a power function (or any other function) is a step away from accurate measurement because the data themselves are precisely correct utility measurements. Nevertheless, there are two reasons for taking an interest in a parametric utility representation like a power utility function. First, human judgment almost always exhibits random variation in the sense that asking the identical assessment question to the same client will produce somewhat different responses at different times. Even if EU theory were descriptively valid, utilities assessed by the standard gamble method, or any other method, for that matter, would not be precisely accurate because they are affected by random variation in judgment. Fitting a parametric utility function to a set of data is one way to reduce the influence of random variation by

---

[5] A power utility function can also be fit by means of linear regression, i.e., if $p^* = (X/A)^r$, a logarithmic transformation yields $\log p^* = r \cdot \log(X/A)$. Therefore one can use linear regression through the origin to solve for r. Miyamoto and Eraker (1985) used a method similar to this to estimate r for individual patients.

[6] It was necessary to omit the initial point, $(0, 0)$, from the data because the utility function is discontinuous at this point.

aggregating across responses. From this perspective, the fitted curve in Figure 3.4 (left panel) is a more accurate representation of preference than are the individual data points because the individual points are subject to greater random variation than a summary constructed from the data.

Second, even if the assessed standard gamble utilities represent true preferences, i.e., even if they are not affected in part by random variation in judgment, the fitting of a power parameter facilitates comparisons of risk posture across individuals, across populations, and across decision analyses. For example, Miyamoto and Eraker (1985) fitted the power utility model to the certainty equivalents data of individual patients. They found that estimates of r were about equally divided between values greater than and less than 1. In other words, risk aversion and risk seeking were found about equally often in their data. The power parameter allows us to state this finding even if the power utility model is not a precisely accurate description of the utilities. To give another example, in the next section we will reinterpret the data in Table 3.1 from the standpoint of rank-dependent utility theory. The analysis will show that under rank-dependent utility assumptions, the estimated power parameter is .618 rather than .446, as found under EU assumptions. This shows that the rank-dependent utility analysis yields a utility function that is less risk averse than the EU analysis. The fitting of a power parameter allows one to state concisely an interesting relationship between different utility functions. This issue will be discussed further later on.

To solve UA Problem 3, assume the descriptive validity of EU theory and the linear QALY model. Let a represent full health, and set $H(a) = 1$. Suppose we want to determine $H(b)$ for a better-than-death health state b. Choose any survival duration y and use the standard gamble method to find the probability p^* that the client judges to satisfy the equivalence

$$(b, y); \quad [(a, y), p^*; (a, 0), 1 - p^*]. \tag{13}$$

By Equation (8) and the linear QALY model (1), we have

$$k \exists H(b) \cdot y = p^* \cdot k \cdot H(a) \cdot y + (1 - p^*) \cdot k \cdot H(a) \cdot 0. \tag{14}$$

Thus,

$$H(b) = p^* \tag{15}$$

because $H(a) = 1$. Evidently, one can use this procedure repeatedly to find the values of $H(b)$ for any finite list of better-than-death health states. Thus, the standard gamble method solves UA Problem 3 under EU assumptions.

To solve UA Problem 4, note first that the assessment of $H(b)$ by means of standard gambles is the same for a power QALY model as for a linear QALY model. To see this, suppose that p^* satisfies (13). By Equation (8) and the power QALY model (4),

$$k \cdot H(b) \cdot y^r = p^* \cdot k \cdot H(a) \cdot y^r + (1 - p^*) \cdot k \cdot H(a) \cdot 0^r. \qquad (16)$$

Thus,

$$H(b) = p^*. \qquad (17)$$

Therefore the empirical relation, (13), determines the health state utility by means of the identical Equations (15) or (17) for either the linear or the power QALY models. To complete the assessment of the power QALY model, one needs to assess r. The solution to this assessment problem was sketched earlier. Choose any fixed better-than-death health state b. Often, one would choose b equal to either current symptoms or to the best health state in the decision analysis, but from the standpoint of logic, any choice of b is permissible. Let 0 and A be the shortest and longest survival durations, respectively. Let $(b, X_1), \ldots, (b, X_n)$ be a list of intermediate outcomes, and let $p_1^*, \ldots, p_n^*$ be the corresponding probability equivalents with respect to the endpoints, $(b, 0)$ and (b, A). According to Equation (4),

$$k \exists H(b) \cdot X_i^r = p_i^* \cdot k \cdot H(b) \cdot A^r + (1 - p_i^*) \cdot k \cdot H(b) \cdot 0^r \qquad (18)$$

where (18) follows from (4) and (11). Therefore

$$p_i^* = (X_i/A)^r, \qquad (19)$$

exactly as was found before. An estimate of r can then be determined by nonlinear regression with $p_1^*, \ldots, p_n^*$ as the values of the dependent variable and $X_1/A, \ldots, X_n/A$ as the values of the predictor variable. Thus, the standard gamble method yields a solution to UA Problem 4 if one assumes EU theory and the power QALY model.

Notice that in all of the applications of the standard gamble method, the validity of the assessment is heavily dependent on the assumption that utility is linear in probability. For each utility that is to be assessed, the client must produce a p^* that satisfies an equivalence of the form of (10) or (13), and the calculation of the utility requires that p^* and $1 - p^*$ constitute the appropriate weights for the superior and inferior utilities, respectively, on the right side of Equation (11). If the perception of probability is systematically distorted, the standard gamble method transfers the distortions into the utility scale by means of Equation (11).

This completes our discussion of the standard gamble method under EU assumptions. Next, we will consider the time trade-off procedure and, finally, the method of certainty equivalents.

The time trade-off method was introduced by Torrance, Thomas, and Sackett (1972) as a measure of health status. Let a denote full health or whatever is the best health state in the utility assessment problem, and let b be any other better-than-death health state. Let $x > 0$ be any survival duration. Then the *time trade-off between a and b with respect to the duration x* is the duration y^* such that

$$(a, y^*) \sim_{pr} (b, x). \tag{20}$$

If y^* satisfies (20), then *the proportional time trade-off between a and b with respect to duration x* is the ratio y^*/x. For brevity, I will refer to time trade-offs as TTOs and proportional time trade-offs as PTTOs. The relation between TTOs and health state utilities depends on the utility assumptions that one adopts. If one assumes the validity of EU theory, but not the validity of the linear or power QALY models, then (20) implies only that $U(a, y^*) = U(b, x)$ and nothing more.

If one assumes the validity of EU theory and the linear QALY model (1), then the TTO method provides a solution to UA Problem 3. Let a be the best health state, and assign $H(a) = 1$. For any better-than-death health state b, determine the y^* that satisfies (20). Then (20) implies that

$$k \cdot H(a) \cdot y^* = k \cdot H(b) \cdot x. \tag{21}$$

Hence,

$$H(b) = y^*/x \tag{22}$$

because $H(a) = 1$. Therefore, assuming EU theory and the linear QALY-model, TTOs with respect to the best health state provide a solution to UA Problem 3. TTOs also contribute to the solution of UA Problem 4, but to explain this, one must first explain the use of certainty equivalents to assess a power parameter.

The method of certainty equivalents is used primarily to solve UA Problems 2 and 4. Let (b, x) and (b, z) denote any two survival durations in a constant health state b. Then we say that (b, y^*) is the certainty equivalent of the lottery, $[(b, x), p; (b, z), 1 - p]$, if and only if

$$(b, y^*) \sim _{pr}[(b, x), p; (b, z), 1 - p]. \tag{23}$$

In this chapter, we will be concerned only with certainty equivalents of even-chance gambles, i.e., lotteries of the form $[(b, x), 0.5; (b, z), 0.5]$. Even-chance gambles are especially useful in utility assessment because the concept of a flip of a fair coin is widely understood by the general public. Suppose that (b, y^*) is the certainty equivalent of the even-chance gamble, $[(b, x), 0.5; (b, z), 0.5]$, that is,

$$(b, y^*); \quad [(b, x), 0.5; (b, z), 0.5]. \tag{24}$$

Equation (8) and the power QALY model imply that

$$k \cdot H(b) \cdot (y^*)^r = .5 \cdot k \cdot H(b) \cdot x^r + .5 \cdot k \cdot H(b) \cdot z^r \tag{25}$$

Therefore

$$(y^*)^r = .5 \cdot x^r + .5 \cdot z^r \tag{26}$$

and

$$y^* = [.5 \cdot x^r + .5 \cdot z^r]^{1/r}. \tag{27}$$

Once again we have a problem in nonlinear estimation. To estimate r, collect data for certainty equivalents with varying values of x and z. Let the certainty equivalents serve as the dependent variable, and let the values of x and z serve as the predictor variables in a nonlinear regression that solves for the value of r. To illustrate this idea, Table 3.2 contains hypothetical certainty equivalents data for five even-chance gambles. The data appear to be slightly risk averse, and the fit of Equation (27) to these data yields an estimate of $r = .74$, which is slightly less than 1. Of course, in actual research, one would prefer to have more data. This solves UA Problem 2 by means of certainty equivalents.

To solve UA Problem 4 by means of certainty equivalents, we also need to consider TTOs. Let a be the best health state, so that $H(a) = 1$. Assuming the validity of EU theory and the power QALY model (4), the

Table 3.2. *Hypothetical
Certainty Equivalents*

| y^* | $y^*; (x, .5; z, .5)$ | |
	x	z
4	10	0
6	12	2
10	25	0
12	24	2
12	24	4

Under EU assumptions:
$$\hat{y}^* = [.5 \cdot x^{.74} + .5 \cdot z^{.74}]^{1/.74}$$
Under RDU assumptions:
$$\hat{y}^* = [.44 \cdot x^{.90} + .56 \cdot z^{.90}]^{1/.90}$$

TTO shown in (20) implies that

$$k \cdot H(a) \cdot (y^*)^r = k \cdot H(b) \cdot x^r. \tag{28}$$

Hence

$$H(b) = \left(\frac{y^*}{x}\right)^r. \tag{29}$$

Notice that EU theory and the linear QALY model imply that (22) gives the value of $H(b)$, whereas EU theory and the power QALY model imply that (29) gives the value of $H(b)$. Because the parameter r represents risk posture in the power QALY model, Equation (29) is sometimes said to define a *risk-adjusted PTTO*. I will refer to an estimate calculated by means of (29) as an *RA-PTTO*.

To gain some intuition for the role of r in Equation (29), consider Figure 3.5. If the client judges that the equivalence (20) holds, $U(a, y^*) = U(b, x)$. The linear QALY model and the power QALY model both imply that

$$\frac{U(b, x)}{U(a, x)} = \frac{H(b)}{H(a)} = H(b). \tag{30}$$

The ratio $U(b, x)/U(a, x)$ is not directly observable; rather, what one observes is the ratio y^*/x. If the utility functions for survival duration are straight lines radiating from the origin, as shown in the left panel of

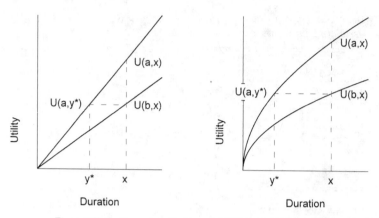

Figure 3.5. Left panel: In the linear QALY model, $U(b, x)/U(a, x) = y^*/x$. Right panel: In a power QALY with a risk-averse utility function, $U(b, x)/U(a, x) > y^*/x$.

Figure 3.5, then $H(b) = U(b, x)/U(a, x) = y^*/x$. As shown in the right panel of Figure 3.5, the curvature of a risk-averse utility function causes the ratio y^*/x to exaggerate the difference between health states a and b. Thus, $H(b) = U(b, x)/U(a, x) > y^*/x$. It is not hard to see that if the utility function is risk seeking, $U(b, x)/U(a, x)$ is less than y^*/x. Therefore, raising the PTTO to the power r, as shown in Equation (24), is a correction for the curvature of the utility functions. It removes a distortion in the assessment of $H(b) = U(b, x)/U(a, x)$ that is introduced by the risk posture of the utility function. The PTTO, y^*/x, overstates the reduction in utility if the utility of survival duration is risk averse, and it understates the reduction if the utility of survival duration is risk seeking.

Certainty equivalents and TTOs provide another solution to UA Problem 4. Certainty equivalents and Equation (27) allow one to estimate the power parameter r. Then TTOs with respect to the best health state and Equation (29) allow one to estimate $H(b)$ for all other health states.

The standard gamble method was introduced by the creators of EU theory, von Neumann and Morgenstern (1944). Torrance et al. (1972) described the measurement of health state utilities by means of a variant of the standard gamble procedure and introduced the TTO method as an alternative method for determining health state utilities in a linear QALY model. Torrance (1986) presented a thorough review of the theoretical foundations of health utility assessment under EU assumptions (for more recent reviews, see Drummond et al., 1997, and Froberg & Kane, 1989a, 1989b, 1989c, 1989d). Miyamoto and Eraker (1985) presented a method for assessing the power parameter of the power QALY model (4) from certainty equivalents data. The method presented in this chapter is an improvement over this method. These authors also emphasized the need to adjust TTOs for risk posture when assessing health state utilities for a power QALY model. Cher et al. (1997) pointed out that Markov process models of clinical decisions can be sensitive to the distinction between TTO and RA-TTO measures of health state utilities.

Summary of EU Assessment Methods

I will summarize the assessment procedures that are sufficient to solve UA Problems 1–4 under EU assumptions.

UA Problem 1. Assess the Utilities of Holistic Outcomes

- The standard gamble method provides the only solution when no attribute structure is specified for the outcomes.

UA Problem 2. Assess the Utility of Survival Duration in Some Fixed Health State

- The standard gamble method can be used to provide a piecewise linear approximation to a utility function for survival duration. One can also fit a power function to the assessed utilities by means of a nonlinear regression procedure.
- Alternatively, certainty equivalents can be collected, and a power function can be fit to these equivalents by means of a nonlinear regression procedure.

UA Problem 3. Assess the Values of H(b), Assuming the Validity of the Linear QALY Model

- The standard gamble method yields values of $H(b)$ for each health state b.
- Alternatively, PTTOs also yield values of $H(b)$ for each health state b.

UA Problem 4. Assess the Values of r and H(b), Assuming the Validity of the Power QALY Model (4)

- The standard gamble method yields utilities for individual survival durations. A power function can be fit to the assessed utilities, as in UA Problem 2. The standard gamble method also yields values of $H(b)$ for each health state b.

- Alternatively, certainty equivalents can be collected and a power function fit to these certainty equivalents, as in UA Problem 2. PTTOs must be adjusted for risk posture, as in Equation (29), to yield values of $H(b)$ for each health state b.

The next section presents solutions to these same assessment problems under rank-dependent utility theory.

Rank-Dependent Utility Theory

The rank-dependent utility (RDU) theory is a major attempt to explain the violations of EU theory by means of a postulated nonlinear transformation of probabilities. A full discussion of RDU theory requires a description of the representation of lotteries as cumulative probability distributions over outcomes, and of the process by which a nonlinear transformation of cumulative probabilities is converted to decision weights (Quiggin, 1982, 1993; Quiggin & Wakker, 1994). Fortunately, the only lotteries required for the utility assessments of this chapter are binary lotteries. Therefore, to explain how these assessments are interpreted under RDU assumptions, it will suffice to describe the RDU representation of binary lotteries and simple outcomes.

For the special case of binary lotteries, RDU theory asserts that the utility of a lottery is determined by the following formula:

$$U(A, p; B, 1 - p)$$
$$= \begin{cases} w(p)U(A) + [1 - w(p)]U(B) & \text{if} \quad A \geq_{pr} B & (31) \\ [1 - w(p)]U(A) + w(1 - p)U(B) & \text{if} \quad B \geq_{pr} A & (32) \end{cases}$$

where w is a nonlinear function from probabilities to the unit interval, that is, $1 \geq w(p) \geq 0$ for every probability p. It can be shown that under the assumptions of RDU theory the utility function is an interval scale (Wakker, 1989). The utility of a lottery is calculated by Equation (31) when $A \geq_{pr} B$ and by Equation (32) when $B \leq_{pr} A$. When $A \sim B, U(A) = U(B)$, so either (31) or (32) produces the same result. In all analyses discussed here, the lotteries that serve as stimuli have the form $(A, p; B, 1 - p)$, where A is preferred to B. Therefore only Equation (31) will be required in the present discussion. Obviously, minor modifications allow one to reformulate the methods with respect to Equation (32) if lotteries are used in which B is preferred to A.

The exact form of the probability weighting function w is presently the subject of intense investigation (Gonzalez, 1993; Tversky & Kahneman, 1992; Wu & Gonzalez, 1996). For purposes of illustration, I will discuss a weighting function suggested by Tversky and Kahneman (1992). They proposed that probability weighting can be represented by the class of transformations

$$w(p) = \frac{p^{\gamma}}{(p^{\gamma} + (1 - p)^{\gamma})^{1/\gamma}}. \tag{33}$$

For the case of binary lotteries, one can interpret $w(p)$ as the weight attached to the utility of the superior outcome.[7] The value of the γ parameter can vary from one individual to the next, corresponding to individual differences in the weight attached to the superior outcome. Figure 3.6 shows the probability weight $w(p)$ when γ equals .61. This

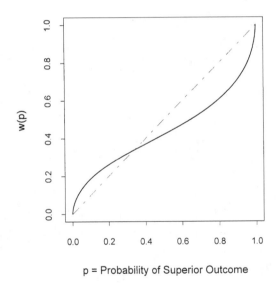

p = Probability of Superior Outcome

Figure 3.6. The probability weighting function for gains based on estimates in Tversky and Kahneman (1992).

---

[7] In a full development of RDU theory or CPT, one interprets w as a transformation that applies to the cumulative or decumulative probability distribution of a lottery. Discussion of cumulative or decumulative probabilities is unnecessary when one restricts attention to binary lotteries and simple outcomes.

value of γ was the median estimate in a sample of 25 Berkeley and Stanford graduate students (Tversky & Kahneman, 1992). The subjects judged certainty equivalents of monetary gambles for gains. In the following discussion, I will assume in some analyses that w has the form (33) with $\gamma = .61$. This assumption is made to illustrate the implications of a specific w for utility assessment. More empirical research will be required to determine what common values of γ are to be found in patient populations.

The hypothesis of nonlinear probability weighting alters the theoretical analysis of risk posture. As a concrete example, let us consider the interpretation of the following certainty equivalent under EU and RDU assumptions.

$$5 \text{ years for sure} \sim {}_{pr}(20 \text{ years, } .5; 0 \text{ years, } .5) \tag{34}$$

Panel A of Figure 3.7 shows the implications of this equivalence under EU assumptions. The utility of 5 years is indicated by an open circle.

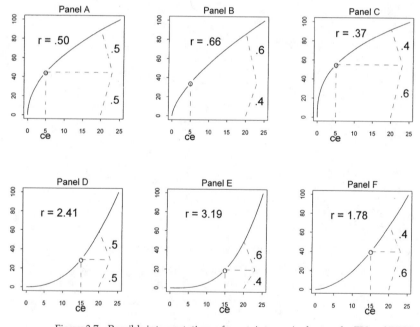

Figure 3.7. Possible interpretations of a certainty equivalent under EU and RDU assumptions. "ce" indicates the location of the certainty equivalent. Panels A and D assume linear probability weighting. Panels B and E assume pessimistic probability weighting. Panels C and F assume optimistic probability weighting.

The height of this circle is halfway between the utility of 0 years and the utility of 20 years, as indicated by the dashed lines, because EU theory implies that the utilities of 20 years and 0 years are weighted by the probability .5. The solid utility curve is a power utility function fit to the datum, $U(5 \text{ years}) = .5U(20 \text{ years})$. The inferred power parameter happens to be .5, i.e., a square root transformation. Panel B depicts an RDU interpretation of the same datum, (34), under the assumption that $w(.5) = .4$. By Equation (31), $U(5 \text{ years}) = .4U(20 \text{ years})$. The open circle in Panel B is 40% of the height of the utility of 20 years, as shown by the dashed lines on the right. Because $U(5 \text{ years})$ is lower in Panel B than in Panel A, the power utility function is less risk averse – the inferred power, $r = .66$, is closer to linearity ($r = 1.0$) than the r of .50 that was inferred under EU assumptions. Conversely, Panel C shows the implication of the certainty equivalent under the assumption that $w(.5) = .6$. In this case, $U(5 \text{ years}) = .6U(20 \text{ years})$, and the utility function must be more risk averse than the utility function inferred under EU assumptions. Panels D, E, and F show the analogous relations for a risk-seeking utility function. If the client judges 15 years for sure (20 years, .5; 0 years, .5), the EU interpretation is that the client is rather risk seeking (Panel D). If $w(.5) < .5$, then the RDU interpretation is that the utility function is even more risk seeking (Panel E), and if $w(.5) > .5$, the RDU interpretation is that the utility function is less risk seeking (Panel F).

Let us say that a probability weighting function w is *optimistic* with respect to p if $w(p) > p$, and it is *pessimistic* with respect to p if $w(p) < p$. Because $w(p)$ is the probability weight for the superior option (see Equation 31), an optimistic weight places greater weight on the superior option than p, and a pessimistic weight places greater weight on the inferior option than $1 - p$. The probability weighting function shown in Figure 3.6 implies that weights will be optimistic for $p < .33$ and pessimistic for $p > .33$, where p is the probability of the superior option in a binary lottery. As argued by Wakker and Stiggelbout (1995), the preference behavior that is attributed to risk aversion or risk seeking under EU assumptions may be due in part to nonlinear probability weighting. For example, Panel B of Figure 3.7 depicts a situation in which a preference that appears to be quite risk averse under EU assumptions is attributed under RDU assumptions to a utility function that is somewhat risk averse and a probability weight that is somewhat pessimistic.

Suppose that U_1 and U_2 are two utility functions for survival duration. Let us say that U_1 is *relatively more risk averse* than U_2 if certainty equivalents assuming U_1 are always lower than corresponding certainty equivalents assuming U_2. Conversely, let us say that U_1 is *relatively more risk seeking* than U_2 if certainty equivalents assuming U_1 are always greater than corresponding certainty equivalents assuming U_2. In the power utility model, U_1 is relatively more risk averse than U_2 if the power parameter for U_1 is less than the power parameter for U_2, and it is relatively more risk seeking than U_2 if the power parameter for U_1 is greater than the power parameter for U_2. Notice that with this terminology, U_1 can be relatively more risk averse than U_2 even if neither function is risk averse in an absolute sense, i.e., in comparison to a risk-neutral utility function. For example, Panels C and F of Figure 3.7 display utility functions that are relatively more risk averse than Panels B and E, respectively, even though Panel F is not risk averse in an absolute sense.

The essential point from the standpoint of utility assessment is that preference behavior that appears to be risk averse or risk seeking under EU assumptions is interpreted under RDU assumptions to be a joint consequence of a nonlinear utility function and a nonlinear probability weighting function. Furthermore, if we compare utility functions that are inferred under EU assumptions to utility functions that are inferred under RDU assumptions, the EU functions will be relatively more risk averse than the RDU functions if probability weighting is pessimistic with respect to the probabilities in the assessment, and the EU functions will be relatively more risk seeking than the RDU functions if probability weighting is optimistic with respect to the probabilities in the assessment. The discussion of utility assessment under RDU assumptions will attempt to disentangle the contributions of nonlinear utility and nonlinear probability weighting to the observed preference behavior.

Next, I will describe solutions to UA Problems 1–4 under RDU assumptions. Equation (31) will be the main analytical assumption. In some assessment methods, it will also be necessary to assume that the weighting function satisfies Equation (33) with $\gamma = .61$. These assumptions will be spelled out as the assessment methods are described. Issues pertaining to risk posture will also be discussed.

Utility Assessment under RDU Assumptions

In the previous section, it was shown that the standard gamble method provides solutions to UA Problem 1–4. The same holds true under RDU assumptions, provided that one knows the values of $w(p^*)$ for the probability equivalents that are produced in the assessment. Consider the following argument due to Wakker and Stiggelbout (1995): Let A designate the best outcome and Z the worst outcome in the health domain under investigation. Let us assign $U(A) = 100$ and $U(Z) = 0$. Let B be any other health outcome, and suppose that p^* is the probability equivalent of B with respect to A and Z, as shown in (10). By Equation (31) of RDU theory.

$$U(B) = w(p^*)U(A) + (1 - w(p^*))U(Z) = w(p^*) \cdot 100. \tag{35}$$

Equation (35) can be used to determine the utility of B, provided that one knows the value of $w(p^*)$.

Evidently, the key to applying the standard gamble method under RDU assumptions is to develop a method for determining the form of w for individual clients. Although some research articles have published estimates of the weighting function w for groups of subjects (Camerer & Ho, 1994; Tversky & Kahneman, 1992), I do not know of published accounts of estimates of w that are tailored to individuals. I believe, however, that research conditions are ripe for the development of methodologies for assessing the weighting function at the level of individuals. Gonzalez and Wu (1999) have completed an extensive study of alternative models of the probability weighting function, including assessments of model parameters at the level of individuals. Their work is restricted to the study of preferences for monetary lotteries in stimulus designs that were chosen to investigate theoretical questions. Abdellaoui (1998) and Bleichrodt and Pinto (1998) have independently undertaken studies of weighting functions at the individual subject level, the former in the domain of money and the latter in the domain of health. These studies attempt to determine qualitative features of the shape of the probability weighting function without assuming a specific parametric model for probability weighting. So far as I know, it is an open question whether an efficient methodology can be developed for assessing probability weighting functions of individual clients, followed by an RDU assessment of individual health utilities by means of standard gambles. Because assessment of the probability weighting function w holds the key to generalizing the standard gamble method to RDU assumptions and also to cumulative prospect theory assumptions, this would appear to be a productive target for further investigation.

Wakker and Stiggelbout (1995) and Bayoumi and Redelmeier (1996) have applied a group estimate of the probability weighting function to the problem of interpreting standard gamble utilities. A potential deficiency of this approach is that it assumes that all individuals have the same probability weighting function, but it has the virtue of being straightforward to implement at a practical level and is also heuristically informative. To illustrate this idea, suppose that we wish to assess the utility of an outcome B under the assumption that w has the form of (33) with $\gamma = .61$, as shown in Figure 3.6. Suppose, further, that the client produces the standard gamble judgment $B \sim_{pr} (A, .8; Z, .2)$. Applying (33) with $\gamma = .61$, we find that $w(.8) = .607$. By Equation (35), we have $U(B) = 60.7$. Evidently, this process can be repeated for each holistic outcome, thereby providing a solution to UA Problem 1.

To solve UA Problem 2, let $Z = 0$ years, and let A denote the longest survival duration in the assessment problem. Assume that health state is fixed at some better-than-death health state. Let $p_1^*, \ldots, p_n^*$ denote the probability equivalents of a series of intermediate durations, $X_1, \ldots, X_n$. Assuming the validity of Equation (33) with $\gamma = .61$, we can find the utilities of the intermediate durations, $100 \cdot w(p_1^*), \ldots, 100 \cdot w(p_n^*)$. For example, the second column of Table 3.1 shows hypothetical probability equivalents (p^*) for the durations, 5, 10, 15, and 20 years. The fourth column of Table 3.1 shows the corresponding values of $w(p^*)$, which can be multiplied by 100 to yield utilities scaled from 0 to 100. The right panel of Figure 3.4 (solid lines) shows a piecewise linear approximation to the utility function for survival duration. The dotted line in the right panel shows a power utility function fitted to these data by means of nonlinear regression, as described in the previous section. Notice that the utility function is less risk averse in the RDU analysis – the power parameter r is .618 in the RDU analysis and .446 in the EU analysis. This finding corresponds to the fact that $w(p^*) < p^*$ (pessimism) for every probability equivalent in the second column of Table 3.1. Whereas EU theory must attribute risk-averse preferences entirely to the curvature of the utility function, yielding a low $r = .446$, RDU theory can interpret the preferences as a consequence of pessimistic probability weighting and a more moderate curvature of the utility function.

To solve UA Problem 3 under RDU assumptions, assume the descriptive validity of the linear QALY model (1) and Equation (33) with $\gamma = .61$. Let a represent full health, and set $H(a) = 1$. To determine $H(b)$, choose any survival duration y and have the client judge the p^* that yields the equivalence:

$$(b, y) \sim_{pr} [(a, y), p^*; (a, 0), 1 - p^*]. \tag{36}$$

According to the linear QALY model and Equation (35),

$$k \cdot H(b) \cdot y = w(p^*) \cdot k \cdot H(a) \cdot y + [1 - w(p^*)] \cdot k \cdot H(a) \cdot 0.$$

(37)

Thus,

$$H(b) = w(p^*).$$
(38)

For example, if $p^* = .75$, then $H(b) = .57$ by Equation (33) with $\gamma = .61$.

To solve UA Problem 4 under RDU assumptions, assume the descriptive validity of the power QALY model (4) and Equation (33) with $\gamma = .61$. Once again, let a represent full health, and set $H(a) = 1$. To determine $H(b)$, have the client judge p^* as in (36). The power QALY model and Equation (35) imply that

$$k \cdot H(b) \cdot y^r = w(p^*) \cdot k \cdot H(a) \cdot y^r + [1 - w(p^*)] \cdot k \cdot H(a) \cdot 0^r.$$

(39)

Thus,

$$H(b) = w(p^*)$$
(40)

because $H(a) = 1$. For example, if $p^* = .75$, $H(b) = .57$, exactly as was found for the linear QALY model under RDU assumptions. As can be seen from Equations (38) and (40), under RDU assumptions the standard gamble method yields the same estimate of $H(b)$ for either the linear or power QALY model.

To complete the assessment of the power QALY model under RDU assumptions, let 0 and A be the shortest and longest survival durations, respectively, let $X_1, \ldots, X_n$ be a list of intermediate durations, and let $p_1^*, \ldots, p_n^*$ be the probability equivalents of $(b, X_1), \ldots, (b, X_n)$, respectively, relative to the endpoints (b, A) and $(b, 0)$. Then the power QALY model and Equation (35) imply that

$$k \cdot H(b) \cdot X_i^r = w(p_i^*) \cdot k \cdot H(b) \cdot A^r + [1 - w(p_i^*)] \cdot k \cdot H(b) \cdot 0^r.$$

(41)

Therefore

$$w(p_i^*) = (X_i/A)^r.$$
(42)

Assuming Equation (33) with $\gamma = .61$, we can compute specific values for $w(p_i^*)$. An estimate of r can then be determined by nonlinear regression, with $w(p_1^*), \ldots, w(p_n^*)$ as the values of the dependent variable and $X_1/A, \ldots, X_n/A$ as the values of the predictor variable.[8] Combining this estimate of r with the previous assessment of $H(b)$ for various values of b yields a solution to UA Problem 4 under RDU assumptions and the assumption of Equation (33) with $\gamma = .61$.

The standard gamble method yields straightforward solutions to UA Problems 1–4 if one assumes a specific probability weighting function like Equation (33) with $\gamma = .61$. Clearly, an important question about this procedure is whether individual differences in probability weighting are sufficiently large to produce substantial deviations from the weighting function with $\gamma = .61$. One should bear in mind that Equation (33) with $\gamma = .61$ is used here simply for illustration. This value of γ was estimated from the preferences of 25 Stanford and Berkeley graduate students for monetary lotteries and should not be taken too seriously in the context of health utility analysis. What are required are estimates of probability weighting functions that are determined from preferences for health lotteries in populations that are relevant to health utility analysis, e.g., among patients or the general public. Such data would permit one to evaluate whether a single choice of weighting function is a poor or good approximation to the weighting functions of individuals.

The TTO procedure provides a solution to UA Problem 3 under RDU assumptions for precisely the same reasons as it does under EU assumptions. If $(a, y^*) \sim _{pr}(b, x)$, as shown in (20), then (21) and (22) follow under RDU assumptions. Therefore $H(b) = y^*/x$, as shown in (22).

The method of certainty equivalents provides alternative solutions to UA Problems 2 and 4. Under RDU assumptions, however, the estimation of r requires that one also estimate $w(.5)$. Let b be any better-than-death health state, and let (b, y^*) be the certainty equivalent of $[(b, x), p; (b, z), 1 - p]$, as shown in (23). I assume that $x > z$. The power QALY model (4) and Equation (35) imply that

$$k \cdot H(b) \cdot (y^*)^r = w(.5) \cdot k \cdot H(b) \cdot x^r + [1 - w(.5)] \cdot k \cdot H(b) \cdot z^r.$$

$$(43)$$

---

[8] As before, an alternative method of estimation is to treat $\log w(p_1^*), \ldots, \log w(p_n^*)$ as the values of the dependent variable and $\log(X_1/A), \ldots, \log(X_n/A)$ as the values of the predictor variable in a linear regression.

Therefore

$$(y^*)^r = w(.5) \cdot x^r + [1 - w(.5)] \cdot z^r \tag{44}$$

and

$$y^* = [w(.5) \cdot x^r + (1 - w(.5)) \cdot z^r]^{1/r}. \tag{45}$$

To estimate r, collect data for certainty equivalents with varying values of x and z. Let the certainty equivalents serve as the dependent variable, and let the values of x and z serve as the predictor variables in a nonlinear regression that solves for estimates of $w(.5)$ and r. This solves UA Problem 2 by means of certainty equivalents under RDU assumptions. Although the estimate of $w(.5)$ may have theoretical interest, it is not directly relevant to the utility assessment. For purposes of utility assessment, the estimate of $w(.5)$ is needed only to provide an accurate estimate of the risk parameter r.

To illustrate this method, Table 3.2 contains hypothetical certainty equivalents data for five even-chance gambles. As shown in the table, the fit of Equation (45) to these data yields an estimate of $r = .90$ and $w(.5) = .44$. Notice that the RDU solution for these data is less risk averse than the EU solution for the same data. This is due to the fact that the apparent risk aversion in the certainty equivalents has been absorbed into a slightly pessimistic value of $w(.5)$, i.e., $w(.5) < .5$, as well as in the slightly risk-averse value of r.

To solve UA Problem 4 under RDU assumptions, we need to combine this method for estimating r with risk adjustment of PTTOs. One must first estimate r, as explained in the previous paragraph. To assess $H(b)$ for a health state b, one must determine a TTO for b, as shown in (20). RDU theory and the power QALY model then imply (28) and (29), the latter equation being the risk adjustment needed to convert the PTTO to $H(b)$. One repeats this procedure for each health state b, thereby solving UA Problem 4 under RDU assumptions.

Wakker and Deneffe (1996) have recently presented a method of utility assessment that is based on quite different principles from any of the methods described in this section. Their method avoids distortions in utility that can be produced by nonlinear probability weighting, as do the methods described in this section. It also has the advantage of not requiring the assumption that all individuals have the same probability weighting function, nor does it require that the utility function be drawn from a known class of parametric functions like the power functions. I have omitted the method of Wakker and Deneffe from this chapter because the methods discussed here are essentially revisions of standard EU assessment methods, whereas Wakker and Deneffe's method is not a variant of a standard EU method. Rather, Wakker and Deneffe's method harkens back to the basic process by which equally spaced points (so-called standard sequences) are constructed in fundamental measurement theory (Krantz et al., 1971).

Summary of RDU Assessment Methods

I will summarize the assessment procedures that are sufficient to solve UA Problems 1–4 under RDU assumptions.

UA Problem 1. Assess the Utilities of Holistic Outcomes

- The standard gamble method provides the only solution when no attribute structure is specified for the outcomes. Probability equivalents p^* must be transformed into corresponding probability weights $w(p^*)$ in order to carry out the utility assessment.

UA Problem 2. Assess the Utility of Survival Duration in Some Fixed Health State

- The standard gamble method yields probability equivalents for a series of survival durations. The probability equivalents must be transformed into probability weights which serve as utilities after multiplying by a scaling constant, e.g., 100. A piecewise linear approximation to the utility function can be inferred from these utilities or a power function can be fit by means of non-linear regression.
- Alternatively, certainty equivalents can be collected, and a power function can be fit to these equivalents by means of a nonlinear regression procedure. This approach yields estimates of $w(.5)$ and r.

UA Problem 3. Assess the Values of H(b), Assuming the Validity of the Linear QALY Model (1)

- The standard gamble method yields probability equivalents p^* for each health state b. These probability equivalents must be transformed into corresponding probability weights $w(p^*) = H(b)$.

- Alternatively, PTTOs also yield values of $H(b)$ for each health state b.

UA Problem 4. Assess the Values of r and H(b), Assuming the Validity of the Power QALY Model (4)

- The standard gamble method yields probability equivalents p^* for individual survival durations. The probability equivalents must be transformed into probability weights which serve as utilities after multiplying by a scaling constant. A power function can be fit to these utilities by means of nonlinear regression, thereby providing an estimate of r. To assess values of $H(b)$, one finds probability equivalents p^* for each health state b. These probability equivalents must be transformed into corresponding probability weights $w(p^*) = H(b)$.
- Alternatively, certainty equivalents can be collected and a power function fit to these certainty equivalents, as in UA Problem 2. PTTOs must be adjusted for risk posture, as in Equation (29), to yield values of $H(b)$ for each health state b.

Note that all of the assessments that involve standard gambles require one to determine $w(p^*)$ for each probability equivalent p^*. The assessments that involve certainty equivalents do not require that the probability weighting function w be known, but they assume that the utility of survival duration is a power function. One can replace this assumption by a different parametric class of functions; for example, one can assume instead that the utility of survival duration is an exponential function.

An Empirical Example of RDU QALY Assessment

To illustrate the implications of RDU utility assessment on QALY assessment, it is informative to consider some empirical results.[9] Data from Miyamoto and Eraker (1988) will be used to estimate the parameters of the power QALY model (4) under EU and RDU assumptions. We will examine the parameter estimates to see how EU and RDU theory differ in their interpretation of the same data.

Miyamoto and Eraker (1988) reported an experiment in which a sample of medical patients judged certainty equivalents of even-chance

---

[9] The work presented in this section is part of a larger project on non-EU utility assessment that is being developed jointly with Richard Gonzalez and Jon Treadwell.

Table 3.3. *High and Low Outcomes*
for Six Even Chance Gambles

Stimulus gamble	High outcome	Low outcome
1	12 years	0 years
2	12 years	1 year
3	12 years	4 years
4	24 years	0 years
5	24 years	2 years
6	24 years	8 years

gambles for survival duration. Table 3.3 lists the high and low out-comes for six even-chance gambles that were presented as stimuli in the "power" condition of the experiment. Subjects in this condition were asked to judge the certainty equivalents of these gambles assuming full health and a second time assuming life with their current symptoms. Each subject also made 8 TTO judgments, as in Equation (20). The TTOs were judged with respect to 15, 16, 20, and 24 years with current symptoms. Every certainty equivalence judgment and TTO judgment was replicated twice. A more complete description of the subjects and experimental procedure is given in Miyamoto and Eraker (1988).

Table 3.4 displays the certainty equivalence data for Subjects 1, 2, 7, and 23. The gambles that elicited these certainty equivalents are the six gambles shown in Table 3.3. Subjects were instructed to assume that survival would be accompanied by full health for the gambles in the upper half of Table 3.4 and by current symptoms for the gambles in the lower half of the table. The complete data are given for these subjects so that the interested reader can reproduce the utility analy-sis as it is presented here. For the sake of brevity, the TTO data are not presented, but the mean PTTOs are listed in the fifth column of Table 3.5.

Let $\hat{r}_{EU}$ stand for an estimate of the risk parameter of the power QALY model (4) computed under the assumption that EU theory is valid. To determine $\hat{r}_{EU}$ for each subject, let Equation (27) define the model to be estimated in a nonlinear regression. The certainty equiv-alents in Table 3.4 serve as the dependent variable, and the high and low outcomes in Table 3.3 serve as the predictor variables. The starting

Table 3.4. *Certainty Equivalents Data for Four Subjects*

Health state	Stimulus gamble	Subject 1 Trial		Subject 2 Trial		Subject 7 Trial		Subject 23 Trial	
		1	2	1	2	1	2	1	2
Full	1	6.00	6.00	6.00	5.50	10.00	10.00	6.50	7.00
Full	2	7.00	6.00	7.00	7.00	9.50	10.50	4.50	8.50
Full	3	9.00	8.00	9.00	9.00	10.50	10.75	7.50	8.50
Full	4	11.00	12.00	10.00	12.00	20.50	21.00	5.50	9.50
Full	5	11.00	12.00	13.00	13.00	20.50	21.50	7.50	12.50
Full	6	11.00	12.00	17.00	18.00	21.00	21.00	13.50	13.50
Current	1	6.00	7.00	5.50	6.00	10.00	10.50	6.50	6.00
Current	2	7.00	6.00	5.50	6.50	10.50	10.50	6.50	6.50
Current	3	8.00	8.00	9.50	9.00	11.00	10.75	7.50	8.50
Current	4	12.00	12.00	7.50	12.00	21.00	21.00	8.50	12.50
Current	5	12.00	9.00	11.00	13.00	21.50	21.50	9.50	9.50
Current	6	16.00	16.00	14.00	17.00	20.00	22.00	13.50	15.50

value of $r = 1$ was employed in a nonlinear, least squares regression. The second column of Table 3.5 displays the estimates of r calculated under EU assumptions.

Let $\hat{r}_{RDU}$ stand for an estimate of r that is computed under the assumption that RDU is valid. To determine $\hat{r}_{RDU}$ for each subject, let Equation (45) define the model to be estimated in a nonlinear regression. The certainty equivalents in Table 3.4 serve as the dependent variable, and the high and low outcomes in Table 3.3 serve as the predictor variables. The risk parameter r and the probability weight $w(.5)$ are the parameters to be estimated in the regression. The starting values of $r = 1$ and $w(.5) = .5$ were employed in a nonlinear, least squares regression.

Table 3.5. *Results for Four Subjects*

Subject	EU theory $\hat{r}_{EU}$	RDU theory $\hat{r}_{RDU}$	$w(.5)$	Linear QALY PTTO	EU theory RA PTTO	RDU theory RA PTTO
1	.89	1.60	.31	.56	.60	.40
2	.89	.65	.58	.76	.78	.84
7	5.15	2.61	.70	.89	.54	.73
23	.72	1.06	.38	.55	.65	.53

The third and fourth columns of Table 3.5 display the estimates of r and $w(.5)$ calculated under RDU assumptions.

Let a = full health and let b = current symptoms. Let $H(a) = 1$. Assuming the linear QALY model (1), the PTTO equals $H(b)$, as shown in Equation (22). The fifth column of Table 3.5 shows the mean PTTO for each subject averaged over eight PTTO judgments. Note that the means shown in the fifth column of Table 3.5 are estimates of $H(b)$ for the linear QALY model under either EU or RDU assumptions because Equation (22) is implied by the linear QALY model under either EU or RDU assumptions.

Suppose now that we drop the assumption of linearity and assume instead that a power QALY model (4) holds. EU theory and RDU theory both imply that the calculation of $H(b)$ must adjust the PTTO for the risk parameter r, as shown in Equation (29), but the RA-PTTOs will differ because EV and RDU theories yield different estimates of r. The sixth and seventh columns of Table 3.5 show the RA-PTTOs for EU and RDU theory, respectively.[10] In other words, the sixth column shows $[\text{mean}(y * /x]^{\hat{r}_{EU}}$, and the seventh column shows $[\text{mean}(y^*/x)]^{\hat{r}_{RDU}}$.

Let us compare the utility assessment under EU and RDU assumptions for these four subjects. For Subject 1, the utility of survival duration is slightly risk averse under EU assumptions ($\hat{r}_{EU} = .89$). The RDU analysis, however, suggests that this subject is actually rather risk seeking ($\hat{r}_{RDU} = 1.60$). The reason for this discrepancy is that the RDU analysis finds that this subject is rather pessimistic with respect to the .5 probability ($w(.5) = .31$). The preference behavior that the EU analysis attributes to risk aversion is associated so strongly with pessimism in the RDU analysis that the curvature in the utility function is reversed from risk aversion to risk seeking. These differing assessments of risk posture impact the assessment of $H(b)$, the utility of current symptoms. Assuming risk neutrality, $H(b) = \text{PTTO} = .56$. Risk adjustment with respect to $\hat{r}_{EU}$ yields $H(b) = .60$. Risk adjustment with respect to $\hat{r}_{RDU}$ yields $H(b) = .40$, a considerably lower utility for b. Although the lower value of $H(b)$ found under RDU assumptions is a direct result of the fact that $\hat{r}_{RDU}$ is rather risk seeking (see Figure 3.5), we should note that the more basic reason for the discrepancy between the EU and RDU

---

[10] Technically, it would be better to apply the power transformations to individual PTTOs prior to averaging them and then average these transformed PTTOs, but the risk-adjusted mean PTTOs reported in Table 3.5 are within ±.01 of the mean RA-PTTOs that would be computed by this alternative method.

assessment of $H(b)$ is that the latter theory allows for pessimism in the probability weighting. Nonlinear probability weighting impacts both the assessment of risk posture and the assessment of health state utilities by TTO methods.

Under EU assumptions, Subject 2 is precisely as risk averse as Subject 1 ($\hat{r}_{EU} = .89$), but the RDU analysis found Subject 2 to be slightly optimistic with respect to the .5 probability ($w(.5) = .58$). Therefore, unlike Subject 1, Subject 2 is more risk averse under the RDU analysis than under the EU analysis. Consequently, $H(b)$ assessed under RDU assumptions is greater than the estimate of $H(b)$ found under either the linear QALY model or the power QALY model and EU theory.

Subject 7 is an example of an individual who appears to be extremely risk seeking under EU assumptions ($\hat{r}_{EU} = 5.15$). When nonlinear probability weighting is taken into account in the RDU analysis, the subject is considerably less risk seeking, although still risk seeking ($\hat{r}_{RDU} = 2.61$), and is found to be rather optimistic ($w(.5) = .70$). Whereas the EU analysis yields an RA-PTTO of .54, which is far below the PTTO of .89 found under linear QALY assumptions, the RDU analysis yields an RA-PTTO of .73, which is approximately midway between .54 and .89. Absorbing some of the apparently risk-seeking preferences into an optimistic estimate of $w(.5)$ reduces the discrepancy between the estimate of $H(b)$ found under the linear QALY model and the estimate of $H(b)$ found under EU assumptions and the power QALY model.

Finally, Subject 23 appears to be somewhat risk averse under EU assumptions ($\hat{r}_{EU} = .72$), but the RDU analysis attributes the apparently risk-averse preferences almost entirely to pessimism ($\hat{r}_{RDU} = 1.06$, $w(.5) = .38$). Therefore the utility of health state b is almost identical under the linear QALY model ($H(b) = .55$) and under the power QALY model and RDU assumptions ($H(b) = .53$), whereas it is somewhat higher under the power QALY model and EU assumptions ($H(b) = .65$).

These examples illustrate several differences between utility assessments under EU and RDU assumptions. First, in general, $\hat{r}_{EU} < \hat{r}_{RDU}$ when $w(.5) < .5$, and conversely, $\hat{r}_{EU} > \hat{r}_{RDU}$ when $w(.5) > .5$. Richard Gonzalez, Jon Treadwell, and I have examined certainty equivalents data for 65 utility functions for survival duration and have found only one exception to this pattern. Equation (29) shows that the PTTO must be adjusted for risk posture in order to estimate $H(b)$. As we have seen here, nonlinear probability weighting has a systematic impact on the degree of risk aversion or risk seeking that will be found in the assessed utility function. Putting these two findings together, we can see that if

$1 > (y^*/x) > 0$, then in general,

$$\left(\frac{y^*}{x}\right)^{\hat{r}_{EU}} > \left(\frac{y^*}{x}\right)^{\hat{r}_{RDU}} \quad \begin{array}{l} \text{if and only if} \quad \hat{r}_{EU} < \hat{r}_{RDU} \\ \text{if and only if} \quad w(.5) < .5. \end{array}$$

Because $(y^*/x)^{\hat{r}_{EU}}$ is the EU assessment of $H(b)$ and $(y^*/x)^{\hat{r}_{RDU}}$ is the RDU assessment of $H(b)$, this shows that the EU assessment of $H(b)$ will exceed the RDU assessment of $H(b)$ for individuals who are pessimistic with respect to the .5 probability.

What these examples show is that nonlinear probability weighting impacts both the measure of risk posture, r, and the RA-TTO. Although this example is confined to estimation of risk posture from certainty equivalents data, I believe that analogous relationships will be found in standard gambles data. In other words, if standard gambles data are collected that allow one to estimate the form of nonlinear probability weighting for individual subjects, the RDU utility assessment will be relatively more risk seeking than the EU utility assessment for individuals who are pessimistic with respect to the probabilities in the utility assessment. For health state utilities, the RDU estimates of $H(b)$ should be lower than the EU estimates of $H(b)$ for individuals who are pessimistic with respect to the probabilities in the utility assessment. In effect, nonlinear probability weighting should impact measures of risk posture and health state utility, regardless of whether utilities are assessed by standard gambles or certainty equivalents and TTOs.

Conclusions

The assessment of utilities under EU assumptions is strongly influenced by the assumption that probabilities contribute linearly to the utility of a lottery. This is certainly true of the standard gamble, in which the probability equivalent of an outcome is interpreted as the utility of that outcome (after possible rescaling – see Equation 11). In the method of certainty equivalents, the .5 probability that appears in the stimulus gamble is assumed to carry a .5 weight in the evaluation of the utility of an outcome (see Equation 27). The only exception is the assessment of health state utilities by means of TTOs under the assumption that the utility of survival duration is linear. If the linear QALY model is assumed to be descriptively valid, then the PTTO equals the health state utility under EU or RDU assumptions. In effect, if one makes the strong assumption that the utility of survival duration is linear, one can use TTOs to assess health state utilities and thereby avoid the assumption that the perception of probability is linear. It can be shown, however, that the utility of survival duration is typically not linear (Miyamoto & Eraker, 1985, 1989), and therefore, descriptive accuracy requires risk adjustment of the PTTOs. Risk-adjusted TTOs are influenced by non-linear probability perception because nonlinear probability weighting affects the estimation of the risk parameter r (see Equation 29).

RDU theory provides a theoretical basis for taking nonlinear probability weighting into account in the process of utility assessment. Given a probability weighting function w, the standard gamble method can be applied under RDU assumptions to assess the utilities of individual outcomes, health state utilities, or the utility of continua like survival duration. At present, only population-based estimates of w are available, and it can be questioned whether a single weighting function is sufficiently close to the weighting functions of individuals. It is likely that research in the near future will determine whether it is possible to estimate weighting functions for individuals from the kinds of small data sets that are common in health utility analysis. This chapter also describes an approach to QALY measurement based on certainty equivalents and TTOs. Richard Gonzalez, Jon Treadwell, and I are currently investigating this approach to QALY measurement. An advantage of this approach is that it requires the estimation of only one probability weight, $w(.5)$, but it requires that one assume that the utility of survival duration is drawn from a specific class of parametric utility functions, like power functions or exponential functions.

As was shown in the examples of utility assessment, nonlinear probability weighting affects both the measurement of risk posture and the assessment of health state utilities. Pessimistic probability weights reduce the degree of risk aversion that is found in the assessments of the utility of survival duration. Not only do changes in risk aversion affect utility trade-offs between short- and long-term survival, they also affect assessments of health state utility through the process of risk adjustment of TTOs. One goal of future research should be to investigate whether decision analyses are sensitive to discrepancies between EU and RDU assessments of health state utilities.

Another goal of future research will be the further generalization of utility assessment methods to the cumulative prospect theory (CPT) of Tversky and Kahneman (1992). The principal difference between CPT and RDU theories is that CPT postulates that outcomes are perceived as gains or losses relative to a reference level rather than as absolute levels of wealth or health. Furthermore, CPT postulates that the utility representation for lotteries can differ, depending on whether the outcomes of a lottery are exclusively nonlosses (gains or "zero" outcomes), exclusively nongains (losses or "zero" outcomes), or a mixture of gains and losses. The CPT representation for lotteries that are nonlosses is isomorphic to the RDU representation, as is the CPT representation for lotteries that are nongains. Hence the methods for RDU assessment that were described in this chapter remain valid for CPT when the domain consists exclusively of nonloss or nongain outcomes. The main issues that arise in the generalization of the present work to CPT are, first, the development of a methodology for identifying reference levels in health domains and, second, the development of assessment methods that take into account preferences for lotteries whose outcomes are mixtures of losses and gains.

References

Abdellaoui, M. (1998). Parameter-free elicitation of utilities and probability weighting functions. Working Paper, GRID, ENS, Cachar, France.

Bayoumi, A. M., & Redelmeier, D. A. (1996). Correcting distorted utilities: An application of cumulative prospect theory to medical economics (abstract). *Medical Decision Making*, 16, 457.

Bleichrodt, H., & Pinto, J. L. (1998). A parameter-free elicitation of the probability weighting function in medical decision making. Working paper, iMTA, Erasmus University, Rotterdam, the Netherlands.

Bleichrodt, H., Wakker, P., & Johannesson, M. (1997). Characterizing QALYs by risk neutrality. *Journal of Risk and Uncertainty*, 15, 107–114.

Bostic, R., Herrnstein, R. J., & Luce, R. D. (1990). The effect on the preference reversal phenomenon of using choice indifferences. *Journal of Economic Behavior and Organization*, 13, 193–212.

Camerer, C. F. (1989). An experimental test of several generalized utility theories. *Journal of Risk and Uncertainty*, 2, 61–104.

Camerer, C. F., & Ho. T. (1994). Violations of the betweenness axiom and nonlinearity in probability. *Journal of Risk and Uncertainty*, 8, 167–196.

Cher, D. J., Miyamoto, J. M., & Lenert, L. A. (1997). Risk adjustment of Markov process models: Importance in individual decision making. *Medical Decision Making*, 17, 340–350.

Drummond, M. F., O'Brien, B., Stoddart, G. L., & Torrance, G. W. (1997). *Methods for the economic evaluation of health care programmes* (second edition). New York: Oxford University Press.

Edwards, W. (Ed.). (1992). *Utility theories: Measurements and applications*. Boston: Kluwer.

Fanshel, S., & Bush, J. W. (1970). A health-status index and its application to health-services outcomes. *Operations Research*, 18, 1021–1066.

Fischer, G. W., & Hawkins, S. A. (1983). Strategy compatibility, scale compatibility, and the prominence effect. *Journal of Experimental Psychology: Human Perception and Performance, 19*, 580–597.

Fishburn, P. C. (1982). *The foundations of expected utility theory.* Dordrecht, NL: D. Reidel.

Fishburn, P. C. (1989). Retrospective on the utility theory of von Neumann and Morgenstern. *Journal of Risk and Uncertainty, 2*, 127–157.

Froberg, D. G., & Kane, R. L. (1989a). Methodology for measuring health-state preferences–I: Measurement strategies. *Journal of Clinical Epidemiology, 42(4)*, 345–354.

Froberg, D. G., & Kane, R. L. (1989b). Methodology for measuring health-state preferences–II: Scaling methods. *Journal of Clinical Epidemiology, 42(5)*, 459–471.

Froberg, D. G., & Kane, R. L. (1989c). Methodology for measuring health-state preferences–III: Population and context effects. *Journal of Clinical Epidemiology, 42(6)*, 585–592.

Froberg, D. G., & Kane, R. L. (1989d). Methodology for measuring health-state preferences–IV: Progress and a research agenda. *Journal of Clinical Epidemiology, 42(7)*, 675–685.

Fryback, D. G. (1999). The Qaly model: Utilities for cost-utility analysis in health care. In J. Shanteau, B. Mellers, & D. Schum (Eds.), *Decision research from Bayesian approaches to normative systems: Reflections on the contributions of Ward Edwards.* Norwell, MA: Kluwer.

Gold, M. R., Siegel, J. E., Russell, L. B., & Weinstein, M. C. (1996). *Cost-effectiveness in health and medicine.* New York: Oxford University Press.

Gonzalez, R. (1993). Estimating the weighting function. Paper presented at the 26th Annual Mathematical Psychology Meeting, Oklahoma City, Oklahoma.

Gonzalez, R., & Wu, G. (1999). On the form of the probability weighting function. *Cognitive Psychology, 38*, 129–166.

Kahneman, D., & Tversky, A. (1979). Prospect theory: An analysis of decision under risk. *Econometrica, 47*, 276–287.

Kahneman, D., & Tversky, A. (1984). Choices, values, and frames. *American Psychologist, 39*, 341–350.

Karni, E., & Safra, Z. (1990). Rank dependent probabilities. *Economics Journal, 100*, 187–195.

Keeney, R. L., & Raiffa, H. (1976). *Decisions with multiple objectives.* New York: Wiley.

Krantz, D. H., Luce, R. D., Suppes, P., & Tversky, A. (1971). *Foundations of measurement* (Vol. 1). New York: Academic Press.

Llewellyn-Thomas, H., Sutherland, H. J., Tibshirani, R., Ciampi, A., Till, J. E., & Boyd, N. F. (1982). The measurement of patients' values in medicine. *Medical Decision Making, 2*, 449–462.

Luce, R. D. (1992). Where does subjective expected utility fail descriptively? *Journal of Risk and Uncertainty, 5*, 5–27.

McNeil, B. J., & Pauker, S. G. (1982). Optimizing patient and societal decision making by the incorporation of individual values. In R. L. Kane & R. A. Kane (Eds.), *Values and long-term care* (pp. 215–230). Lexington, MA: D. C. Heath.

McNeil, B. J., Weichselbaum, R., & Pauker, S. G. (1978). Fallacy of the five-year survival in lung cancer. *New England Journal of Medicine, 299*, 1397–1401.

Miyamoto J. M. (1992). Generic analysis of utility models. In W. Edwards (Ed.), *Utility: Theories, measurement, and applications* (pp. 73–106). Boston: Kluwer.

Miyamoto, J. M. (1999) Quality-adjusted life years (QALY) utility models under expected utility and rank-dependent utility assumptions. *Journal of Mathematical Psychology, 43,* 201–237.

Miyamoto, J. M., & Eraker, S. A. (1985). Parameter estimates for a QALY utility model. *Medical Decision Making, 5,* 191–213.

Miyamoto, J. M., & Eraker, S. A. (1988). A multiplicative model of the utility of survival duration and health quality. *Journal of Experimental Psychology: General, 117,* 3–20.

Miyamoto, J. M., & Eraker, S. A. (1989). Parametric models of the utility of survival duration: Tests of axioms in a generic utility framework. *Organizational Behavior and Human Decision Processes, 44,* 166–202.

Miyamoto, J. M., Wakker, P., Bleichrodt, H., & Peters, H. (1998). The zero condition: A simplifying assumption in QALY measurement. *Management Science, 44,* 839–849.

Patrick, D. L., Starks, H. E., Cain, K. C., Uhlmann, R. F., & Pearlman, R. A. (1994). Measuring preferences for health states worse than death. *Medical Decision Making, 14,* 9–18.

Pliskin, J. S., Shepard, D. S., & Weinstein, M. C. (1980). Utility functions for life years and health status. *Operations Research, 28,* 206–224.

Quiggin, J. (1982). A theory of anticipated utility. *Journal of Economic Behavior and Organization, 3,* 323–343.

Quiggin, J. (1993). *Generalized expected utility theory – The rank-dependent model.* Boston: Kluwer.

Quiggin, J., & Wakker, P. (1994). The axiomatic basis of anticipated utility theory: A clarification. *Journal of Economic Theory, 64,* 486–499.

Roberts, F. S. (1979). *Measurement theory with applications to decision making, utility, and the social sciences* (pp. 13–47, 101–148). London: Addison-Wesley.

Slovic, P., & Lichtenstein, S. (1968). Relative importance of probabilities and payoffs in risk taking. *Journal of Experimental Psychology, 78,* 1–18.

Slovic, P., Lichtenstein, S., & Fischhoff, B. (1988). Decision making. In R. C. Atkinson, R. J. Herrnstein, G. Lindzey, & R. D. Luce (Eds.), *Steven's handbook of experimental psychology* (Vol. 2), pp. 673–738. New York: Wiley.

Sox, H. C., Blatt, M. A., Higgins, M. C., & Marton, K. I. (1988). *Medical decision making.* Boston: Butterworths.

Stalmeier, P. F. M., Bezembinder, T. G. G., & Unic, I. J. (1996). Proportional heuristics in time tradeoff and conjoint measurement. *Medical Decision Making, 16,* 36–44.

Sutherland, H. J., Llewelynn-Thomas, R. N. J., Boyd, N. F., & Till, J. E. (1982). Attitudes toward quality of life: The concept of "Maximal Endurable Time." *Medical Decision Making, 2,* 299–309.

Torrance, G. W. (1986). Measurement of health state utilities for economic appraisal: A review. *Journal of Health Economics, 5,* 1–30.

Torrance, G. W., Thomas, W. H., & Sackett, D. I., (1972). A utility maximization model for evaluation of health care programs. *Health Services Research, 7,* 118–133.

Tversky, A., & Kahneman D. (1992). Advances in prospect theory: Cumulative representation of uncertainty. *Journal of Risk and Uncertainty, 5,* 297–323.

Tversky, A., Sattath, S., & Slovic, P. (1988). Contingent weighting in judgment and choice. *Psychological Review*, 95, 371–384.

von Neumann, J., & Morgenstern, O. (1944). *The theory of games and economic behavior*. Princeton, NJ: Princeton University Press.

von Winterfeldt, D., & Edwards, W. (1986). *Decision analysis and behavioral decision theory*. New York: Cambridge University Press.

Wakker, P. P. (1989). *Additive representations of preferences: A new foundation of decision analysis*. Boston: Kluwer.

Wakker, P. P., & Deneffe, D. (1996). Eliciting von Neumann–Morgenstern utilities when probabilities are distorted or unknown. *Management Science*, 42, 1131–1150.

Wakker, P. P., & Stiggelbout, A. (1995). Explaining distortions in utility elicitation through the rank-dependent model for risky choices. *Medical Decision Making*, 15, 180–186.

Weinstein, M. C., Fineberg, H. V., Elstein, A. S., Frazier, H. S., Neuhauser, D., Neutra, R. R., & McNeil, B. J. (1980). *Clinical decision analysis*. Philadelphia: W. B. Saunders.

Wu, G., & Gonzalez, R. (1996). Curvature of the probability weighting function. *Management Science*, 42, 1676–1690.

4 Evidence-Based Medicine: A Quantitative Approach to Decision Making

John P. A. Ioannidis, MD, and Joseph Lau, MD

Introduction

"Evidence-based medicine" is a common, if somewhat loose, term that refers to a spectrum of attempts, including decision analyses, to introduce more objective, quantifiable estimates of clinical variables to the practice of medicine (Sackett 1995). The concept is not new – some clinicians have always suggested that real data are better than speculation or opinion – but the application of formal syntheses of evidence is complementing, if not replacing, traditional "experienced-based" medicine as health care comes under closer scrutiny.

The value of any decision depends largely on the accuracy and validity of the information on which it is based. Recent studies indicate that expert opinion can often be outdated and misleading (Antman et al. 1992, Mulrow 1987), whereas the results of high-quality, controlled experimental studies have long been seen as preferable to those of poor-quality, uncontrolled studies. The use of randomized, controlled trials as the reference standard for scientific investigation in medicine reflects the demand for more and better scientific evidence, as opposed to experiential evidence, on which to base decisions. Clearly, good evidence is compatible with good medicine.

We describe here some basic principles, strengths, and weaknesses of the major techniques for obtaining, evaluating, and synthesizing evidence from the medical literature: evidence-based medicine is essentially literature-based medicine. Understanding the potential and

From the Therapeutics Research Program, DAIDS, National Institute of Allergy and Infectious Diseases, Bethesda, Maryland; and the Division of Clinical Care Research, New England Medical Center Hospitals, and Tufts University School of Medicine, Boston, Massachusetts.

limitations of these techniques is essential to their appropriate use in clinical decision making.

Issues in Data Collection and Quality

The range of data needed for decision analyses can be wide and is limited only by the detail of the model and the ingenuity of the analyst. Typically, estimates and ranges of the risk of a disease or outcome of interest are almost always needed, as are prevalence and incidence data. Life expectancies and probabilities of survival in natural and treated states are commonly transformed from Kaplan–Meier analyses to create transition probabilities in Markov models. The efficacy and adverse effects of the modeled interventions also need to be quantified. Adverse effects may include toxicity of medications, undesirable experiences, and complications from surgical procedures.

No two decision models are identical. Although some models may share a similar decision-tree structure, the data needed to create the chance and decision nodes are quite different between models, and the amount of evidence needed varies greatly among the models. Also, information from different sources may be contradictory. To select the best information and to specify acceptable ranges for different variables, the analyst needs to consider the reliability of different sources of information.

Advantages of Experimental Control: The Hierarchy
of Evidence

The designs of clinical studies provide different levels of control for bias. Depending on the robustness of the comparison, the following types of studies can be ranked by the degree of control each can offer, from highest to lowest (Byar, cited in Olkin 1995):

1. Double-masked (subjects and evaluators), randomized, placebo-controlled trials
2. Single-masked (subjects), randomized, placebo-controlled trials
3. Open-label (unmasked), randomized, placebo-controlled trials
4. Nonrandomized, controlled observational studies with concurrent control groups
5. Observational studies with historical control groups

6. Uncontrolled observational studies, especially individual case reports, case series, and descriptive reports based on large databases and clinical registries

Strict experimental conditions, as exemplified by the fully concealed allocation, double-masked, randomized design, are, in theory, the least susceptible to bias. Empirical research has shown that the lack of allocation concealment (techniques used to prevent manipulating patients into specific groups at enrollment) may inflate the magnitude of the observed treatment effects in therapeutic comparisons (Schultz et al. 1995). The results of open-label (unmasked) drug trials may conflict with those of double-masked studies in the estimate of the treatment effect (Ioannidis et al. 1997a) and, typically, unmasked studies are more optimistic (Schultz et al. 1995). Similarly, the use of historical controls rather than concurrent, randomly assigned controls may also inflate the estimate of the treatment effects (Sacks et al. 1982). Observational data need to be adjusted for potential confounding variables, and it is unlikely that all of these variables are known, measured, or even measurable (Byar 1991).

Studies without control groups are even more prone to bias and often may lead to spurious claims about large treatment effects or inflated associations between a diagnosis and prognostic factors. Case reports are likely to provide the most uncommon data because their publication is largely driven by the rarity and unusual features of a condition. As stated in the *Instruction to the Authors* of a major clinical journal in infectious diseases, "articles reporting ... cases of infection with organisms seldom encountered clinically will not be considered unless they contain the first description of such infection or there is something else unique about the case" (*Clinical Infectious Diseases* 1997).

Data from double-masked, randomized trials for all comparisons would be ideal. However, because this level of quality is unlikely to ever be available even for a modest portion of comparisons, clinical policies may have to be based on observational data (Hornberger and Wrone 1997). Further, double masking in a study is sometimes impossible when the intervention has easily identifiable characteristics, such as procedural differences or side effects. Even random assignment may be unethical when uncontrolled or partially controlled trials already indicate that interventions are effective (Kadane 1996).

Randomized studies require time and money: the average randomized efficacy trial may span 5 to 7 years from conception to publication, and others may take more than a decade. With the flourishing of basic laboratory sciences that consume most research funds, money for randomized clinical research is relatively limited. Moreover, although we believe in the need to promote and support controlled trials, under some circumstances a specific clinical trial may not be cost-effective; in fact, a sizable literature has recently been generated on the cost-effectiveness of conducting clinical trials (Detsky 1989, 1990, Hornberger et al. 1995). Finally, as mentioned earlier, many estimates needed for decision analyses, such as the prevalence and incidence of a disease or outcome or life expectancies, must be derived from observational data.

Quality Considerations: Internal Validity

Data from randomized trials may sometimes be far from perfect for several reasons. The internal validity of a randomized trial depends not only on whether the initial study design creates a robust comparison, but also on whether this comparison is maintained during the conduct of the trial. Lack of adherence to the experimental treatment and crossover to the opposite arm of the trial tend to decrease the observed treatment effects. Patients lost to follow-up (Ioannidis et al. 1997b) and missing measurements may introduce potentially large biases into the analysis. Imputation methods for addressing the effect of missing data and losses to follow-up have been developed for making sample size calculations (Lakatos 1986), as well as for analyzing datasets in which missing data are prominent (Rubin and Schenker 1991), but when losses and missing data are nonrandom and are associated with the group assignment, the bias is often impossible to account for completely with even modest certainty.

Moreover, the serendipitous use of the experimental treatment by the control group may also narrow the observed difference between the groups. For example, in a recent mega-trial comparing transdermal nitrates to placebo, about half of the placebo patients received some nitrates therapy (ISIS-4 1995, Woods 1995). Monitoring actual drug levels or a surrogate marker in blood or urine may help detect any serendipitous use of experimental treatment in the control groups and adherence in the experimental arm. Adherence to the treatment protocol was assessed in zidovudine trials through the drug's effect on the mean corpuscular volume (Concorde 1994), and trials of metoprolol therapy after myocardial infarction used assays of metoprolol in urine (Hjalmarson et al. 1981). Pill-taking behavior can also be monitored by electronic pill containers.

Pragmatic Considerations: Different Approaches to Analysis

Traditionally, intention-to-treat analysis has been the standard approach for analyzing the results of randomized trials. In this approach, all patients are analyzed as part of the group to which they were originally assigned, whether or not they completed the protocol for that group. This approach is likely to be the most unbiased. In some situations, however, on-treatment analyses (analyzing only those patients who completed the assigned protocol) may provide estimates of quantitative variables that are more useful in decision analyses than those provided by intention-to-treat estimates. For example, decision models frequently consider adverse and nonadverse outcomes of an intervention separately in two different branches of the decision tree. Estimates based on intention-to-treat analysis combine these outcomes, whereas those based on on-treatment analysis are reported separately. If adverse reactions require that the treatment be discontinued, there is no benefit to the treatment, so on-treatment estimates are therefore more appropriate than intention-to-treat estimates for modeling efficacy in these branches of the decision tree. The preference for on-treatment approaches has also been discussed for exploratory phase I (safety) and early phase II (efficacy) trials in which nonadherent patients and withdrawals may need to be excluded if one wants to get an accurate picture of the biological potency of a tested regimen rather than its clinical effect (Pocock 1983).

The informed researcher should determine whether any of these components of internal validity might have been a problem in a specific trial and whether they have been appropriately accounted for in the design and results of a randomized trial that will be used in a decision analysis.

Generalizability Considerations: External Validity

Another issue in assessing the adequacy of randomized trials is the external validity or generalizability of the results. The strict experimental control of randomized trials may decrease the generalizability of their results. Some trials may have narrow eligibility criteria, and it may not always be prudent to extrapolate the study results to different patient populations, especially to patients with different levels of risk (Bailey 1994).

The baseline risk of the disease should be seriously considered in any decision analysis. Moreover, patients enrolled in a clinical trial may be different from those who are eligible but who decide not to enroll; indeed, some patient subpopulations have no chance of enrolling in a clinical trial (Cowan and Wittes 1994). Ideally, an eligibility-enrollment log should be kept so that the representativeness of the enrolled patients can be evaluated. Some researchers (Peto 1996) argue that in many situations, such a log is impractical to create, and the results for the nonenrolled patients are impossible to impute anyhow. Nevertheless, when feasible, comparing the enrolled patients with eligible, nonenrolled patients may be helpful in assessing whether the sample was representative of the target population.

Adjusted and Unadjusted Estimates: Subgroup Analyses

There is general consensus that nonrandomized studies should try to adjust for as many potential variables as possible. Such adjustments, which necessitate subgroup analyses, although likely to lead to more relevant estimates, also usually increase the uncertainty about the magnitude of the effect (the confidence intervals become wider) as more subgroups are analyzed (Kelsey et al. 1996).

For binary outcomes, a common technique for controlling for the influence of additional variables is the Mantel–Haenszel procedure, which can assess whether the treatment effect is still significant after adjusting for another explanatory variable (Mantel and Haenszel 1959). When several adjustments must be made, regression analyses should be considered. For continuous outcomes, least-squares linear regression analyses with adjustment for covariates may be used. The regression method of choice for time-to-event analyses is typically Cox proportional hazards regression (Cox 1972), and that for binary outcomes is logistic regression (Hosmer and Lemeshow 1989).

Both confounding variables (variables associated both with the treatment effect and with the treatment) and modifying variables (variables that affect the magnitude of the treatment effect by their presence but that are not associated with the treatment) need to be considered. A simple approach for detecting modifiers is to test for the significance of an interaction term between the therapy and the potential modifier. This approach is preferable to looking for the efficacy of the treatment in different subgroups. Subgroup analyses that are not defined a priori are problematic in that (a) the definition of subgroups is likely to be arbitrary, (b) the lack of statistical significance in a given subgroup may be the result only of the smaller size of the subgroup, and (c) multiple statistical comparisons increase the chances of wrongly attributing a result to treatment (Oxman and Guyatt 1992).

Adjustments and Stratification in Randomized Trials

In randomized trials, the need to adjust for statistical imbalances among groups is debated. Some researchers (Peto et al. 1976, Yusuf et al. 1984) believe that randomization alone should be sufficient to protect against baseline imbalances among groups, especially in larger trials; thus, confounding is thought to be unlikely. However, for small and moderate-sized trials, imbalances in important prognostic factors are likely to occur and may result in some surprising outcomes. Small trials are particularly vulnerable (Ioannidis and Lau 1997).

We believe that the problem of modifiers is not solved by random assignment, even with large samples, and that the problems listed earlier for subgroup analyses in observational studies apply to randomized trials as well. Remedies include stratifying the sample on these variables before group assignment (to ensure adequate representation of the variables in each group) and adjusting for them in the statistical analysis after the end of the trial. Neither remedy is likely to solve the problem completely. In small trials, stratification before assignment is impractical and cumbersome. Moreover, stratifying a continuous variable into a series of ordinal categories may not preserve the underlying relationship between the independent and dependent variables. The post hoc definition of the categories may be arbitrary, and extensive stratification and adjustments increase any uncertainty in the results.

Some variables are often routinely adjusted for, such as when study site is used as a stratification factor, during either the assignment process or the analysis of the results. Most adjustment and stratification approaches are equivalents of fixed-effects models (which assume that all study results are approximations of a single fixed "truth") and do not routinely consider the heterogeneity in the treatment effects between the different sites. Although random-effects models (which assume that the results of different studies are approximations of a "truth" that itself has a random variation within a range of values) are not very intuitive for analyzing site effects, and although there is little consensus on how to handle treatment–site interactions (Fleiss 1986), the belief that all sites participating in a multicenter trial provide equally reliable data may be an oversimplification. Sites may vary in terms of the enrollment and retention of patients and the quality of data collection (Sylvester et al. 1981), so investigators in multicenter trials should ensure that performance standards are met across all sites (Rosendorf et al. 1993, Wilcosky et al. 1986). Even so, different sites may conceivably enroll different populations of patients who experience different treatment effects (Horwitz et al. 1996).

Multiple and Secondary Endpoints

Well-designed trials make clear a priori the specific endpoints to be addressed and the statistical analyses to be performed. However, despite half a century of clinical trials, trial reports are often vague about their endpoints and analytic methods and even deviate from the prespecified analysis plan. Data from such studies should be viewed with caution; the phenomenon of "moving the goal posts," or adjusting the question to correspond with the results, is probably more frequent in uncontrolled studies. Manipulating the definitions of endpoints and the methods of analysis may lead to false-positive results.

Even trials with clearly defined endpoints commonly have several primary endpoints (often arising from the presence of multiple arms with multiple potential comparisons) and an even larger number of secondary endpoints (Tukey 1977). In this case, appropriate adjustments may need to be made to the reported P values and associated confidence intervals to adjust for multiple comparisons (Miller 1981). In general, researchers should avoid relying on statistical significance and should use confidence intervals to indicate the magnitude of the treatment effect, particularly when estimates are to be used for sensitivity analyses in decision making.

Another special situation may arise when a trial uses interim analyses to meet the needs of safety monitoring boards. Appropriate adjustments for multiple comparisons need to be made in this case as well, even if the interim analyses are planned (DeMets et al. 1995, O'Brien and Fleming 1979). Stopping trials early because interim results were statistically significant is likely to lead to overestimates of the magnitude of the treatment effect. Finally, secondary endpoints should be interpreted with even more caution, and their results should be seen and reported as exploratory analyses.

Data on Safety and Adverse Reactions

Besides efficacy endpoints, clinical drug studies almost invariably collect data on safety and toxicity. Such data are often indispensable for performing a decision analysis, in which both benefit and harm need to be quantified as precisely as possible. Be aware, however, that all the problems pertaining to efficacy data pertain to safety and toxicity data as well, to the same or a larger degree, and that, unfortunately, safety and toxicity data are often reported more sporadically, in less detail, and have been less carefully verified than efficacy data. Descriptive studies of large databases may provide information about toxic effects or adverse reactions, but they are unlikely to avoid the problems inherent in their lack of rigorous controls.

Many side effects are described in adverse reaction case reports after the drug is marketed (Kessler 1993). Despite improvements in adverse reaction notification and surveillance efforts, the reporting may still be sporadic, and there can be long delays in recognizing and quantifying the frequency of even important side effects (Venning 1983). In addition, some side effects may be ambiguous (Koch-Wesser et al. 1977), although many medical disciplines are beginning to use standardized toxicity scales.

Techniques for Synthesizing Evidence

Meta-analysis is a set of quantitative methods for statistically combining the results of different studies on the same topic to explore the degree of and reasons for heterogeneity and bias in the combined results and to provide a quantitative synthesis of these results (Lau et al. 1997). Some of these methods will now be described.

A General Perspective on Meta-analysis of Randomized Trials

Meta-analyses are appearing in the medical literature at an exponential rate. We estimate that more than 2,500 meta-analyses of randomized trials were published as of late 1998. Yet, this number is still small when compared to the several hundred thousand randomized trials performed in the last 50 years. The vast majority of meta-analyses to date have been retrospective, but interest is increasing in conducting prospective meta-analyses (Meinert 1989), in which a set of trials on a given topic are prospectively designed with the intention of analyzing the composite data with meta-analytic techniques. The evolution of prospective meta-analysis has been hindered by the traditional belief that any single trial should be adequately powered to answer the question on the basis of its own data ("a trial is an end to itself") (Chalmers and Lau 1993, 1996) and by the difficulty of coordinating a multitude of international trialist groups. Hopefully, such barriers will be reduced in the future.

Current initiatives, such as the Cochrane Collaboration, aim to perform and disseminate systematic reviews (if not the more quantitative meta-analyses) of all the randomized trials ever conducted and to update them with data from new randomized trials yet to be conducted (Bero and Rennie 1995). The extent of the success of such initiatives cannot be predicted, but it is likely that in the near future we may have a more complete picture of the broader state of evidence from randomized trials. A large number of randomized trials may be irrelevant or not pertinent to current medical practice; be found to be overtly biased after the fact; or be unusable for a variety of other reasons.

Along the same lines, to date meta-analyses have dealt mostly with problems believed to be important for clinical decision making; have been composed of trials likely to be of better-than-average quality; and have been performed in areas in which adequate information was available. These factors should be considered when evaluating a meta-analysis. However, some meta-analyses may have been preferentially conducted and published primarily for marketing or other reasons, and others have limited themselves to information provided in published trial reports and have excluded studies not published or not published in English. Individual research conducted for personal or economic motives may lead to bias in meta-analyses as well. Hopefully, prospective meta-analysis will not be subject to these limitations.

The overall quality of meta-analyses is already becoming a concern (Bailar 1997, Moher and Olkin 1995). The quality of meta-analyses improved during the 1990s (Sacks et al. 1987), but quality and standardization can be improved further. There is much interest in assessing the reliability of meta-analyses and in comparing their results to the results of large trials (Cappelleri et al. 1996, LeLorier et al. 1997, Villar et al. 1995). These analyses have stressed differences in the conclusions arrived at by the two methodologies, but they also show that large trials and meta-analyses often agree (Ioannidis et al. 1998). The discrepancies may involve both study quality and heterogeneity (combinability) issues and may provide a unique opportunity to learn how to improve the quality of both randomized trials and meta-analyses in the long term.

Developing a Meta-analysis Protocol

The previous observations highlight the importance to meta-analysts of having a robust protocol, a detailed analytical plan, and a careful presentation plan equal to that of any good-quality clinical trial. Issues of multiple comparisons, specification of endpoints, and data analysis also pertain to meta-analyses. Exploratory analyses suggested by the data need not be prohibited and may even lead to hypotheses more interesting than the original ones, but such analyses should be identified as exploratory. The main questions to be answered should be clearly defined. The search strategy, data sources, and inclusion and exclusion criteria for the studies considered should be delineated. The modes of data extraction and validation should be specified. Analysis plans should be specified before the study begins, and the presentation of the results should follow a specified format. Deviations from these principles may lead to spurious conclusions.

Sources of Data for Meta-analyses

Data for a meta-analysis may need to be collected from several different sources. Generally, electronic databases are good places to start. Ideally, both MEDLINE and EMBASE (the electronic equivalent of Excerpta Medica) should be screened, with no language restrictions. Recent investigators have suggested the presence of a "Tower of Babel bias" (or English bias) in the publication of randomized trials (Egger et al. 1996). Studies published in non-English journals may be more likely to report negative results (Egger et al. 1996) or positive results (Vickers et al. 1998), depending on the topic; thus, limiting the search to English-language evidence may distort results for different interventions. The extent of this potential language bias is not known, but its detection has strengthened the perception that the non-English literature on a topic should be scrutinized carefully.

In many medical disciplines, the non-English literatures of randomized trials have never been large, are shrinking even further, or are of generally dubious quality (although quality issues are probably not a problem for some European literatures or the Japanese literature at least).

Bibliographic databases are likely to become more inclusive and even larger in the future. However, electronic search strategies currently fail to identify all pertinent studies. Depending on the specific topic, MEDLINE searches may identify 30–90% of relevant randomized, controlled trials (Dickersin et al. 1994), although our experience suggests that the problem may not be that serious. Reasons for missed retrievals include indexing errors and incorrect terms in the search strategy. Moreover, MEDLINE currently indexes only about 4,000 of the 16,000 biomedical journals currently published, and EMBASE indexes only 1,000 journals that are not included in MEDLINE, although non-MEDLINE indexed journals tend to publish lower-quality research. Subject-specific databases, such as BIOSIS, CINAHL, PsychLit, and CancerLit, should be searched when appropriate.

Other methods for identifying information include manually searching through relevant journals, screening reference lists, screening study registries, and personally contacting pharmaceutical and medical device companies, as well as colleagues and researchers who may know of other published or unpublished studies. Surveys of authors of previous research studies, content experts, and colleagues who may know of additional studies may have low response rates (Hetherington et al. 1989). The Cochrane Collaboration is creating a registry of controlled trials from all medical disciplines (Cochrane Collaboration 1996). When completed and standardized, the registry may contain an invaluable core of the randomized trials' literature. Other initiatives are encouraging the prospective registration of trial protocols in various medical fields, a concept proposed as the only means of ensuring access to complete information (Simes 1986, Stern and Simes 1997).

Data Extraction for Meta-analyses

Despite improvements in the reporting of randomized trials and steps taken to standardize their reports (Begg et al. 1996), different trials may present their results differently. This "presentation bias" may be overcome by focusing on data that are likely to be reported in a standard way, by transforming presented data into a standard form if possible, and by communicating with individual investigators who may provide additional or more detailed data.

Data should be extracted from relevant studies with the utmost care because errors may substantially affect the conclusions. Ideally, two researchers should extract the data independently. The two sets of extracted data should then be compared and all discrepancies resolved, either by discussion and consensus or by a third independent reviewer. The practice of masking researchers to the authors' names and affiliations, the results and conclusions of the study, and the journal of publication during data extraction had been controversial, but recent evidence suggests that masking is probably not necessary, which could substantially reduce the time and effort required to extract data (Berlin 1997).

Communicating with the sponsors and trial investigators of the studies included in a meta-analysis may help clarify inconsistencies and may make the detailed information on individual patients available for the meta-analysis. The drawback of such communication is that the meta-analysis may be delayed or even distorted for mostly political reasons, which can arise in any large collaborative effort. It is also possible that the inclusion of "data on file" may sometimes lead to conclusions different from those published. In such situations, separating the scientific and quality issues of the unpublished databases and from political issues can be difficult. Stelfox et al. (1998) present a classic example of conflict of interest in clinical research and meta-analysis in which the results of studies on calcium-channel antagonists were associated with whether the investigators had or had not received funding from the pharmaceutical industry.

Qualitative Assessment of the Evidence

The quality of randomized trials may be assessed with standardized scales that attempt to score various components of the study design, analysis, and report. The most commonly used scale, developed by Chalmers, assesses over 30 different elements (Chalmers et al. 1981). Study design issues, such as adequacy of random assignment and double masking, are heavily weighted in the final quality score. Other scales, such as the one proposed by Jadad (1993), focus on reporting and presentation. A comprehensive review of the various scales has been published by Moher et al. (1995). For specific clinical questions, it may be equally good or even preferable to create individualized quality assessment scales for elements most pertinent to the specific medical question.

Quality scores can be incorporated into a meta-analysis by weighting high-quality studies more than low-quality studies in the calculations or by performing sensitivity and subgroup analyses (e.g., estimate separately the pooled results of good-quality trials) (Detsky et al. 1992). However, quality scores are not consistently related to the magnitude of the treatment effect (Emerson et al. 1990). Thus, it may be better to examine the impact of individual quality factors such as the adequacy of random assignment or masking on the pooled estimate (Ioannidis and Lau 1998).

Quantitative Synthesis of the Evidence

Measures of Treatment Effect. The magnitude of the treatment effect may be expressed and summarized by different measures. For continuous outcomes, correlation coefficients or the mean difference in event rate between treatment and control groups and the standardized mean difference can be used when the scales used to measure the treatment effect differ among trials. The standardized mean difference (or "effect size") is the ratio of the difference between the mean in the treatment group and the mean in the control group divided by the standard deviation in the control group.

For binary data, measures of the treatment effect include the risk difference (and its inverse, the number needed to treat) (McQuay and Moore 1997), the risk ratio, and the odds ratio. The risk difference is the difference in the event rates of the treatment and control groups, whereas the odds ratio and risk ratio provide relative measures of the treatment effect. Ideally, all measures should be considered because they provide complementary information (Sinclair and Bracken 1994). In practice, risk and odds ratios tend to be more consistent across studies than the mean differences, effect size, or correlation coefficients. In some cases, either the odds or the risk ratio may seem more appropriate, but in most circumstances, one ratio is as good as the other for summarizing the data (Deeks et al. 1997). The practical advantages of the odds ratio include the ability to take any positive value and its direct correspondence to logistic regression when binary data are considered. The advantage of the risk ratio is that it does not inflate the magnitude of the treatment effect, as does the odds ratio, especially when the event rates are high. In clinical trials, the odds ratio is often used as an approximation of the risk ratio. The selection of a specific measure of the treatment effect in decision analysis may also depend largely on the structure and specification of the decision model.

Combining Treatment Effects. To summarize the data, each study is given a weight that depends on the precision of its results. (The precision is generally given by the inverse of the variance of the estimated treatment effect in each study.) This variance of the estimated treatment effect has two components: the variance of the individual study (the within-study variance) and the variance between different studies (the between-study variance). The simplest approach to thinking about combining different results is to assume that all studies have approximated the same fixed truth and that differences among the observed treatment effects are only the results of random error. In this case, the between-study variance is assumed to be zero, and the calculations are performed with what are called "fixed-effects models." Fixed-effects models are exemplified by the Mantel–Haenszel method (Mantel and Haenszel 1959) and the Peto method (Fleiss 1993) in the case of dichotomous data.

On the other hand, if the "truth" itself is not fixed but is believed to vary within a range of values, then each study can be seen as addressing a different true treatment effect, and these treatment effects come from a distribution of truths with a variance equal to the between-study variance. In this case, calculations are performed with random effects models, which add the between-study variance to the within-study variance of each study. The most commonly used random effects model is that proposed by DerSimonian and Laird (1986). More sophisticated, fully Bayesian approaches may also be used to calculate the between-study variance (Smith et al. 1995). Fixed- and random-effects methods have also been developed for continuous outcomes (Hedges and Olkin 1985).

Ideally, both fixed- and random-effects calculations should be performed and their results compared. When the results are greatly and significantly heterogeneous, the fixed-effects models are counterintuitive and should be avoided. Usually, fixed- and random-effects estimates are similar, but exceptions can occur (Borzak and Ridker 1995). In terms of precision, random effects are almost invariably associated with larger confidence intervals when heterogeneity is present because between-trial uncertainty is introduced. Compared to the DerSimonian and Laird estimates, fully Bayesian methods may result in even wider confidence intervals.

Some simple formulas for calculating treatment effects and weights are provided in the Appendix. These formulas work well for large numbers but sometimes not for small ones (Emerson 1994). Generally, Mantel–Haenszel estimates work well even with small numbers (Emerson 1994), whereas random-effects estimates are more unstable. The Peto fixed-effects model may be associated with large bias when the data are unbalanced (Greenland and Salvan 1990). With the increasing popularity of meta-analysis, several easy-to-use software programs to combine data have become available (Egger et al. 1998). However, the informed researcher should be aware of the preceding caveats and should understand which formulas are used by the software.

Presenting the Results. Figure 4.1 shows the typical summary presentation of the results of a meta-analysis. Each study is shown with its point estimate and confidence intervals (CI, typically the 95% CI). The pooled estimate and its 95% CI are also presented.

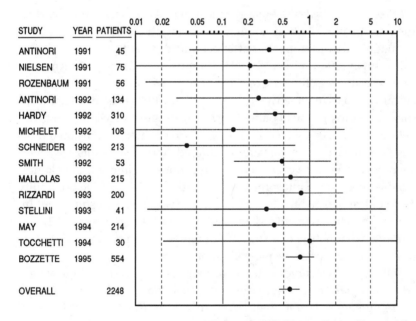

Favors TMP/SMX   Favors Pentamidine

Figure 4.1. Typical presentation of a meta-analysis of randomized trials. Each study is shown as a point estimate with a CI (typically 95%). The pooled estimate is shown at the bottom. This meta-analysis compared sulfamethoxazole with aerosolized pentamidine for the prophylaxis of *Pneumocystis carinii* pneumonia. Although most studies, including the largest, were inconclusive, the meta-analysis shows convincingly that trimethoprim/sulfamethoxazole is superior to pentamidine (Ioannidis et al. 1996). Reprinted from the *Archives of Internal Medicine* with permission.

Assessing Heterogeneity among Study Results

There is a widespread misconception that the goal of meta-analyses is to force heterogeneous results into a single estimate. Although obtaining a single treatment effect may be appropriate and functional in many circumstances, a more interesting application of meta-analysis is to explore any heterogeneity among different trials and to understand possible reasons for these differences. The tests most commonly used to refute heterogeneity are based on the chi-square distribution and tend to be insensitive, so they should probably be considered significant at $P < 0.10$ (Lau et al. 1997), although there is no consensus on this issue (Fleiss 1981). Regardless of the type I criterion used, however, the failure to detect heterogeneity among different trial results does not mean that it does not exist.

Meta-regression Analysis. Meta-regression analysis uses the individual study as the unit of observation in assessing the relationship between the magnitude of the treatment effect and different predictors (Berlin and Antman 1994; Smith et al. 1993, Thompson 1993). Predictors may be study-specific (e.g., the dose or route of administration of a drug) or ecological variables in which a mean or median value is taken as characteristic of the study group of patients (e.g., mean age or percentage of men). Meta-regressions may be presented as two- or three-dimensional plots when one or two predictors are considered, and their results are generally reported as slope coefficients with confidence intervals. Ecological variables need to be interpreted with caution because of the possibility of ecological bias, which occurs when study averages misrepresent individual patients (Greenland and Robins 1994, Morgenstern 1982). For example, what is true of a study with patients of mean age of 50 years may not be true for a specific patient of age 50.

The statistical techniques for meta-regression analysis include weighted least squares for continuous outcomes and logistic regression for binary outcomes. Random-effects regression equivalents have been developed (Berkey et al. 1995). In addition, for variables subject to measurement error, such as the use of the event rate in the control group as the baseline risk of the study population (Schmid et al. 1998), adjustments can be made with Bayesian hierarchical models (McIntosh 1996).

Meta-regression should be viewed cautiously when it is performed a posteriori because the selection of covariates may have been suggested spuriously by the data. The selection of covariates is also dictated to a large extent by the availability of data (variables collected and reported across all trials) and by the subjective selection of the meta-analysts, who choose covariates that they believe may be important to the specific problem. In addition to these potentially subjective covariates, others are always available in clinical trials, regardless of the topic, and may thus be used as standard probes in the assessment and interpretation of among-study heterogeneity. These other covariates include the sample size, the variance of the results, and the rate of events in the control group.

Differences in Sample Size and Variance. Meta-regression analyses of the treatment effect on sample size or variance may be useful in assessing the potential for publication bias, in particular, the lack of publication of small studies with negative results (Egger et al. 1997). When the treatment effect is more favorable in smaller, less precise studies, it is possible that data from some small negative studies are not represented in the literature. The presence of publication bias has been documented both in retrospective analyses (Dickersin and Min 1993, Dickersin et al. 1987, Easterbrook et al. 1991, Scherer et al. 1994) and in prospective registries of clinical trials (Ioannidis 1998). Publication bias is more prominent in uncontrolled studies and in small Phase I studies, but even randomized efficacy studies are affected.

The term "completion" or "publication lag" may describe publication bias more appropriately. In a prospective evaluation of 109 federally sponsored (National Institutes of Health) efficacy trials, the median time to publication from the start of enrollment was 4.3 years for studies with positive results and 6.5 years for studies with negative results. Negative trials were delayed at all phases of their implementation: they took slightly longer to complete their follow-up activities, longer to submit once complete, and longer to publish after submission to peer review (Ioannidis 1998). Industry-sponsored trials may be more widely affected by this phenomenon.

Regression analysis for assessing publication bias (Egger et al. 1997) may not be the optimal method for assessing publication bias; instead, a standardized correlation coefficient between treatment effect and study variance may be preferable (Begg and Mazumdar 1994). But for practical purposes, even simpler methods may be just as good, such as the traditional inverted funnel plot, in which the sample size or variance is plotted against the size of the treatment effect. Asymmetric funnel plots may suggest publication bias (Figure 4.2). However, such "publication

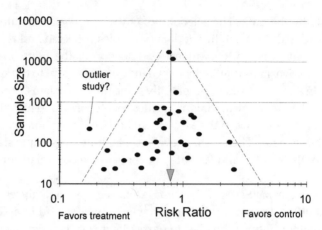

Figure 4.2. An inverted funnel plot for the identification of asymmetry of the trial results as a function of their precision (Lau et al. 1997). Reprinted from the *Annals of Internal Medicine* with permission.

bias diagnostics" may point out heterogeneity among treatment effects resulting from factors other than publication bias.

Differences in the Duration of Follow-up. If the treatment effect decreases over time, studies with longer follow-ups will have smaller variances (more outcome events and smaller treatment effects). Time-dependent treatment effects will thus show up as a false-positive publication bias on the previously mentioned diagnostic funnel plot (Ioannidis et al. 1997a). Similarly, false-positive results may be obtained if the treatment effect is different in patients at varying levels of risk; trials of high-risk populations suffering more events (and thus with smaller variances) will then show different treatment effects than trials of low-risk populations. Trials enrolling low-risk patients will take longer to complete, are more likely to have negative results (as a results of lower power), and may thus take longer to be published as well (Ioannidis 1998).

Effect of the Event Rate in the Control Group. The preceding observations suggest that in addition to sample size and variance, the relationship of the treatment effect with the event rate in the control group should also be assessed. This rate is another objective and ubiquitous meta-regression covariate (Boissel et al. 1993, Smith et al. 1993). It reflects the severity of illness in the study cohort, but it is also modulated by the duration of follow-up, the use of concomitant treatments, and other factors. It can be used to assess whether patient populations at different levels of risk experience different levels of benefit or harm from treatment. The regression models ideally should adjust for measurement error (because the event rate is a measured variable and the number of patients is finite) and must account for the built-in association between the observed treatment effect and the control rate because the treatment effect contains the control rate in its definition (Senn 1994, Sharp et al. 1996).

An assessment of 112 meta-analyses found that the size of the treatment effect was related to the control rate in 14% of studies when the odds ratio or risk ratio was considered and in 31% of studies when the risk difference was considered (Schmid et al. 1998). The control rate reflects the risk of the study cohort and should therefore be interpreted cautiously because it does not predict for individual patients. Patients enrolled even in trials with fairly strict enrollment criteria may still be widely heterogeneous (Ioannidis and Lau 1997). Generally, the minority of high-risk patients tend to contribute the majority of the events of interest. Thus, a meta-regression analysis suggesting that benefit is seen only when the event rate of the entire control group is above, say, 7% may simply be reflecting the fact that a high-risk portion of the control group experienced an event rate of, say, 30% or higher and that these patients were the ones benefiting from the treatment.

Meta-analysis of Diagnostic Tests

Decision analyses often require accurate knowledge of the performance of diagnostic tests. Methods for assessing the performance of diagnostic tests have been used increasingly in the last 20 years (Swets 1988). Besides typical test characteristics, such as sensitivity, specificity, likelihood ratios, and positive and negative predictive values, many researchers prefer to present the characteristics of diagnostic tests through receiver operating characteristics (ROC) curves, which show the trade-off between sensitivity and specificity for different thresholds of classification (Hanley and McNeil 1982) (see Figure 4.3).

The area under the ROC curve is a measure of the overall test performance across different thresholds and may vary from 0.5 (an uninformative test) to 1.0 (a test that discriminates perfectly). When the points along the curve represent independent studies, the area under the ROC curve is equivalent to the Wilcoxon nonparametric statistic. This property can be used to generate estimates of the standard error of the area

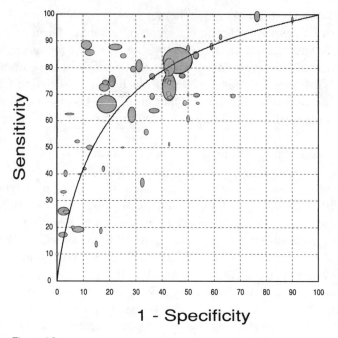

Figure 4.3.

under the curve, to determine the sample size required to provide reliable estimates of the area under the curve, and to have enough power to detect differences in the accuracy of diagnostic systems (Hanley and McNeil 1982). A special correction to the standard error is needed to compare ROC curves when observations are not independent but are derived from the same set of patients, in which case correlation is induced by the paired nature of data (Hanley and McNeil 1983). Finally, confidence bands can be estimated for ROC curves, for example, by employing Working–Hotteling-type confidence bands for simple regression (Guangqin and Hall 1993). These methods are beyond the scope of this chapter, but the decision analyst may be interested in using the range of estimates suggested by confidence intervals.

The results of diagnostic test evaluations may also be combined with meta-analytic methods (Moses et al. 1993). Developing a protocol, retrieving the pertinent documents, and extracting the data are performed as in meta-analyses of randomized trials. The quality of diagnostic test evaluations may be assessed by several different scales, which share some features. Mulrow et al. (1989) discuss various scales and propose the most widely used quality assessment scale for diagnostic tests. Priorities in this scaling system include the description of the purpose of the test; appropriate selection and description of the patient population; appropriate performance and description of the diagnostic test; appropriate selection and performance of the reference standard; and adequate presentation of the test characteristics.

The quantitative combination of diagnostic test data presents some special challenges. Because sensitivity and specificity are correlated, separate pooling of these rates across different studies may underestimate the performance of a diagnostic test (Shapiro 1995).

Meta-analysis of Observational Studies

The principles of meta-analysis can be extended to observational, nonrandomized studies. These applications are more controversial because the problems encountered in the meta-analysis of randomized trial data may be magnified severalfold when nonrandomized trial data are considered. Typical magnified problems include publication bias, presentation bias (incomplete or inconsistent reporting of the purpose, methods, or results), and ecological fallacy issues (in which summary statistics hide important variations in the data). All the disadvantages of nonrandomized trial data are also potentially incurred. Additional problems include the potentially larger heterogeneity in the data, the overall lower quality of nonrandomized studies, and the ambiguity surrounding small effects that are likely to be the target of current observational studies (Shapiro 1994).

Nevertheless, meta-analyses of observational data are more likely to be performed in the future. Coordinated efforts to carefully analyze data from several observational cohorts may lead to more reliable estimates than isolated analyses looking at the strength of specific associations that may be of interest to a decision analyst and in general. Moreover, defenders of the approach have argued that observational heterogeneity is in fact a blessing and that meta-analysis should be viewed primarily as a tool for exploring heterogeneity, generating new hypotheses, and planning new research (Berlin 1995, Petiti 1994). Some areas of application are particularly attractive, such as dose–response meta-analyses (Berlin et al. 1993, Greenland and Longnecker 1992, Tweedie and Mengersen 1995). The discussion of the methodological peculiarities are beyond the scope of this chapter; readers may wish to see a specialized overview of the subject (Greenland 1987).

Meta-analysis of Individual Patient Data

Most meta-analyses conducted to date used summary data from individual studies or subgroups thereof. Meta-analyses using individual patient data (MIPD) from all the pertinent studies are not new, but only a relatively small number have been conducted (see, for example, Early Breast Cancer Trialists' Collaborative Group 1995). The MIPD approach provides several clear advantages, such as closer involvement of the participating investigators and trialists; the ability to verify and update the raw data collected by the included studies; the possibility of more detailed time-to-event analyses; the ability to generate individual-based predictive models; and the chance to assess the effect of various predictors at the individual patient level through bypassing ecological fallacies (Stewart and Clarke 1995).

The disadvantages of these trials include the potential for retrieval bias when trials whose data are not retrievable are excluded; the potentially lower quality of updated data that have been accumulated after the end of the main follow-up period of a randomized trial (such as extensive crossovers or incomplete information on many patients); and the time and effort required to obtain data from a multitude of investigators and trialists groups. The first two reasons could theoretically make MIPD even less reliable than meta-analyses of published group data in some circumstances. Such studies should be encouraged, however, and may become the way of the future, especially with prospective meta-analyses. Early reports have suggested that the estimates obtained by MIPD may occasionally differ from the estimates of conventional meta-analyses of the literature on the same topic (Jeng et al. 1995, Stewart and Parmar 1993), but the extent and frequency of the discrepancies need to be evaluated in a larger number of examples.

Special Issues in Evidence-Based Decision Making

What to Do with Statistically Nonsignificant Results

Observational evidence, clinical trials, and meta-analyses are often reported in a yes–no fashion: "predictor x is important for the disease outcome," "treatment w works," "treatment f does not work." This approach reflects the traditional frequentist heritage that emphasizes the acceptance or rejection of the null hypothesis being tested. Typically, readers accept a 5% type I error rate and are willing to interpret the results as acceptable or not, depending on whether the calculated P value is above or below 0.05.

However, P values say nothing about the magnitude of a treatment effect or the strength of an association, and these are the aspects of evidence of most interest in a decision analysis. From that perspective, we strongly recommend not dropping or simplifying variables to unity on the basis of a recorded nonsignificant effect when selecting probabilities and effect sizes for a decision model. For variables with nonstatistically significant effects, it is preferable to use the range suggested by generous confidence intervals (95% or even 99%). Otherwise, important effects can be missed only because too little evidence was collected to prove their presence.

Differences between Individual and Population or Policy Applications

Decision models can use either average estimates for variables representing a population or variables for individual patients. Reasonably available variable estimates for specific individual patient profiles should be preferred over population averages. Averages are good enough for determining broad policy needs, such as the relative effectiveness of different chains of interventions in an entire population. However, patients at different levels of risk may require different management to optimize the use of resources and individual outcomes. Modeling the outcomes of individual patients with different baseline risks and different responses to treatment may be more rewarding and may even lead to a more diversified policy perspective. As discussed earlier, clinical trials are typically underpowered for detecting subgroup and individual diversity, but meta-analyses may have a better chance of suggesting such diversity.

The Importance of Sensitivity Analysis for Exploring Heterogeneity

Even if subgroup differences are not statistically significant, sensitivity analyses, in which key estimates are varied over their probable range of values to determine their overall impact on the outcome, should be an integral part of meta-analysis. Even when the relative risk reduction is constant across different patient subgroups or individuals, an intervention may be appropriate for patients at high risk and largely inappropriate for patients at low risk. Sensitivity analyses based on the likelihood of the disease should be routinely performed. The situation may be even more interesting when the efficacy or toxicity of different treatments is linked with the baseline risk of the disease (Lau et al. 1998). In such cases, the credibility of the decision models may be enhanced by linking these covarying variables, as suggested by meta-regression approaches. Overall, maximal use of evidence requires a thorough use of wide ranges of estimates and exploitation of associations found by clinical trials and meta-analyses. The optimal use of such information may help create models that can be applied efficiently in the care of individual patients.

Appendix: Common Formulas for Pooled Estimates by the General-Variance Fixed and Random Effects Models

Suppose that the results of κ studies are to be pooled. Let t_i and c_i be the number of treated and control patients, respectively, with the event of interest in the ith study. Also, let T_i and C_i be the number of patients in the treatment and control groups, respectively, in the ith study. Then the estimated standardized treatment effects and their variance in the ith study are given as follows:

Logarithm of the risk ratio

$$\ln(RR_i) = \ln[t_i C_i / c_i T_i] \quad \sigma_i^2 = [(T_i - t_i)/t_i T_i] + [(C_i - c_i)/C_i c_i]$$

Logarithm of the odds ratio

$$\ln(OR_i) = \ln[t_i(C_i - c_i)/c_i(T_i - t_i)] \quad \sigma_i^2 = 1/(T_i) + 1/(T_i - t_i) + 1/(C_i)$$
$$+ 1/(C_i - c_i)$$

Risk difference

$$RD_i = (c_i/C_i) - (t_i/T_i) \quad \sigma_i^2 = \left[(T_i t_i - t_i^2)/T_i^2\right] + \left[(C_i c_i - c_i^2)/C_i^2\right]$$

The pooled treatment effect (TE) measures are obtained in general from the treatment effect measures in the ith study by

$$TE_{\text{pooled}} = \left(\sum w_i TE_i\right) / \left(\sum w_i\right)$$

where w_i is the weight ascribed to the ith study.

The weight of a study is generally given by

$$w_i = \left(\tau^2 + \sigma_i^2\right)^{-1}$$

where σ_i^2 is the variance of the (standardized) treatment effect in the ith study. For fixed-effects calculations, τ^2 is set at 0. For random-effects calculations according to the DerSimonian–Laird model, τ^2 is calculated as

$$\tau^2 = (Q - [n-1])\Big/\left(\sum w_i - \left[\sum w_i^2 \Big/ \sum w_i\right]\right)$$

where $Q = \sum w_i(\text{TE}_i - \text{TE}_{\text{pooled, fixed}})^2$.

The Q statistic follows a χ^2 distribution with $n-1$ degrees of freedom and is the test typically used to test the hypothesis that the κ underlying treatment effects are equal (that there is no between-study heterogeneity). When the τ^2 estimate is negative, then 0 is imputed instead. The variance of a pooled treatment effect is given by the sum of the w_i values.

References

Antman EM, Lau J, Kupelnick B, Mosteller F, Chalmers TC (1992). A comparison of results of meta-analyses of randomized controlled trials and recommendations of clinical experts. *JAMA* 268:240–8.

Bailar JC 3rd (1997). The promise and problems of meta-analysis. *N Engl J Med* 337:559–61.

Bailey KR (1994). Generalizing the results of randomized clinical trials. *Control Clin Trials* 15:15–23.

Begg CB, Mazumdar M (1994). Operating characteristics of a rank correlation test for publication bias. *Biometrics* 50:1088–1101.

Begg C, Cho M, Eastwood S, Horton R, Moher D, Olkin I, Pitkin R, Rennie D, Schultz KF, Simel D, Stroup DF (1996). Improving the quality of reporting of randomized controlled trials. The CONSORT statement. *JAMA* 276:637–9.

Berkey CS, Hoaglin DC, Mosteller F, Colditz GA (1995). A random-effects regression model for meta-analysis. *Stat Med* 14:395–411.

Berlin JA, Longnecker MP, Greenland S (1993). Meta-analysis of epidemiologic dose–response data. *Epidemiology* 4:218–28.

Berlin JA, Antman EM (1994). Advantages and limitations of meta-analytic regressions of clinical trials data. *Online J Curr Clin Trials* (Doc No 134).

Berlin JA (1995). Invited commentary: benefits of heterogeneity in meta-analysis of data from epidemiologic studies. *Am J Epidemiol* 142:383–7.

Berlin JA (1997). Does blinding of readers affect the results of meta-analyses? *Lancet* 350:185–6.

Bero L, Rennie D (1995). The Cochrane Collaboration: preparing, maintaining, and disseminating systematic reviews on the effects of health care. *JAMA* 274:1935–8.

Boissel JP, Collet JP, Lievre M, Girard P (1993). An effect model for the assessment of drug benefit: example of antiarrhythmic drugs in postmyocardial infarction patients. *J Cardiovasc Pharmacol* 22:356–63.

Borzak S, Ridker PM (1995). Discordance between meta-analyses and large-scale randomized, controlled trials. *Ann Intern Med* 123:873–7.

Byar DP (1991). Problems with using observational databases to compare treatments. *Stat Med* 10:663–6.

Cappelleri JC, Ioannidis JPA, Schmid CH, de Ferranti SD, Aubert M, Chalmers TC, Lau J (1996). Large trials vs. meta-analyses of small trials: how do their results compare? *JAMA* 276:1332–8.

Chalmers TC, Smith H Jr, Blackburn B, Silverman B, Schoeder B, Reitman D, Ambroz A (1981). A method for assessing the quality of a randomized control trial. *Controlled Clin Trials* 2:231–49.

Chalmers TC, Lau J (1993). Meta-analysis stimulus for changes in clinical trials. *Stat Meth Med Res* 2:161–72.

Chalmers TC, Lau J (1996). Changes in clinical trials mandated by the advent of meta-analysis. *Stat Med* 15:1263–8.

Clinical Infectious Diseases (1997). Instruction to the Authors.

Cochrane Collaboration (1996). *The Cochrane Controlled Trials Register*. Oxford: Update software.

Concorde Coordinating Committee (1994). Concorde: MRC/ANRS randomised double-blind controlled trial of immediate and deferred zidovudine in symptom-free HIV infection. *Lancet* 343:871–81.

Cowan CD, Wittes J (1994). Intercept studies, clinical trials, and cluster experiments: to whom can we extrapolate? *Control Clin Trials* 15:24–9.

Cox DR (1972). Regression models and life tables. *JRSS* 34 (series B):187–220.

DeMets DL, Fleming TR, Whitley RJ, Childress JF, Ellenberg SS, Foulkes M, Mayer KH, O'Fallon J, Pollard RB, Rahal JJ, Sande M, Straus S, Walters L, Whitley-Williams P (1995). The Data and Safety Monitoring Board and Acquired Immune Deficiency Syndrome Trials. *Controlled Clin Trials* 16:408–21.

Deeks JJ, Altman DG, Dooley G, Sackett DLS (1997). Choosing an appropriate dichotomous effect measure for meta-analysis: empirical evidence of the appropriateness of the odds ratio and relative risk. *Controlled Clin Trials* 18: 84S–85S.

DerSimonian R, Laird N (1986). Meta-analysis in clinical trials. *Controlled Clin Trials* 7:177–88.

Detsky AS (1989). Are clinical trials a cost-effective investment? *JAMA* 262:1795–1800.

Detsky AS (1990). Using cost-effectiveness analysis to improve the efficiency of allocating funds to clinical trials. *Stat Med* 9:173–84.

Detsky AS, Naylor CD, O'Rourke K, McGeer AJ, L'Abbe KA (1992). Incorporating variations in the quality of individual randomized trials into meta-analysis. *J Clin Epidemiol* 45:225–65.

Dickersin K, Chan S, Chalmers TC, Sacks HS, Smith H (1987). Publication bias and clinical trials. *Controlled Clin Trials* 8:343–53.

Dickersin K, Min Y-I (1993). Publication bias: the problem that won't go away. *Ann NY Acad Sci* 703:135–48.

Dickersin K, Scherer R, Lefebvre C (1994). Identifying studies for systematic reviews. *BMJ* 309:1286–91.

Early Breast Cancer Trialists' Collaborative Group (1995). Effects of radiotherapy and surgery in early breast cancer: an overview of the randomized trials. *N Engl J Med.* 333:1444–55.

Easterbrook P, Berlin JA, Gopalan R, Matthews DR (1991). Publication bias in clinical research. *Lancet* 337:867–72.

Egger M, Zellweger T, Antes G (1996). Randomised trials in German language journals. *Lancet* 347:1047–8.

Egger M, Smith GD, Schneider M, Minder C (1997). Bias in meta-analysis detected by a single, graphical test. *BMJ* 315:629–34.

Egger M, Sterne JAC, Smith GD (1998). Meta-analysis software [BMJ Web site]. January 17, 1998. Available at: http://bmj.com.archieve/7126/7126ed9.htm. Accessed February 7, 1998.

Emerson JD, Burdick E, Hoaglin DC, Mosteller F, Chalmers TC (1990). An empirical study of the possible relation of treatment differences to quality scores in controlled randomized clinical trials. *Controlled Clin Trials* 11:339–52.

Emerson JD (1994). Combining estimates of the odds ratio: the state of the art. *Stat Meth Med Res* 3:157–78.

Fleiss JL (1981). *Statistical methods for rates and proportions.* 2nd ed. New York: John Wiley & Sons.

Fleiss JL (1986). Analysis of data from multiclinic trials. *Controlled Clin Trials* 7:267–75.

Fleiss JL (1993). The statistical basis of meta-analysis. *Stat Meth Med Res* 2:121–45.

Greenland S (1987). Quantitative methods in the review of epidemiologic literature. *Epidemiol Rev* 9:1–30.

Greenland S, Longnecker MP (1992). Methods for trend estimation from summarized dose–response data, with applications to meta-analysis. *Am J Epidemiol* 135:1301–9.

Greenland S, Robins J (1994). Invited commentary: ecologic studies – biases, misconceptions, and counterexamples. *Am J Epidemiol* 139:747–60.

Greenland S, Salvan A (1990). Bias in the one step method for pooling study results. *Stat Med* 9:247–52.

Guangqin MA, Hall WJ (1993). Confidence bands for receiver operating characteristics curves. *Med Decis Making* 13:191–7.

Hanley JA, McNeil BJ (1982). The meaning and use of the area under a receiving operating characteristics (ROC) curve. *Radiology* 143:29–36.

Hanley JA, McNeil BJ (1983). A method for comparing the areas under receiver operating characteristic curves derived from the same cases. *Radiology* 148:839–43.

Hedges LV, Olkin I (1985). *Statistical methods for meta-analysis.* Orlando, FL: Academic Press.

Hetherington J, Dickersin K, Chalmers I, Meinert CL (1989). Retrospective and prospective identification of unpublished controlled trials: lessons from a survey of obstetricians and pediatricians. *Pediatrics* 84:374–80.

Hjalmarson A, Elmfeldt D, Herlitz J, Holmberg S, Malek I, Nyberg G, Ryden L, Swedberg K, Vedin A, Waagstein F, Waldenstrom A, Waldenstrom J, Wedel H, Wilhelmsen L, Wilhelmsson C (1981). Effect on mortality of metoprolol in acute myocardial infarction. *Lancet* 2:823–7.

Hornberger JC, Brown BW, Halpern J (1995). Designing a cost-effective clinical trial. *Stat Med* 14:2249–59.

Hornberger JC, Wrone E (1997). When to base clinical policies on observational versus randomized trial data. *Ann Intern Med* 127:697–703.

Horwitz RI, Singer BH, Makuch RW, Viscoli CM (1996). Can treatment that is helpful on average be harmful to some patients? A study of the conflicting information needs of clinical inquiry and drug regulation. *J Clin Epidemiol* 49:395–400.

Hosmer DW, Lemeshow S (1989). *Applied logistic regression*. New York: John Wiley & Sons.

Ioannidis JP, Cappelleri JC, Lau J (1998). Issues in companies between meta-analyses and large trials. *JAMA* 279:1089–93.

Ioannidis JP, Cappelleri JC, Skolnik PR, et al. (1996). A meta-analysis of the relative efficacy and toxicity of P. carinii prophylactic regimens. *Arch Intern Med* 156:177–88.

Ioannidis JP, Cappelleri JC, Sacks HS, Lau J (1997a). The relationship of study design, results, and reporting in randomized trials of HIV infections. *Controlled Clin Trials* 18:431–44.

Ioannidis JP, Bassett R, Hughes MD, Volberding P, Sacks HS, Lau J (1997b). Predictors and impact of patients lost to follow-up in a randomized trial of early versus deferred antiretroviral treatment. *J Acq Immune Defic Syndr Human Retrovirol* 16:22–30.

Ioannidis JP, Lau J (1997). The impact of high risk patients on the results of clinical trials. *J Clin Epidemiol* 50:1089–98.

Ioannidis JP (1998). Effect of the statistical significance of results on the time to completion and publication of randomized efficacy trials: a survival analysis. *JAMA* 279:281–6.

Ioannidis JP, Lau J (1998). Can quality of clinical trials and meta-analyses be quantified? [commentary]. *Lancet* 352:590–1.

ISIS-4 (Fourth International Study of Infarct Survival Collaborative Group (1995). ISIS-4: A randomized factorial trial assessing early oral captopril, oral mononitrate, and intravenous magnesium sulphate in 58, 050 patients in suspected acute myocardial infarction. *Lancet* 345:669–85.

Jadad AR· (1993). *Meta-analysis of randomised clinical trials in pain relief* [thesis]. Oxford University.

Jeng GT, Scott JR, Burmeister LF (1995). A comparison of meta-analytic results using literature vs. individual patient data. Paternal cell immunization for recurrent miscarriage. *JAMA* 274:830–6.

Kadane JB (1996). *Bayesian methods and ethics in a clinical trial design*. New York: John Wiley & Sons.

Kelsey JL, Whitemore AS, Evans AS, Thompson WD, eds (1996). *Methods in observational epidemiology*, 2nd edition. New York: Oxford University Press.

Kessler DA (1993). Introducing MEDWatch: a new approach to reporting medication and device adverse effects and product problems. *JAMA* 269: 2765–8.

Koch-Weser J, Sellers EM, Jacest R (1977). The ambiguity of adverse drug reactions. *Eur J Clin Pharmacol* 11:75–8.

Lakatos E (1986). Sample size determination in clinical trials with time-dependent rates of losses and noncompliance. *Controlled Clin Trials* 7:189–99.

Lau J, Ioannidis JPA, Schmid CH (1997). Quantitative synthesis in systematic reviews. *Ann Intern Med* 127:820–6.

Lau J, Ioannidis JP, Schmid CH (1998). Summing up evidence: one answer is not always enough. *Lancet* 351:123–7.

LeLorier J, Gregoire G, Benhaddad A, Lapierre J, Derderian F (1997). Discrepancies between meta-analyses and subsequent large randomized, controlled trials. *N Engl J Med* 337:536–42.

Mantel N, Haenszel W (1959). Statistical aspects of the analysis of data from retrospective studies of disease. *J Natl Cancer Inst* 22:719–48.

McIntosh M (1996). The population risk as an explanatory variable in research synthesis of clinical trials. *Stat Med* 15:1713–28.

McQuay HJ, Moore RA (1997). Using numerical results from systematic reviews in clinical practice. *Ann Intern Med* 126:712–20.

Meinert CL (1989). Meta-analysis: science or religion? *Controlled Clin Trials* 10:257S–263S.

Miller RG, Jr (1981). *Simultaneous statistical inference*. New York: Springer-Verlag.

Moher D, Jadad AR, Nichol G, Penman M, Tugwell P, Walsh S (1995). Assessing the quality of randomized controlled trials: an annotated bibliography of scales and checklists. *Controlled Clin Trials* 16:62–73.

Moher D, Olkin I (1995). Meta-analysis of randomized controlled trials: a concern for standards. *JAMA* 274:1962–4.

Morgenstern H (1982). Uses of ecologic analysis in epidemiologic research. *Am J Public Health* 72:1336–44.

Moses LE, Shapiro D, Littenberg B (1993). Combining independent studies of a diagnostic test into a summary ROC curve: data-analytic approaches and some additional considerations. *Stat Med* 12:1293–1316.

Mulrow CD (1987). The medical review articles: state of the science. *Ann Intern Med* 106:485–8.

Mulrow CD, Linn WD, Gaul MK, Pugh JA (1989). Assessing quality of a diagnostic test evaluation. *J Gen Intern Med* 4:288–95.

O'Brien PC, Fleming TR (1979). A multiple testing procedure for clinical trials. *Biometrics* 35:549–56.

Olkin I (1995). Statistical and theoretical considerations in meta-analysis. *J Clin Epidemiol* 48(1):133–46.

Oxman AD, Guyatt GH (1992). A consumer's guide to subgroup analyses. *Ann Intern Med* 116:78–84.

Petiti DB (1994). Of babies and bathwater. *Am J Epidemiol* 140:779–82.

Peto R (1996). Clinical trial reporting. *Lancet* 348:894–5.

Peto R, Pike MC, Armitage P, Breslow NE, Cox DR, Howard SV, Mantel N, McPherson K, Peto J, Smith PG (1976). Design and analysis of randomized clinical trials requiring prolonged observation on each patient. I. Introduction and design. *Br J Cancer* 34:585–607.

Pocock SJ (1983). *Clinical trials: a practical approach*. Chichester: John Wiley & Sons.

Rosendorf LL, Dafni U, Amato DA, Lunghofer B, Bartlett JG, Leedom JM, Wara DW, Armstrong JA, Godfrey E, Sukkestad E, Counts GW. (1993). Performance evaluation in multicenter clinical trials: development of a model by the AIDS Clinical Trials Group. *Controlled Clin Trials* 14:523–37.

Rubin DB, Schenker N (1991). Multiple imputation in health-care databases: an overview and some applications. *Stat Med* 10:585–98.

Sackett DL, Haynes RB (1995). On the need for evidence-based medicine. *Evidence-Based Med* 1:5–6.

Sacks H, Chalmers TC, Smith H (1982). Randomized versus historical controls for clinical trials. *Am J Med* 72:233–40.

Sacks HS, Berrier J, Reitman D, Ancona-Berk A, Chalmers TC (1987). Meta-analyses of randomized controlled trials. *N Engl J Med* 316:450–5.

Scherer RW, Dickersin K, Langenberg P (1994). Full publication of results initially presented as abstracts. A meta-analysis. *JAMA* 272:158–62.

Schmid CH, Lau J, McIntosh M, Cappelleri JC (1998). An empirical study of the effect of the control rate as a predictor of treatment efficacy in meta-analysis of clinical trials. *Stat Med* 17:1923–42.

Schulz KF, Chalmers I, Hayes RT, Altman DG (1995). Empirical evidence of bias. Dimensions of methodological quality associated with estimates of treatment effects in controlled clinical trials. *JAMA* 273:408–12.

Senn S (1994). Importance of trends in the interpretation of an overall odds ratio in the meta-analysis of clinical trials. *Stat Med* 13:293–6.

Shapiro DE (1995). Issues in combining independent estimates of the sensitivity and specificity of a diagnostic test. *Acad Radiol* 2:S37–S47.

Shapiro S (1994). Meta-analysis/shmeta-analysis. *Am J Epidemiol* 140:771–8.

Sharp SJ, Thompson SG, Altman DG (1996). The relation between treatment benefit and underlying risk in meta-analysis. *BMJ* 313:735–8.

Simes RJ (1986). Publication bias: the case for an international registry of clinical trials. *J Clin Oncol* 4:1529–41.

Sinclair JC, Bracken MB (1994). Clinically useful measures of effect in binary analyses of randomized trials. *J Clin Epidemiol* 47:712–20.

Smith GD, Song F, Sheldon RA (1993). Cholesterol lowering and mortality: the importance of considering initial level of risk. *BMJ* 306:1367–73.

Smith TC, Spiegelhalter DJ, Thomas A (1995). Bayesian approaches to random-effects meta-analysis: a comparative study. *Stat Med* 14:2685–99.

Stelfox HT, Chua G, O'Rourke K, Detsky AS (1998). Conflict of interest in the debate over calcium channel antagonists. *N Engl J Med* 338:101–16.

Stern JM, Simes R (1997). Publication bias: evidence of delayed publication in a cohort study of clinical research projects. *BMJ* 315:640–5.

Stewart LA, Clarke MJ (1995). Practical methodology of meta-analyses (overviews) using updated individual patient data. Cochrane Working Group. *Stat Med* 14:2057–79.

Stewart LA, Parmar MKB (1993). Meta-analysis of the literature or of individual patient data: is there a difference? *Lancet* 341:418–22.

Swets J (1988). Measuring the accuracy of diagnostic systems. *Science* 240:1285–93.

Sylvester RJ, Pinedo HM, DePauw M, Staquet MJ, Buyse ME, Renard J, Bonadonna G (1981). Quality of institutional participation in multicenter clinical trials. *N Engl J Med* 305:852–5.

Thompson SG (1993). Controversies in meta-analysis: the case of the trials of serum cholesterol reduction. *Stat Meth Med Res* 2:173–92.

Tukey JW (1977). Some thought on clinical trials, especially problems of multiplicity. *Science* 198:679–84.

Tweedie RL, Mengersen KL (1995). Meta-analytic approaches to dose–response relationship, with application in studies of lung cancer and exposure to environmental tobacco smoke. *Stat Med* 14:545–69.

Venning GR (1983). Identification of adverse reactions to new drugs. II–how were 18 important adverse reactions recognized and with what delays? *BMJ* 286:289–92.

Vickers A, Goyal N, Harland R, Rees R (1998). Do certain countries produce only positive results? A systematic review of controlled trials. *Controlled Clin Trials* 19:159–66.

Villar J, Carroli G, Belizan JM (1995). Predictive ability of meta-analyses of randomised controlled trials. *Lancet* 345:772–6.

Wilcosky TC, Phillips JA, Gillings DB (1986). Simple ranking procedures for evaluating members of multicenter collaborative groups. *Controlled Clin Trials* 7:276–81.

Woods KL (1995). Mega-trials and management of acute myocardial infarction. *Lancet* 346:611–14.

Yusuf S, Collins R, Peto R (1984). Why do we need some large, simple, randomized trials? *Stat Med* 3:409–22.

Part II

Health Policy and Economics

5 Linking Modeling with Health Policy Formation and Implementation

David B. Matchar, MD, and Greg P. Samsa, PhD

Introduction

Every day is filled with responses to changing circumstances. Some of the responses follow an identifiable moment of personal decision making. What makes these moments particularly memorable is that they engender some conflict, conflict emerging from the complexity of multiple options, uncertainty about the likelihood of possible outcomes, and the distressing effect of attempting to weigh inherently dissimilar outcomes. As difficult as these personal decisions may be, at least they only involve the knowledge and judgment of a small number of participants.

Some decisional acts, usually by virtue of being common, controversial, or expensive, rise to the level of policy relevance. In this arena the conflicts become more complex, especially because the number of participants rises and the conflicts are not only personal but also interpersonal. In our pluralistic society, all potentially interested parties are apt to register their opinion.

Traditionally, medical decision making has been highly personal, consisting of physicians using their expert and largely experience-based knowledge (Polyani 1958) to tailor diagnosis and therapy to the specific needs of individual patients. However, the idea that the art of medicine is a purely private activity is hardly realistic today. A host of other players ranging from hospitals to insurance companies to government now actively participate in medical encounters. Contemporary medicine has become a vast industry (Starr 1982), and medical decision making has emerged as an issue of public policy.

The policy implications of medical decision making have become even more evident with the rise of managed care. In managed care a variety of controls and incentives change the dynamic of traditional decision making. In traditional practice, the structure of autonomous physicians receiving a fee for service encourages the default position of "when in doubt, do it." The managed care environment, through mechanisms of "decision supervision" and displacement of financial risk to the practitioner, promotes the default position of "when in doubt, don't do it." This massively increases the tension in clinical decision making. As managed care expands and matures, both physicians and administrators recognize that the process of "cutting closer to the bone" cannot be haphazard but requires guidance.

Chapter Goals

As discussed earlier, many more health-related decisions are coming under public scrutiny and thus are becoming health policy decisions. Because health policy decisions should be made systematically, the methodology of policy modeling particularly suggests itself. The questions we seek to address in this chapter are: exactly how does and how should policy modeling link to health policy formation and implementation? To do this, we will first discuss how policy models can help make better health policy decisions. Then we will describe a taxonomy of policy models. Next, we will review examples of the application of policy modeling to policy issues, focusing particularly on the question of anticoagulation services for stroke prevention in patients with atrial fibrillation. The chapter concludes with a discussion of what we believe represents the ideal relationship between policy modeling and policy formation and implementation.

What Is Health Policy?

Before considering the role of decision analysis in the formation and implementation of health policy, it is important to clarify the term *health policy*. To provide as a working definition, we denote two relatively distinct areas: clinical health policy and social health policy. Clinical health policy focuses on the decisions that relate *to the clinical enterprise*, including the decisions themselves (e.g., Should a physician perform noninvasive testing of the carotid arteries? Should women between the ages of 40 and 49 have a mammogram?), as well as the structures that support those decisions (e.g., When should electronic medical records be used? Should anticoagulation management be provided through anticoagulation services?). By contrast, social health policy focuses on decisions that relate to the *context of the clinical enterprise*, including law, reimbursement, access to care, and so forth. Here we discuss applications of modeling to clinical health policy.

As a rule, a clinical health policy is a statement intended to guide a class of health-related decisions. The term *health policy* is also used to relate to the process of forming a health policy and then implementing that policy. When a health policy analyst participates in this process, he or she is responsible for evaluating available options and, usually, for making recommendations to the policy maker. The policy maker then formulates the health policy statement and establishes a plan for translating intent into action.

Who Are Health Policy Makers?

A health policy maker, then, is anyone who either makes health-related decisions directly or influences the health-related decisions of others. These individuals have been classified as micro-, meso-, and macro-level decision makers (Singer 1997). Those making health care decisions directly involving individual patients are micro-level decision makers. Health care delivery organizations decide what services to provide and how to influence the actions of providers through financial incentives; these are meso-level decision makers. In the government, those who influence the health-related decisions of others include agencies that create regulations (e.g., the Food and Drug Administration), those that fund research (e.g., the National Institutes for Health), and those that are involved with reimbursement and mandated health care (e.g., the Health Care Financing Administration). In industry, policy makers decide what products to develop, which potential drugs and devices deserve further evaluation, which patient and provider groups to target, and how to price and market. These public and private units are the macro-level decision makers.

What Are the Objectives of Health Policy Makers?

What do policy makers want? Like any decision makers, policy makers typically want to do the right thing. They are somewhat uncertain about what to do and would like to examine the problem in a calm, rational environment. They also want to minimize the tension and discomfort they experience in the process (Phillips 1984). In the end, they want to feel satisfied that the action chosen represents the best choice under the circumstances. They would also like to feel that their decisions are defensible under outside scrutiny.

Like any decision makers, health policy makers also face the challenge of balancing numerous considerations. Although optimal patient outcomes are important and desirable, other factors such as budgets, organizational dynamics, and politics are also relevant. Of course, each decision maker is swayed by different types of information, depending on his or her perspective. For example, costs may loom large for macro-level decision makers responsible for husbanding public or corporate resources but may be irrelevant to a micro-level decision maker with comprehensive coverage. Decision makers require the flexibility to make trade-offs between competing considerations. Thus, as a rule, they prefer information to be presented in a nonprescriptive fashion that allows them to maintain their decision-making prerogatives (Ascher 1978).

What Are Health Policy Models?

Although the reader of this book should by now be quite familiar with health policy models, as a working definition the term *health policy models* includes decision modeling, simulation modeling, cost-effectiveness analysis, and related techniques that operate by defining the critical components of the medical decision under consideration, using evidence-based data (e.g., the efficacy of a surgical procedure) as inputs, and producing quantitative information (e.g., survival, quality-adjusted survival, incremental cost-effectiveness ratios) as outputs.

In describing the application of modeling to health care decisions, Weinstein describes health policy models as "intended to guide the choices of persons and organizations that, by virtue of regulatory authority, direct control of resources or the power to influence the actions of others, affect the aggregate allocations of resources to a health care problem" (Weinstein 1989). Combining these definitions, then, health policy models are quantitative tools that are intended to influence the agents of health policy – namely, policy makers.

How Can Policy Models Help Make Better Health Policy Decisions?

In this context, policy modeling has been promoted as a useful aid for this complex task of making and implementing health policy (Ascher, 1978). Policy models can be useful in two ways: prescriptively and nonprescriptively. First, to the extent that one subscribes to the notion that the real world does (or should) conform to the axioms of utility theory, prescriptive models can lead policy makers directly to an optimal decision (i.e., optimal in the sense of maximizing expected utility). Since we recognize that most decision makers consider factors other than maximizing expected utility, a second reason that policy modeling can be useful – and a reason that does not require adherence to the prescriptive school of decision analysis – is that incorporating models into the process of policy making can provide a framework supporting (but not necessarily prescribing) policy. In particular, apart from any quantitative insights that the model may provide, simply developing a health policy model requires making explicit statements about which components of the clinical issue are most important, obtaining precisely specified estimates of the parameters of the relevant decision model, and so forth, all of which are beneficial. Although decision making will always contain a component of art in addition to science, these steps help meet the decision maker's need for a fair, rational, repeatable, scientific process which can be described and (if necessary) defended.

Taxonomy of Policy Models

Although the technical details of various modeling approaches are covered elsewhere in this book, it is nevertheless useful to consider the range of models that have been used in service to policy goals. Weinstein has provided a taxonomy of policy models based on their scope, methodology, and intent (Weinstein 1989). According to this taxonomy, policy models may be narrow in scope, focusing on a specific patient type and intervention, or broad, including an entire population defined by a region or provider organization. Models may consider a brief time horizon or long-term outcomes, including multiple competing risks and downline interventions. Descriptive models are designed primarily to make projections of a variety of outcomes relevant to a particular disease and its management. Prescriptive models focus more directly on the question of which of several strategies are preferred.

Another way to classify health policy models is by considering how they fit into the policy process: the sequence of analysis, policy formation, and policy implementation. Accordingly, and in order of increasing integration into the policy process, models may be classified as free-standing, facilitative, and embedded. A *free-standing* model, one of the most noteworthy examples of which is the Coronary Heart Disease

Policy Model (Goldman et al. 1989, 1991, Tosteson et al. 1990, 1997, Weinstein et al. 1987), focuses primarily on the initial analytic step. Models in this class tend to be developed as an activity *separate* from the policy-making activity; the application of the model to policy formation and implementation occurs when (and if) a receptive policy maker chooses to embrace the model's insights and/or results.

The second class of policy model consists of models specifically developed to facilitate the deliberations of policy makers. The efforts of the Office of Management and Research (OMAR) to develop models to assist in technology assessments (Jacoby and Pauker 1986) illustrate this class, as do models developed to support the work of guideline development panels and other consensus-based groups. *Facilitative* models consider issues of policy analysis and policy formation but not necessarily policy implementation. Also, facilitative models tend to be *one-time* applications – for example, to be used for the duration of an expert panel or perhaps for a single step of a panel's deliberations.

The third class of policy models is the *embedded* model, which is directly linked to *ongoing* efforts at practice improvement. Examples include the modeling efforts of groups connected to practice organizations, such as the Henry Ford Medical Center and Kaiser. Another example is the Patient Outcome Research Team for the Secondary and Tertiary Prevention of Stroke (Stroke PORT), in which a comprehensive effort to evaluate and improve stroke prevention practices has been organized around a policy model (Matchar 1994, Matchar et al. 1997). In the stroke PORT application, the policy model not only provided a mechanism for developing specific policy recommendations but also served as a central organizing focus for the entire research effort – for example, influencing the choice of research questions, data sets, data elements, and analyses.

One way to think about the distinctions between free-standing, facilitative, and embedded models is to consider the relationship between the model and its "customer" (i.e., the health policy maker). The free-standing model is developed with no explicit customer in mind; presumably these models are placed in the public domain (e.g., the medical literature) in the hope that their conclusions will be so convincing that implementation will follow as a matter of course. In contrast to the free-standing model, the facilitative model has a customer (e.g., a guideline development panel), who has commissioned the model for a one-time application. Broader considerations – in particular, those involving implementation – are left outside the purview of the model. Finally, an embedded model has a customer, and this customer has additionally chosen to use the model as a critical element or central organizing focus for decision making. The embedded model need not be prescriptive – that is, it need not be the only input into the decisions – but it does play a critical role.

Applications to Anticoagulation for Stroke Prevention among Patients with Atrial Fibrillation

To clarify the preceding taxonomy of health policy models, it is useful to consider specific examples. We will consider models that relate to a specific content area, namely, anticoagulation for stroke prevention in atrial fibrillation (AF).

An illustration of the free-standing class of models is the model developed by Caro and colleagues (Caro et al. 1993). The model was designed to answer a specific clinical question regarding the value of warfarin in a real-world setting. The conclusion of this effort was that anticoagulation for AF is a highly effective therapy for reducing the risk of stroke if the treatment is provided safely. While its applicability to clinical policy is apparent, the model and its results were not developed in conjunction with a specific clinical policy activity (e.g., Caro's analysis implies that warfarin is cost-effective, but it does not suggest how warfarin therapy can be optimally organized).

One example of the facilitative class of model is exemplified by a precursor to the Stroke Prevention Policy Model (SPPM) developed as part of the Patient Outcome Research Team for the Secondary and Tertiary Prevention of Stroke (Stroke PORT) (Matchar 1994, Matchar et al. 1997). This simplified model of the epidemiology of stroke was used to assist the investigators and the project advisory board in selecting a target for the intervention phase of the Stroke PORT. Several options were possible, including efforts to improve the use of antiplatelet agents in symptomatic patients, optimize the safety of carotid endarterectomy, and increase the quality and appropriateness of warfarin use for patients with AF. Modeling suggested that increasing the appropriate use of warfarin in patients with AF was the stroke prevention intervention likely to have the greatest impact on public health. This analysis led to the development of an implementation project, the Managing Anticoagulation Service Trial (MAST), a randomized practice improvement trial to test the effectiveness and cost-effectiveness of anticoagulation services in managed care organizations (Samsa et al. 1998).

Finally, in its full application, the SPPM has also come to represent the embedded class of policy models. As discussed earlier, the SPPM was used as the central organizing focus for the stroke PORT. In addition, for potential MAST sites, it became clear that the decision to embrace anticoagulation services depends on the impact of these services on the health of the local population and the financial incentives or disincentives for a physician to allow his or her patient to be enrolled. To allow this sort of "tailored" evaluation, the SPPM has been modified to incorporate local data and to provide outputs based on the financial perspective of the major players in the local health care community. Since the cost-effectiveness of the anticoagulation service, estimated using the SPPM, is a critical component in the sites' decision on whether or not to continue the anticoagulation service at the conclusion of the MAST, the SPPM thus serves as an embedded model, helping to improve the practice of stroke prevention within the participating managed care organizations.

Discussion

In this chapter, we have described the rationale for health policy modeling, presented a new taxonomy of health policy models based on how they fit within the policy process, and provided examples of the application of various types of models to the clinical question of whether anticoagulation for patients with AF should be given within the context of an anticoagulation service. We have paid particular attention to embedded models – that is, models that are designed with implementation and practice improvement in mind – since this topic is both little studied and crucial for policy modeling to have its maximum possible impact.

How might policy modeling best contribute to efforts at implementation and practice improvement? One way to answer this question is within the framework of a conceptual model for practice improvement (Samsa et al. 1998). In particular, a practice improvement effort might be considered to have the following steps: (1) identify the potential target of opportunity; (2) synthesize information about optimal practice; (3) synthesize information about current practice; (4) identify reasons for discrepancies between current and optimal practice; (5) develop a strategy for practice improvement; (6) assess the effectiveness and cost-effectiveness of the practice improvement strategy; and (7) determine whether the practice improvement strategy should be implemented.

Policy models can be particularly useful in steps 1, 2, and 7. In the topic selection phase (steps 1 through 3), policy models can help to determine which targets are especially worthy of a concerted intervention. For example, a decision model might first be used to identify the optimal clinical management strategy. Combining this knowledge with external data about current practice patterns would thus provide an upper bound on the potential for improvement (e.g., in cost, survival, and quality-adjusted survival) which could be obtained by replacing the current management strategy with its optimal counterpart. Also, presenting information about discrepancies between current and optimal practice can help local providers develop support for practice improvement efforts, which are unlikely to be successful unless a general consensus exists regarding the need for practice patterns to change. In any event, the policy models used at this stage need not necessarily be extraordinarily complex; they need only be sufficient in form and function to satisfy the decisional needs of the policy maker(s) in question (Phillips 1984).

Step 7 illustrates one of the differences between facilitative and embedded models. In contrast to a general-purpose cost-effectiveness or decision analysis model (e.g., as would be sufficient for a typical guideline development panel), the policy model in question must be structured to accommodate tailoring by local policy maker(s). For example, a hospital must be able to replace national norms for length of stay with its particular experience, an insurer must be able to limit the analysis to the subset of the components of cost for which it is financially responsible, and so forth. The need for local tailoring – of outputs as well as inputs – suggests that dedicated, user-friendly software may have great potential in facilitating the use of these models by decision makers who do not necessarily have formal training in the decision sciences. Such software is currently being developed by various corporations (as well as others), and we anticipate that the interest in software development will continue.

Another way to approach the question of how clinical policy modeling can be made useful in health policy is to examine not just the recent experience with health policy modeling but also the broader topic of modeling for public policy as a whole. Ascher (1978), in a description of an extensive study of predictive models used in a variety of policy settings (including the National Resource Planning Board in the 1930s and 1940s, the Planning-Programming-Budgeting System of the 1960s, ongoing Census Bureau forecasts, and the "limits to growth" model of the 1970s), sought to understand what made such efforts effective. He made the following generalizations:

- Acceptability of the effort depends on the prominence of the sponsor, especially if the sponsor is perceived to be impartial.
- Firm projections based on simple models, all things being equal, are preferred.
- Explicit policy recommendations based on "mechanized" optimization calculations tend not to be well received by policy makers, as they usurp their role (i.e., being relevant to policy making is good; automating policy making is bad).
- Organizations with high degrees of goal consensus (i.e., typically corporate but not governmental) tend to be more receptive to using models in guiding policy.

These generalizations are supported by other researchers (Caplan 1977, Knorr, 1977, Weiss 1977) and are likely to be relevant to the use of modeling in health care policy making.

A final insight from the literature on public policy is that the putative impact of a model is strongly dependent on the method used to measure that impact. In particular, if we believe that models must be used prescriptively (i.e., as the single criterion for decision making) rather than descriptively (i.e., to frame the question and as one criterion among many), then we are likely to be disappointed. Similarly, even though they are not as fully integrated into the practice improvement process as embedded models are, both facilitative and free-standing models can have strong influences on health policy, albeit in ways which can be difficult to quantify explicitly. For example, how can one fully assess the impact of a facilitative model which serves to influence the recommendations of a guideline panel, which in turn serves to influence practice? How can one fully assess the impact of a free-standing model that leads to a scholarly article suggesting that a 3-day course of antibiotics for treating sinusitis is essentially as effective as a 10-day course? The impact of such a free-standing model is likely to be a change in the general medical culture – a recognition that "less is more" when treating sinusitis – even though the original citation many not be remembered or even read by many of the providers now using the 3-day course.

Applying this reasoning, the most important use made of the work of analysts is often indirect – in other words, the impact is through enlightenment rather than direct linkage (Weiss 1977). Thus, Weiss suggests that academic researchers should not necessarily follow the conventional wisdom, which would direct them to "identify the customer and accept the fundamental goals, priorities, and political constraints of the key decision-making group." Nor must policy makers necessarily accept the technocratic worldview of academic decision analysts, complete with expected utility optimization and other arcane constructs, in order to be influenced. An *enlightenment model* suggests that academic researchers may be most useful if they present challenging ideas that may lead to reframing of policy discussions and, in subtle ways, to the ultimate policy result.

Whether as problems solvers or as enlighteners, this is a particularly propitious time for policy analysts. First, the reaction (among corporations, government, and the general public) to the dramatic rise in the cost of medical care has made common knowledge of the need to consider not just efficacy but also cost. Second, financial survival is requiring providers, insurers, and others to attach much more importance to issues such as cost-effectiveness than had been the case in the past. The interplay between these forces and other forces supporting the rationalization of medical is leading to wholesale changes in medical practice – embracing clinical guidelines, disease management systems, and computerized decision support systems (among others). Suddenly, it seems, clinicians and other decision makers are thinking about system-level changes that encompass even what were previously minor details of care, and often doing so using the conceptual and technical approaches of the policy analyst.

We have not yet entered the golden age of model-enlightened clinical policy making. Most organized efforts to influence clinical practice continue to focus almost solely on cost containment. In part this reflects the developmental stage of organized health care. If we may be permitted to anthropomorphize, it is difficult for managed care organizations to contemplate self-actualization (enlightened clinical policy making) when survival is threatened. There are other reasons why the prospects for modeling in health policy are not entirely glowing (Matchar 1994). One issue is that there are technical barriers to performing analyses of complex clinical problems. Another issue is that the members of the community of quantitative health scientists are not of one mind regarding the validity of modeling. Some have argued that traditional analytic approaches do not mesh smoothly with the modeling enterprise (Feinstein 1977). Others question the clinical plausibility justifying many of the simplifying assumptions required to make modeling tractable (Schwartz 1979).

Although we are far from an ideal application of models to clinical policy, we are unmistakably on the path. For the discipline of policy analysis to make the most of this opportunity, it is essential for the methods and results of policy modeling not only to be methodologically sound (e.g., in the academic sense) but also to serve the needs of decision makers as much as possible. This will require ongoing consideration of how decisions are actually made – for example, to ensure that the results of policy modeling are presented in the most useful format possible for decision makers – and the field of medical decision making is currently benefiting from extensive cross-disciplinary fertilization in coming to grips with this question. This will also require consideration of how decisions are actually implemented – a question which we feel is also critically important but that is considerably less well studied.

In terms of the all-important issue of framing the question, one can argue that even though the results may be difficult to quantify, the most important battle has already been won since all of the participants in the process of making clinical health policy have already accepted the paradigm of evidence-based medicine – one which (we would argue) supports and even necessitates the role of health policy modeling (Matchar et al. 1997). As health policy researchers, then, our challenge is no longer to justify our efforts in general, but rather to continue to refine our methods, paying particular attention that the links between policy modeling and the policy maker, both direct and indirect, are as strong as possible. This will help policy modeling have its maximum impact on its ultimate goal, namely, to improve the quality of medical practice.

References

Ascher, W. *Forecasting: An Appraisal for Policy-makers and Planners*. Baltimore: Johns Hopkins University Press, 1978.

Caplan, N. A Minimal Set of Conditions Necessary for the Utilization of Social Science Knowledge in Policy Formulation at the National Level, in *Using Social Research in Public Policy-Making*, ed. CH Weiss. Lexington, Mass: Lexington-Health, 1977, pp 183–97.

Caro JJ, Groome PA, Flegel KM. Atrial fibrillation and anticoagulation: from randomised trials to practice. *Lancet* 1993;341:1381–4.

Feinstein AR. Clinical biostatistics. XXXIX. The haze of Bayes, the aerial palaces of decision analysis, and the computerized Ouija board. *Clin Pharmacol Ther* 1977;21:482–96.

Goldman L, Weinstein MC, Goldman, PA, Williams LW. Cost-effectiveness of HMG-CoA reductase inhibition for primary and secondary prevention of coronary heart disease. *Journal of the American Medical Association* 1991;265:1145–51.

Goldman L, Weinstein MC, Williams LW. Relative impact of targeted versus population-wide cholesterol interventions on the incidence of coronary heart disease. *Circulation* 1989;80:254–60.

Jacoby I, Pauker SG. Technology assessment in health care: group process and decision theory. *Isr J Med Sci* 1986;22:183–90.

Knorr, K. Policy-Makers' Use of Social Science Knowledge: Symbolic or Instrumental? in *Using Social Research in Public Policy-Making*, ed. CH Weiss. Lexington, Mass: Lexington-Health, 1977, p. 180.

Matchar DB. Application of Decision Analysis to Guideline Development, in *Clinical Practice Guideline Development: Methodology Perspectives*, ed. KA McCormick, SR Moore, R Siegel. AHCPR pub. No. 95-009. Rockville, MD: Agency for Health Care Policy and Research; 1994, pp 35–40.

Matchar DB, Samsa GP, Matthews JR, Ancukiewicz M, Parmigiani G, Hasselblad V, Wolf PA, D'Agostino RB, Lipscomb J. The stroke prevention policy model: linking evidence and clinical decisions. *Ann Intern Med* 1997;127:704–11.

Phillips JD. A theory of requisite decision models. *Acta Psychol (Amst)* 1984;56:29–49.

Polyani M. *Personal Knowledge: Towards a Post-Critical Philosophy*. Chicago: Univ of Chicago Press, 1958.

Samsa GP, Matchar DB, Cohen SJ, Lipscomb J, Abrahamse P, McCormick M. A seven-step model for practice-improvement research: description and application to the Managing Anticoagulation Services Trial (MAST). *New Med* 1998;2:39–146.

Schwartz WB. Decision analysis: a look at the chief complaint. *N Engl J Med* 1979;300:556–9.

Singer PA. Resource allocation: beyond evidence-based medicine and cost-effectiveness analysis. *ACP J Club* 1997;127(3):A16–180.

Starr P. *The Social Transformation of American Medicine*. New York: Basic Books, 1982.

Tosteson ANA, Weinstein MC, Hunink MGM, Mittleman MA, Williams LW, Goldman PA, Goldman L. Cost-effectiveness of population wide educational approaches to reduce serum cholesterol levels. *Circulation* 1997;95:24–30.

Tosteson ANA, Weinstein MC, Williams LW, Goldman L. Long-term impact of smoking cessation on the incidence of coronary heart disease. *Am J Public Health* 1990;80:1481–6.

Weinstein MC. Methodologic issues in policy modeling for cardiovascular disease. *JACC* 1989;14:38A–43A.

Weinstein MC, Coxson PG, Williams LW, Pass TM, Stason WB, Goldman L. Forecasting coronary heart disease incidence, mortality, and cost. *Am J Public Health* 1987;77:1417–1426.

Weiss CH. Research for policy's sake: the enlightenment function of social research. *Policy Analysis* 3:1977:531–45.

6   Cost-Effectiveness Analysis

Louise B. Russell, PhD

Cost-effectiveness analysis (CEA) defines a framework for evaluating the health effects and costs of health interventions. Many of the techniques discussed in other chapters of this book, such as decision analysis and quality-adjusted life years, can be components of a CEA. In addition, CEA adds two new ingredients: estimation of costs, which requires estimating and valuing the resources used for interventions, and comparison of costs with health effects. To facilitate this comparison, results are typically presented in the form of cost-effectiveness ratios. For example, an analysis of screening for mild thyroid failure found that screening patients every 5 years, starting at age 35, cost $9,200 per quality-adjusted life year for women and $22,600 for men compared with not screening (1994 dollars; Danese et al., 1996).

CEA is conventionally distinguished from cost–benefit analysis by its measure(s) of health effects. Cost–benefit analysis values health effects in monetary terms, which makes them directly comparable to costs and also permits comparison of health and nonhealth investments. By contrast, CEA measures health effects in terms specific to health, such as cases of disease or life years. In this chapter I use the term "cost-effectiveness analysis" inclusively, to mean not only analyses that use cases, lives, or life years as the measure of health outcome, but also cost-consequence analyses, which present costs and effects but not ratios, and cost-utility analyses, which use health measures that incorporate judgments about the quality or utility of different states of health.

The chapter begins by discussing what CEA contributes to medical decision making that other methods do not. It then reviews how CEAs are conducted. The first subject of this review is the framing of a CEA, those initial decisions that define the questions an analysis can answer and the main elements involved in its conduct. The chapter then briefly outlines the steps of an analysis: estimating and valuing outcomes; estimating and valuing resource use; discounting; and reporting and interpreting results. Throughout the chapter I refer to the work of the Panel on Cost-Effectiveness in Health and Medicine, which I cochaired. For brevity, I refer to it as the Panel. The Panel was convened by the U.S. Public Health Service in 1993, and was asked to develop recommendations to improve the quality of studies and encourage consistent practice across conditions and interventions. Its recommendations were published in 1996 (Gold et al., 1996; Russell et al., 1996; Siegel et al., 1996; Weinstein et al., 1996).

CEA in Medical Decision Making

Table 6.1 presents some typical cost-effectiveness ratios. In 1997 dollars, propranolol used to treat mild to moderate hypertension in people aged 35 to 64 cost $19,700 per year of life saved (Edelson et al., 1990), while lovastatin used to reduce elevated cholesterol, in men aged 35 to 44 with no history of heart disease or risk factors other than gender and high cholesterol, cost $1,084,000 per life year (Goldman et al., 1991).

Cost-effectiveness ratios tend to focus attention on money spent. The true cost of an intervention is not, however, the dollars spent on it, or even the resources they represent, but the health benefits that could have been achieved if the resources had been used another way. Economists call the benefits foregone when one course of action is chosen over another the "opportunity cost" of the decision. More precisely, the opportunity cost of an intervention is the benefits of the best alternative use of the resources. If the benefits lost are greater than the benefits gained, the decision is not optimal.

The information provided by CEAs can be presented in another way that focuses more directly on the opportunity costs of alternatives. Table 6.1 also shows the life years that could be achieved with an expenditure of $1 million on each of the same interventions. For example, $1 million spent on propranolol yields 51 life years, while the same amount spent on lovastatin for low-risk men aged 35–44 yields a bit less than 1 life year. This method of presentation shows more clearly than cost-effectiveness ratios how CEA provides information about trade-offs in medical choices. If $1 million is spent on lovastatin for low-risk men, the true cost is not $1 million but the health benefits foregone because some other service was not funded.

Table 6.1. *Cost-Effectiveness Ratios and Life Years per $1 Million, 1997 Dollars, Selected Interventions*

Intervention	Cost/year	Life years/$1M
Propranolol, U.S. pop.	$19,700	51
Pap smear every 3 years	27,500	36
Bypass surgery, left main disease, middle-aged men	10,800	93
Lovastatin, low-risk men aged 35–44 with no heart disease	1,084,000	1
Influenza vaccine for persons aged 65+	130	7,750
CCU for low-risk patients	435,372	2
Thyroid screening every 5 years for women	10,300	98
Total hip arthroplasty for osteoarthritis of hip, white men aged 85+	6,064	165
Tetanus booster every 10 years	275,247	4

Note: The comparator for bypass surgery is medical management, for CCU is intermediate-care unit. For all others, the comparator is care for condition when it develops.

Note: Updated to 1997 dollars using the medical care component of the consumer price index.

Sources: In order from top: Edelson et al., 1990; Eddy, 1990; Weinstein and Stason, 1982; Goldman et al., 1991; Office of Technology Assessment, 1981; Fineberg et al., 1984; Danese et al., 1996; Chang et al., 1996; Balestra and Littenberg, 1993.

The interventions compared in Table 6.1 are quite different from each other. Many medical decisions, however, and many CEAs involve choices not about different interventions but about the appropriate intensity of an intervention or the appropriate groups to receive it. Table 6.2 shows the number of life years produced when each of four interventions is applied to different risk groups. For example, monitoring chest pain patients in a coronary care unit (CCU) produces 10 life years when preadmission evaluation shows that the patient's probability of a myocardial infarction is 20% but only 2 life years when the probability is 5% (Fineberg et al., 1984). Table 6.3 compares different intensities of an intervention for the same patients. Compared with no screening, a Papanicolaou smear every 3 years yields 36 life years (Eddy, 1990). Increasing the frequency of screening to every 2 years adds one

Table 6.2. *Life Years per $1 Million When the Same Intervention Is Applied to Patients in Different Risk Groups, 1997 Dollars*

CCU for chest pain patients	
5% risk of MI	2 life years
20% risk of MI	10 life years
Bypass surgery, middle-aged men	
Left main disease	93 life years
One-vessel disease	12 life years
20 mg/day lovastatin, primary prevention, men, cholesterol 300+	
55–64, high risk	42 life years
35–44, low risk	2 life years
Thyroid screening every 5 years	
Women	98 life years
Men	40 life years

Note: Updated to 1997 dollars using the medical care component of the consumer price index.
Sources: In order from top: Fineberg et al., 1984; Weinstein and Stason, 1982; Goldman et al., 1991; Danese et al., 1996.

Table 6.3. *Life Years per $1 Million When an Intervention Is Applied at Different Intensities, 1997 Dollars*

Pap smear	
Every 3 years	36 life years
Every 2 years	1 life years
Every year	<0.5 life year
Lovastatin, secondary prevention, men 55–64 years of age, cholesterol 250+	
20 mg/day	398 life years
40 mg/day	37 life years
80 mg/day	9 life years
Tetanus booster	
At age 65	115 life years
Decennial versus at age 65	2 life years

Note: Updated to 1997 dollars using the medical care component of the Consumer Price Index.
Sources: Eddy, 1990; Goldman et al., 1991; Balestra and Littenberg, 1993.

more life year for each additional $1 million, compared with screening every 3 years, and annual screening adds less than half a year per $1 million spent compared with biennial screening. Similarly, each increase in the dose of lovastatin brings fewer years of life for each $1 million (Goldman et al., 1991), and decennial tetanus boosters bring fewer life years than a single booster at age 65 (Balestra and Littenberg, 1993). The possibility that the resources could be put to better use elsewhere grows as the intensity of these interventions increases.

Focusing on opportunity costs suggests questions like "How many life years will be lost if more money is allocated to this intervention rather than that one?" "In terms of better health, what are the most productive investments for new resources?" "The least productive?" The notion of opportunity costs provides a way to address these questions without losing sight of the goal of improving health. To serve that goal best, the interventions selected should have the smallest opportunity costs – the smallest foregone health benefits – which is just another way of saying that decision makers should choose interventions that produce the most health for the resources spent. CEA is built on this principle: it is designed to identify the interventions that will produce the most health for a given expenditure of resources.

The principle, and the notion of opportunity cost, focus attention on the world beyond the decision at hand. A decision made for a particular patient or group of patients has implications that go far beyond those patients. Benefits will be lost to others because this course was chosen, and the loss should be kept as small as possible. Costs are a proxy for these lost benefits, a reminder that choices have effects that go beyond those immediately involved. This is the crucial additional information that CEA contributes to medical decisions.

Thus the purpose of CEA is to help decision makers compare alternatives and decide which interventions, for whom, and at what intensity are the best use of medical resources. Comparability is essential, certainly within studies, and, for broader decisions, across studies as well, if CEA is to serve this purpose, hence the Panel's charge to promote consistent practice. The examples given in Tables 6.1 through 6.3 are comparable within the same study (e.g., different frequencies for cervical cancer screening) but are not entirely comparable across studies. The studies from which they were drawn were based on somewhat different decisions about which items to include. Thus the comparisons made in this section should be considered suggestive, not definitive.

Framing the Analysis

"Framing" refers to a series of decisions made at the outset of an analysis about the perspective(s) to be used in the analysis, the target population(s) for the intervention, the alternatives or "comparators" with which the intervention will be compared, and the time horizon of the study.

Perspective

The perspective of a study is the point of view it represents. It answers the question "Whose benefits and costs matter to this decision?" Typical perspectives, or points of view, are those of an individual, of society, of providers, or of payers like health maintenance organization, insurers, employers, or government programs. Clearly, the perspective needs to correspond to the kinds of decisions the analysis is intended to inform. Moreover, analyses based on different perspectives cannot be compared because, reflecting the interests associated with each perspective, they count different health effects and resources and value them differently. Thus comparisons across studies are valid only for studies that use the same perspective.

The Panel argues that the societal perspective is appropriate for analyses that are designed to inform decisions made in the public interest about the broad allocation of medical resources – for example, decisions by an expert advisory group about whether to recommend a new vaccine or decisions by the federal government about whether to propose a program to provide new health benefits (Gold et al., 1996, Chapter 1; Russell et al., 1996). In a CEA conducted from the societal perspective, the analyst counts all significant costs and health effects that accrue to anyone affected by the intervention. Health effects include harms as well as benefits, even those experienced by people who are not the intended recipients of the intervention. Resource costs include all resources used, whether or not money changes hands and regardless of who incurs the costs. No significant cost or health effect is excluded. Such comprehensive information is necessary to support decision makers who want to consider the impact of their decisions on all affected parties.

An analysis done from the societal perspective will, by definition, define the time horizon and population to include all significant health effects and uses of resources. It will use methods for measuring and valuing health effects and costs that reflect the value of these to society. Thus the choice of perspective implies many other choices for the analysis.

The primary purpose of a study may require the use of another perspective, perhaps that of an employer or a third-party payer. But most analyses also aim to influence the larger public debate about medical choices. For this debate, only the societal perspective, which considers the impact of an intervention on everyone, is appropriate. Thus the Panel recommends that studies include as a special case, called the "reference case," an analysis that is based on the societal perspective and that follows the other guidelines set out for the reference case.

Since each possible perspective has detailed implications for how a CEA should be conducted, it is not possible to consider all possible perspectives in the space of a single chapter. Nor, so far as I am aware, has anyone spelled out the implications of other perspectives in the detail that the Panel does for the societal perspective. The rest of this chapter will focus primarily on the societal perspective and on CEA done from that perspective (societal CEA).

Comparators

Another crucial choice that is made early in a study involves which alternatives to compare. Should a new intervention be compared with an old one or with no intervention? If an old one, which one(s)? What intensities of the intervention should be considered – what frequencies of screening, dosages of medication, or schedules of vaccination? As the examples in Tables 6.1 to 6.3 suggest, the choice can make an enormous difference in the cost-effectiveness of an intervention. Screening every 2 years for cervical cancer might seem very cost-effective compared with no screening but not when compared with the more realistic alternative of screening every 3 years.

The selection of comparators is crucial because the elements in a cost-effectiveness ratio are calculated as differences between two alternatives. The numerator of the ratio, net costs, is the difference in costs between the intervention and the comparator. The denominator, net health effects, is the difference in health effects between the two. Table 6.4 shows the calculations for a particular case using detail from a recently published analysis of vaccination against pneumococcal bacteremia in the elderly (Sisk et al., 1997). The intervention in this study was a single vaccination against pneumococcal bacteremia. The comparator was "no vaccination," that is, people were treated for pneumococcal bacteremia if and when they contracted it.

Table 6.4. *Vaccination Against Pneumococcal Bacteremia among People Aged 65 and Older: Costs and Effects of Vaccination, No Vaccination, and the Differences between Them, per Person Vaccinated, 1993*

	Vacc.	No vacc.	Diff.
Costs			
Vaccine and administration	$12.00	0	$12.00
Adverse effects of			
vaccination	0.01	0	0.01
Treatment of bacteremia	76.41	$96.69	−20.28
Total	88.42	96.69	−8.27
Effects			
Quality-adjusted days	2,273.26*	2272.05	1.21

*Net of adverse effects. Adverse effects were so small (−0.00000252) that they cannot be shown separately without adding several places to the numbers and have no effect on net quality-adjusted days at the level of accuracy shown in the table.

Source: Sisk et al., 1997. Detail provided by William Whang.

The vaccination strategy involves costs for the vaccine and its administration and for treatment of the side effects sometimes caused by the vaccine (Table 6.4). Costs are also incurred for treatment of bacteremia since not all bacteremia is of the kind prevented by the vaccine, nor is the vaccine 100% effective. The costs of treating bacteremia are less under the vaccination strategy, so much less that the net result is a saving of $8.27 per person vaccinated. At the same time, the vaccine extends lives and improves health: the net gain in health, allowing for the adverse effects of the vaccine as well as the reduction in cases of bacteremia, is 1.21 quality-adjusted days per person vaccinated.

Different schedules for an intervention offer examples of another, more complex, kind of comparator. When annual Papanicolaou smears are compared to no screening, they cost about $40,000 per life year saved (1985 dollars). But compared with the more realistic alternative of screening every 2 years, the cost per life year is more than $1 million. An analysis of different schedules for tetanus boosters showed that compared to immunization by age 6 with no subsequent boosters, booster shots delivered every 10 years yielded a year of life at a cost of $143,000 (1986 dollars). The epidemiology of tetanus suggested, however, that a single booster at age 65 might capture most of the benefit. Compared with that alternative, decenniel boosters cost $282,000 per life year.

It is relatively rare that the most reasonable or only comparator is to do nothing. Usually, current medical practice suggests a more reasonable option (medical management versus surgery, for example). Often, as noted, it is also useful to analyze alternative intensities of the intervention. Sometimes the most reasonable alternative is a mixture of possibilities, reflecting the fact that different clinicians treat the same condition differently. The Panel suggests that when this is the case, the analyst can either use all the major possibilities as comparators in the analysis or create a comparator that includes each possibility in proportion to its use.

Elements of an Analysis

Once the framing decisions have been made for an analysis, the analyst can begin the work of measuring and valuing health outcomes for each alternative, measuring and valuing resource use for each, and combining the various items under each heading into cost-effectiveness ratios. The choices made at the framing stage help ensure that these steps will be carried out in a consistent fashion. In the following discussion I will generally refer to a single intervention. The process for each alternative is the same.

Measuring and Valuing Health Outcomes

The societal perspective requires that all significant benefits and harms to health be counted in arriving at an estimate of the net health effects of an intervention. To estimate net health effects, the analysis needs to identify the states of health that patients may experience, the probabilities that each state will occur, and the length of time each state is likely to last. Health states depend on the natural progress of the condition as well as on the events that take place during the intervention. A thorough description of both condition and intervention, sometimes called the "clinical pathway" or "event pathway," is the starting point for estimating health effects.

In the analysis of pneumococcal vaccine, for example, the pathway starts with the unvaccinated target population, the elderly. For the intervention, the events that follow are vaccination, diagnosis, and treatment of any adverse effects of vaccination, bacteremia for those who contract it despite vaccination, and treatment of bacteremia, together with the probabilities of death and normal health associated with each of these events (Sisk et al., 1997). The event pathway for the comparator, no vaccination, includes only bacteremia and its sequelae or, for those who escape bacteremia, normal health. As another example, the sequence of events associated with a screening test includes the test itself, follow-up tests, treatment for those with positive results on screening and follow-up, and all the states of health, good and bad, that can result from the condition, tests, and treatment. The pathway encompasses all events necessary to produce the final health outcome – a case of disease avoided, say, or a life saved.

The time period for which states and probabilities are defined will depend on the nature of the condition and the intervention. One year is a common choice. The analyst then estimates the probabilities that an individual will experience different events each year – the probability that disease will occur, the probability that the patient will survive if the intervention is used, the probabilities that the patient will experience improvement or deterioration in function if the intervention is used, and so on. For many conditions, a year is insufficient and the analysis is carried out over as many years as are necessary to capture the main effects and costs.

In some cases, however, a year is too long. Acute conditions, for example, may involve important changes in the patient's condition, including the patient's probability of survival, in a few days or weeks. For these conditions the appropriate time period may be 1 week or 1 month. Or a mixture of time periods may be necessary. Events in the immediate aftermath of the condition and its treatment may require short periods of time to define important health states and their probabilities appropriately, while later events may be sufficiently well represented by the changes that occur between one year and the next.

Because CEA is based on differences between alternatives, the pathway needs to be carefully worked through for each alternative in the analysis. At points where the differences between alternatives are expected to be important, particular attention should be paid to identifying all the possible health effects that could occur.

It is sometimes possible to get all the information needed to estimate the probabilities along the pathway from a single study. More often no study includes all population groups of interest or extends over a long enough period of time to provide information on all significant events and health outcomes. Thus the analyst typically has to develop a model that incorporates information from many different studies (Buxton et al., 1997; Gold et al., 1996, Chapter 5; Russell, in press).

Decision analysis, discussed in Chapter 2 by Roberts and Sonnenberg, is often used for modeling the pathway of events, defining time
periods and attaching probabilities to each event, and carrying out the
calculations necessary to arrive at the impact of the entire chain of events
on the final health outcome, such as years of life. State-transition models,
which include Markov models as a special case, are another common
form. Modeling techniques are reviewed by Roberts and Sonnenberg
(Chapter 2 of this book), in Chapter 5 of the Panel's report (Gold et al.,
1996), and in other sources. Chapter 4 by Ioannidis and Lau discusses
the evaluation and use of data on the probabilities of events.

Effectiveness estimates, and the model on which they are based,
should be validated. Eddy (1985) has suggested a hierarchy of tests
for models. In order from least to most rigorous, (1) the structure of
the model should make sense to experts, (2) the model should replicate
the outcomes reported in the studies used to estimate its parameters,
and (3) the model's predictions should correspond well with results of
studies not used in its construction. A fourth and even tougher test, not
often possible, would be to use the model to predict outcomes for a new
program and compare the predictions with experience under the program. The Panel suggests that sensitivity analyses, in which base-case
values for elements of the model are replaced with other values, particularly extreme ones, can help test the model's validity (Gold et al., 1996,
Chapter 5).

The probabilities of the events and health states along the pathway
determine the effect of the intervention on some final measure of health
outcome, such as cases of disease prevented or lives saved or, as in
many of the examples presented earlier in this chapter, years of life
saved. Years of life are the most general measure. They allow not only
for the lifesaving capacity of an intervention, but also for the length of
life it provides, and unlike cases, they can be compared across interventions aimed at different diseases. None of the three measures, however,
captures the effects of interventions on the quality of life, including
symptoms, pain, and ability to function. Thus interventions with important effects on symptoms, pain, and function (including possible
adverse effects) are not well represented by these measures.

To allow for more comprehensive and complete comparison of interventions, techniques have been developed for assigning numerical values, called "weights," to different states of health and combining them
with survival in a single summary measure called "quality-adjusted

life years (QALYs)." The weights are usually measured on a scale that extends from 0 (death) to 1 (perfect health). For use in CEAs, a QALY system needs to have certain other properties as well (Gold et al., 1996). Chapter 3, by Miyamoto, discusses the definition and calculation of QALYs. QALYs were used as the measure of health effect in the study of vaccination against pneumococcal bacteremia shown in Table 6.4.

Just as it is especially important to have accurate data when the probabilities of events are expected to be different for the intervention and the comparator, it is especially important to have accurate quality weights for health states that are expected to represent the most important differences between alternatives. Quality weights can be elicited from professionals with expertise in the condition and intervention, from patients with the condition, or from the general public.

Some research has suggested that people who have not experienced a particular condition of ill health attach lower numerical values to states of poor health than do people in those states (see Gold et al., 1996, Chapter 4; Russell et al., 1996). Because of this, it has been argued that weights elicited from the general population discriminate against people in poor health, in the sense that CEAs based on them will show smaller net health effects when an intervention is applied to someone with illness or disability than if the patient's own weights were used (see Russell et al., 1996, for a numerical example).

This argument assumes that a lower weight for a health state means a lower estimated health effect for CEA. But since cost-effectiveness ratios are based on differences between an intervention and a comparator, it is differences between weights that are important, not levels. If those with ill health or disability value their state more highly than those in good health do, the consequence is not that those in ill health value all interventions that might apply to them more highly. Instead, the effect is to value interventions that prevent deterioration in the initial state more highly than healthy people would but to value interventions that improve health or function from its current level less highly.

Which source of weights – experts, patients, or the public – is appropriate for an analysis depends on the perspective adopted for the analysis. The Panel recommended that QALY weights for use in the reference case, which is based on the societal perspective, be derived from representative samples of the community. It also recommended that the weights used to represent normal health be less than 1, in recognition of the reality that most people's health is not perfect. Fryback and Lawrence

(1997) have shown that the mistaken practice of equating the absence of a condition with perfect health tends to overstate the number of QALYs gained from an intervention.

Measuring and Valuing Resource Use

From a societal perspective, all resources necessary to produce the health effects of an intervention should be counted in calculating costs. These resources include the goods and services used to provide health care, the time patients spend to receive care, the services of caregivers (paid or unpaid), and costs such as those for travel to and from doctors' offices, child-care expenses, and the like. Resources used (or saved) outside the health care system because of a health intervention are also included, such as changes in educational or environmental costs (Gold et al., 1996, Chapter 6).

The crucial distinction is whether resources are used, not whether money changes hands. Thus it is just as important to count the time spent by friends and relatives caring for a patient as it is to count the time of a salaried visiting nurse or home health aide. By the same token, since patients' time is a scarce resource, the time they devote to undergoing care should be counted and valued. To omit unpaid resources means that analyses will tend to favor investment in interventions that use them over interventions that use paid resources.

Resource use is appropriately measured as the marginal or incremental amount required by the intervention, that is, the difference between the amount of a resource used for the intervention and the amount used for the comparator. From the societal perspective, these differences should be measured over the long run. The long run is defined as a period of time long enough that all resources are "variable," meaning that they could be moved out of their current use. In the short term, for example, a hospital building is a fixed resource; the hospital already exists, it is equipped for use as a hospital, and the only costs associated with its existence in the near future are maintenance costs. In the long run, however, the hospital could be converted to some other use or allowed to fall down. The long-run perspective requires that the full cost of the hospital, depreciation plus maintenance, be considered in a CEA.

Studies done from other perspectives might well consider resource changes over a shorter period of time (Davidoff and Powe, 1996). They would certainly exclude some categories of costs. An individual's perspective does not include resources that are paid for by third-party payers, for example, and a third-party payer's perspective does not include those that are paid for by individuals. Gold et al. (1996, Table 6.1, p. 187) show the costs likely to be considered under different perspectives.

In principle, the process of estimating costs proceeds through three separate steps: identifying all resources used by the intervention; measuring the quantities used; and valuing the quantities at an appropriate cost per unit. Careful description of the sequence of events involved in an intervention is as essential to the correct estimation of costs as it is to the estimation of health effects. Events that cause changes in health states also trigger costs. Screening that uncovers disease necessitates a visit to a physician, which requires the patient's time, the cost of the physician visit, and the cost of tests or procedures conducted during the visit. Any treatment that follows will not only change the patient's health, but it will also generate further costs for procedures, visits, drugs, and perhaps hospital stays and help from family members. There may also be events that produce costs but not health effects along the way. When a model is used, it should include all events thought to be important for either effects or costs.

In addition to identifying cost-generating events, the analyst needs to catalog the nature of each step of the intervention – the services required, kinds of personnel, equipment, medications, and so on. A careful and complete description of the resources or "inputs" needed to produce the intervention delineates what economists call the "production function." It is an important foundation for and check on the validity of the subsequent costing process.

Micro-costing is the method of choice for costing (Gold et al., 1996, Chapter 6). The term "micro-costing" refers to a process that goes through all three steps – identification of resources, measurement of quantities, and valuation of quantities – separately and in detail. An intervention is broken into its components, such as hours of nursing time and milligrams of medication per patient per day, and the use of each component is measured. Individual components are then valued at prices appropriate to them and summed to arrive at the total cost of the intervention.

Often the cost differences that drive the comparison between alternatives can be accurately identified only when resources are measured at this level of detail. Eisenberg et al. (1984) compared a cephalosporin antibiotic that was administered once daily with cephalosporins that had to be given three or four times daily. Using time-and-motion studies, they measured differences in labor and materials associated with the two schedules. National savings from the once-daily regimen were estimated to amount to $85–$115 million per year. That difference would not have been detected without micro-costing.

The example suggests the methods required to carry out micro-costing. Administrative and billing systems can be used as a starting point, but they will usually need to be supplemented by more detailed study of the content of the services tracked by the systems. Some randomized controlled trials allow resources to be tracked prospectively. For resources that are not captured by administrative and billing systems, analysts may need to use observational studies or surveys and interviews. The latter are particularly likely to be appropriate for resources that are best known to individual patients, such as the patient's time devoted to the intervention, family time, and out-of-pocket expenses.

Because it requires that the components of an intervention be identified in detail, micro-costing permits users of an analysis to see how well their practice corresponds to the one analyzed. This helps them to decide whether the analysis is relevant to their situation. In addition, micro-costing has the advantage of allowing the analyst to select unit costs or prices appropriate for each resource and avoids much of the problem of adjusting for cost-to-charge ratios that arises in gross costing (see the later discussion).

Micro-costing is, however, more time-consuming and expensive than gross costing. And there are some uses of resources, such as general medical care or hospital stays years in the future, for which micro-costing is not possible because their components are not known in detail or are not yet knowable. As a rule, then, micro-costing is most important and most appropriate for resources that are an essential part of the intervention being analyzed over the shorter term, perhaps a few years at most.

Gross costing involves the collection of costs for large aggregates of resources, such as a hospital stay. While the method can be used alone, it is better thought of as a supplement to micro-costing. For gross costing, analysts may rely on the billing data of providers or payers to estimate the costs of hospital stays, physician visits, or nursing home days related to the intervention. For example, hospital stays for patients undergoing hip replacements might be selected from the data base and charges for those stays used as a basis for estimating costs. But little effort is made to determine what resources actually go into producing the stay.

Medicare cost data are used increasingly for gross costing because they are readily available and nationally representative (e.g., Cromwell et al., 1997; Sisk et al., 1997; see also the discussion in Gold et al., 1996,

Chapter 6). For example, studies can use average national diagnosis related group (DRG) rates to represent the resources used in a hospital stay for a particular condition or procedure. Medicare's schedule of physicians' fees, which uses the Resource-Based Relative Value Scale, provides a basis for estimating the cost of physician services. While Medicare data are most appropriate for the elderly, it has been argued that they are preferable to charges for the rest of the population as well, since few third-party payers reimburse charges (Cromwell et al., 1997). It is worth noting that gross costing is not an option in many national health systems, which do not have bills or the extensive administrative data systems necessary to prepare them.

In gross costing, resource use and valuation are already combined in the data. When the data are collected from providers, they often show the charges for a stay or a visit rather than true costs. Since charges can include profit in excess of the fair return considered a necessary component of economic cost, the analyst must then attempt to adjust them to arrive at a better approximation of true costs. Cost-to-charge ratios may be defined for the institution as a whole or, in an attempt to control for the variability in the ratio across services, for cost centers within the institution.

In micro-costing, the measurement of resource use and the valuation of resources are separate steps. Just as the resources counted will vary with the perspective of the study, so will the way they are valued. For analyses conducted from the societal perspective, resources should be valued at their opportunity cost, their value in their best alternative use (Gold et al., 1996, Chapter 6). Under the right conditions, market prices are good proxies for opportunity costs, and they are generally used even when those conditions are not met for lack of a better alternative. Prices should correspond to the population for which health effects are estimated; for example, if health effects are for the U.S. population, U.S. average prices should be used for valuing resources. All prices should be for the same year. They can be adjusted to a common year using the Consumer Price Index, or its medical care component, as appropriate.

For goods and services that are not marketed, an alternative measure of opportunity cost is needed. The time of patients and unpaid caretakers is an important example. For working-age adults, economic theory suggests that their wage is a reasonable measure of the opportunity cost of their time. For those not engaged in paid work, the wage of similar adults is a reasonable proxy. The Panel recommends that age-gender-specific wage rates be used to value time.

Patients' time and the time of unpaid caregivers have not generally been included in past studies. There are no readily available sources of data on the amount of time patients and caregivers spend in different interventions, although reasonable guesses are not difficult to make for many services. Valuation is a problem for groups that are not normally in the labor force, particularly children and the disabled, but also the elderly, for whom the restrictions and incentives of retirement programs mean that the wages of those who still work are not likely to measure opportunity cost well.

Sensitivity analyses are a reasonable way to handle these costs until research provides a better basis for estimating them. For example, base-case estimates could exclude time costs, but a sensitivity analysis could show the impact of adding them. A recent study of smoking cessation interventions handled time costs this way (Cromwell et al., 1997). Other sensitivity analyses could suggest the imporance of various assumptions made in the estimation of time costs. For example, the point has been raised that, because women's wages are generally less than those of men, their time costs will usually be less, which could make interventions more cost-effective when applied to women than to men. Sensitivity analyses could be conducted using an average wage to suggest how important the differences are (Gold et al., 1996, Chapter 6).

Note that the time costs discussed here are not the same as the "productivity" or "lost productivity" costs that are included in some studies. These estimates represent the value of time lost from work because of ill health or premature death. Their inclusion has been criticized on the ground that it values people solely for their paid labor and not for their other contributions to their own and others' well-being. Health, good or ill, and gains or losses in life expectancy are represented by health effects in a CEA; thus, productivity estimates, which are another way of valuing these effects, should not be included.

Cost estimates should be validated, just as effectiveness estimates are, by testing and comparing them in various ways, although this is not usually done. Elsewhere, I have suggested that Eddy's tests for models could be extended to costs (Russell, in press). More generally, costs have not usually been given as much attention as health effects in the analysis of interventions. Accurate cost estimates are as important to the validity of cost effectiveness as accurate estimates of health effects. The Panel's recommendations recognize and encourage a trend to improve the quality of costing in CEA.

Discounting

Net costs and net health effects often extend over a period of years. Before they can be summed to yield total net costs and health effects, the quantities for each year must be discounted. The brief discussion of discounting in this section will begin by considering net costs, primarily to avoid the awkwardness of having to refer to both costs and effects in every sentence.

The purpose of discounting is to adjust for the fact that people generally prefer to have resources now rather than later, so that a given quantity of resources that must be given up today will be valued more highly than the same quantity a year from now. And the quantity a year from now will be valued more highly than the same quantity 10 years from now. The logic behind this preference is easy to understand. Resources that are available today can be invested and will earn a return. If the rate of return is 5%, then $1 invested today will be worth $1.05 next year and $1.63 10 years from now. If the rate of return is 10%, $1 will be worth $2.59 after 10 years.

The process of discounting values dollars today at $1 and converts future dollars to "present value," so that they can be added to today's dollars, by deflating them by the rate of return that could be earned over the period. The standard formula follows, where PV denotes present value, C is net costs in each year (C_0 is costs at baseline, C_1 is costs of the first year, and so on), r is the rate of return, and T is the maximum number of years in the analysis.

$$PV = C_0 + \frac{C_1}{(1+r)^1} + \frac{C_2}{(1+r)^2} + \frac{C_3}{(1+r)^3} + \cdots + \frac{C_T}{(1+r)^T}$$

Net health effects are discounted the same way before they are summed to yield total net effects. The C's for each year in the preceding formula are simply replaced by E's.

While discounting is generally accepted for costs, many people are less comfortable with discounting health effects and with the assumption implicit in discounting them: that health effects gained (or lost) in the future are less valuable than health effects gained or lost today. Various arguments have been put forward to justify the practice. Keeler and Cretin (1983) showed that if health effects are discounted at a lower rate than costs, as is frequently proposed, then it will always be better to wait until next year to begin a health investment. Raiffa et al. (1977) have argued that future health effects must be discounted exactly because they are being compared with future dollars, which are discounted.

There is also controversy over whether the discount rate should be constant, as it is in the formula, or should vary over time in some fashion that better reflects people's preferences. Various alternative approaches have been put forward (Gold et al., 1996, Chapter 7).

While neither of these issues has been resolved to everyone's satisfaction, current practice is to discount both health effects and costs, and to do so at a constant rate. The appropriate rate is also a matter of some disagreement and studies have used different rates, although the majority use 5% per year or rates close to 5%. Russell (1986) proposed that in the interest of comparability across studies, analysts should agree to use 5% as the standard rate and to present other rates in sensitivity analyses. Based on the concept of the social opportunity cost of capital, and on evidence suggesting what that rate might be, the Panel proposes that analysts use a rate of 3% per year for the reference case, with 5% used in sensitivity analysis to preserve some comparability with past studies (Gold et al., 1996; Weinstein et al., 1996).

Reporting and Using CEAs: Decision Making Again

In the report of the analysis, costs and effects will be presented separately for each of the alternatives analyzed, as well as combined into cost-effectiveness ratios. As a rule, cost-effectiveness ratios should compare each intervention to the next most effective alternative.

If users are to understand the work that has gone into an analysis to make it useful and credible, and how that work might apply to their situations, the analyst needs to meet high standards for reporting as well as for conducting the analysis. As obvious as this may seem, experience shows that reporting practices are highly variable and that readers cannot always count on finding even basic information (Udvarhelyi et al., 1992). The Panel offers general reporting guidelines and makes specific recommendations for reporting reference case results designed to make it easier for users to compare studies (Gold et al., 1996, Chapter 9; Siegel et al., 1996).

At the beginning of this chapter, I discussed the information decision makers could expect from cost-effectiveness studies. Costs are a proxy for benefits foregone. They remind decision makers to consider the benefits that will be lost if an intervention is undertaken, benefits that are suggested by CEAs, of other interventions. Other chapters in this book discuss errors in perception and reasoning and habits of thought that lead to poor choices. Cost-effectiveness analysis can help prevent these kinds of errors by providing accurate estimates of costs and health outcomes, both beneficial and adverse, and by showing how the costs of an intervention compare with its health effects. Considering costs in relation to benefits, as CEA does, means trying to use health resources to achieve as much health as possible. Ignoring costs, or guessing at them, means achieving less with the same resources.

Nonetheless, CEA should not be used mechanically to make decisions. The factors that drive cost-effectiveness results differ from one place, or one situation, to another – incidence of the condition, content and cost of the intervention, skills of clinicians, circumstances of patients. A CEA done for one set of values may not closely approximate the values appropriate to the decision maker's problem.

In addition, as comprehensive as CEA, and especially CEA done from the societal perspective, tries to be, there are factors that may be relevant to a decision that cannot be included in an analysis. Because of the way health effects are measured, for example, CEA cannot incorporate all the nonhealth benefits (and adverse effects) of an intervention. The impact of an intervention on civil liberties, or its place in the moral philosophy of clinicians and patients, are not part of the calculations of CEA. In Chapter 9, Cohen, Asch, and Ubel discuss some of the ethical issues that can arise when decision makers consider how to make use of CEA results. Decision makers need to be aware of these issues and to consider CEA results in light of them.

At the same time, the discussion earlier in this chapter made the point that CEA brings ethical issues to the table that are not well represented in other decision-making techniques – particularly issues of the well-being of others affected by a decision, or even of the patient in other circumstances. These issues are represented by opportunity costs. CEA done from the societal perspective takes a broad view of opportunity costs. It provides information in support of the principle that good decisions balance the benefits gained and lost to all parties affected by a decision, not just those most immediately involved.

References

Balestra DJ, Littenberg B (1993). Should adult tetanus immunization be given as a single vaccination at age 65? A cost-effectiveness analysis. *Journal of General Internal Medicine*, 8 (8), August, 405–412.

Buxton MJ, Drummond MF, van Hout BA, et al. (1997). Modelling in economic evaluation: an unavoidable fact of life. *Health Economics*, 6 (3), May–June, 217–228.

Chang RW, Pellissier JM, Hazen GB (1996). A cost-effectiveness analysis of total hip arthroplasty for osteoarthritis of the hip. *Journal of the American Medical Association*, 275 (11), March 20, 858–865.

Cromwell J., Bartosch WJ, Fiore MC, et al. (1997). Cost-effectiveness of the clinical practice recommendations in the AHCPR guideline for smoking cessation. *Journal of the American Medical Association*, 278 (21), 1759–1766.

Danese MD, Powe NR, Sawin CT, Ladenson PW (1996). Screening for mild thyroid failure at the periodic health examination: a decision and cost-effectiveness analysis. *Journal of the American Medical Association*, 276 (4), July 24/31, 285–292.

Davidoff AJ, Powe NR (1996). The role of perspective in defining economic measures for the evaluation of medical technology. *International Journal of Technology Assessment in Health Care*, 12 (1), 9–21.

Eddy DM (1985). Technology assessment: the role of mathematical modeling. In Committee for Evaluating Medical Technologies in Clinical Use, Institute of Medicine, *Assessing Medical Technologies*, Washington, D.C.: National Academy Press, 144–154.

Eddy DM (1990). Screening for cervical cancer. *Annals of Internal Medicine*, 113, 214–226. Reprinted in DM Eddy, *Common Screening Tests*, Philadelphia: American College of Physicians, 1991.

Edelson JT, Weinstein MC, Tosteson ANA, et al. (1990). Long-term cost-effectiveness of various initial monotherapies for mild to moderate hypertension. *Journal of the American Medical Association*, 263 (3), January 19, 407–413.

Eisenberg JM, Koffer H, Finkler SA (1984). Economic analysis of a new drug: potential savings in hospital operating costs from the use of a once-daily regimen of parenteral cephalosporin. *Reviews of Infectious Diseases*, 6, S909–S923.

Fineberg HV, Scadden D, Goldman L (1984). Care of patients with a low probability of acute myocardial infarction. *New England Journal of Medicine*, 310, May 17, 1301–1307.

Fryback DG, Lawrence WF Jr (1997). Dollars may not buy as many QALYs as we think: a problem with defining quality-of-life adjustments. *Medical Decision Making*, 17 (3), July–September, 276–284.

Gold MR, Siegel JE, Russell LB, Weinstein MC (1996). *Cost-Effectiveness in Health and Medicine*, New York: Oxford University Press.

Goldman L, Weinstein MC, Goldman PA, Williams LW (1991). Cost-effectiveness of HMG-CoA reductase inhibition. *Journal of the American Medical Association*, 265, March 6, 1145–1151.

Keeler EB, Cretin S (1983). Discounting of life-saving and other nonmonetary effects. *Management Science*, 29, 300–306.

Office of Technology Assessment, U.S. Congress (1981). *Cost-Effectiveness of Influenza Vaccination*, Washington, D.C.: Office of Technology Assessment, December.

Raiffa H, Schwartz WB, Weinstein MC (1977). Evaluating health effects of societal decisions and programs. In *Decision Making in the Environmental Protection Agency*, Washington, D.C.: National Research Council (U.S.) Committee on Environmental Decision Making.

Russell LB (1986). *Is Prevention Better Than Cure?* Washington, D.C.: The Brookings Institution.

Russell LB (1992). Opportunity costs in modern medicine. *Health Affairs*, 11, Summer, 162–169.

Russell LB (in press). Modeling for cost-effectiveness analysis. *Statistics in Medicine*.

Russell LB, Gold MR, Siegel JE, Daniels N, Weinstein MC for the Panel on Cost-Effectiveness in Health and Medicine (1996). The role of cost-effectiveness analysis in health and medicine. *Journal of the American Medical Association*, 276 (14), October 9, 1172–1177.

Siegel JS, Weinstein MC, Russell LB, Gold MR for the Panel on Cost-Effectiveness in Health and Medicine (1996). Recommendations for reporting cost-effectiveness analyses. *Journal of the American Medical Association*, 276 (16), October 23/30, 1339–1341.

Sisk JE, Moskowitz AJ, Whang W, et al. (1997). Cost-effectiveness of vaccination against pneumococcal bacteremia among elderly people. *Journal of the American Medical Association*, 278 (16), October 22/29, 1333–1339.

Udvarhelyi S, Colditz GA, Rai A, Epstein AM (1992). Cost-effectiveness and cost-benefit analyses in the medical literature: are the methods being used correctly? *Annals of Internal Medicine*, 116, 238–244.

Weinstein MC, Siegel JS, Gold MR, Kamlet MS, Russell LB for the Panel on Cost-Effectiveness in Health and Medicine (1996). Recommendations of the Panel on Cost-Effectiveness in Health and Medicine. *Journal of the American Medical Association*, 276 (15), October 16, 1253–1258.

Weinstein MC, Stason WB (1982). Cost-effectiveness of coronary artery bypass surgery. *Circulation*, 66, Suppl III, III-56–III-66.

Part III

Psychology of Medical Decision Making

7 Cognitive Processes and Biases in Medical Decision Making

Gretchen B. Chapman, PhD, and
Arthur S. Elstein, PhD

Research on the psychology of decision making often compares actual decision making to some normative standard or benchmark of rationality. Deviations from normative standards represent decision biases and are important for two reasons. First, they offer clues to the cognitive processes underlying decision making, and second, they indicate areas where improvement is needed. This latter point is particularly important in clinical decision making, where improved decision processes can mean better patient care and health outcomes. A number of decision biases have been demonstrated in both physician and patient decision making (Dawson & Arkes, 1987; Redelmeier, Rozin, & Kahneman, 1993).

In the past couple of decades, much has been written about decision biases in medicine and other domains (Arkes & Hammond, 1986; Kahneman, Slovic, & Tversky, 1982). Rather than retread old ground, in this chapter we focus on decision biases that have been the subject of recent research in health and medicine applications. Thus, we do not discuss the classic biases such as representativeness, availability, and anchoring (Tversky & Kahnenmen, 1974), although these phenomena play an important role in medical decisions (see Dawson & Arkes, 1987, for a review). Instead, we focus on 12 decision biases that are the subject of current research. The purpose of this review is therefore to summarize recent research on decision biases in medicine.

For each of the 12 biases, we describe the normative theory or principle that is violated, the implications for descriptive theories of decision processes, and applications to medical decision making by both physicians and patients. The 12 biases are organized into three sections. First, biases can occur when judging the probability of events such as potential diagnoses and treatment outcomes. Second, deviations from normative principles can occur in preferences or evaluations of the utility of an outcome, as when choosing a treatment or management course. Finally, time and temporal sequencing can affect decision making, a topic of recent research.

Judging the Likelihood of Events

Many decisions involve uncertainty. For example, a physician may need to make treatment decisions when the patient's diagnosis is not clear or when the outcome of a treatment is uncertain. Often the prevalence of a disease or the frequency of a treatment outcome is available from epidemiological databases or outcome studies. The frequency of an outcome over a large population can then serve as the probability estimate of the outcome in an individual case. In some situations, however, a frequency-based probability is unavailable (for example, for outcomes of a new or experimental treatment) or does not seem appropriate for an individual patient, who may differ from the reference population. In this case, the physician must make an intuitive estimate of the probability based on the information available. We will now review three biases that can occur when judging uncertainty.

Support Theory and Unpacking

According to normative decision theory, the likelihood of an event (such as a diagnosis or treatment outcome) should be expressed as a probability, and probability judgments should obey the laws of probability theory. The rules of probability apply even when the likelihood is an intuitive estimate.

Redelmeier, Koehler, Liberman, and Tversky (1995) demonstrated one way in which probability theory is violated: alternative representations of the same event can give rise to different probability judgments. In one of their studies, house officers were given a case description of a 22-year-old woman with right lower quadrant abdominal pain of 12 hours' duration. Half of the physicians were asked to estimate the probabilities of two diagnoses (gastroenteritis and ectopic pregnancy) and of the residual category of "none of the above." The other half of the physicians were asked to estimate the probabilities of five diagnoses (the two specified for the first group plus three others: appendicitis, pyelonephritis, and pelvic inflammatory disease), as well as a residual category. Physicians in both groups were told that their probability judgments must sum to 100%.

Normatively, the probability of the "none of the above" category in the short-list condition should be equal to the sum of the probabilities of the "none of the above" category, appendicitis, pyelonephritis, and pelvic inflammatory disease in the long-list condition. The residual category in the short-list condition logically includes these other possibilities. In contrast to this normative prescription, the judged probability of the residual in the short-list condition was smaller than the sum of the corresponding probabilities in the long-list condition (50% versus 69%). These results are explained by Support Theory (Tverksy & Koehler, 1994), a descriptive theory that posits an *unpacking principle*: providing a more detailed description of an event increases its judged probability. Thus, unpacking the residual category by specifying particular diagnoses in the long-list condition increased the judged probability of that category, either by reminding physicians of possibilities they hadn't considered or by making some possibilities more salient.

In a second demonstration, Redelemeier et al. (1995) asked physicians to judge the probability of one of four possible outcomes of a patient's hospital admission during a myocardial infarction: dying during this admission, surviving this admission but dying within 1 year, living for more than 1 year but less than 10 years, or surviving for more than 10 years. Logically, the probabilities of these outcomes should sum to 100%; however, the average probability judgments for the four outcomes were 14%, 26%, 55%, and 69%, summing to 164%. Because each physician judged the probability of only one of the four outcomes, the other three outcomes formed an unspecified residual category. According to the unpacking principle, unspecified possibilities are discounted. Thus, physicians overestimated the specified possibility they were judging and therefore by corollary underestimated the residual category, leading to the superadditivity result. This unpacking phenomenon influences the judged probability of clinical events and consequently can affect the treatment decision made.

Hindsight Bias

Hindsight bias occurs when decision makers inflate the probability that they would have correctly diagnosed a patient (Fischhoff, 1975). Arkes, Wortmann, Saville, and Harkness (1981) presented a clinical case to five groups of physicians. The case described a patient with a mix of symptoms and listed four potential diagnoses. Physicians in the control group were asked to judge the likelihood of each of the four diagnoses given the information presented in the case. Those in the four other groups were told the actual diagnosis (each of the four groups was given a different "actual" diagnosis). They were asked for the probabilities they would have assigned to each of the four diagnoses if they had not been told the correct diagnosis. Physicians in these four hindsight groups gave judgments that were systematically different from those given by the control group. Specifically, each inflated the probability of the diagnosis they had been told was correct.

The hindsight bias is nonnormative because the information about the correct diagnosis should be irrelevant, since physicians were asked for the likelihood judgments they would have given had they not known the true outcome. What does this bias reveal about the decision processes used in judging the likelihood of potential diagnoses? Several studies indicate that knowledge of the outcome focuses the decision maker's attention on case information that is consistent with that outcome; that is, outcome knowledge draws attention to reasons why the diagnosis was predictable but not reasons why alternative diagnoses were plausible. Evidence consistent with the diagnosis is more easily recalled than facts that contradict the outcome (Dellarosa & Bourne, 1984). Hindsight bias is reduced by asking subjects how they would explain alternate outcomes if they had occurred (Arkes, Faust, Guilmette, & Hart, 1988; Slovic & Fischoff, 1977). For example, Arkes et al. (1988) asked neuropsychologists to read a case and estimate the probability of three diagnoses. Physicians in the hindsight condition (who were told the actual diagnosis) gave a higher estimate of the diagnosis than did those in the foresight condition (who were given no outcome information). This hindsight bias was reduced when physicians in both conditions were asked to list one reason why each of the possible diagnoses might be correct.

Dawson and Arkes (1988) point out an important clinical implication of hindsight bias. If physicians assume that they would have predicted a clinical outcome, then they may fail to learn from a case. For example, unusual or noteworthy cases presented at grand rounds may seem quite predictable because of hindsight bias. Audience members may conclude that "I know this already" and consequently fail to learn the lessons illustrated by the case.

Another nonnormative influence of outcome knowledge, similar to hindsight bias, is the outcome bias (Baron & Hershey, 1988; Caplan, Posner, & Cheney, 1991; Gruppen, Margolin, Wisdom, & Grum, 1994). Decisions are evaluated more favorably if they resulted in a good outcome rather than a poor outcome. Caplan et al. (1991) constructed pairs of anesthesiology cases. The two cases in each pair were identical except that one described a temporary adverse outcome, while the other described a permanent adverse outcome. Anesthesiologists then rated the appropriateness of care in each case. Cases that resulted in permanent outcomes received lower ratings of appropriateness of care than those that resulted in temporary outcomes. For the two cases in a pair, the actions taken by the physician and the information available to her or him were identical; thus, the patient outcome cannot indicate the quality of the clinical decision making. It nevertheless influenced evaluations of the quality of care delivered. This result is similar to hindsight bias in that the evaluators behaved as if the case physician should have been able to predict the outcome. This type of outcome bias can prevent evaluators from viewing outcomes as unexpected and may lead to inappropriate evaluations of the acting physician.

Confirmation Bias

One important aspect of diagnostic reasoning is hypothesis testing. Physicians must determine which of several diagnoses (or hypotheses) is most likely given the evidence available from the patient's history, exam, and laboratory tests. The normative theory for hypothesis testing is Bayes' Theorem. Accordingly, the probability of a diagnosis is determined by combining the prior probability (or prevalence) of the diagnosis with the information value (or likelihood ratio) of each piece of relevant information. A sizable body of psychological research has explored the ways in which the hypothesis testing of physicians and lay people deviates from this normative theory. The term "confirmation bias" has been used to refer to many of these hypothesis testing biases. Klayman (1995) reviews the various phenomena that have been subsumed under this label. For example, a decision maker may start out overconfident in an initial belief about a particular hypothesis, or may search for evidence in a way that biases the data to support the favored hypothesis, for example by avoiding tests thought to be likely to contradict the hypothesis. A decision maker could also interpret the data in a biased way by, for example, discarding disconfirming information, or she may revise her confidence in the hypothesis insufficiently given the data.

One classic example of a confirmation bias is "pseudodiagnosticity." Kern and Doherty (1982) asked medical students to determine which of two diagnoses was more likely for a hypothetical patient by selecting the appropriate information about two symptoms. According to Bayes' Theorem, one needs to know the probability of a particular symptom given each of the two diseases in order to determine if the symptom is diagnostic. In contrast, the medical students tended to request the probability of each of the two symptoms given only a single diagnosis. That is, they wished to know how typical (as opposed to diagnostic) each symptom was of the focal disease. Wolf, Gruppen, and Billi (1985) found a similar result with medical residents.

Klayman and Brown (1993) demonstrated a method for debiasing this type of error. They presented subjects with information on various symptoms associated with each of two diseases. Some subjects learned about each disease individually by seeing a number of cases of each disease with a symptom profile for each case. Later, when asked to diagnose new cases, these subjects relied on symptoms that were typical or representative of a disease, rather than on symptoms that were diagnostic and differentiated one disease from another. Other subjects learned about the two diseases jointly in a contrastive format in which cases of the two disease were intermixed. These subjects diagnosed new cases by relying on diagnostic rather than typical symptoms.

Confirmation biases have two implications for clinical practice. First, a desire to confirm one's favored hypothesis may contribute to increasing inefficiency and costs by the ordering of additional laboratory tests that can contribute little to revising one's opinion, considering the other clinical data already at hand, since their results are expected to be consistent with the focal hypothesis. A second clinical implication of confirmation biases is that having additional laboratory tests in hand may cause physicians to increase their confidence in the focal diagnosis, even though the additional data do not alter the Bayesian probability of the diagnosis. That is, additional data can increase confidence without increasing accuracy. For example, Dawson, Connors, Speroff, Kemka, Shaw, and Arkes (1993) found that experienced physicians were more confident, but not more accurate, than less experienced physicians, indicating that the additional expertise and knowledge that come with experience may influence confidence but not accuracy. The earliest demonstration of this phenomenon is by Oskamp (1962).

Preferences and Values

In addition to probability estimation, medical decisions involve evaluating outcomes with respect to one's preferences and values. For example, the patient and physician must decide whether the benefits of a treatment outweigh the side effects or whether the risks of a diagnostic test are worth taking, given the information it will provide. Psychological research indicates that choices and values are often quite labile. These results suggest that preference elicitation does not merely reveal stable preferences; instead, preferences are constructed by the elicitation procedure (Slovic, 1995). Consequently, minor differences in the assessment method can lead to major differences in preference and choice. Here we review seven biases in preference judgments. Some of these are expressed in choice, while others occur in quantitative measures of preference such as utility assessment.

Framing Effects

Perhaps the most well-known example of labile preferences is the framing effect. In a classic example, the Asian flu problem, Kahneman and Tversky (1984) presented lay people with one of two public health scenarios. In both scenarios, subjects were told that health officials were preparing for an outbreak of Asian flu expected to kill 600 people. Two plans to combat the outbreak were available. One version of the scenario, the "lives saved" frame, described one plan that would save 200 people for sure and a second plan that would save all 600 people with a one-third probability. Another version of the scenario, the "lives lost" frame, described one plan by which 400 people would die for sure and a second plan in which all 600 people would die with a two-thirds probability. The two frames describe exactly the same options since saving 200 people implies that the other 400 will die. Subjects nevertheless reacted differently to the two frames, preferring the less risky choice in the lives saved frame but the more risky choice when the outcomes were presented as lives lost.

McNeil, Pauker, Sox, and Tversky (1982) conducted a similar study using patients and physicians (radiologists) as subjects. A hypothetical decision scenario presented a choice between surgical and radiation treatment for lung cancer. In one frame, the treatments were described in terms of survival rates, whereas in the other they were described as mortality rates. For both treatments, the outcomes presented were immediate, 1-year and 5-year survival (or mortality) rates. Radiation therapy had a higher immediate survival rate but a lower 5-year survival rate compared to surgery. Although survival rate and mortality rate describe exactly the same information, both patients and physicians expressed different preferences in the two frames. In the survival frame, there was a strong preference for surgery (78% of patients and 84% of physicians chose this option), while in the mortality frame, preferences for the two therapies were more equal (60% of patients and 50% of physicians preferred surgery). Thus, immediate mortality from the surgery itself had a larger impact on choice in the mortality frame than in the survival frame.

Framing effects, such as shown in these examples, violate the normative principle of descriptive invariance, which prescribes that equivalent descriptions of the same decision should lead to the same choice. The descriptive explanation of framing effects is that decision makers evaluate outcomes as gains or losses relative to a reference point. Furthermore, reference points are easily redefined, such that the same outcome can be viewed either as a gain or a loss. Prospect Theory (Kahneman and Tversky, 1979) proposed an S-shaped value function defined around a reference point. In the gain domain, value is a decelerating function of lives saved, leading to risk-averse choices for gains. In the loss domain, negative value is a decelerating function of the (absolute) number of lives lost, leading to risk-seeking choices for losses. Furthermore, the function is steeper for losses than for gains, indicating that a change in losses (e.g., a change in mortality rate) has a larger influence on evaluations than an equal change in gains. This value function can account for the framing effects described previously.

The formulation that choices are generally risk averse for gains and risk seeking for losses has been challenged by Mellers, Schwartz, and Weber (1997). They propose that people are generally risk averse in both domains and that the observed preference shift occurs because in the loss domain the sure loss is perceived as more risky than the gamble.

Framing effects can have implications for clinical practice because they indicate that subtle differences in outcome description can potentially determine the choice that is made. As with many decision-making biases, one crucial question regarding framing effects is how prevalent they are. Do they bias a large number of decisions made by patients and physicians, or do they represent only an occasional aberration from rational choice? Gain/loss framing has been explored in a number of studies of medical decisions, resulting in framing effects sometimes but not always. For example, O'Connor and colleagues (1989; O'Connor, Boyd, Tritchler, Kriukov, Sutherland, and Till, 1985) found that framing outcomes in terms of survival or mortality (or both) influenced hypothetical trade-offs between the toxicity of a cancer treatment and the survival rate that it offered. On the other hand, O'Connor, Pennie, and Dales (1996) found that actual decisions to receive an influenza vaccine were not influenced by whether information was framed positively (as a percentage who remain free of the flu) or negatively (as a percentage who acquire the flu). Christensen, Heckerling, Mackesy-Amiti, Bernstein, & Elstein (1995) looked for framing effects in 12 medical scenarios presented to physicians, residents, and medical students. Only 2 of the 12 problems showed a framing effect; one of those was in the predicted direction, with the loss frame increasing the preference for the more risky option, while the other was in the counterpredicted direction. These results indicate that framing effects may occur only in some cases. We still do not know what features of a decision will evoke this effect (but see Kuhlberger, 1998; Levin, Schneider, & Gaeth, 1998).

Preference Reversals

Framing effects (when they occur) violate the normative principle of descriptive invariance. Another related normative principle is procedural invariance, which states that different methods of eliciting a preference should lead to the same preference order. For example, a person who chooses A over B should also be willing to pay more for A than for B and should give a higher preference rating to A than to B. Violations of procedural invariance are known as "preference reversals" and have been demonstrated in a large number of studies (e.g., Slovic and Lichtenstein, 1983), most involving evaluation of monetary lotteries. A few studies, however, have examined preference reversals in health contexts.

Chapman and Johnson (1995) asked college students to evaluate health items (e.g., having 20–20 vision) and consumer items (e.g., five bus tickets). The subjects evaluated the items in two ways: by indicating the amount of money for which they would sell the item and by indicating the amount of additional life expectancy they would demand in exchange for giving up the item. If procedural invariance holds, then the rank order of the items according to monetary amounts should be the same as the rank order according to life expectancy amounts. The results of the experiment showed, however, that in monetary evaluations the consumer items were likely to receive higher evaluations than the health items, whereas in the life expectancy evaluations the reverse was true. That is, preference for consumer versus health items reversed, depending on the response scale. Chapman and Johnson (1995) explained this result in terms of "semantic compatibility," a concept introduced by Tversky, Sattath, and Slovic (1988). Accordingly, features of a target item that are meaningfully related to the response scale will receive more weight in the evaluation. Thus, consumer features are given more weight in monetary judgments and health features more weight in life judgments. These results imply that quality of life will be seen as more valuable when traded off against length of life (a compatible dimension) than when traded for monetary savings (an incompatible dimension).

Another example of preference reversals was demonstrated by Stalmeier and colleagues (Stalmeier, Bezembinder, & Unic 1996; Stalmeier, Wakker, & Bezembinder, 1997). These authors found that many college students regarded a particular aversive health state (constant migraines) so aversive that they would rather live only 10 years in this health state rather than 20 years. Subjects were then given a time trade-off task in which they were asked to specify the number of years in perfect health that is equally attractive to 10 years with constant migraine and the number of years in perfect health equivalent to 20 years with constant migraine. Since 10 years of migraine are preferable to 20 years of migraine, the equivalent number of years in perfect health should be larger for the 10 years of migraine than for the 20 years of migraine. In fact, a majority of the subjects gave a higher time trade-off response for the 20 years of migraine, indicating a preference reversal. A subsequent study (Stalmeier & Chapman, unpublished data) found similar results using patients who suffered from migraine headaches.

These studies, as well as the framing effects reviewed earlier, indicate that the procedures or questions used to elicit preferences can influence the preferences themselves. These findings pose problems in the elicitation of patient preferences. Normative decision theory assumes that preferences are revealed by utility assessment methods, not constructed by the elicitation technique. Studies demonstrating procedural variance challenge this assumption and point to one more normative-descriptive difficulty.

Adding Decision Alternatives

Framing effects and preference reversals both represent choice biases in which altering some normatively irrelevant aspect of the problem (such as the description or response mode) changes the choice. That is, some factor that should have no effect (such as frame) has an effect.

Still other factors in choice problems affect the decision in the opposite direction from that prescribed by normative theory. Imagine that a decision maker is choosing between two alternatives. For example, a physician might be deciding between medications A and B. Suppose that a third alternative, medication C, is added to the choice set. This addition could potentially decrease the probability that the physician will select A or B (that is, C might steal "market share" from A or B or both). According to the normative principle of "regularity," however, the addition of C to the menu of options should not increase the probability of choosing A or B, since the expected utility of each option is unaffected by the number of options available.

Redelmeier and Shafir (1995) found a violation of regularity in physician choice. In one study, family physicians were presented with the case of a patient with osteoarthritis of the hip who has tried several nonsteroidal anti-inflammatory medications without success and who has agreed to a referral to an orthopedist for consideration of hip replacement. The physician participants were asked to chose among two or three management plans. In the two-option condition, the case specified that there was one nonsteroidal medication (ibuprofen) that the patient had not yet tried. The physicians thus chose between (a) refer to an orthopedist and do not start any new medications and (b) refer to an orthopedist and also start ibuprofen. About half of the physicians (53%) chose the first option. In the three-option condition, the case specified that two nonsteroidal medications (ibuprofen and piroxicam) had not yet been tried and physicians were offered three options: (a) refer to an orthopedist and do not start any new medications, (b) refer to an orthopedist and also start ibuprofen, and (c) refer to an orthopedist and also start piroxicam. In this condition, most of the physicians (72%) chose the first option, the no-medication alternative. Thus, the addition of alternative C increased the preference for alternative A, a violation of regularity.

This choice pattern can be explained in terms of the reasons that decision makers use to justify or explain their choices (Shafir, Simonson, & Tversky, 1997). In the three-option condition, it may be difficult to explain why one selected the ibuprofen over the piroxicam, or vice versa. This decision conflict can be avoided by selecting the "default" option of referring the patient to an orthopedist without starting any new medication, making this option particularly attractive. In the two-option condition, there is no such decision conflict between two similar options that can be resolved by selecting a third.

Another type of choice bias that occurs as the result of adding an additional choice option is the "attraction effect" (Huber, Payne, & Puto, 1982). Once again, the addition of a third alternative increases the preference for one of the other two options. In this case, the third alternative is worse in every way than one of the other two options (that is, it is dominated). Thus, the third option (called the "decoy") is seldom chosen itself, but it does influence the choice between the other two by "attracting" market share to the option that is superior in every way to the decoy. For example, Schwartz and Chapman (1999) presented internal medicine residents with hypothetical cases that posed a choice among medications. One medication (A) was very effective but had frequent side effects, while another (B) was moderately effective and had no side effects. In some versions of the cases, a third, decoy medication (C) was also available. It was moderately effective but had occasional side effects. Option C is obviously worse than B, so it was not chosen; however, its presence increased the likelihood of selecting option B over option A. Chapman and Malik (1995) found a similar result with college student subjects.

This attraction effect can also be explained in terms of the reasons used to explain a choice (Shafir et al. 1997). In the three-option condition, the choice of B offers the easy explanation that it was better than C, whereas the two-option condition offers no such defense. Biases induced by adding additional choice alternatives are particularly relevant to medical practice, where new medications and other treatments frequently become available (Redelmeier & Shafir, 1995). While one might hypothesize that additional options for medical treatment would likely improve medical care, the studies reviewed in this section suggest that additional options may alter decisions in ways that are not necessarily improvements.

Sunk Cost Bias

According to normative decision theory, decisions should be made to maximize future utility. Past utility is irrelevant because a decision now cannot influence outcomes that have already occurred. In contrast to this prescription, decision makers are sometimes influenced by sunk costs or by resources that have already been expended. The sunk cost bias (Arkes & Blumer, 1985; Brockner, 1992) occurs when a decision maker continues to invest resources in a previously selected action or plan even after it is perceived to be suboptimal. For example, Arkes and Blumer (1985, Experiment 1) told participants to imagine that they had inadvertently purchased tickets for two nonrefundable ski trips on the same weekend. Even though they were told to assume further that they would enjoy more the trip they had purchased second, a majority of participants chose the trip they had purchased first, which had cost them more money. From an economic perspective, choosing the first trip is suboptimal; because the money for both trips has been irretrievably sunk, one ought to choose the trip that would be more enjoyable.

There have not been many demonstrations of the sunk cost bias in medical decision making. Bornstein, Emler, and Chapman (1999; Chapman, Bornstein, & Emler, 1996) examined whether it could be found in medical management. Residents in internal medicine and family practice were presented with four cases that required decisions about whether to continue a current management strategy. For example, in one case, a patient was started on antisecretory medication because of gastroesophageal reflux. The medication was ineffective and produced drowsiness. The physicians were asked to decide whether to maintain the original treatment or discontinue the medication and also to select one of several potential reasons for their decision. Four nonmedical scenarios were also included. The amount of resources already invested in the current plan was varied in each scenario.

Residents were more likely to advocate staying with the original plan so as not to waste the resources sunk if a high level of resources had already been invested, but this effect was most evident in the nonmedical scenarios. Thus, there is some evidence that physicians are able to avoid the sunk cost fallacy in their own area of expertise. It is possible that decision rules specific to medicine, such as choosing the most effective treatment, were able to override the sunk cost fallacy in the medical domain. More research is needed on whether the sunk cost bias influences medical decision making. Demonstrations in other decision domains, however, suggest that physicians and patients may be somewhat reluctant to abandon ineffective management plans if they have already invested a lot of time, thought, or expense in those plans.

Omission Bias

Decision theory is a consequentialist theory, meaning that the optimal decision is defined as the one that, on average, will achieve the best consequence. The action taken to achieve the consequence is not relevant (except insofar as the action produces additional consequences that are relevant to the decision). For example, in deciding on the best strategy to manage localized prostate cancer, the relevant consequences include length of life, quality of life, treatment side effects, and so on. If expectant management (watchful waiting or essentially doing nothing) achieves better overall outcomes than prostatectomy (doing something), then expectant management is the optimal decision. (Some decision analyses show this to be the case, although the issue is quite controversial.) The fact that expectant management is a passive strategy and surgery an active strategy is irrelevant. Surgery does not get an extra advantage because it involves doing something (as opposed to doing nothing). The fact that prostatectomy remains a frequent procedure suggests that patient and physician decision makers may be influenced by factors other than the consequences. Specifically, they may have a preference for actions over omissions (or vice versa).

Ritov and Baron (1990) examined this distinction experimentally. They presented college student subjects with a scenario concerning a decision to vaccinate a child. In the scenario, subjects imagined that they were the parent of a 1-year-old child and that 10 in 10,000 such children would die from the flu. A vaccination was available that eliminated flu infection but that had some side effects that could be fatal. Subjects were asked what fatality risk from the vaccine would cause them to decide not to vaccinate. According to decision theory, the relevant consequence in this decision is risk of death. Any vaccine that lowers the risk of death from the 10 in 10,000 risk posed by the flu is preferable to the alternative of not vaccinating. Thus, subjects should accept a vaccine with a 9 in 10,000 risk. More than half of the subjects would not accept such a vaccine, however. They viewed a death resulting from an omission (not vaccinating) as preferable to a death resulting from an act (vaccinating). This omission bias was even more pronounced when the risks involved were ambiguous.

Some related studies (Baron & Ritov, 1994; Spranca, Minsk, & Baron, 1991) found that decision makers saw omissions that led to harmful outcomes as less immoral or less bad than acts that led to the same outcomes. In addition, omissions were often preferred to commissions even in decisions leading to good outcomes (Spranca et al., 1991). One explanation for the omission–commission distinction is that decision makers evaluate each by comparing them to different reference points. A commission is compared to the status quo, whereas an omission is compared to itself, yielding a neutral evaluation. Thus, for example, when evaluating surgical treatment for prostate cancer (a commission), the outcome (not having cancer) is compared to the status quo (having cancer) and appears to be an improvement. Expectant management (an omission) is given a neutral evaluation.

Another clinical example of the omission–commission distinction may occur in the decision to prescribe hormone replacement therapy for postmenopausal women (Elstein, Holzman, Ravitch, Metheny, et al., 1986). A harmful outcome (say, uterine or breast cancer) that could result from the commission (prescribing) is evaluated by comparing it to the status quo (the patient's good health status before treatment begins). In contrast, a harmful outcome (say, bone fracture) that could result from the omission (not prescribing) is evaluated by comparing it to what would have happened had no decision been made and the patient's health progressed naturally. Thus, the harmful outcome from prescribing is evaluated more harshly than the harmful outcome from not prescribing. The omission–commission distinction can also explain why passive euthanasia is viewed more favorably than active euthanasia (Singer, Choudhry, Armstrong, Meslin, & Lowry, 1995). Passive euthanasia (withdrawing life support) may be compared to the patient's natural progression had medicine not intervened. It is thus evaluated more neutrally than active euthanasia.

Regret

Comparing a decision outcome to alternatives appears to be an important component of decision making (Kahneman & Miller, 1986). One important example is the emotion of regret, which results when a decision outcome is compared to the outcome that would have occurred had a different decision been made. (This is in contrast to disappointment, which results from comparing an outcome to another that could have resulted from the same decision.) According to Regret Theory (Loomes & Sugden, 1982), large contrasts with a counterfactual have a disproportionate influence on decision making.

Since regret results from comparing the decision outcome with what might have been, it depends on the feedback available to decision makers about what outcome the alternative option would have yielded. For example, if a patient experiences impotence as a result of surgery for prostate cancer, he may not know whether to feel regret or to rejoice because the alternative of watchful waiting may have yielded a better or worse outcome. Ritov (1996; see also Josephs, Larrick, Steele, & Nisbett,

1992) found that decision making was affected by whether uncertainty was resolved for the chosen option only or for all options. Altering the potential for regret by manipulating uncertainty resolution reveals that decision-making behavior that appears to be risk aversion can actually be attributed to regret aversion (Zeelenberg, Beattie, van der Plight, & de Vries, 1996).

There is some indication that regret may be related to the distinction between acts and omissions. Some studies have found that regret is more intense following an action than an omission (Landman, 1987). For example, in a study by Kahneman and Miller (1986), subjects judged that a decision maker who switched stock funds from one company to another and lost money would feel more regret than another decision maker who decided against switching stock funds and also lost money. Gilovich, Medvec, and Chen (1995) also found a difference in regret between acts and omission. Subjects assigned a higher value to an inferior outcome when it resulted from an act than from an omission, presumably as a way of counteracting the regret that could result from an act. Another study, however, found that regret was no larger for acts than for omissions (Connolly, Ordonez, & Coughlan, 1997), while still others showed that inaction can lead to different forms for regret (Gilovich, Medvec, & Kahneman, 1998).

Regret has been little studied in clinical situations, most likely because the outcome of the unchosen treatment can rarely be known for certain. Ritov and Baron (1995) presented college students with hypothetical scenarios about fetal testing and vaccination. In some conditions, subjects expected to learn the outcome of only the option they had chosen, whereas in another condition they expected to learn the outcomes of both the chosen and foregone alternatives, and in a third condition they did not expect to learn the outcome of either option. Subjects anticipated feeling more regret in conditions where they expected outcome feedback. Although more research is needed on regret in medical decisions, the high stakes and the possibility of dire consequences in many medical decisions suggest that regret may play a large role.

Decision Weights

Many medical decisions involve uncertainty. Normative expected utility theory prescribes that the utilities of decision outcomes should be weighted by the probability of their occurrence. In addition, probability should be treated as a linear scale. For example, a decrease of

1% in mortality risk should have the same impact on expected utility whether it is a decrease from, say, 10% to 9% or from 1% to 0%. Descriptively, decision makers do not treat uncertainty in this manner. Specifically, changes from certainty to uncertainty have more influence than similar-sized changes from more to less uncertainty (Kahneman & Tversky, 1979). For example, in one study (Viscusi, Magat, & Huber, 1987), consumers were asked to consider a $10 container of pesticide with a toxicity risk of 15 in 10,000. Respondents were willing to pay $1.04 extra for the reduction in risk from 15 to 10 per 10,000 but would pay $2.41 extra for the reduction from 5 to 0 per 10,000. Redelmeier et al. (1993) refer to this phenomenon as the "enchanting appeal of zero risk." Public outcry about the desirability of reducing to zero risks that are already minuscule vividly illustrates this phenomenon.

Tverksy and Kahneman (1986) demonstrated a similar phenomenon called the "certainty effect." A group of physicians was presented with three cases involving a choice between two treatments for a tumor. The treatments described in each case and the percentage of physicians preferring each treatment are as follows:

Case 1

Treatment A	20% chance of imminent death and 80% chance of normal life, with longevity of 30 years (35%)
Treatment B	certainty of normal life with longevity of 18 years (65%)

Case 2

Treatment C	80% chance of imminent death and 20% chance of normal life, with longevity of 30 years (68%)
Treatment D	75% chance of imminent death and 25% chance of normal life, with longevity of 18 years (32%)

Case 3

Consider a new case where there is a 25% chance that the tumor is treatable and a 75% chance that it is not. If the tumor is not treatable, death is imminent. If the tumor is treatable, the outcomes of the treatments are as follows:

Treatment E	20% chance of imminent death and 80% chance of normal life, with longevity of 30 years (32%)
Treatment F	certainty of normal life, with longevity of 18 years (68%)

In case 1, a majority of physicians prefer treatment B, which has no uncertainty. The relative consequences of the treatments in case 2 are the same as those in case 1 except that each treatment's probability of survival has been divided by 4. Since the expected utility (EU) of each option is the product of the probability of survival and the utility of the survival outcome, the expected utilities for the case 2 options are the same as for the case 1 options except that the case 2 EUs have been divided by 4. (This is true regardless of what utilities are assigned to the outcomes.) Thus, if EU(B) > EU(A), then EU(D) > EU(C). However, the physicians' choice behavior contradicts this normative property, since the majority of physicians favored treatment C. Psychologically, the difference between the two cases is that case 1 offers a certainty, while case 2 does not. Given the lack of certainty, the physicians preferred the option with the better outcome in case 2.

Case 3 illustrates the "pseudo-certainty effect" (Tversky & Kahneman, 1986). It presents a two-stage lottery that is formally identical to case 2. For example, treatment E actually yields an overall 20% probability of living for 30 years, considering that there is only a 25% chance that the tumor is treatable. Nevertheless, the physicians' responses were similar to those reported for case 1. They appear to focus on the certainty offered by treatment F in the second stage of the lottery.

These results indicate how uncertainty is incorporated into decision making. Specifically, probability is not treated as a linear scale. If it were, then dividing probabilities by a factor of 4 in the preceding cases would not change the preference order. The choice patterns in these cases suggest that, instead, decision makers weight outcomes using a nonlinear function of probability known as the "pi function" (Tversky & Kahneman, 1992) or as "decision weights." This function gives disproportionate weight to movement away from certainty (probabilities of 0 or 1.0) and less weight to changes in the middle of the probability scale. Thus, the comparison between a 100% and an 80% chance of survival seems more than four times as large as the comparison between 25% and 20%.

The Role of Time in Decision Making

Uncertainty is not the only factor that makes medical decisions subject to bias. Many medical decisions also involve outcomes that occur at different points in time. For example, surgery often presents a fairly immediate risk of mortality or complications but a long-term survival advantage over medical management. Similarly, a decision to engage in a preventive health behavior (for example, to quit smoking) involves a fairly immediate sacrifice and a benefit that accrues over time, reaching an appreciable level only after a period of time. One explanation for why patients find it so difficult to adopt preventive health behaviors is that they place less weight on future outcomes than they do on present ones (Christensen-Szalanski & Northcraft, 1985). Like other decision phenomena, intertemporal choice also shows biases; two types will now be discussed.

Variable Discount Rates

Discounted utility theory is the normative theory of choices between outcomes that occur at different times into the future. According to this theory, the (absolute) value of future outcomes should be discounted by a factor known as a "discount rate." The discount rate is the percentage increase in value needed to offset a given delay. For example, if $100 now were just as attractive at $110 one year from now, then the annual discount rate would be 10%. Normative theory (Fishburn & Rubenstein, 1982; Loewenstein & Prelec, 1992; Weinstein & Stason, 1977) specifies that the discount rate should be a constant positive rate, and most decision analyses use a low rate such as 3% (Gold, Siegel, Russell, & Weinstein, 1996).

Actual decision making deviates from this normative theory in a number of ways. First, the discount rates implicitly used in intertemporal choice for health outcomes are often very high, sometimes 100% or more (Cairns, 1992; Chapman, 1996b; Chapman & Elstein, 1995). Other studies have found discount rates in a more plausible range; however, sometimes discount rates are zero or negative (Redelmeier & Heller, 1993). Moderate changes in the discount rates applied to a decision analysis can substantially alter the results. If descriptive preferences were used as the basis for decision analytic discount rates, the results would depend heavily on the circumstances under which subjective discount rates were elicited.

Subjective discount rates are influenced by several nonnormative factors representing a second deviation from normative theory. For example, subjective discount rates are higher for gains than for losses, higher for small-magnitude than for large-magnitude outcomes, and higher for short delays than for long delays (e.g., Chapman, 1996b; MacKeigan, Larson, Draugalis, Bootman, & Bruns, 1993; see Chapman, 1998, for a review). This last effect is particularly interesting because it can lead to a type of preference reversal (Kirby & Herrnstein, 1995). For example, someone may prefer $200 8 years from now to $100 6 years from now, but 6 years later the same person would prefer $100 right away to $200 2 years from now. Note that both situations involve whether one wishes to delay payment for 2 years in order to receive double the money, but the second situation takes place 6 years after the first. Because both delays are longer in the first situation, the subjective discount rate is lower and the person is willing to wait for the larger reward. As another example, a person may resolve in the evening to get up early the next morning to reap the long-term reward of a good day's work. The next morning, however, the preference switches to the short-term rewards of sleeping in.

Christensen-Szalanski (1984) demonstrated such a preference reversal in women deciding whether to have anesthesia for childbirth. One month before labor and 1 month postpartum, the women preferred to avoid using anesthesia during labor. During active labor, their preference suddenly shifted toward using anesthesia to avoid pain. The anesthesia offers immediate pain relief but also the risk of long-term side effects. At short delays (during labor), the women showed a stronger preference for the immediate relief. This demonstration indicates that time preferences measured at any one time may not be representative of long-term time preferences.

A third way in which behavioral decision making deviates from discounted utility theory is that discount rates differ across different decision domains. Discount rates used in health decisions are typically not correlated with discount rates used in financial decisions (Cairns, 1992; Chapman, 1996b; Chapman, & Elstein, 1995). Thus, decision makers may use one discount rate for medical decisions and another for investment decisions. Keeler and Cretin (1983) have demonstrated that the use of different discount rates for separate domains results in decision paradoxes. For example, if money is discounted at a higher rate than health, then any program that spends money to improve health will become more cost effective if the program is delayed infinitely. Similarly, if health is discounted at a higher rate than money, then such programs become more cost effective when expedited infinitely.

Evaluation of Sequences

One area of research on the role of time in decision making has focused on how decision makers evaluate sequences of outcomes. As with other forms of intertemporal choice, the normative theory for the evaluation of sequences is discounted utility theory (Fishburn & Rubenstein, 1982; Loewenstein & Prelec, 1992; Weinstein & Stason, 1977). Accordingly, each outcome in the sequence should be discounted in value according to the delay until its occurrence. The overall value of the sequence is then the sum of the discounted values.

Whereas the same normative theory applies to intertemporal choice for individual outcomes and sequences of outcomes, in actual decision making these two cases are treated quite differently. In evaluating individual outcomes, decision makers generally prefer to have good outcomes sooner rather than later (a positive time preference). In contrast, when evaluating sequences of outcomes, decision makers usually prefer improving sequences that put the best outcomes off until last (a negative time preference) (Chapman, 1996a; Loewenstein & Prelec, 1993).

Treadwell (1998) found that if a negative discount rate was assumed, then discounted utility theory provided a good account of evaluations of sequences of health outcomes. Specifically, evaluations satisfied the normative principle of preferential independence. For example, if a sequence (E, S, M) of 10 years of excellent health (E) followed by 10 years of severe headaches (S) and 10 years of mild coughing (M) was preferred to a sequence of S, E, M, then E, S, E should be (and was) preferred to S, E, E. In this example, both options within each pair end in the same health state (M for pair 1 and E for pair 2). Thus, the choice between sequences within each pair should be *independent* of the final health state. Consequently, changing the final health state from M for both options to E for both options should not influence the preference for the first sequence over the other. Participants in Treadwell's studies showed just this pattern.

Other types of studies have not found such strong support for discounted utility theory. Redelmeier and Kahneman (1996) queried patients undergoing colonoscopy or lithotripsy for repeated real-time ratings of the intensity of the pain experienced. Later, the patients were also asked for retrospective global evaluations of the total pain caused by the procedure. Normatively, the retrospective evaluations should be equal to the sum of the minute-by-minute ratings, with appropriate discounting of later time periods. Specifically, the retrospective evaluations should be related to the duration of the experience, since, on average, a longer experience means more total pain. In contrast, patients' retrospective ratings were unrelated to duration, a result known as "duration neglect." Instead, they were strongly related to peak intensity of the pain and the pain during the final few minutes of the procedure.

In a related study, Kahneman, Fredrickson, Schreibner, and Redelmeier (1993) found that the preference for a sequence of painful stimulation (a cold pressor test) could be increased by extending the sequence by 30 seconds so that it lasted longer but ended at a less painful level. That is, a sequence that ended with 30 seconds of moderate pain was preferred to a (dominant) sequence that ended 30 seconds earlier. The pattern violates the normative principle of dominance. It can be explained by postulating that decision makers neglect the duration of a sequence but instead base their evaluation on the concluding level of pain. These results indicate that patient preferences can be greatly influenced by whether the health events being evaluated are framed as individual events or as sequences of outcomes.

Conclusions

Prevalence of Decision Biases

The research reviewed here indicates that medical decision making by both patients and physicians is influenced by a number of biases. Most of the biases reviewed here (e.g., hindsight bias, framing, effect of adding alternatives) have been repeatedly demonstrated in medical decision making. Some other biases, most notably sunk cost and regret, have received much less attention in medical decision making than in studies of decision making in other domains. Demonstrations of decision errors do not indicate how prevalent these effects are in everyday decision making. Only a few studies (e.g., Christensen et al., 1995) have examined a particular bias in a large number of cases. Furthermore, recent psychological research (e.g., Gigerenzer & Goldstein, 1996) suggests that decision making is often close to optimal on problems representative of the decision maker's usual environment. Thus, the impact of decision biases on clinical practice and patient outcomes is an important topic that requires further research. Decision biases that frequently influence clinicians and patients in actual practice and that impact patient outcomes would be the most important to identify.

Correcting Decision Biases

Another area needing additional investigation is how to correct decision biases when they occur. Research identifying biases is much more prevalent than research on debiasing. An understanding of the psychological processes underlying a decision bias is necessary for the success of a debiasing effort. Arkes (1991) identified three categories of decision biases. Strategy-based errors result from applying a suboptimal heuristic because it is faster or easier than the normative rule. The decision maker judges that the extra accuracy achieved with the normative rule is not worth the additional effort. These errors can be corrected by providing an incentive to use the more accurate rule or by making the normative rule easier to execute. Computerized decision aids are an example of a method to make a normative rule easier to execute. Clinical practice guidelines also reduce the effort involved in making case-by-case decisions.

A second type of decision error is association-based. These errors occur when semantic associations bring to mind information that is normatively irrelevant to the decision. Hindsight bias and confirmation bias are both examples of association-based errors. In hindsight bias, for example, knowledge of the outcome brings to mind case information that is consistent with the outcome that actually occurred. This information is, of course, no more relevant than case information consistent with an alternative outcome. Association-based errors are unlikely to be debiased by incentives or by warning the decision maker to avoid the error. Instead, they can be corrected by cueing the decision maker to perform a debiasing behavior or to consider a neglected piece of information. For example, prompting decision makers to consider reasons why a different outcome might have occurred can reduce the hindsight bias (Arkes et al., 1988).

Psychophysical errors, a third type of decision bias (Arkes, 1991), result from nonlinear mapping of physical stimuli into psychological representations. The S-shaped value function and the decision weight function of Prospect Theory (Tversky & Kahneman, 1992) are both examples of psychophysical functions. Framing effects and the certainty effect result from the fact that equivalent information (for example, survival and mortality) is coded psychologically in different ways. Psychophysical errors are difficult to debias in the same way that visual illusions are difficult to eliminate; they are a function of how the cognitive system encodes information. Arkes (1991) suggests that psychophysical errors can be corrected by reframing the options, for example, by changing the reference point.

An understanding of the errors that can occur in medical decision making is important for two reasons: (1) Clinically, they identify areas where the quality of care can be improved and where decision supports are likely to be helpful. (2) From a basic science viewpoint, these errors illuminate the cognitive processes used in decision making. An accurate characterization of decision processes can, in turn, suggest debiasing techniques. Thus, at its best, research on decision biases can both advance the psychology of decision making and improve medical care.

References

Arkes, H.R. (1991). Costs and benefits of judgment errors: Implications for debiasing. *Psychological Bulletin, 110*, 486–498.

Arkes, H.R. & Blumer, C. (1985). The psychology of sunk cost. *Organizational Behavior and Human Decision Processes, 35*, 124–140.

Arkes, H.R., Faust, D., Guilmette, T.J., & Hart, K. (1988). Eliminating the hindsight bias. *Journal of Applied Psychology, 73*, 305–307.

Arkes, H.R. & Hammond, K.R. (Eds.). (1986). *Judgment and Decision Making: An Interdisciplinary Reader*. New York: Cambridge University Press.

Arkes, H.R., Wortmann, R.L., Saville, P.D., & Harkness, A.R. (1981). Hindsight bias among physicians weighing the likelihood of diagnoses. *Journal of Applied Psychology, 66*, 252–254.

Baron, J. & Hershey, J.C. (1988). Outcome bias in decision evaluation. *Journal of Personality and Social Psychology, 54*, 569–579.

Baron, J. & Ritov, I. (1994). Reference points and omission bias. *Organizational Behavior and Human Decision Processes, 59*, 475–498.

Bornstein, B.H., Emler, A.C., & Chapman, G.B. (1999). Is there a sunk cost effect in medical treatment decisions? *Social Science and Medicine, 49*, 215–222.

Brockner, J. (1992). The escalation of commitment to a failing course of action: Toward theoretical progress. *Academy of Management Review, 17*, 39–61.

Cairns, J.A. (1992). Health, wealth and time preference. *Project Appraisal, 7*, 31–40.

Caplan, R.A., Posner, K.L., & Cheney, F.W. (1991). Effect of outcome on physician judgments of appropriateness of care. *Journal of the American Medical Association, 265*, 1957–1960.

Chapman, G.B. (1996a). Expectations and preferences for sequences of health and money. *Organizational Behavior and Human Decision Processes, 67*, 59–75.

Chapman, G.B. (1996b). Temporal discounting and utility for health and money. *Journal of Experimental Psychology: Learning, Memory, and Cognition, 22*, 771–791.

Chapman, G.B. (1998). Sooner or later: The psychology of intertemporal choice. In D.L. Medin (Ed.), *The Psychology of Learning and Motivation*, Vol. 38, pp. 83–113. New York: Academic Press.

Chapman, G.B., Bornstein, B.H., & Emler, A.C. (1996). The sunk cost fallacy in medical management decisions. *Medical Decision Making, 16*, 452 [abstract].

Chapman, G.B. & Elstein, A.S. (1995). Valuing the future: Temporal discounting of health and money. *Medical Decision Making, 15*, 373–386.

Chapman, G.B. & Johnson, E.J. (1995). Preference reversals in monetary and life expectancy evaluations. *Organizational Behavior and Human Decision Processes, 62*, 300–317.

Chapman, G.B. & Malik, M.M. (1995). The attraction effect in prescribing decisions and consumer choice. *Medical Decision Making, 15,* 414 [abstract].

Christensen, C., Heckerling, P., Mackesy-Amiti, M.E., Bernstein, L.M., & Elstein, A.S. (1995). Pervasiveness of framing effects among physicians and medical students. *Journal of Behavioral Decision Making, 8,* 169–180.

Christensen-Szalanski, J.J.J. (1984). Discount functions and the measurement of patients' values: Women's decisions during childbirth. *Medical Decision Making, 4,* 47–58.

Christensen-Szalanski, J.J.J. & Northcraft, G.B. (1985). Patient compliance behavior: The effects of time on patients' values of treatment regimens. *Social Science and Medicine, 21,* 263–273.

Connolly, T., Ordonez, L.D., & Coughlan, R. (1997). Regret and responsibility in the evaluation of decision outcomes. *Organizational Behavior and Human Decision Processes, 70,* 73–85.

Dawson, N.V. & Arkes, H.R. (1987). Systematic errors in medical decision making: Judgment limitations. *Journal of General Internal Medicine, 2,* 183–187.

Dawson, N.V., Arkes, H.R., Siciliano, C., Blinkhorn, R., Lakshmanan, M., & Petrelli, M. (1988). Hindsight bias: An impediment to accurate probability estimation in clinicopathologic conferences. *Medical Decision Making, 8*(4), 259–264.

Dawson, N.V., Connors, A.F., Speroff, T., Kemka, A., Shaw, P., & Arkes, H.R. (1993). Hemodynamic assessment in managing the critically ill: Is physician confidence warranted? *Medical Decision Making, 13,* 258–266.

Dellarosa, D. & Bourne, L.E. (1984). Decisions and memory: Differential retrievability of consistent and contradictory evidence. *Journal of Verbal Learning and Verbal Behavior, 23,* 669–682.

Elstein, A.S., Holzman, G.B., Ravitch, M.M., Metheny, W.A., Holmes, M.M., Hoppe, R.B., Rothert, M.L., & Rovner, D.R. (1986). Comparison of physicians' decisions regarding estrogen replacement therapy for menopausal women and decisions derived from a decision analytic model. *American Journal of Medicine, 80*(2), 246–258.

Fischhoff, B. (1975). Hindsight $\neq$ foresight: The effect of outcome knowledge on judgment under uncertainty. *Journal of Experimental Pschology: Human Perception and Performance, 1,* 288–299.

Fishburn, P.C. & Rubenstein, A. (1982). Time preference. *International Economic Review, 23,* 677–694.

Gigerenzer, G. & Goldstein, D.G. (1996). Reasoning the fast and frugal way: Models of bounded rationality. *Psychological Review, 103*(4), 650–669.

Gilovich, T., Medvec, V.H., & Chen, S. (1995). Commission, omission, and dissonance reduction: Coping with regret in the "Monty Hall" problem. *Personality and Social Psychology Bulletin, 21,* 182–190.

Gilovich, T., Medvec, V.H., & Kahneman, D. (1998). Varieties of regret: A debate and partial resolution. *Psychological Review, 105,* 602–605.

Gold, M.R., Siegel, J.E., Russell, L.B., & Weinstein, M.C. (1996). *Cost Effectiveness in Health and Medicine.* New York: Oxford University Press.

Gruppen, L.D., Margolin, J., Wisdom, K., & Grum, C.M. (1994). Outcome bias and cognitive dissonance in evaluating treatment decisions. *Academic Medicine, 69,* S57–S59.

Huber, J., Payne, J.W., & Puto, C. (1982). Adding asymmetrically dominated alternatives: Violations of regularity and the similarity hypothesis. *Journal of Consumer Research, 9*, 90–98.

Josephs, R.A., Larrick, R.P., Steele, C.M., & Nisbett, R.E. (1992). Protecting the self from the negative consequences of risky decisions. *Journal of Personality and Social Psychology, 62*, 26–37.

Kahneman, D., Fredrickson, B.L., Schreibner, C.A., & Redelmeier, D.A. (1993). When more pain is preferred to less: Adding a better end. *Psychological Science, 4*, 401–405.

Kahneman, D. & Miller, D.T. (1986). Norm theory: Comparing reality to its alternatives. *Psychological Review, 93*, 136–153.

Kahneman, D., Slovic, P., & Tversky, A. (Eds.). (1982). *Judgment Under Uncertainty: Heuristics and Biases*. New York: Cambridge University Press.

Kahneman, D. & Tversky, A. (1979). Prospect theory: An analysis of decision under risk. *Econometrica, 47*, 263–291.

Kahneman, D. & Tversky, A. (1984). Choices, values, and frames. *American Psychologist, 39*, 341–350.

Keeler, E.G. & Cretin, S. (1983). Discounting of life-saving and other non-monetary effects. *Management Science, 29*, 300–306.

Kern, L. & Doherty, M.E. (1982). "Pseudodiagnosticity" in an idealized medical problem-solving environment. *Journal of Medical Education, 57*(2), 100–104.

Kirby, K.N. & Herrnstein, R.J. (1995). Preference reversals due to myopic discounting of delayed reward. *Psychological Science, 6*, 83–89.

Klayman, J. (1995). Varieties of confirmation bias. In J. Busemeyer, R. Hastie, and D.L. Medin (Eds.), *Decision Making from a Cognitive Perspective. The Psychology of Learning and Motivation*, Vol. 32, pp. 385–418. New York: Academic Press.

Klayman, J. & Brown, K. (1993). Debias the environment instead of the judge: An alternative approach to reducing error in diagnostic (and other) judgment. *Cognition, 49*, 97–122.

Kuhlberger, A. (1998). The influence of framing on risky decisions: A meta-analysis. *Organizational Behavior and Human Decision Processes, 75*, 23–55.

Landman, J. (1987). Regret and elation following action and inaction: Affective responses to positive versus negative outcomes. *Personality and Social Psychology Bulletin, 13*, 524–536.

Levin, I.P., Schneider, S.L., & Gaeth, G.J. (1998). All frames are not created equal: A topology and critical analysis of framing effects. *Organizational Behavior and Human Decision Processes, 76*, 149–188.

Loewenstein, G. & Prelec, D. (1992). Anomalies in intertemporal choice: Evidence and interpretation. *Quarterly Journal of Economics, 107*, 573–597.

Loewenstein, G. & Prelec, D. (1993). Preferences for sequences of outcomes. *Psychological Review, 100*, 91–108.

Loomes, G. & Sugden, R. (1982). Regret theory: An alternative theory of rational choice under uncertainty. *Economic Journal, 92*, 805–824.

MacKeigan, L.D., Larson, L.N., Draugalis, J.R., Bootman, J.L., & Bruns, L.R. (1993). Time preference for health gains versus health losses. *Pharmaco Economics, 3*, 374–386.

McNeil, B.J., Pauker, S., Sox, H., Jr., & Tversky, A. (1982). On the elicitation of preferences for alternative therapies. *New England Journal of Medicine, 306*, 1259–1262.

Mellers, B.A., Schwartz, A., & Weber, E.U. (1997). Do risk attitudes reflect in the eye of the beholder? In A.A.J. Marley (Ed.), *Choice, Decision, and Measurement: Essays in Honor of R. Duncan Luce.* Mahwah, NJ: Lawrence Erlbaum Associates, pp. 570–571.

O'Connor, A.M. (1989). Effects of framing and level of probability on patients' preferences for cancer chemotherapy. *Journal of Clinical Epidemiology, 42,* 119–126.

O'Connor, A.M., Boyd, N.F., Tritchler, D.L., Kriukov, Y., Sutherland, H., & Till, J.E. (1985). Eliciting preferences for alternative cancer drug treatments: The influence of framing, medium, and rater variables. *Medical Decision Making, 5,* 453–463.

O'Connor, A.M., Pennie, R.A., & Dales, R.E. (1996). Framing effects on expectations, decisions, and side effects experienced: The case of influenza immunization. *Journal of Clinical Epidemiology, 49,* 1271–1276.

Oskamp, S. (1962). The relationship of clinical experience and training methods to several criteria of clinical prediction. *Psychological Monographs, 76* (28, Whole No. 547).

Redelmeier, D.A. & Heller, D.M. (1993). Time preferences in medical decision making and cost-effectiveness analysis. *Medical Decision Making, 13,* 212–217.

Redelmeier, D.A. & Kahneman, D. (1996). Patients' memories of painful medical treatments: Real-time and retrospective evaluations of two minimally invasive procedures. *Pain, 66,* 3–8.

Redelmeier, D.A., Koehler, D.J., Liberman, V., & Tversky, A. (1995). Probability judgement in medicine: Discounting unspecified possibilities. *Medical Decision Making 15*(3):227–230.

Redelmeier, D.A., Rozin, P., & Kahneman, D. (1993). Understanding patients' decisions: Cognitive and emotional perspectives. *Journal of the American Medical Association, 270*(1), 72–76.

Redelmeier, D.A. & Shafir, E. (1995). Medical decision making in situations that offer multiple alternatives. *Journal of the American Medical Association, 273*(4), 302–305.

Ritov, I. (1996). Probability of regret: Anticipation of uncertainty resolution in choice. *Organizational Behavior and Human Decision Processes, 66,* 228–236.

Ritov, I. & Baron, J. (1990). Reluctance to vaccinate: Omission bias and ambiguity. *Journal of Behavioral Decision Making, 3*(4), 263–277.

Ritov, I. & Baron, J. (1995). Outcome knowledge, regret, and omission bias. *Organizational Behavior and Human Decision Processes, 64,* 119–127.

Schwartz, J.A. & Chapman, G.B., (1999). Are more options always better? The attraction effect in physicians' decisions about medications. *Medical Decision Making, 19,* 315–323.

Shafir, E., Simonson, I., & Tversky, A. (1997). Reason-based choice. In W.M. Goldstein & R.M. Hogarth (Eds.), *Research on Judgment and Decision Making: Currents, Connections, and Controversies.* New York: Cambridge University Press, pp. 69–94.

Singer, P.A., Choudhry, S., Armstrong, J., Meslin, E.M., & Lowry, F.H. (1995). Public opinion regarding end-of-life decisions: Influence of prognosis, practice and process. *Social Science and Medicine, 41*(11), 1517–1521.

Slovic, P. (1995). The construction of preferences. *American Psychologist, 50,* 364–371.

Slovic P. & Fischhoff, B. (1977). On the psychology of experimental surprises. *Journal of Experimental Psychology: Human Perception and Performance, 3*, 544–551.

Slovic, P. & Lichtenstein, S. (1983). Preference reversals: A broader perspective. *American Economic Review, 73*, 596–605.

Spranca, M., Minsk, E., & Baron, J. (1991). Omission and commission in judgment and choice. *Journal of Experimental Social Psychology, 27*, 76–105.

Stalmeier, P.F.M., Bezembinder, T.G.G., & Unic, I.J. (1996). Proportional heuristics in time tradeoff and conjoint measurement. *Medical Decision Making, 16*, 36–44.

Stalmeier, P. F.M, Wakker, P.P., & Bezembinder, T.G.G. (1997). Preference reversals: Violations of unidimensional procedure invariance. *Journal of Experimental Psychology: Human Perception and Performance, 23*(4) 1196–1205.

Treadwell, J.R. (1998). Tests of preferential independence in the QALY model. *Medical Decision Making, 18*, 418–428.

Tversky, A. & Kahneman, D. (1974). Judgment under uncertainty: Heuristics and biases. *Science, 185*, 1124–1131.

Tversky, A. & Kahneman, D. (1986). Rational choice and the framing of decisions. *Journal of Business, 59*, S251–S278.

Tversky, A. & Kahneman, D. (1992). Advances in prospect theory: Cumulative representations of uncertainty. *Journal of Risk and Uncertainty, 5*, 297–323.

Tversky, A. & Koehler, D.J. (1994). Support theory: A nonextensional representation of subjective probability. *Psychological Review, 101*, 547–567.

Tversky, A., Sattath, S., & Slovic, P. (1988). Contingent weighting in judgment and choice. *Psychological Review, 95*, 371–384.

Viscusi, W.K., Magat, W.A., & Huber, J. (1987). An investigation of the rationality of consumer valuations of multiple health risks. *RAND Journal of Economics, 18*, 465–479.

Weinstein, M.C. & Stason, W.B. (1977). Foundations of cost-effectiveness analysis for health and medical practices. *New England Journal of Medicine, 296*, 716–721.

Wolf, F.M., Gruppen, L.D., & Billi, J.E. (1985). Differential diagnosis and the competing-hypotheses heuristic. A practical approach to judgment under uncertainty and Bayesian probability. *Journal of the American Medical Association, 253*(19), 2858–2862.

Zeelenberg, M., Beattie, J., van der Plight, J., & de Vries, N.K. (1996). Consequences of regret aversion: Effects of expected feedback on risky decision making. *Organizational Behavior and Human Decision Processes, 65*, 148–158.

8 Physician Judgments of Uncertainty

Neal V. Dawson, MD

Introduction

The primary aims of this chapter are to describe three valuable methods of assessing the accuracy of physicians' judgments and to review examples of studies that have examined the accuracy of physicians' judgments about actual patients. The three methods for assessing accuracy are receiver operating characteristic (ROC) curves (with or without calibration curves), mean probability score ($\overline{PS}$) (with or without decompositions), and lens model analyses. The area under the ROC curve is currently a standard method for assessing the accuracy of diagnostic tests and prognostic models and has been used many times to assess the accuracy of physicians' judgments. The relative familiarity of ROC curve analysis among those doing health care research and the plethora of articles in the medical literature devoted to its use and interpretation have led me to devote more space in this chapter to the other two techniques. Although they are valuable methods of assessing accuracy, $\overline{PS}$ and lens model analysis are much less commonly seen in medical studies and are not widely known among health care researchers. For the section on studies of physician judgment, I have selected studies that

I would like to thank several colleagues who took the time to read an earlier version of this chapter and provide substantive feedback. This list includes Hal Arkes, Ph.D.; Ray Cooksey, Ph.D.; Jack Dowie, Ph.D.; Ken Hammond, Ph.D.; Amy Justice, M.D., Ph.D.; Theodore Speroff, Ph.D.; and J. Frank Yates, Ph.D. I would also like to thank an anonymous reviewer and Gretchen Chapman, Ph.D., for their thoughts on how to better organize and clarify my presentation. I, of course, must take credit for any remaining errors and any less than clear portions of the chapter.

Lastly, I would like to thank Charles Thomas for his programming and statistical contributions and Mignon Gray for her typing skill and cheerful acceptance of my many requests for "just a few more changes" to the manuscript.

(1) assessed physician (not medical student) judgmental accuracy, (2) involved judgments about actual patients (not paper-and-pencil cases), and (3) used ROC, $\overline{PS}$, or lens model analyses. Many valuable studies did not meet these criteria. Other studies were not used because they demonstrated results very similar to those that are included. Although the sample of included studies was not intended to be exhaustive, it does include cogent examples of published studies that met the selection constraints. Nearly all of the cited studies deal with binary outcomes (survival, death; disease present, absent) that are appropriate for analysis by ROC and PS. The study by Speroff et al. (1989) assessed a continuous outcome by lens model techniques. Methods for decomposing judgments about continuous outcomes using correlations have been described (Stewart, 1990; Stewart and Lusk, 1994), but I have been unable to find a medical example for judgments about actual patients.

In general, when describing formulas, I have used word definitions rather than mathematical symbols. For those who prefer the symbolism of math, they are included in the Glossary[1] along with the definitions of several technical terms used in this chapter.

Several chapters in this book highlight difficulties that physicians have in making medical judgments[2] and offer techniques or prescriptive methods that may enhance physician judgments in order to improve the decision-making process. A basic aspect of the usefulness of physicians' judgments is their judgmental accuracy. Understanding overall accuracy, its essential components, the sufficiency of judgment, and its relationship to maximal achievable accuracy are fundamental to understanding and improving physicians' judgments.

Making clinical judgments or predictions involves integrating information derived from one or more of our five primary senses and information from our memory systems. From these sources come multiple pieces of information (i.e., cues) that, by their very nature, are imperfectly related to the outcome being predicted (i.e., there are multiple fallible indicators) (Hammond, 1996b). Judgments may be influenced not only by perceptual and cognitive processes but also by issues related to presentation or measurement (e.g., categorical vs. dimensional data), to

---

[1] Word and phrases included in the Glossary are marked with an asterisk.
[2] In this chapter, the terms "judgments," "prediction," "estimates," and "forecasts" will be used interchangeably. The term "judges" will refer to physicians making judgments unless noted otherwise.

task characteristics (e.g., time pressure and available information), and to noncognitive factors (e.g., emotional and social influences).

The formal evaluation of the accuracy of judgments, sometimes called "accuracy analysis," involves the assessment of overall accuracy plus meaningful and distinct components of overall accuracy, often performed as mathematical decompositions. Some characteristics of accuracy analysis include: (1) it doesn't assume a specific model of judgments (i.e., it doesn't matter how the judgments/predictions are made), (2) it can be used for any current or future event (e.g., diagnosis or prognosis), and (3) the results may or may not map well onto our impressions of what makes a good judge. In this chapter, it will be shown that: (1) discrimination can be described as three related, but dramatically different, phenomena (separation by labeling, rank order, or probability value), (2) calibration involves the realistic use* of probability values), and (3) summary accuracy scores, like $\overline{PS}$, reflect aspects of both outcome group separation and realistic probability use.

One way of assessing the goodness of judgments is to determine how the forecasts of outcomes relate to the actual outcomes, i.e., determine their empirical accuracy or their external "correspondence." This is contrasted with assessment by "coherence," in which the goodness of judgments is assessed by the degree to which the judgment is consistent with an underlying theory or set of axioms (Hammond, 1996a; Hammond, 1996b; Yates, 1982).

One can compare the performance of different types of physician judges, e.g., best judge, a typical expert, or an average peer. Additional comparisons with "artificial judges" can sometimes be very informative (Yates, 1994). These include hypothetical judges that provide a constant judgment such as a uniform estimate (e.g., always .5), the historical base rate, or the current sample base rate for each and every "judgment." An artificial judge also could be a statistical or actuarial model with which physicians' judgments can be compared.

Baseline Assumptions

The following four assumptions should be kept in mind as we investigate aspects of accuracy analysis.

1. How you observe and measure a phenomenon influences what you see and the conclusions you may infer.

This has been shown clearly in disciplines as disparate as particle physics and survey research. Consistent with assumption 4 (see later), differences in results among methods of measuring accuracy may not imply "right" or "wrong," "better" or "worse." Apparent paradoxes may provide opportunities for new insights.

2. Performance cannot exceed the predictive information content of the available cues.

In this context, "information content" refers to the aggregate predictiveness of cues as determined by cue validity, reproducibility, strength,* and form*. As is the case with diagnostic tests, information content is reflected in the aggregate cue "test characteristics" and is influenced by spectrum* (i.e., the types of patients about whom judgments are made) and bias.

3. Observed maximally accurate prediction will rarely (if ever) equal perfect prediction.

The analogy between physician prediction and diagnostic tests can be continued by recalling the adage "there are no perfect tests." By selecting appropriate cutoffs and circumstances, we may observe either perfect sensitivity or perfect specificity but not both at the same time.

4. The goal(s) of prediction will define the requisite accuracy of prediction.

What is viewed as good enough or even optimal will be influenced by the underlying purpose for making the predictions. If the underlying goal is labeling or classification, discrimination should be optimized. If creating equivalent risk groups* is the ultimate purpose of prediction, calibration should be optimized.

Measures of Accuracy

The accuracy measures to be detailed relate to external correspondence, i.e., the relationship between predicted events or outcomes and actual events or outcomes. In assessing accuracy, one should consider three fundamental issues: base rate, discrimination, and calibration. From the diagnostic testing literature, we know that spectrum can vary with base rates and that test characteristics can vary with spectrum (Begg, 1987; Hlatky et al., 1984; Knottnerus, 1987; Ransohoff and Feinstein, 1978;

Weiner et al., 1979). These same issues apply to physician judgment tasks. In thinking about discrimination and calibration, it is helpful to consider discrimination as reflecting occurrence group* prediction and calibration as reflecting risk group* prediction. This should become more evident as the descriptions of discrimination and calibration unfold.

A familiar method for assessing the performance of many diagnostic tests and for probabilistic prognostic estimates (human or statistical) is the receiver operating characteristic (ROC) curve* (Centor, 1991; Hanley and McNeil, 1982, 1983; McNeil and Hanley, 1984). The area under the ROC curve provides information about a type of discrimination, more specifically, rank order discrimination. The ROC area represents the proportion of times (among all possible pairs of those with and without the outcome of interest) that the member of the outcome pair with the outcome of interest was given the higher probability estimate (or the higher likelihood rank). ROC area for a binary outcome (as represented by the C statistic) also has a straightforward relationship with rank correlation, that is, Somer's $Dyx = 2$ (C statistic $-.5$) (Lee et al., 1986). Somer's rank correlation reflects the proportion of the ROC area between .5 (no rank order discrimination) and 1.0 (perfect rank order discrimination) that is associated with the set of test results, estimates, or judgments of interest.

Another familiar assessment technique is the calibration curve* (e.g., Yates, 1990; Dawson, 1993). Calibration provides information about the degree to which the relationship between probability estimates and actual outcomes is realistic. The better the numerical match between predicted probability and observed proportion, the better the degree of calibration.

Other, less familiar, summary measures of external correspondence include $\overline{PS}$, also known as the "Brier score" (Brier, 1950). $\overline{PS}$ reflects a construct of overall accuracy. A probability score can be calculated for each prediction or forecast. $PS = $ (forecast $-$ outcome)$^2 = (f - d)^2$, where "forecast" (f) is the stated probability of the event or outcome and "outcome" (d) is an index such that it equals 1.0 when the outcome being predicted occurs and 0 otherwise. The average probability score across all stated probability estimates (N) of a given judge is the mean probability score or Brier score for the judge. $\overline{PS}$ is like a golf score in the lower scores mean better performance. Perfect prediction is represented when $\overline{PS} = 0$.

$\overline{PS}$ is a "proper" scoring rule (Yaniv, Yates, and Smith, 1991; Yates, 1982, 1990, 1994). Although properness is not necessary for a scoring rule to be used to assess external correspondence, it provides an incentive against "hedging"; for example, if judges were rewarded according to the value of their $\overline{PS}$ (lower values reaping higher rewards), it is in the judges' best interest to report their forecasts truthfully. Physicians may feel it is in the patients' best interest for them to report higher probabilities of disease than the physicians really believe (Wallsten, 1981). Although empirically unproven for physicians, the use of proper scoring rules could conceivably provide incentives against this form of "value induced bias" (Dawson and Arkes, 1987).

In addition, $\overline{PS}$ can be partitioned into parts that are interpretable and have important meaning. Various decompositions of $\overline{PS}$ have been devised, and several have been reviewed by Yates (Yaniv et al., 1991; Yates, 1982, 1988). For the Murphy decomposition, $\overline{PS}$ can be algebraically partitioned into three component parts. $\overline{PS}$ = outcome index variance − discrimination index + calibration index] = [Var(d)− DI +CI] = [(a prevalence-determined variance measure) − (a pure separation measure) + (a measure of realistic probability use)]. Formulae for Murphy's decomposition of the mean probability score are shown here (Yates, 1982, 1990, 1994) and are further defined in the Glossary. Redelmeier et al. (1991) have described a statistical method to compare two Brier scores. Statistical bootstrap methods can be used to compare components of decompositions between judges.

Mean Probability Score

$$\overline{PS} = \frac{\sum_{i=1}^{N}(f_i - d_i)^2}{N} \tag{1}$$

Murphy Decomposition

$$\overline{PS} = \overline{d}(1 - \overline{d}) \quad - \frac{\sum_{j=1}^{J} N_j(\overline{d}_j - \overline{d})^2}{N} \quad + \frac{\sum_{j=1}^{J} N_j(f_j - \overline{d}_j)^2}{N}$$

Mean probability score = [outcome index variance] − [discrimination index] + [calibration index]

$$\overline{PS} = \text{Var}(d) \quad - \quad \text{DI} \quad + \quad \text{CI}$$

Var(d) is a prevalence-dependent measure. It is prevalence ($\overline{d}$) multiplied times the complement of prevalence, i.e., $\overline{d}(1 - \overline{d})$. (This is similar to the binomial variance measure, $Np(1-p)$ or Npq). The discrimination index (DI) is a measure of pure separation by labeling or categorization. This designation reflects the fact that neither "rational"* nor "realistic" probability use is required to have good discrimination by this measure. The probability estimates serve only as labels for distinguishing instances in which the outcome of interest will or will not occur and thus reflects rational label use as opposed to rational probability use. (Note that for the purpose of "labeling," nonnumerical labels such as words or symbols also could be used.) As can be seen in the formula for DI, the numerical properties of probabilistic forecasts are not entailed in the DI as such. Rather, the conditional base rate (i.e., the observed outcome occurrence rate, $\bar{d}_j$) within a given forecast category (e.g., a decile of probability) is subtracted from the overall outcome occurrence rate, $\bar{d}_j$. Thus, $(\bar{d}_j - \bar{d})$ denotes the degree of "separation" of the conditional outcome occurrence rate in each forecast category from the sample prevalence rate.

If, for example, a physician designated the instances in which patients were predicted to survive as .1, .3, .5, .7, .9 (and all survived) and designated instances in which patients were predicted to die as 0, .2, .4, .6, .8, 1 (and all died), perfect discrimination by this measure will have been achieved since those who lived are labeled differently from those who died. When labeling is perfect, $DI = \text{Var}(d)$ and these two terms drop out of Murphy's decomposition, leaving only the calibration term. In the previous example, the $\overline{PS}$ will be greater than zero, i.e., will reflect nonperfect probability based prediction, since CI is greater than 0. CI requires realistic probability use; for example, an estimate of .2 should be associated with an observed proportion of .2. When perfect calibration exists across all estimates, $CI = 0$.

Two properties of Murphy's decomposition of the mean probability score are the following:

1. Perfect prediction occurs only with perfect "0,1" discrimination and calibration, i.e., when all nonoccurrences were predicted as "zero" and all occurrences were predicted as "one." When this occurs, $CI = 0$, $DI = \text{Var}(d)$, and thus, $\overline{PS} = 0$. The smallest (best) $\overline{PS}$ will occur under circumstances where the judge applies labels to predictions of outcomes that will occur that are different from the labels applied to nonoccurrences and uses probabilities realistically.
2. Even with perfect calibration (i.e., $CI = 0$), nonperfect 0,1 discrimination will lead to $DI < \text{Var}(d)$ and $\overline{PS} > 0$.

Although perfect discrimination is highly valued by both judges (e.g., physicians) and consumers (Yates et al., 1996) of predictions (e.g., patients), cues in medical settings (symptoms, signs, lab tests, radiological exams, etc.) rarely, if ever, allow perfect 0,1 prediction across all cases. This would require sensitivity and specificity to both be 100%. Since there are no perfect tests, some reliance on calibration will be necessary. This suggests that maximally, accurate prediction will rarely, if ever, be equivalent to perfect prediction.

A formal evaluation of components of calibration can be achieved by the covariance decomposition of $\overline{PS}$. Calibration here refers to "calibration-in-the-small," that is, calibration of multiple forecast categories along the "line of identity," the 45 degree line of predicted probabilities versus observed proportions of the outcome. Within each prediction category, e.g., each decile of probability, this can be seen to be the conditional base rate of each category. This is contrasted with "calibration-in-the-large," which represents the match between the overall base rate or prevalence and the average of the assigned probability values across all cases.

The covariance decomposition provides an alternative to Murphy's decomposition. In this decomposition, DI (the pure separation by labeling or categorization term) is both added to and subtracted from the right side of the equation and is thus algebraically eliminated (Yates, 1982). This leaves the following relationship:

$$\overline{PS} = [\text{outcome index variance} + \text{minimum forecast variance}$$
$$+ \text{excess forecast variance} + \text{calibration-in-the-large}$$
$$- 2(\text{forecast-outcome covariance})]$$
$$= [\text{Var}(d) + (\text{slope}^2)(\text{Var}(d)) + \text{scatter} + (\text{bias}^2)$$
$$- 2(\text{slope})(\text{Var}(d))]$$

"Outcome index variance" is the same prevalence-determined variance measure, $d(1 - d)$ as in the Murphy decomposition. "Minimum forecast variance" is the amount of variation among forecasts that is necessary to predict outcomes given the observed prevalence and slope. "Excess forecast variance" or "scatter" is variation in predictions beyond that necessary to predict outcomes and may be seen to represent "noisy" predictions. "Calibration-in-the-large" or "bias^2" represents the goodness of fit between the overall prevalence or base rate and the average of the assigned probability values across all cases. "Forecast-outcome covariance" reflects the degree to which predictions and outcomes covary. As such, it can be seen to be a type of discrimination-related measure. Forecast-outcome covariance is calculated from "slope" and Var(d). Slope is another type of separation measure and is the arithmetic difference between the mean forecast when the outcome occurred $\bar{f}_1$ and the mean forecast when the outcome did not occur $\bar{f}_0$, i.e., ($\bar{f}_1 - \bar{f}_0$).

For a set of perfect predictions, an evaluation using the covariance decomposition will lead to the following observations. The terms for excess forecast variance (i.e., scatter) and calibration-in-the-large (i.e., bias^2) will equal zero. This will leave outcome index variance + minimum forecast variance = 2(forecast $-$ outcome covariance) and $\overline{PS} = 0$.

Several aspects of the previously described accuracy measures (ROC, calibration, $\overline{PS}$, Murphy's decomposition, covariance decomposition) can be highlighted by examining similarities and differences that are outlined in Table 8.1. At the top of Table 8.1 are six hypothetical judges' (A through F) estimates of survival for 110 patients. Below the letter representing each judge are summarized the number of estimates in each forecast category (0.0 through 1.0) made for patients who lived ($n = 50$) and for those who died ($n = 60$). Just below the forecasts are descriptions of "unique labeling" (i.e., the degree to which those who lived were given labels that are unique from labels given those who died and vice versa). Next is a description of "calibration" (i.e., the degree to which probability values were used realistically within forecast categories). Below these descriptions are three different types of discrimination measures: separation by rank order (ROC), separation by categorization (DI), and separation by probability value (slope). Below the ROC area row is the overall accuracy score, $\overline{PS}$. Below this are shown the components of Murphy's decomposition of $\overline{PS}$ (Var(d), DI, CI), and portions of the covariance decomposition, (min Var(f), scatter, bias, slope). The covariance decomposition of $\overline{PS}$ includes Var(d), excludes DI, and further decomposes CI.

Comparisons with the $\overline{PS}$ of two artificial judges, one who always provides the sample base rate ($\overline{PS} = .248$) and one who uniformly guesses 50% ($\overline{PS} = .250$), also can be informative. Since the artificial judges' forecasts and sample prevalence do not vary, $\overline{PS}$ for each artificial judge is invariant. (If, for example, the survival rate had been 90/110 instead of 50/110, the $\overline{PS}$ of the base rate judge would have been .149; however, the $\overline{PS}$ of the uniform judge would be unchanged [$\overline{PS} = .250$]).

Each hypothetical judge's data set is accompanied by a figure (8.1 a–f), in which the judged probability of survival (horizontal axis) is

Table 8.1. *Illustrative Judgments by Six Hypothetical Judges*

Estimated Survival	A Lived	A Died	B Lived	B Died	C Lived	C Died	D Lived	D Died	E Lived	E Died	F Lived	F Died
0.0		10				10		6		20		60
.1	10	10						34	1	9		
.2	10	10			5	15	8		2	8		
.3	10	10							3	7		
.4	10	10		60					4	6		
.5	10	10			30	30	11	11				
.6			50						6	4		
.7					15	5	21	9	7	3		
.8									8	2		
.9									9	1		
1.0							10		10		50	
n = 110	50	60	50	60	50	60	50	60	50	60	50	60
Unique labeling	Perfect (100%)		Perfect (100%)		Poor (9%)		Fair (15%)		Good (27%)		Perfect (100%)	
Calibration	Awful		Very poor		Good		Outstanding		Perfect		Perfect	
ROC area	.5		1.0		.717		.817		.9		1.0	

PS	.350	.160	.206	.166	.127	0
Var(d)	.248	.248	.248	.248	.248	.248
DI	.248	.248	.043	.082	.121	.248
CI	.350	.160	.002	.000	0	0
MinVar(f)	0	.010	.005	.026	.059	.248
Scatter	.1	0	.023	.055	.063	0
Bias	.046	.036	.009	.004	.000	0
Slope	0	.2	.140	.326	.487	1.0

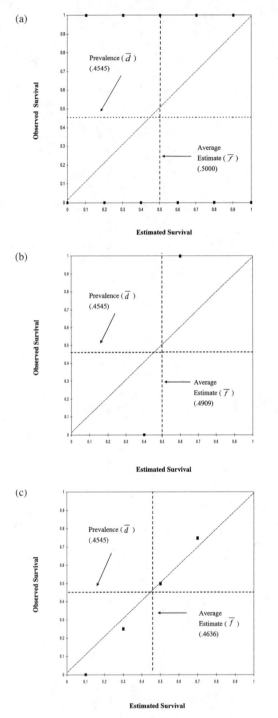

Figure 8.1. (Opposite page and above). Calibration plots (predicted vs. observed survival) for the data presented in Table 8.1. See text for details.

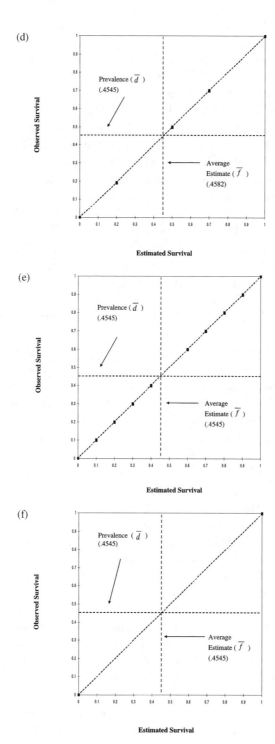

Figure 8.1. (*continued*)

plotted against the observed proportion of patients who actually survived (vertical axis). The intersection of the average forecast ($\bar{f}$) and prevalence ($\bar{d}$) also is demonstrated.

Judge A and Figure 8.1a demonstrate perfect "labeling" in that no forecast category was used for both patients who lived and for those who died. No rank order discrimination is demonstrated (ROC area = .5), but perfect separation by categorization is shown (DI = Var(d)). Rational probability use is not demonstrated in that there is no separation by probability value (slope = 0). Calibration is nearly nonexistent (only 0.0 is calibrated and .9 is somewhat calibrated). Calibration-in-the-small is awful (CI = .350) and is the sole contributor to $\overline{PS}$ = .350, which is worse than the performance of either of the artificial judges ($\overline{PS}$ base rate = .248 and $\overline{PS}$ uniform = .250). The match or goodness of fit of the average estimate with the overall prevalence is not bad ($\bar{f} - \bar{d}$ = bias = .046) but the estimates are noisy (scatter = .1)

Judge B and Figure 8.1b also demonstrate perfect labeling, as shown numerically by DI = Var(d), but also have perfect rank order discrimination (ROC = 1.0). Separation by probability value is relatively low (slope = .2). Similar to judge A, judge B demonstrates very poor calibration-in-the-small (CI = .160), which again is the sole contributor to $\overline{PS}$ = .160. The goodness of fit of the average of the assigned probability values with the overall prevalence is improved compared with judge A (bias = .036). Overall accuracy is clearly better for B than for A, both in terms of a much smaller $\overline{PS}$ and relative to the artificial judges ($\overline{PS}$ base rate = .248; $\overline{PS}$ uniform = .250). Forecast variance is limited to that needed to make the forecasts (min Var(f) = .010) and estimates are not noisy (scatter = 0).

Judges C, D, and E and Figures 8.1c–e have patterns of estimates that demonstrate both improving discrimination and calibration as we move from judge C to judge E. Poor labeling discrimination is reflected by judge C, with only 9% of observations being uniquely labeled (10 deaths) and improves through D and E. DI is much smaller than Var(d) (.043/.248 = 17%) for judge C and improves considerably for judge E(DI/Var(d) = 49%). Good rank order discrimination is shown by judge C (ROC = .717) and improves to excellent for judge E (ROC = .9). Separation by probability value (slope) also improves from C to E (slope = .140 and .487, respectively). Calibration is good for judge C, nearly perfect for D, and perfect for E. Numerically this is reflected in values of CI that are .002 in set C, zero to three decimal places for judge D (estimation category .2 is associated with an observed proportion of .19), and zero for judge E. Bias also improves from .009 to .004 to .000, respectively, for judges C, D, and E. Total forecast variance (min Var(f) + scatter) also increases from C to E, but an increasing proportion of the total is contributed by Min Var(f) (18%, 32%, and 48%, respectively), i.e., the portion of total forecast variance necessary to predict outcomes given the observed prevalence and slopes. Since Var(d) is constant, this reflects increasing slope (min Var(f) = (slope^2) (Var(d))). Overall accuracy, as summarized by $\overline{PS}$, also increases from judge C to judge E ($\overline{PS}$ = .206, .166, and .127, respectively). Perfect calibration (data set E) is always associated with less than perfect discrimination (Diamond, 1991), i.e., ROC < 1, DI < Var(d), and slope < 1, unless one has perfect 0,1 prediction.

Judge F represents perfect 0,1 prediction. It reflects perfect discrimination (DI = Var(d), ROC = 1.0, slope = 1.0) and perfect calibration (CI = 0, [Var(d) + min Var(f) = 2(slope)(Var(d))], bias = 0); thus PS = 0.

Three summary points can be gleaned from the discussion of Table 8.1. (1) Discrimination can be described as three related, but demonstratively different, phenomena: separation by labeling, rank ordering, and probability value. At its core, discrimination involves the prediction of occurrence groups. (2) Calibration involves the realistic use of probability values. At its core, calibration involves predicting risk groups. (3) Summary accuracy scores, like the $\overline{PS}$, reflect aspects of both outcome group separation and realistic probability use. Perfect calibration will not be accompanied by perfect discrimination (unless the discrimination involves perfect 0,1 prediction). The predictive information content of medical data will not support perfect 0,1 prediction across a spectrum of medical cases; thus some degree of concern about calibration will always be necessary.

Improvements on and extensions of Murphy's decomposition recently have been published. Yaniv and colleagues (1991) have provided methods to adjust DI for differences in base rates across judges (normalized discrimination index, NDI*). A second measure (adjusted normalized discrimination index, ANDI*) additionally adjusts for the number of judgment categories and the number of cases. Yates (1988) also has provided a method of extending the covariance decomposition to multiple events, e.g., for predictions among two specific diseases and all others rather than a single disease and its complement. Stewart (1990) has provided decompositions of predictive skill, i.e., the match between a judge's predictive accuracy relative to the accuracy of a reference prediction for a continuous outcome.

After the accuracy (external correspondence) of a set of predictions has been determined), a potential advantage of the use of decompositions is the ability to examine the effects of aspects of accuracy that are and are not under the potential control of the judge (Stewart and Lusk, 1994; Yates, 1994). Through various types of feedback and/or training, future judgmental accuracy may be improved.

Outcome index variance ($\bar{d}(1 - \bar{d})$) is determined by prevalence and is, therefore, not under the judge's control. Although cue access and cue quality are not generally under the control of the judge, cue selection and appropriate cue use (to rule in and rule out specific instances as part of discrimination) are under the judge's control. Aspects of calibration also may be under the judge's control. Excess forecast variance or scatter is potentially under the judge's control. The value of the term is increased by the use of invalid cues and by the inconsistent use of valid cues. Calibration-in-the-large may be improved by an awareness of the appropriate prevalence, by cue access and selection, and by the judge's not hedging in one direction or the other. Forecast–outcome covariance can be enhanced by appropriately recalling a typical judgment in which an outcome did or did not occur (conditional matching recall) (Yates, 1994) and by appropriately "regressive" cue use, i.e., not placing more emphasis on a very abnormal value than it deserves.

By using decompositions in the evaluation of predictive performance, one can determine the effects of prevalence, discrimination, and calibration on accuracy. In studying forecasting processes, one can construct reasonable hypotheses about variation in the components of predictions and potentially design experiments or observational studies to evaluate the effects of variation in the underlying factors.

Methodological Issues

Much of what we know empirically about human judgmental accuracy evaluated by decompositions in nonmedical settings comes from many classroom experiments and from a smaller number of prospective observational studies. A basic component of these investigations is that the same set of subjects have been evaluated by different judges.

In most naturalistic settings in medicine, physicians often see and make judgments about similar types of patients but rarely see exactly the same set of patients as other physicians. Because the subjects of the judgment task are not identical, several methodological challenges need to be addressed that are not pertinent when the same patients are seen by each physician. The challenges include issues related to case selection and patients' baseline susceptibility to the target outcome being predicted. Referral filters and other selection pressures may lead to shifts in the distributions of patient characteristics such that a given type of physician may tend to see, for example, somewhat older or more severely ill patients. The distributional shift in characteristics may be associated with a larger (or smaller) proportion of a given physician's patients being more susceptible to the outcome of interest at baseline. Such patients also may have other characteristics (e.g., primary disease or comorbidity) that increase or decrease their baseline susceptibility. ·

To compare judgmental accuracy across physician groups (e.g., by specialty) or between individual physicians in this setting, one must ensure comparability among sets of patients. Although comparing identical sets of patients is usually impossible in day-to-day clinical practice, the key goal is to have sufficiently comparable patient groups so that a fair comparison will result. It is possible that the only important difference between two groups of similar but nonidentical patients about whom judgment data have been collected is the base rate of the target outcome. If this is the case, both the Murphy and covariance decompositions of the $\overline{PS}$ permit controlling for differing base rates.

The analytic methods that will be proposed to facilitate fair comparisons will be quite familiar to clinical epidemiologists and health services researchers, but many of these methods have not been used in much of the research done on judgment. A major challenge in observational medical studies is selection bias, which can affect the distribution of characteristics among physicians' patients. Although not new, methods to adjust for selection bias directly and explicitly have only recently been applied to research in medical areas.

In larger data sets, selection bias can be addressed by the use of the propensity score* methodology (Rosenbaum, 1991; Rosenbaum and Rubin 1983, 1984; Rubin, 1997). The propensity score methodology has been adapted recently to other medical problems (Connors et al., 1996). Use of the propensity score methodology will provide sets of patients with comparable baseline characteristics that influence patients' tendency to be seen by different types of physicians. Remaining (independent) characteristics that influence the outcome can be addressed by matching, stratification, or multivariable adjustment. Which specific techniques will be desirable will depend on factors such as sample size and the number of remaining independent characteristics that need to be addressed. Some of these methodological challenges are being addressed currently (Cooksey, 1996; Dawson et al., 1998), while the remainder will provide challenging research topics for the foreseeable future.

Examples of Studies of Physician Accuracy

In this and the following sections, we will review examples of published studies of physicians' judgments in naturalistic settings. Increasingly over the past 20 years, common physician judgment tasks performed during the actual care of patients have been examined to determine physician accuracy. As seen in Table 8.2, the tasks may be conveniently grouped as those involving diagnosis and those involving prognosis. Accuracy in this group of published studies has been evaluated by ROC area and calibration curves.

In two common outpatient tasks, the evaluation of patients with sore throats and coughs, experienced physicians have demonstrated a surprising amount of difficulty in accurately predicting low-prevalence events such as streptococcal pharyngitis ("strep throat") among patients with sore throats (Poses et al., 1985) and outpatient pneumonia among patients with cough (Christensen-Szalanski and Bushyhead, 1981; Dawson and Speroff, 1989). ROC areas have been modest, and overestimation of prevalence has been prominent. Performance in estimating the likelihood of bacteremia among hospitalized patients (Poses and Anthony, 1991) by house staff showed similarly modest discrimination and prominent overestimation. House staff evaluation of patients with chest pain in an Emergency Department (Tierney et al., 1986) demonstrated much better performance, with very good discrimination (ROC area = .87) and small to moderate overestimation.

Physician prediction of in-hospital mortality for adult intensive care unit (ICU) and non-ICU patients has been very good to excellent for house staff and ICU fellows (Detsky et al., 1981; Kruse et al., 1988; Poses et al., 1989), as well as for more senior physicians (Marks et al., 1991; McClish and Powell, 1989; Poses et al., 1989). Physicians generally underestimated survival (i.e., overestimated mortality), but this was less prominent than for the previously discussed diagnostic predictions of strep throat, pneumonia, and bacteremia.

Estimating the longer-term prognosis (beyond hospitalization) has proven somewhat more difficult and often varies by disease. Physicians (mostly attending physicians) in the SUPPORT study (Knaus et al., 1995)

Table 8.2. *Examples of Studies of Physicians' Judgments*

Task	Prevalence	ROC Area	Description of Calibration
Diagnosis			
Strep throat			
Poses et al., 1985 (attendings)	5%	.67	Large overestimation[c]
Outpatient pneumonia			
Christensen-Szalanski, and			
Bushyhead, 1981 (attendings)	3%	[a]	Large overestimation
Dawson and Speroff, 1989			
(house staff and attendings)	10%	.73	Large overestimation
Bacteremia			
Poses and Anthony, 1991 (house staff)	12%	.69	Large overestimation
Myocardial infarction			
Tierney et al., 1986 (house staff)	12%	.87	Estimates ≤30%: small underestimation[d]
			Estimates >30%: moderate overestimation
Prognosis: Survival – Adults			
Hospital: Detsky et al., 1981 (house staff)	91%	.83[b]	Moderate underestimation
ICU: Kruse et al., 1988 (house staff and			
fellows	60%	.89	Small over- and underestimation[e]
Poses et al., 1989 (ICU attendings)	77%	.86	Small underestimation
(primary care)	77%	.84	Over- and underestimation
(residents)	77%	.83	Moderate underestimation

(*Continued*)

Table 8.2. (Continued)

Task	Prevalence	ROC Area	Description of Calibration
McClish and Powell, 1989 (attendings)	75%	.89	Underestimation
Marks et al., 1991 (senior registrars)	54%	.82	Moderate underestimation
SUPPORT: Knaus et al. 1995, 9 diseases (6 month)	52%	.78	Small underestimation
Cancer: Dawson et al., 1998 (2 month) (generalists)	56%	.81	Small underestimation
(oncologist)	52%	.76	Small overestimation
Congestive heart failure: Poses et al., 1997 (90 days) (trainees, ED physicians)	81%	.66	Moderate underestimation
(1 year) (trainees, ED physicians)	64%	.63	Small–moderate underestimation
Coronary artery disease: Kong et al., 1989 (3 year) (cardiologists)	a	.76	Underestimation
Survival–Neonatal ICU: Stevens et al., 1994 (attendings)	96%	.85	Underestimation

[a] Not provided in article.

[b] Calculated from data provided in the published paper.

[c] Overestimation: the tendency for estimated probabilities to be numerically higher than the associated observed proportion of outcomes.

[d] Underestimation: the tendency for estimated probabilities to be numerically lower than the associated observed proportion of outcomes.

[e] Over- and underestimation: refers to different portions of the calibration plots that are either above or below the 45 degree line or line of identity.

had good discrimination for 6-month prognosis of the entire cohort of seriously ill hospitalized adult patients who had one of nine illnesses (ROC area = .78) but had less good discrimination (ROC = .70) in the subgroup with chronic illnesses (chronic obstructive pulmonary disease, congestive heart failure, and cirrhosis). These physicians demonstrated only a small amount of underestimation of survival. A recent report from this study (Dawson et al., 1998) found better discrimination by nonspecialists in predictions of 2-month survival and significantly different patterns of calibration. Predicting survival at 90 days and 1 year for patients with congestive heart failure has been shown to be particularly difficult (Poses et al., 1997). Discrimination is only fair (ROC = .66 and .63), and small to moderate underestimation is again demonstrated. Predictions by cardiologists (Kong et al., 1989) of 3-year survival of patients with coronary artery disease have shown good discrimination (ROC = .76) and general underestimation of survival. Prognostic estimates of survival of seriously ill neonates have been shown to have accuracy similar to that for adults in ICUs. Stevens et al. (1994) found excellent discrimination (ROC = .85) and a general tendency to underestimate survival.

Examples of Decomposition Studies of Physician Accuracy

Although the overall accuracy measure, $\overline{PS}$, is seen in medically related articles (e.g., McClish and Powell, 1989; Poses et al., 1989), decompositions are currently uncommon. Two recent examples of decompositions include outpatient pneumonia diagnosis (Yates, 1994) and survival estimates for seriously ill hospitalized adults (Arkes et al., 1995). Yates (1994) has provided both Murphy and covariance decompositions for pneumonia diagnosis (from Tape et al., 1991) and Murphy decomposition of survival estimates for ICU patients (from McClish and Powell, 1989). The reanalyses are displayed in the first four columns of Table 8.3.

The first three columns of Table 8.3 summarize measures of accuracy of physicians' diagnoses of pneumonia in outpatients from three teaching hospitals' Emergency Departments (Tape et al., 1991). In the second row, we can see that the prevalence of pneumonia varies markedly among the sites. These differences may or may not influence the meaningfulness or fairness of comparative accuracy analyses. Several factors can lead to variations across sites or samples. These factors may

Table 8.3. *Examples of $\overline{PS}$ and Decompositional Analyses of Physicians' Judgments*

	Pneumonia: Outpatients			Prognosis: Survival	
	Illinois[a]	Virginia[a]	Nebraska[a]	ICU[a]	Support (2 month)[b]
$N =$	1105	140	119	523	692
Prevalence	.114	.214	.319	.75	.847
ROC area	c	c	c	.89	.74[e]
Calibration	Moderate overestimation	Moderate overestimation	Small over- and underestimation	Moderate underestimation	Small underestimation
$\overline{PS}$	.1231	.1245	.0986	.1240	.134
Var(d)	.1010	.1684	.2173	.1875	.1296
DI	.0214	.0914	.1370	.0845	.0186[e]
(NDI)	(.2119)	(.5431)	(.6303)	(.4507[d])	(.1435)[e]
(ANDI)	(.2053)	(.5117)	(.6001)	c	c
CI	.0434	.0476	.0183	.0210	.0237[e]
minVar(f)[d]	.0112	.0294	.0423	c	.0057
Scatter	.0600	.0464	.0293	c	.039
Bias	.135	.146	.036	c	-.121
Slope	.333	.418	.441	c	.209
$\overline{PS}$ base rate	.1010	.1684	.2173	.1875	.1296
$\overline{PS}$ uniform	.2500	.2500	.2500	.2500	.2500

[a] Adapted from Yates, 1994.
[b] Adapted from Arkes et al., 1995.
[c] Not provided in the article.
[d] Calculated from data provided in the article.
[e] Calculated from original data not found in the article.

232

affect clinical predictions in the same way that they affect medical tests (Dawson, 1993) and involve the concepts of spectrum and bias (Ransohoff and Feinstein, 1978; Begg, 1987). "Spectrum" refers to the types of patients about whom predictive judgments are made and is determined by the sample selection process. In the Tape et al. (1991) study, physicians decided which patients needed chest radiographs. Readings of the radiographs were then used as the gold standard for pneumonia diagnosis. Unless physicians have 100% sensitivity for ordering chest radiographs for persons with outpatient pneumonia, some degree of "verification bias" will occur (Begg, 1987). Verification bias (also called "workup bias") leads to inflated estimates of test (or judgmental) sensitivity and has a variable effect on specificity.

Even with equal prevalence, spectrum differences could involve varying proportions of types of pneumonia (e.g., typical vs. atypical pneumonia), which may, in turn, influence judgmental accuracy. Judgmental accuracy could be influenced by the chronicity and severity of symptoms and signs, by the extent and location of pneumonia, and by the type and degree of comorbid illnesses. For example, in the Tape et al. study, Nebraska patients were older, and significantly higher proportions of these patients had chronic obstructive pulmonary disease and respiratory rates greater than 25 beats per minute. Tape and colleagues (1991) appropriately attempted to account for possible differences in physicians' selection of patients for chest radiography across the three sites. Their analytic efforts were necessarily limited, however, to those patients for whom physicians had ordered radiographs.

Other investigators have found that physicians' judgmental sensitivity for detecting patients who have pneumonic infiltrates on their chest radiographs may be as low as 30% to 67% (Bushyhead and Christensen. Szalanski, 1981; Dawson et al., 1986). When physicians' ordering patterns for the gold standard test are less than 100% sensitive, verification bias must be considered as potentially influencing physician accuracy measures. A method to alleviate verification bias involves performing the gold standard test on all patients who meet study entry criteria (regardless of physician ordering patterns) (Ransohoff and Feinstein, 1978). Alternatively, the effect of verification bias can be estimated by performing the gold standard test on a sufficiently large random subsample of study patients who did not have the test performed by physicians' orders (Begg, 1987).

For the purpose of discussing the listed accuracy measures, we will assume, at least for now, that the only important differences among the sites are the prevalence differences. In the fourth row of Table 8.3, we see that Nebraska physicians had the best calibration: mild over- and underestimation by description, the lowest CI, and the smallest bias. The Nebraska physicians' discrimination was best: highest DI, NDI (adjusts for prevalence), ANDI (additional adjustments for number of cases and number of judgment categories), and slope. Their judgments also were least noisy, i.e., they had the least scatter. Given the superiority of the Nebraska physicians' components of $\overline{PS}$, it is not surprising that they also were most accurate overall. They had the lowest $\overline{PS}$ and far exceeded the performance of the sample base rate and uniform judges. Although the Illinois physicians performed much better than the uniform judge, they did not have a lower $\overline{PS}$ than the sample base rate judge.

A possible explanation for the observed superiority of the Nebraska physicians' judgments is the predominance of board-certified physicians among Nebraska physicians (62%) compared with Virginia (30%) and Illinois (11%). We will return to the presumption of equality of judgment tasks in the following section discussing lens model analysis. Given the study structure, other biases such as test review bias, incorporation bias, and diagnostic review bias (Dawson, 1993) seem to be unlikely explanations of judgmental accuracy differences. The effect of dropout rates (Nebraska 21%, Virginia 2%, Illinois 1%) on performance is less apparent.

Two examples of decompositions of the accuracy of survival estimates are provided in the last two columns of Table 8.3. In the fourth column, physicians' accuracy of the likelihood of ICU patients' survival to hospital discharge is shown. The overall survival rate to discharge was 75%. Physicians' rank order discrimination (ROC area) was .89, which represents 78% of the area between .5 and 1.0. Labeling discrimination (DI = .0845) represents 45% of the theoretical maximum (DI/Var(d) = NDI = .4507). Calibration is described as moderate underestimation of survival and is associated with a CI of .0210. Overall accuracy, denoted by the $\overline{PS}$ of .1240, is better than that obtained by the two artificial judges' performance at the bottom of the fourth column.

The accuracy of estimates of 2-month survival (from study entry into SUPPORT) for seriously ill adults is shown in the last column (Arkes et al., 1995). These estimates are for the subset of SUPPORT patients who were able to provide prognostic estimates for themselves at study entry (and were thus less severely ill than SUPPORT patients as a whole). Nearly 85% of these less severely ill patients lived for 2 months. Physicians' rank order discrimination was less than that seen for the ICU

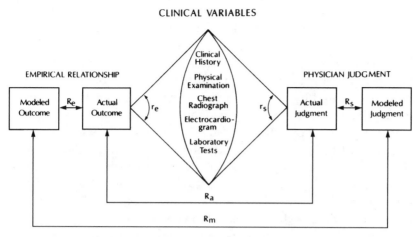

Figure 8.2. Lens model analysis describes how clinical data are related to both physicians' judgments and the outcome of interest. The following relationships can be formally evaluated: r_e (cue validity), r_s (cue utilization), R_a (achievement), R_e (environmental predictability), R_s (consistency), and R_m (matching). See text for details.

patients (ROC = .74, which represents 48% of the area between .5 and 1.0). Labeling discrimination (DI = .0186) represents 14% of the theoretically maximal value (NDI = .1435). Discrimination using realistic probability values also is limited (slope = .209). Descriptively, calibration demonstrated only small underestimation of survival at 2 months and was associated with a CI of .0237 and a bias of −.121. Scatter, as a percentage of total forecast variance, was relatively large at 83% (.039/.0447), indicating noisy estimates. Although $\overline{PS}$ was only .01 larger than that in the ICU prognosis study (fourth column), physicians' overall performance was slightly worse than that of the base rate judge ($\overline{PS}$ base rate = .1296).

Lens Model Analysis

Additional aspects of judgments can be evaluated by employing lens model analysis (Cooksey, 1996; Hammond, 1996; Wigton, 1988). As shown in Figure 8.2, lens model analysis provides a method for formally comparing the correlations among available clinical data (cues), the importance of the cues to judgments, and the "inherent" (empirical) predictive capabilities of the available cues. In Figure 8.2, "r_e" represents how the cues correlate with the actual outcome (cue validity), r_s

represents the relationship between the cues and physician judgments (cue utilization), and R_a describes how well physicians' predictions correlate with the actual outcome (achievement). After statistical regression models are created to represent cue relationship with both the judgment and the outcome, R_e is used to describe how well the outcome is captured by its model (environmental predictability) and R_s to describe how well physician judgment has been modeled (consistency). The model of judgment can then be compared with the model of outcome (R_m = matching). For lens model analyses, statistical bootstrapping can be used to build distributions that can be used to compare cue weights within a judge's policy or to compare respective cue weights across judges. Sampling distributions also can be built so that statements about correlations in the lens model can be made (Cooksey, 1996).

Typically, lens model analyses have been performed in circumstances where each judge in the study assesses the same series of subjects. This approach allows an understanding of cue use and overall performance at an individual judge level and often is referred to as the "ideographic" approach (Cooksey, 1996). As previously discussed, the study of physicians' judgments in day-to-day practice often requires the identification of sufficiently similar, but not identical, patients who have been evaluated by the sample of physicians. In this approach, physicians are treated as replicates of each other, and averaging is used to gain more reliable estimates of judgment performance. This latter approach is sometimes called "aggregated" or "nomothetic" (Cooksey, 1996). The two lens model examples to be discussed are of the aggregated type. The study by Tape et al. (1991) addresses judgments about a binary outcome (presence of pneumonia), while Speroff et al. (1989) studied a continuous outcome (hemodynamic status, i.e., measures of heart and lung functioning).

Numerous formulations of the lens model and multiple analytic approaches (including one for logistic regression) have been compiled and evaluated recently by Cooksey (1996). Decisions about which specific techniques to employ should be tempered by considering the goals of the analysis. For example, studies designed to provide cue-level feedback to individual physicians (ideographic approach) will have different needs than studies designed to examine specialty-level differences in judgment (nomothetic approach).

Lens model analyses and related analyses are valuable for exploring reasons why physicians' judgments may be inaccurate. As demonstrated in the two studies to be discussed, this may be because the events physicians are trying to predict may be relatively unpredictable. Alternatively, the events may be quite predictable but physicians may be using invalid cues or may give valid cues improper weights.

Examples of Medical Lens Models

Tape and colleagues (1991) used lens model analysis to capture physicians' clinical policies for diagnosing pneumonia at three teaching hospitals. Although physicians were more accurate at the Nebraska site (see Table 8.3), these investigators found that pneumonia was more easily predictable in Nebraska (environmental predictability, $R_e = .64$) than it was in Illinois ($R_e = .39$) and that differences in achievement score (how well physicians' predictions related to actual pneumonia) paralleled the differences in environmental predictability. Thus, although Illinois physicians were least accurate, they had the most difficult prediction task.

After several earlier studies had found that physicians had difficulty accurately predicting hemodynamic status (cardiac index and pulmonary capillary wedge pressure) in critically ill ICU patients, Speroff et al. (1989) evaluated this prediction task by 123 physicians in 440 patients using lens model analysis. These investigators found that the available clinical data were better able to predict hemodynamic status ($R_e = .67$) than were physicians' judgments ($R_a = .42$). Physicians' judgments were mainly represented by history (Hx) and physical examination (PE) data (93% of the explained variance of the physician judgment model came from the Hx and PE data, and only 7% came from chest radiograph (CXR), electrocardiograph (ECG), and laboratory (lab) data). In the model of the empirical relationship, Hx and PE data contributed to explaining 70% of the variation in hemodynamic status, and subsequent testing contributed 30%. Physicians apparently did not use some valuable lab data (e.g., hematocrit) and overweighted some important Hx and PE data (e.g., the subjective impression of the presence of congestive heart failure).

Examples of Potential Modifiers of Physician Accuracy

Elsewhere in this book, the reader will find examples of other phenomena that can affect physicians' judgments. For example, in Chapter

7, the effects of heuristics and bias on judgments were discussed. In subsequent chapters, the decision making of medical teams (Chapter 10) and ways of improving medical decision making (Chapter 15) are discussed. In this section, we will examine some examples of how experience, expertise, feedback, confidence, and combining predictions may influence the accuracy of physicians' judgments.

Experience and Expertise

Experience in medicine could be represented by many potential characteristics, including age, training level, faculty status, the number of years in practice (or since graduation from medical school), or prior experience with a specific phenomenon such as the number of dying patients for whom physicians have provided care. The experience of caring for large numbers of dying patients is not limited to physicians, however. In three recent studies, nurses were found to have prognostic judgments for ICU patients that were similar to those of physicians. Kruse and colleagues (1988) found that the rank order discriminations of 18 interns, 22 residents, and 17 ICU fellows were not significantly different from one another but that ICU fellows' ROC curve areas (ROC = .89) were significantly different from that of 33 nurses (ROC = .84, $p < .01$). Marks et al. (1991) found physicians' (senior registrars) and nurses' discrimination to be equivalent (ROC = .82 and .80, respectively). In a neonatal ICU, Stevens and coworkers (1994) found a trend in rank order discrimination that favored nurses' discrimination (18 attending physicians' ROC = .85; > 100 primary nurses' ROC = .93, $p = .069$).

Poses et al. (1989) found no significant differences in rank order discrimination of survival of ICU patients by house staff and attending staff (house staffs' ROC = .825, primary care attendings' ROC = .839, critical care attendings' ROC = .856). Analysis of Brier scores demonstrated differences by experience and by expertise (house staffs' $\overline{PS}$ = .126, critical care attendings' $\overline{PS}$ = .119, primary care attendings' $\overline{PS}$ = .109; all p values < .01). "Expertise" here denotes physician specialty, i.e., critical care versus other. Dawson and coworkers (unpublished data) examined the relationship between several physician characteristics (age, training level, faculty status, experience with dying patients during the prior year, number of predictions made) and accuracy of survival estimates (Brier scores) for seriously ill hospitalized adult (SUPPORT) patients who entered the study during the observational phase of the study (first 2 years). They found that among the physician characteristics assessed, only the degree of experience with dying patients in the prior year was significantly associated with overall accuracy of survival estimates ($p = .0003$).

The assessment of hemodynamic status (estimation of cardiac output and pulmonary capillary wedge pressure) is common to many diagnostic evaluations among hospitalized patients. Dawson and colleagues (1993) found no differences in accuracy among physicians (interns, residents, and ICU fellows) who assessed the hemodynamic status of ICU patients. Berwick and Thibodeau (1983) looked at the effect of training level of pediatric trainees who estimated the likelihood of pneumonia and strep throats for pediatric patients in an Emergency Department. They found that trainees in the higher levels of training were better calibrated and had higher ROC areas than more junior trainees. They found no consistent patterns between accuracy and trainee level in predicting streptococcal pharyngitis.

From these examples, the following hypotheses seem to be supported. (1) The level of general experience of physicians (e.g., training level) does not seem to have a strong effect on the accuracy of physicians' judgments about prognosis. (2) The degree of specific experience (e.g., prior experience with dying patients) may be a more important consideration. In fact, experienced nonphysicians may do as well as physicians in some prognostic tasks. (3) For diagnosis, the general level of experience may play an important role in judgmental accuracy, but the effect may be disease or problem dependent (pneumonia vs. streptococcal pharyngitis and hemodynamic status).

Feedback

Valid feedback may be a way in which more experience can lead to more accurate judgments. In day-to-day clinical care, however, ethical, cost, or other pragmatic considerations may lead to test ordering patterns that contribute to inadequate feedback about the presence of disease. Imperfect test ordering patterns and incomplete feedback have been suggested to contribute to physicians' low sensitivity in diagnosing pneumonia in outpatients (Bushyhead and Christensen-Szalanski, 1981). Feedback about cue validity and disease prevalence has been shown to improve physician performance in predicting streptococcal pharyngitis (Poses et al., 1995). When multiple cues have only a probabilistic relationship with the predicted state or event, even veridical outcome feedback (i.e., learning the true diagnosis) may not lead to more accurate judgments, however (Brehmer, 1980).

Confidence

Although accuracy may or may not increase with experience, confidence often does. Einhorn and Hogarth (1978) have suggested that confidence is directly proportional to the prior number of judgments made in a given domain, regardless of the correctness of the judgments. Frequently in the psychology literature the word "confidence" refers directly to a subjective probability estimate. In the following discussion, "confidence" denotes a second-order probability that represents the ambiguity or perceived imprecision of a physician's point estimate of a subjective probability (Curley et al., 1989). Dawson et al. (1993) found that confidence in estimates of hemodynamic status increased significantly in trainees in postgraduate years 1 through 5. The accuracy of estimates, however, was unrelated to levels of confidence. This finding is typical of many studies of confidence and accuracy.

If confidence is known to be related to accuracy for a given type of prediction, however, this is very useful knowledge. It implies that the judges have some degree of insight into the reasons for variability of probability estimates. Confidence also may be related to behaviors such that high levels of confidence in either high or low probability estimates may lead to action based on those estimates, and lack of confidence may lead to gathering additional information or may provide an appropriate opportunity to use validated statistical or actuarial predictive models.

In Phase I of the SUPPORT study, Connors and coworkers (1992) found that physicians' prognostic accuracy varied directly with confidence. Brier scores were consistently and significantly lower (indicating greater accuracy) when confidence in the estimates was high. McNeil and colleagues (1998) studied the judgments of psychiatrists who prospectively estimated the likelihood of aggressive behavior of recently admitted psychiatric patients, as well as their confidence in their estimates. When the psychiatrists had high confidence in their violence estimates, their rank order discrimination for acts of violence was outstanding (ROC = .97). However, when their confidence in their estimates of violence was low, their assessments were uninformative (ROC = .52).

These examples of studies of physician confidence in probabilistic forecasts (prognosis for survival or for exhibiting aggressive behavior) suggest that knowing the explicit relationship between confidence and accuracy is important. Such knowledge may help differentiate instances that are, in essence, simply bravado from instances that contribute important insights.

Combining Predictions

Combining estimates may enhance accuracy when estimates are valid (i.e., unbiased) but noisy or when each potential source contains independent predictive information. Poses et al. (1990) demonstrated that averaging the prognostic estimates of resident physicians and critical care fellows produced estimates very comparable in accuracy to those of experienced ICU attending physicians. When SUPPORT physicians' estimates (ROC = .78) were combined statistically with those of the SUPPORT model (ROC = .78), rank order discrimination was significantly enhanced (ROC = .82) (Knaus et al., 1995). When Stevens and coworkers (1994) combined physicians' estimates of neonatal survival (ROC = .85) with a validated model's estimates (ROC = .94), both were statistically significant, independent predictors of survival. When they added nurses' estimates (ROC = .93) to the model, the nurses' estimates did not add significantly to the prediction of survival ($p = .09$). McClish and Powell (1989) combined physicians' survival estimates for ICU patients (ROC = .89) with those from the APACHE II model (ROC = .83). The combined model had significantly better discrimination (ROC = .90) than the APACHE estimates alone and significantly better calibration than the physician estimates alone. Kong et al. (1989) found that a previously validated model added significantly to physicians' accuracy in predicting survival of patients with coronary disease, but physicians' predictions did not add to the model's accuracy.

The results of these example studies seem to suggest that more accurate estimates may be obtained by the simple averaging of noisy but valid forecasts or the statistical combination of physicians' estimates and a model's estimates.

Summary and Conclusions

Although a modest amount of research has described the rank order discrimination of physicians' judgments (using ROC analysis) and degree of calibration (using calibration curves) in the care of actual patients, relatively few studies have been published that examine reasons for their levels of performance, especially to evaluate which cues seem to be used and how. An increase in the use of both $\overline{PS}$ and lens model analyses should aid our understanding of both the overall levels of accuracy of physicians' judgments and how their judgments may be improved.

ROC curve analysis has the advantage of being familiar. It also can be used to evaluate rank order likelihoods as independent variables ($\overline{PS}$ requires probabilistic forecasts) and to explicitly examine the trade-offs between false negatives and false positives as different operating positions are examined. The ROC curve, however, is not a summary accuracy score. It has not been partitioned, and the addition of a calibration curve does not yield a formal decomposition. Its use does not explicitly suggest ways in which judgments may be improved. It also may be relatively statistically insensitive to differences between judgments when compared with statistical methods used to compare $\overline{PS}$. Lastly, it is not a proper scoring rule and provides no theoretical incentive for the elimination of value-induced bias. Knowing about rank order discrimination, nonetheless, is important. In combination with a calibration curve, two important qualities of accuracy can be assessed.

The $\overline{PS}$ is a summary accuracy score that is proper and partitionable, provides results that can suggest ways in which judgments can be improved, separates factors that are potentially under judges' control from factors that are not, and involves relatively simple calculations even for the decompositions.

Use of lens model techniques provides an opportunity to examine the validity and consistency of judgments both for individual judges and across judges. One can examine overall judgments, the use of individual cues or groups of cues, and the difficulty of the task (inherent predictability of the disease or outcome). This methodology remains relatively unfamiliar to physicians and many other health care researchers and is more computationally challenging than $\overline{PS}$ and ROC analyses.

The empirical accuracy of physicians' judgments ranges from remarkably good to surprisingly poor. In general, physicians have demonstrated better accuracy for judgments about prognosis than for judgments about diagnosis. This suggests that short-term prognostic tasks (hospitalization for up to 6 months) may be cognitively easier than many diagnostic tasks.

No single measure of accuracy captures all the potentially important dimensions of judgmental accuracy, although for a given purpose, one measure may be quite satisfactory. Perfect prediction may occur in limited circumstances but should not be expected to occur across the entire spectrum of predictive occasions. Changes in the prevalence of the predicted outcome may alter predictive accuracy both directly (by affecting the absolute number of false positive and false negative predictions) and through associated changes in spectrum (by affecting the sensitivity and/or specificity of judgment). Discrimination can involve the ability to classify (DI), rank order correctly (ROC) or to separate by probability value (slope) those instances in which the outcome will occur from those in which it will not. Calibration reflects the ability to use probability values realistically. Decompositions of accuracy measures and use of the lens model methodology can lead to insights into how judgments can be improved. In order to implement methods to improve judgments, factors that are under the control of the judge should be differentiated from those that are not.

Glossary

Word or Phrase	Definitions and Comments
calibration curves	Calibration curves are created by plotting the average forecasts of outcomes within a prediction category (e.g., probabilistic forecasts within deciles of probability) against the associated observed occurrence rate for the forecasts within that prediction category. Perfect calibration occurs when the points representing the associated predicted and observed outcomes line up along the 45 degree line of the graph or along the "line of identity." The degree of calibration can be tested by calculating the Hosmer–Lemeshow statistic (Hosmer and Lemeshow, 1989).
cue form	In many approaches to examining the relationship between cues and the predicted outcome, especially regression, an assumption of linearity is made. One also should consider nonlinear forms and interactions.
cue strength	This represents the degree of relationship between cues and the predicted outcome. For a predictor of prognosis for survival, the

degree of relationship could be represented by the relative risk or estimated by an odds ratio. For diagnosis, this could be represented by a likelihood ratio.

equivalent risk groups

This assumes that the available predictive information will not support "unique labeling" discrimination or perfect prediction. Groups are said to be of equivalent risk if, based on their characteristics, they have sufficiently similar likelihoods of disease (for diagnosis) or survival (for prognosis). One could logically produce equivalent risk groups (e.g., .7 probability of survival) by combining appropriate numbers of patients who will live and die (e.g., 7 and 3, respectively) to form each group. If the patients' fates could be deterministically predicted beforehand, combining them to create the risk group would be a great disservice to the patients and a waste of information, however.

occurrence groups

For a two-outcome prediction task (disease present or absent; survive or die), each occurrence group would be homogeneous for one or the other of the two possible outcome states. For example, for survival, one occurrence group would contain all patients in the sample who will live, and the other occurrence group would contain all patients who will die. Occurrence group predication may involve the use of 0,1 prediction or it may simply involve the use of unique labels for each of the outcome groups, e.g., "live, die."

propensity score

The basic idea is to derive a single function to replace a number of covariates in an observational study. The score from this function is then used as if it were a single covariate. The propensity score is derived by developing a statistical model to predict selection to one of two groups. If, for example, one wanted to compare the judgments of two physicians (A and B) who saw similar, but not identical, patients, one could use patients' characteristics (independent variables) to predict the likelihood of patients seeing physician A (the dependent variable) using a logistic regression. Based on patient-level characteristics, each patient could be given a probability of being cared for by physician A. The probability of being cared for by physician A is the propensity score used to adjust for selection bias. When patients are subclassified into about five groups, e.g., by quintile of propensity, the propensity score will adjust for all covariates that were included in the estimation. Judgments about, say, prognosis for survival could be assessed by comparing $\overline{PS}$ in comparable patient groups, i.e., within quintiles of propensity (e.g., Dawson et al., 1998).

rational probability use

Probability use is said to be rational if patients who were judged to be likely to have the disease (or outcome) of interest were given probability estimates of 1 or near 1 and those judged to be unlikely to have the disease (or outcome) of interest were given probability estimates of 0 or near 0. This is contrasted with the arbitrary use of .1, .3 (to denote patients who would live) and .8 and 1.0 (to denote patients who would die) in Table 8.1 and Figure 8.1a.

realistic probability use

Probability use is said to be realistic if the probability estimates are associated with an equivalent observed proportion of outcomes. For example, if a group of patients were judged to have a .4 probability of survival and 40% survived, the physician would be using probabilities realistically.

receiver operating characteristic curve (ROC)

An ROC curve is created by plotting "1 − specificity" or false positive (FP) rates (the number of times the outcome was predicted to occur divided by all occasions when it did not, in fact, occur) on the horizontal axis against sensitivity or true positive (TP) rates (the number of times the outcome was predicted to occur divided by all occasions when it did, in fact, occur) on the vertical axis. The associated TP and FP rates are defined by selecting a series of cutoff points along the dimension of the variable used to judge the likelihood of the outcome (e.g., from lowest to highest rank-ordered likelihood or deciles of probability). Rank order discrimination can be compared statistically using familiar methods for ROC curves (Centor, 1991; Hanley and McNeil, 1982, 1983; McNeil and Hanley, 1984). Although they are good descriptors of overall rank order discrimination, ROC analyses may be relatively insensitive to differences between tests.

risk groups

This type of prediction involves only rank order likelihood predictions or probabilistic forecasts. Although risk group predictions may involve 0,1 predictions (as in occurrence group prediction), unlike occurrence group prediction, risk group prediction also may include any probability between 0 and 1.0.

spectrum

This reflects the kinds of patients included in a given study of physician judgment. Its dimensions include three components: pathologic (e.g., extent and location of disease), clinical (e.g., severity and chronicity of symptoms), and comorbid diseases (which may influence rates of false negative or false positive predictions). Spectrum should be examined in both groups of patients, i.e., those who have and those who do not have the disease or outcome of interest.

Formula or Component of Formula	Definitions and Synonyms*
f_i	An individual probabilistic forecast, $i = 1, \ldots, N$
f_j	A probabilistic forecast within a forecast category, e.g., within a decile of probability
d_i	An outcome index ($= 1$ if outcome occurs; $= 0$ if it does not occur) within a forecast category which matches f_i
$\bar{f}_i$	Mean forecast when outcome event occurred
$\bar{f}_0$	Mean forecast when outcome event did not occur
$\bar{f}$	Mean forecast (across all forecasts)
$\bar{d}$	Mean outcome index value, prevalence, base rate, outcome occurrence rate
$(1 - \bar{d})$	Complement of the mean outcome index, outcome nonoccurrence rate
$(\bar{f}_1 - \bar{f}_0)$	Slope, separation
$\bar{d}_j$	Conditional base rate, conditional observed proportion, observed outcome occurrence rate in forecast category f_j
N_j	Number of forecasts in forecast category f_j
$(\bar{f}_i - d_i)^2$	Probability score, $PS_i(f, d)$
$(\frac{1}{N})\sum_{i=1}^{N}(f_i - d_i)^2$	Mean probability score, $\overline{PS}(f, d)$, Brier score
$\bar{d}(1 - \bar{d})$	Outcome index variance, outcome variance, Var(d), [similar to binomial variance $= npq = np(1 - p)$]
$(\frac{1}{N})\sum_{j=1}^{J} N_j(\bar{d}_j - \bar{d})^2$	Murphy's resolution, Murphy's discrimination, measure of pure separation (sorting outcomes into categories),

discrimination index (DI)

$\dfrac{DI}{\text{Var}(d)}$

Normalized discrimination index (NDI); the interpretation of DI as a separation measure is conditional on Var(d), i.e., is prevalence dependent; NDI can be interpreted as the percentage of the outcome variable variance accounted for by the forecasts [conditional on number of cases (N) and number of judgment categories (J)]

$\dfrac{(N)(NDI) - J + 1}{N - J + 1}$

Adjusted normalized discrimination index (ANDI); removes the bias in NDI that varies with the number of cases (N) and the number of judgment categories (J) [similar to adjusted R^2]

$(\frac{1}{N}) \sum_{j=1}^{J} N_j (f_j - \bar{d}_j)^2$

Reliability-in-the-small, calibration-in-the-small, calibration index (CI)

Var(f)

Forecast variance, total forecast variance, S_f^2

min Var(f)

Minimum forecast variance, total forecast variance minus excess forecast variance, $S_{\tilde{f}}^2$, min [Slope^2][Var(d)], conditional minimum forecast variance, minimum value statistically necessary given the observed prevalence and slope, i.e., necessary to predict the outcome of interest

Scat(f)

Excess forecast variance, total forecast variance minus minimum forecast variance, scatter, noise, ΔS_f, variability in a set of forecasts not due to min Var(f), i.e., not necessary to predict the outcome of interest $[N_1 \text{Var}(f^1) + N_0 \text{Var}(f^0)]/N_1 + N_0]$

N_1

Cases in which the outcome of interest occurs

N_0

Cases in which the outcome of interest does not occur

N

$N_1 + N_0$

$\left(\frac{\text{Var}_1(f_1)}{N_1}\right) \sum_{j=1}^{N_1} (f_{1j} - f_1)^2$

Conditional variance of the probability judgments for the outcome of interest on those occasions when it occurred (N_1)

$\mathrm{Var}(F_0)$

$\left(\frac{1}{N_0}\right) \sum_{j=1}^{N_0}(f_{0j} - \bar{f}_0)^2$

$(\bar{f} - \bar{d})^2$

$(\bar{f} - \bar{d})$

S_{fd}

Conditional variance of the probability judgments for the outcome of interest on those occasions when it did not occur (N_0)

Reliability-in-the-large, calibration-in-the-large, bias^2

Bias

Forecast-outcome covariance, [Slope][Var(d)], FOCOV

*From Yates (1982, 1984, 1988).

References

Arkes HR, Dawson NV, Speroff T, Harrell FE, Alzola C, Phillips R, Desbiens N, Oye RK, Knaus W, Connors AF. (1995) The covariance decomposition of the probability score and its use in evaluating prognostic estimates. *Med Decis Making* 15:120–31

Begg CB. (1987) Biases in the assessment of diagnostic tests. *Stat Med* 6:411–23

Berwick DM, Thibodeau LA. (1983) Receiver operating characteristic analysis of diagnostic skill. *Med Care* 21:876–85

Brehmer B. (1980) In one word: Not from experience. *Acta Psychol* 45:223–41

Brier GW. (1950) Verification of forecasts expressed in terms of probability. Monthly Weather Rev 78:1–3

Bushyhead JB, Christensen-Szalanski JJ. (1981) Feedback and the illusion of validity in a medical clinic. *Med Decis Making* 1:115–23

Centor RM. (1991) Signal detectability: The use of ROC curves and their analyses. *Med Decis Making* 11:102–6

Christensen-Szalanski JJ, Bushyhead JB. (1981) Physicians' use of probability information in a real clinical setting. *J Exp Psychol* [*Hum Percept*] 4:928–35

Connors AF, Dawson NV, Speroff T, Arkes H, Knaus WA, Harrell FE, Lynn J, Terro J, Goldman L, Califf R, Fulkerson W, Oye R, Bellamy P, Desbiens N. (1992) Physicians' confidence in their estimates of the probability of survival: Relationships to accuracy. *Med Decis Making* 12: (abstract) 336

Connors AF, Speroff T, Dawson NV, Thomas C, Harrell FE, Wagner D, Desbiens N, Goldman L, Wu AW, Califf RM, Fulkerson WJ, Vidaillet H, Broste S, Bellamy P, Lynn J, Knaus WA. (1996) The effectiveness of right heart catheterization in the initial care of critically ill patients. *JAMA* 287:889–97

Cooksey RW. (1996) *Judgment Analysis: Theory, Methods, and Applications.* Academic Press, San Diego

Curley SP, Young MJ, Yates JF. (1989) Characterizing physicians' perceptions of ambiguity. *Med Decis Making* 9:116–24

Dawson N, Siciliano C, Goldberg H, Hershy C, Cohen D. (1986) Health care providers have limited ability to predict pneumonitis in outpatients. *Clin Res* 34: (abstract) 814A

Dawson NV, Arkes HR. (1987) Systematic errors in medical decision making: Judgment limitations. *J Gen Intern Med* 2:183–7

Dawson NV, Speroff T. (1989) Validated decision aid for outpatient pneumonia. *Clin Res* 37: (abstract) 74

Dawson NV. (1993) Physician judgment in clinical settings: Methodological influences and cognitive performance. *Clin Chem* 93:1468–80

Dawson NV, Connors AF, Speroff T, Kemka A, Shaw P, Arkes H. (1993) Hemodynamic assessment in managing the critically ill: Is physician confidence warranted? *Med Decis Making* 13:258–66

Dawson NV, Rose JH, Thomas C, O'Toole E, Connors AF, Cohen HJ, Lynn J, Hamel MB, Desbiens NA, Wenger N. (1998) Survival estimates and accuracy of prognostic predictions for cancer patients vary by physician specialty. *J Gen Intern Med* 13 (Supplement): (abstract) 18

Detsky AS, Stricker SC, Mulley AG, Thibault GE. (1981) Prognosis, survival, and expenditure of hospital resources for patients in an intensive care unit. *N Engl J Med* 305:667–72

Diamond GA. (1991) What price perfection? Calibration and discrimination of clinical prediction models. *J Clin Epidemiol* 45:85–9

Einhorn HJ, Hogarth RM. (1978) Confidence in judgment: Persistence of the illusion of validity. *Psychol Rev* 85:395–416

Hammond KR. (1996a) How convergence of research paradigms can improve research on diagnostic judgment. *Med Decis Making* 16:281–7

Hammond KR. (1996b) *Human Judgment and Social Policy: Irreducible Uncertainty, Inevitable Error, Unavoidable Injustice.* Oxford University Press, New York

Hosmer DW Jr, Lemeshow S. (1989) *Applied Logistic Regression.* New York: John Wiley and Sons.

Hanley JA, McNeil BJ. (1982) The meaning and use of the area under a receiver operating characteristic (ROC) curve. *Radiology* 143:29–36

Hanley JA, McNeil BJ. (1983) A method of comparing the areas under receiver operating characteristic curves derived from the same cases. *Radiology* 148:839–43

Hlatky MA, Pryor DB, Harrell FE, Califf RM, Mark DB, Rosati RB. (1984) Factors affecting sensitivity and specificity of exercise electrocardiography: Multivariable analysis. *Am J Med* 77:64–71

Kong DF, Lee KL, Harrell FE, Bostwick JM, Marks DB, Hlatky MA, Califf RM, Pryor DB. (1989) Clinical experience and predicting survival in coronary disease. *Arch Intern Med* 149:1177–81

Knaus WA, Harrell FE, Lynn J, Goldman L, Phillips RS, Connors AF, Dawson NV, Fulkerson WJ, Califf RM, Desbiens N, Layde P, Oye RK, Bellamy PE, Hakim RB, Wagner DP. (1995) The SUPPORT prognostic model: Objective estimates of survival for seriously ill hospitalized adults. *Am Intern Med* 122:191–203

Knottnerus JA. (1987) The effects of disease verification and referral on the relationship between symptoms and diseases. *Med Decis Making* 7:139–48

Kruse JA, Thill-Baharozian MC, Carlson RW. (1988) Comparison of clinical assessment with APACHE II for predicting mortality risk in patients admitted to a medical intensive care unit. *JAMA* 260:1739–42

Lee KL, Pryor DB, Harrell FE, Califf RM, Behar VS, Floyd WL, Morris JJ, Waugh RA, Whalen RE, Rosati RA. (1986) Predicting outcome in coronary disease: Statistical models vs. expert clinicians. *Am J Med* 80:553–60

Marks RJ, Simons RS, Blizzard RA, Browne DRG. (1991) Predicting outcome in intensive therapy units – a comparison of APACHE II with subjective assessments. *Intensive Care Med* 17:159–63

McClish DK, Powell S. (1989) How well can physicians estimate mortality in a medical intensive care unit? *Med Decis Making* 9:125–32

McNeil BJ, Hanley JA. (1984) Statistical approaches to the analysis of receiver operating characteristic (ROC) curves. *Med Decis Making* 4:137–50

McNeil DE, Sandberg DA, Binder RL. (1998) The relationship between confidence and accuracy in clinical assessment of psychiatric patients' potential for violence. *Law Hum Behav* 6:655–69.

Poses RM, Cebul RD, Collins M, Fager SS. (1985) The accuracy of experienced physicians' probability estimates for patients with sore throats. *JAMA* 254:925–9

Poses RM, Bekes C, Copare FJ, Scott WE. (1989) The answer to "What are my chances, Doctor?" depends on whom is asked: Prognostic disagreement and accuracy for critically ill patients. *Crit Care Med* 17:827–33

Poses RM, Bekes C, Winkler RL, Scott WE, Copare FJ. (1990) Are two (inexperienced) heads better than one (experienced) head? Averaging house officers' prognostic judgments for critically ill patients. *Arch Intern Med* 150:1874–8

Poses RM, Anthony M. (1991) Availability, wishful thinking, and physicians' diagnostic judgments for patients with suspected bacteremia. *Med Decis Making* 11:159–68

Poses RM, Cebul RD, Wigton RS. (1995) You can lead a horse to water – improving physicians' knowledge of probabilities may not affect their decisions. *Med Decis Making* 15:65–76

Poses RM, Smith WR, McClish DK, Huber EC, Clemo ELW, Schmitt BP, Alexander-Forti D, Racht EM, Colenda CC, Centor RM. (1997) Physicians' survival predictions for patients with acute congestive heart failure. *Arch Intern Med* 157:1001–7

Ransohoff DF, Feinstein AR. (1978) Problems of spectrum and bias in evaluating diagnostic tests. *N Engl J Med* 299:926–30

Redelmeier DA, Bloch DA, Hickam DH. (1991) Assessing predictive accuracy: How to compare Brier scores. *J Clin Epidemiol* 44:1141–6

Rosenbaum PR. (1991) Discussing hidden bias in observational studies. *Ann Intern Med* 115:901–5

Rosenbaum PR, Rubin DB. (1983) The central role of the propensity score in observational studies for causal effects. *Biometrika* 70:41–55

Rosenbaum PR, Rubin DB. (1984) Reducing bias in observational studies using subclassification on the propensity score. *J Am Stat Assoc* 79:516–24

Rubin DB. (1997) Estimating causal effects from large data sets using propensity scores. *Ann Intern Med* 127:757–63

Speroff T, Connors AF, Dawson NV. (1989) Lens model analysis of hemodynamic status in the critically ill. *Med Decis Making* 9:243–52

Stevens SM, Richardson DK, Gray JE, Goldmann DA, McCormick MC. (1994) Estimating neonatal mortality risk: An analysis of clinicians' judgments. *Pediatrics* 93:945–50

Stewart TR. (1990) A decomposition of the correlation coefficient and its use in analyzing forecasting skill. *Weather Forecast* 5:661–6

Stewart TR, Lusk CM. (1994) Seven components of judgmental forecasting skill: Implications for research and the improvement of forecasts. *J Forecast* 13:579–99

Tape TG, Heckerling PS, Ornato JP, Wigton RS. (1991) Use of clinical judgment analysis to explain regional variations in physicians' accuracies in diagnosing pneumonia. *Med Decis Making* 11:189–97

Tierney WM, Fitzgerald J, McHenry R, Roth BJ, Psaty B, Stump DL, Anderson FK. (1986) Physicians' estimates of the probability of myocardial infarction in emergency room patients with chest pain. *Med Decis Making* 12:12–17

Wallsten TS. (1981) Physician and medical student bias in evaluating diagnostic information. *Med Decis Making* 1:145–64

Weiner DA, Ryan TJ, McCabe GH, Kennedy JW, Schloss M, Tristani F, et al. (1979) Correlations among history of angina, ST-segment response, and prevalence of coronary artery disease in the Coronary Artery Surgery Study (CASS). *N Engl J Med* 301:230–5

Wigton RS. (1988) Use of linear models to analyze physicians' decision. *Med Decis Making* 8:241–52

Yaniv I, Yates JF, Smith JEK. (1991) Measures of discrimination skill in probabilistic judgment. *Psych Bull* 110:611–17

Yates JF. (1982) External correspondence; decompositions of the mean probability score. *Org Behav Hum Perf* 30:132–56

Yates JF. (1988) Analyzing the accuracy of probability judgments for multiple events: An extension of the covariance decomposition. *Org Behav Hum Decis Process* 41:281–99

Yates JF. (1990) *Judgement and Decision Making.* Prentice Hall, Englewood Cliffs, NJ

Yates JF. (1994) Subjective probability analysis. In *Subjective Probability*; Wright FG, Ayton P (ed.). John Wiley and Sons, New York, Ch. 16, pp. 381–410

Yates JF, Price PC, Lee J-W, Ramirez J. (1996) Good probabilistic forecasters: The "consumer's" perspective. *Int J Forecast* 12:41–56

9 Bioethics and Medical Decision Making: What Can They Learn from Each Other?

Joshua Cohen, PhD, David Asch, MD, and Peter Ubel, MD

1. Introduction

Bioethics addresses the moral conflicts and tensions that arise in healthcare. At the theoretical level, bioethics establishes principles and guidelines governing medical practice. At the empirical level, bioethics examines the moral practices of healthcare participants to see how ethical decisions are made and conflicts resolved. Medical decision making addresses many facets of clinical practice and, in particular, how to assess the clinical- and cost-effectiveness of alternative medical treatments. At the theoretical level, medical decision making employs well-established decision-analytic principles, while at the empirical level, medical decision making examines everyday clinical decisions.

Bioethical and decision-analytic principles are both put forth as normative guides to medical decision making. However useful these may be as normative guides, it is important to understand whether they are applicable in everday decisions in clinical practice. It is also important to understand whether these normative guides are compatible, complementary, or at odds.

This chapter addresses how bioethics and medical decision making can and do learn from each other. This pairing enables the two disciplines to bring medical decisions in line with individual and social moral values. Sections 2 and 3 outline bioethical and decision-analytic principles and their limitations. Section 4 describes the interplay between bioethics and medical decision making, using actual clinical case studies to demonstrate mutual feedback mechanisms. Section 5 summarizes the main points.

2. Bioethical Principles and Their Limitations

In their highly influential book *Principles of Biomedical Ethics*, Beauchamp and Childress (1989) argue that most ethical decisions in medicine can be made with the guidance of four principles: autonomy, nonmaleficence, beneficence, and justice.[1] The first principle described by Beauchamp and Childress is respect for patient autonomy: the right a patient has to make independent decisions about his/her care, together with a patient's right to receive adequate and truthful information from healthcare providers (informed consent). The second principle outlined by Beauchamp and Childress is the "do no harm" principle (nonmaleficence). The third principle is beneficence: benefiting the patient by preserving life, treating disease, and reducing pain. These individualistic ethical principles are put forth as the foundation of the fiduciary relationship in which physicians are expected to serve their patients' best interests as defined by the patients themselves. As appealing as these principles may be, adherence to them is sometimes difficult. For example, patient autonomy is difficult to preserve for unresponsive patients who have not assigned proxies. Furthermore, tension often exists among these principles. For example, the beneficence and nonmaleficence principles seem to collide when medical care that supports life also causes pain.

In addition to these individualistic principles, there are also social bioethical principles that address fairness with respect to the distribution of resources across the population. Fairness is often thought of in egalitarian terms. For example, a fair division of cake implies giving everybody an equal slice. However, other competing notions of fairness (libertarian, utilitarian) do not necessarily imply an egalitarian allocation of resources. A fair distribution from a utilitarian standpoint is one that allocates health resources to maximize overall well-being. This may mean that some patients, those who are expected to benefit most from the resources, are given more resources than others. It is easy to see how social justice principles can conflict with the individualistic principles outlined earlier. For example, organ transplantation programs often must make hard choices with regard to the allocation of scarce organs.

---

[1] It should be noted that while the principles of biomedical ethics outlined by Beauchamp and Childress have been highly influential, they are far from being the sole principles proposed to guide and justify ethical decision making in medicine. Moreover, many contemporary bioethicists blend elements of these principles with utilitarianism, as well as with common sense and reasoning by precedent.

Sometimes these allocation decisions serve the purpose of maximizing populationwide benefits in a way that may conflict with the individualistic beneficence principle.

The analysis of ethical principles purports to provide a guidepost for making difficult clinical decisions or at least helping people understand their moral implications. But there are limits to how much this kind of analysis can illuminate clinical practice without empirical feedback. Empirical research suggests that ethical principles are limited in their capacity to direct moral decision making in real-world settings (Pearlman et al. 1993). For example, numerous empirical studies indicate how professional behaviors in healthcare settings diverge from the norms implied by the principles (Asch and DeKay 1997, Ubel 1995). In addition, empirical research demonstrates when moral distinctions are evidently too subtle for people to understand as a way of guiding their moral decision making. It has been shown, for example, that even bioethicists have difficulty maintaining the supposedly morally relevant distinctions between active euthanasia, passive euthanasia, and assisted suicide (Flynn 1993, Hall 1994, Ubel and Asch 1997). The distinctions are analytically useful in that they contribute to the debate on euthanasia, in which a multiplicity of defensible views is expressed. Nevertheless, the distinctions appear to have limited real-world value in actually guiding moral decisions.

Empirical research can also indicate whether the goals implied by ethical principles are obtainable. For example, the principle of autonomy urges that patients receive adequate and truthful information regarding medical treatment alternatives. Empirical research can show how well patients process the information provided to them and whether, in fact, the kind of probabilistic information they are provided is processed accurately.

In short, empirical investigations help to sharpen the focus on the most relevant ethical issues facing real-world participants. These investigations make observations about the world and, in so doing, identify practical limitations to the application of theoretical principles. At the same time, they uncover new ethical issues, revealing the complexity and conflict that might otherwise be understated.

It is clear from empirical bioethical research that clinical circumstances and patient preferences do not uniquely determine ethical decisions. One prominent example of the contribution of empirical bioethics research concerns patients near the end of life. Over the past two decades, a great deal of work in bioethics, largely based on theory, resulted in the conclusion that patients' autonomy in end-of-life settings could be fostered through the use of advance directives, such as living wills or the designation of surrogate decision makers. The Patient Self-Determination Act was enacted in 1991 to support this view. Empirical studies show that the theoretical promise of advance directives has been largely unfulfilled. Despite the plausibility and theoretical appeal of advance directives as means to improve end-of-life decision making, a large collection of empirical studies demonstrate severe limitations in their practical utility. Advance directive completion rates remain low, surrogate and patient views are often discordant, and clinicians often ignore advance directives that are available or consider them too vague and difficult to interpret (Gross 1998). Alternative theoretically defined decision rules, such as medical futility principles that might apply in certain situations, have confronted similar practical constraints as well as significant theoretical disagreement.

3.   Decision-Analytical Principles and Their Limitations

Decision-analytic principles address individual and social rational decision making. The foundation of decision analysis is utility theory: the theory of how to measure and maximize utility individually and socially. A normative decision-analytic exercise numerically measures the extent to which each consequence of each alternative chosen achieves each goal for each person. The measure of goal achievement is called "utility" (Baron 1994). Uncertain outcomes are weighted by multiplying the utility of each outcome by its probability of occurring. Decisions become utility-maximization exercises. The philosophy underlying utility theory, utilitarianism, is itself ethically laden. Its most fundamental idea is that we treat each moral decision as a choice among competing alternatives. Each alternative implies defined consequences with different probabilities. To decide which alternative is "morally best," utilities of consequences are added across people. The best alternatives are those with the highest expected utility across the population. Normative decision analysis is then a general theory of how we should choose among possible alternatives given our goals and values and the resource constraints imposed on us. The alternatives involved may be medical interventions, while values may be the preferences we have for their clinical consequences. In the case of health policy, it is assumed that the utilities of different outcomes of medical treatment for different people can be measured, combined, and interpersonally compared.

Analogous to bioethical principles, tension exists between decision-analytic principles at the individual and social levels. In the Prisoner's Dilemma,[2] for example, each person has a strictly dominant individual strategy that, no matter what others do, his/her own goals are better served by following. At the same time, everyone's goals are better served if each follows a different (more cooperative) strategy. Numerous experimental games demonstrate the existence and relevance of the Prisoner's Dilemma in situations where individual and social rationality conflict. A patient's exercise of his/her autonomy, for example, may be the patient's dominant strategy. Yet, collectively, it may be more in the patient's interest (and in the interest of society as a whole) to pursue a more cooperative, less selfish strategy, which entails having each person give up some autonomy.

Cost-effectiveness analysis (CEA) is a form of decision analysis used to make choices among alternative treatments that consume those common scarce resources (see Chapter 6). Accordingly, CEA shows how to use resources efficiently, that is, in ways that maximize the amount of health benefits to patients within a resource constraint. An important purpose of CEA is to make hard-to-balance trade-offs explicit, for instance, the trade-off between money spent and lives saved.

In most countries, including the United States, CEA is a decision guide or tool, not the decision maker per se (Siegel et al. 1996). The limited role of CEA in guiding health care policies may reflect the perceived ethical shortcomings of CEA. CEA is criticized typically on ethical grounds for ignoring issues of fairness in distributing health resources. Given its focus on overall efficiency, CEA generally ignores equity concerns regarding health resource distribution. Egalitarian critics of CEA are concerned with the relative positions of individuals as a result of a utilitarian distribution of resources that may discriminate against people with disabilities or may undervalue the benefits of treating severely ill as opposed to moderately ill patients (Nord 1992). More generally, specific bioethical principles sometimes conflict with the process and outcomes of decision analysis and, for some, constitute an argument against the wide application of decision analysis (Blumstein 1997).

---

[2] The classic Prisoner's Dilemma involves two individuals implicated in a crime. They can either confess to the crime or claim their innocence. Each prisoner sees that it is definitely in his/her interest to confess no matter what the other does (the two prisoners have no knowledge of each other's pleas). Guided by rational self-interest, the two prisoners confess. If, however, neither had confessed, both would have been better off.

Normative decision analyses, despite their rigor and axiomatic base, often fail to explain observed behavior due to the role of apparently irrational factors such as emotion and intuition (Kahneman and Tversky 1979, Redelmeier et al. 1993). Generally, normative decision analysis fails to incorporate certain intuitive considerations that are important to decision makers – psychological feelings associated with anticipation or regret, ethical and cultural attitudes, and other values that are difficult to quantify (Ubel and Loewenstein 1997). These intuitive thought processes often lead to suboptimal decisions, that is, behavior that does not maximize expected utility.

Decision studies in psychology suggest that people tend to be more sensitive to certain types of risk than they ought to be, according to the normative model, because their subjective risk perception differs from more objective assessments of risk. For example, some parents exhibit "omission bias" when deciding whether to vaccinate their children. They decide not to vaccinate even though they know that the risk of vaccination is less than the risk of contracting the diseases for which the child is being vaccinated (Meszaros et al. 1996). People also tend to be influenced by the "framing" of questions, the ways in which vignettes with the same descriptive content are presented (Kahneman and Tversky 1979). An enlarging literature has cataloged numerous biases, and a less well developed literature has begun to identify ways to overcome these biases in order to help people achieve clinical goals (see Chapter 7).

As with tensions between theoretical and empirical approaches to bioethics, theoretical and empirical approaches to understanding medical decision making are complementary. Although we can look narrowly at studies of actual decisions and conclude that they reveal that people are irrational, we can also see them as agendas for useful prescriptive change. In general, what we have learned from decision studies in psychology should alert us to the importance of emotions and intuition in reasoning.

4. Patient Autonomy, Informed Consent, and Decision Analysis

The relationship between decision analysis and informed consent, as described in Ubel and Loewenstein (1997), illustrates the potential for interaction and feedback between bioethics and medical decision making. By stating that physicians have the duty to inform patients adequately and truthfully, the doctrine of informed consent plays a fundamental role in upholding the positive rights patients have to autonomy. Using decision analysis, physicians can present information to patients in a structured way that may assist patients in deciding which medical options are best for them, in accordance with the patients' preferences. Note that the kind of information necessary for decision analysis, including knowledge of clinical alternatives and the chance and value of their likely outcomes, is also required for adequate informed consent in clinical settings.

Decision analysis is well suited to decomposing complex situations into a set of simple decision situations. Consider the following example of a couple's decision on whether to have their fetus tested for Down syndrome. This decision can be presented using a decision tree (the example used here is adapted from Baron 1994, pp 337–338). The decision is to test or not to test (see Figure 9.1). Without a test there is a $p1$ probability of delivering a child with Down syndrome and a $1 - p1$ probability of delivering a child without Down syndrome. Testing carries with it a slightly increased risk of miscarriage (probability $p2$).

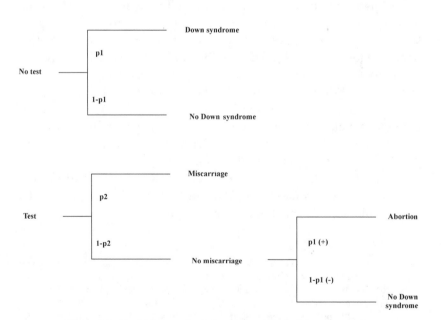

Figure 9.1. Decision tree depicting a couple's decision on whether to screen their fetus for Down syndrome. Note that in this figure, for simplicity's sake, we have ignored the chance of both false negative and false positive test results. From Baron (1994) with permission.

If there is no miscarriage $(1 - p2)$, then a positive test result (probability p1) would imply termination of the pregnancy (abortion), while the chance of delivering a child without Down syndrome is $1 - p1$. To assess the utility attached to miscarriage, the couple can imagine a decision in which they must choose between a miscarriage for sure and a gamble between a child with Down syndrome and a child without it. From a prescriptive decision-analytic perspective, the choice of whether to do the test depends strictly on the parents' relative utilities for the four possible outcomes. Attaching utility numbers to the four possible outcomes of Down syndrome, no Down syndrome, miscarriage, and abortion is all the couple needs to make the ultimate choice.[3]

It can be argued that the physician who uses the decision tree in Figure 9.1 to elicit preferences is assisting the couple in their struggle to arrive at a choice that reflects their preferences. The physician is not only complying with the requirements for informed consent, but he/she is also making the decision explicit for the couple. But a potential problem with this decision-analytic method of arriving at choices is that it may seem too prescriptive.[4] This method assumes that the decision to test is based only on outcomes and their utilities, and that there is no reason to do the test unless the couple is prepared to act on the consequences (Asch et al. 1990, 1996, Baron 1993). This means that before doing the test, couples should be willing to have an abortion if the test turns out positive. However, other issues may play a role in the decision on whether to do the test. These issues may include the reassurance a test result gives a couple or simply the knowledge the test provides. For example, a couple unwilling to have an abortion if the test turns out positive may still decide to test in order to prepare themselves for the possibility of having a child with Down syndrome.

We now turn to the area of health resource allocation, where bioethics and medical decision making overlap greatly. Several studies have used the techniques and methods of empirical decision psychology to

---

[3] On a scale from 0 to 1, the utility attached to delivering a child with Down syndrome is set arbitrarily at 0, while the utility attached to delivering a child without Down syndrome is set arbitrarily at 1. Intermediate utilities, those attached to miscarriage and abortion, can be calculated using the indifference procedure outlined earlier.

[4] It should also be noted that the prescriptive decision-analytic method does not easily incorporate future effects, such as regret, which may be powerful motivators and enduring factors in these decisions. Couples who decide to terminate or continue a pregnancy based on the test result may regret having made that decision later on. Their anticipation of that regret may influence their current decision.

investigate public preferences in this ethically charged area and, in turn, these studies challenge some of the conceptual foundations of CEA in particular and medical decision-making more broadly. For example, surveys on the social distribution of health resources suggest that the public does not uniformly support the utilitarian principles that underlie CEA. Ubel et al. (1993, 1996b) found that a substantial proportion of the public, more than 60% of 380 persons surveyed, favored a health policy that would have as its premise the equitable availability of kidneys to all members of the population, regardless of race and differences in antigen-matching status (implying differences in the likelihood of transplant success), despite the fact that such a distribution would result in fewer overall successful transplants. Evidently, in the public's mind, equal access to healthcare services is an important goal even when it increases costs or reduces effectiveness. Related studies reveal that the public also considers the social benefits of treating severely ill patients as outweighing those of treating moderately ill patients, even if the improvement in quality of life (and therefore quality-adjusted-life-years) is greater for the moderately ill patients (Ubel et al. 1996a). These findings, derived from descriptive studies of decision making, have important implications for many of the normative foundations of CEA. Decision analyses such as CEA typically do not incorporate concerns about the distribution of clinical outcomes – only their average across a population. Yet, the public, patients, and physicians care about how these outcomes are distributed. For many, equity is an important independent goal.

CEA can become more compatible with the public's egalitarian intuition if the ways in which individual and societal values are measured change. First, CEA's ability to capture societal notions of fairness may improve if, instead of measuring preferences related to health states in isolation, preferences regarding health state intervals (improvements from one health state to another) are measured (Nord 1992). Furthermore, if not only health state intervals, but also the societal values related to the health programs responsible for bringing about such health state shifts are measured, then CEA may be in an even better position to incorporate fairness. The latter measurement may represent a more accurate reflection of society's views on treating severely ill as opposed to moderately ill patients. These steps can be seen as broadening the perspective of patient values so that they encompass public health concerns. Indeed, a fundamental challenge in reconciling common ethical principles and the methods of CEA is that the former typically derive their authority from individualistic notions of patient autonomy and the like and leave little room for issues of distributive justice.

End-of-life care is another important area in which research in bioethics and medical decision making overlap. Using clinical vignettes, self-reported data, and other clinical observation methods, numerous studies have examined clinicians' willingness to withhold or withdraw life support and the processes they use. The decision to withdraw treatment precedes the decision regarding which life support system to withdraw and when. A patient may be attached to a variety of life support systems which can be sequentially or concurrently withdrawn. The order in which life support systems are withdrawn may affect the "rapidity, dignity, and painlessness of patients' death" (Christakis and Asch 1993, p 642). For these reasons, this setting has attracted considerable attention from bioethicists and those who study decision processes.

The decision to withdraw life support has a sound and generally well-accepted moral basis when the patient (or surrogate) and the physician have together determined that further medical treatment is not beneficial. However, in the real world of conflicting interests and principles, physicians and patients (or their surrogates) may decide unilaterally to forego life support. When the patient decides unilaterally to forego life support, how does the physician respond to this request? Some physicians may go against the patient's wish because they have a built-in bias against discontinuing life-sustaining treatment. In a study done by Asch et al. (1995), 34% of 879 physicians surveyed continued life-sustaining treatment despite the wish of the patient or surrogate that it be discontinued. On the other hand, in the same study, 25% of physicians reported having withheld life-sustaining treatment that they judged to be futile without the written or oral consent of the patient or family, and 3% of physicians reported having withheld life-sustaining treatment despite the objections of the patient or family.

Once the decision to withdraw life support has been made, the patient's interests should remain the primary concern. However, a large collection of studies show that decisions to forego life support often run counter to patients' previously stated goals or at least reflect physicians' social and professional characteristics in addition to clinical circumstances. For example, physician age, religion, and specialization are associated with differences in how these decisions are made (Asch and Christakis 1996; Asch et al. 1995; Christakis and Asch 1995a, 1995b). Age and specialization appear to be particularly significant factors, as younger physicians are more likely to withdraw life support, with specialized physicians preferring to withdraw "familiar" life-support systems (Christakis and Asch 1995a).

The discussion surrounding the decision on whether to forgo life-sustaining treatment, rather than being an isolated bioethical discussion, serves as a thought-provoking example in a much broader bioethical context concerning the level of care, goals of therapy, and variety of treatment options available to patients. This context includes discussions on cardiopulmonary resuscitation (CPR) and do-not-resuscitate (DNR) orders.

The decision on whether or not to attempt to revive a patient after a cardiopulmonary arrest offers a unique opportunity to observe the interaction between bioethics and medical decision making. Studies on the efficacy of widespread use of CPR have raised questions concerning its effectiveness in certain groups of critically and chronically ill patients (Pearlman et al. 1993). This research has led some to reconsider the scope of patient autonomy when dealing with cases in which CPR offers only a low probability of survival. The empirical survey data are of interest not only at the individual patient–physician level but also at the social level. It can be asked whether healthcare policies should allow patients to demand treatments with high opportunity costs, such as CPR, even when they are very unlikely to achieve reasonable therapeutic goals.

The importance of involving patients in DNR decisions is widely recognized. Empirical research suggests that current DNR policies may not be sufficiently aligned with the principle of patient autonomy. This research has provided the impetus for a new set of guidelines and recommendations to encourage early discussions about advance directives and hospital policies which require patients be asked about life-sustaining treatment on admission to the hopsital.

An extensive study involving more than 5,000 terminally ill patients identified serious shortcomings in clinical care and patient–physician communication on issues related to advance directives and life-sustaining treatment (SUPPORT 1995). In the first phase of the study, researchers used both self-reported data and observations of actual behavior to identify deficiencies in care. It was found that in a majority of cases, patient preferences concerning both CPR and DNR were unknown to the clinical caregivers. Often, excessively aggressive life-sustaining treatment was given to patients spending their last days in intensive care units (ICUs). The aim of the second phase of the study was to examine the effects of improvements in patient–physician communication and prognostic information on end-of-life decision making. This phase of the study used a similar patient dataset (terminally ill patients with similar prognostic indicators). Informed consent guidelines were strictly adhered to; prognostic information was more accurate; and communication with patients was strengthened. Despite these extensive efforts to improve communication and prognostic information and to involve patients in decision making, little or no change occurred in a number of target outcomes, including the incidence, prevalence, and timing of DNR orders and the median number of days spent in the ICU. Even patient–physician agreement and mutual knowledge of CPR preferences remained the same. While this study suggests the gaps in aligning end-of-life decisions with the principle of patient autonomy, it simultaneously raises doubts about the efficacy of actually implementing guidelines aimed at achieving those goals.

5. Concluding Remarks

Through mutual feedback, bioethics and medical decision making can assist in the difficult task of improving individual and social decision making in healthcare settings. For this symbiotic relationship to work, medical decision making must remain informed by theoretical bioethics and the empirical results of both bioethical and psychological decision studies. These decision studies bring to light certain unrealistic assumptions underlying the normative models of medical decision making. Furthermore, these studies serve to inform medical decision makers of the importance that intuitive values such as fairness play in clinical decisions. It has been shown, for instance, how sensitive bioethicists and lay people are to fairness in medical resource allocation decisions. This high sensitivity suggests the need for clinical cost-effectiveness analysis to recognize and, if feasible, explicitly incorporate fairness in their decision or interpretation.

At the same time, bioethics can learn from decision-analytic aspects of medical decision making. Decision analysis can help to establish a more systematic basis for the implementation of ethical principles such as patient autonomy and its complement, informed consent. In addition, decision analysis can be a useful tool in decomposing difficult medical decisions in which weights attached to utilities and probabilities play an important role. The same decision studies that demonstrate high sensitivity to fairness also reveal certain inconsistencies in people's decision making. Given that consistency across contexts, or invariance to framing, are themselves important moral precepts, studies of decision processes may reveal areas where intuition is a poor moral guide or where principles previously felt to be inviolable deserve reconsideration. For example, it has been shown that people's sensitivity to fairness can be influenced by the ways in which resource allocation problems are framed. This empirical observation may temper the enthusiasm of those bioethicists who consider fairness to be an inviolable principle. Although bioethical scholarship is conventionally viewed as abstract and theoretical, empirical studies designed to explore decision making contribute importantly to bioethical thought, move it forward, and often challenge previous assumptions. At the same time, widely held principles, such as the importance of fairness, often raise concerns about observed decision processes or the conclusions of presumably normative decision-analytic studies.

References

Asch DA, Patton JP, Hershy JC. Knowing for the sake of knowing: the value of prognostic information, *Medical Decision Making* 1990; 10: 47–57.

Asch DA, Hansen-Flaschen J, Lanken P. Decisions to limit or continue life-sustaining treatment by critical care physicians in the United States: conflicts between physicians' practices and patients' wishes, *American Journal of Respiratory Critical Care Medicine* 1995; 1515: 288–292.

Asch DA, Christakis NA. Why do physicians prefer to withdraw some forms of life support over others?, *Medical Care* 1996; 34: 103–111.

Asch DA, Hershey JC, Pauly MV, Patton JP, Jediziewski MK, Mennuti MT. Genetic screening for reproductive planning: methodologic and conceptual issues in policy analysis, *American Journal of Public Health* 1996; 86: 684–690.

Asch DA, DeKay ML. Euthanasia among U.S. critical care nurses: practices, attitudes, and social and professional correlates, *Medical Care* 1997; 35: 890–900.

Baron J. 1994 *Thinking and Deciding*, 2nd ed. New York, Cambridge University Press.

Beauchamp T, Childress J. 1989 *Principles of Biomedical Ethics*, New York, Oxford University Press.

Blumstein JF. The Oregon experiment: the role of cost–benefit analysis in the allocation of Medicaid funds, *Social Science and Medicine* 1997; 45: 545–554.

Christakis NA, Asch DA. Biases in how physicians choose to withdraw life support, *The Lancet* 1993; 342: 642–647.

Christakis NA, Asch DA. Medical specialists prefer to withdraw familiar technologies when discontinuing life support, *Journal of General Internal Medicine* 1995a; 10: 491–494.

Christakis NA, Asch DA. Physican characteristics associated with decisions to withdraw life support, *American Journal of Public Health* 1995b; 85: 367–372.

Flynn, T. A case for mercy killing, *Free Inquiry* 1993; 13: 60–61.

Gross MD. What do patients express as their preferences in advance directives? *Archives of Internal Medicine* 1998; 158: 363–365.

Hall, R. Final act: sorting out the ethics of physician-assisted suicide, *The Humanist* 1994; 54: 10–15.

Kahneman D, Tversky A. Prospect theory: an analysis of decision under risk, *Econometrica* 1979; 47: 262–291.

Meszaros JR, Asch DA, Baron J, Hershey JC, Kunreuther H, Schwartz-Buzaglo J. Cognitive processes and the decisions of some parents to forego pertussis vaccination for their children, *Journal of Clinical Epidemiology* 1996; 49: 697–703.

Nord E. An alternative to QALYs: the saved young life equivalent (SAVE), *British Medical Journal* 1992; 305: 875–877.

Pearlman RA, Miles SH, Arnold RM. Contributions of empirical research to medical ethics, *Theoretical Medicine* 1993; 14: 197–210.

Redelmeier DA, Rozin P, Kahneman D. Understanding patients' decisions: cognitive and emotional perspectives, *Journal of the American Medical Association* 1993; 270: 72–76.

Siegel JE, Weinstein MC, Russell LB, Gold MR. Recommendations for reporting cost-effectiveness analysis, *Journal of the American Medical Association* 1996; 276: 1339–1342.

SUPPORT. A controlled trial to improve care for seriously ill hospitalized patients, *Journal of the American Medical Association* 1995; 274: 1591–1598.

Ubel PA. Elevator talk: observational study of inappropriate comments in a public space, *American Journal of Medicine* 1995; 99: 190–194.

Ubel PA, Arnold RM, Caplan AL. Rationing failure: the ethical lessons of the retransplantation of scarce vital organs, *Journal of the American Medical Association* 1993; 270: 2469–2475.

Ubel PA, DeKay ML, Baron J, Asch DA. Cost-effectiveness analysis in a setting of budget constraints: is it equitable? *The New England Journal of Medicine* 1996a; 334: 1174–1178.

Ubel PA, DeKay ML, Baron J, Asch DA. Public preferences for efficiency and racial equity in kidney transplant allocation decisions, *Transplantation Proceedings* 1996b; 28: 2997–3002.

Ubel PA, Asch DA. Semantic and moral debates about hastening death: a survey of bioethicists, *Journal of Clinical Ethics* 1997; 8: 242–249.

Ubel PA, Loewenstein G. The role of decision analysis in informed consent: choosing between intuition and systematicity, *Social Science and Medicine* 1997; 44: 647–657.

10 Team Medical Decision Making

Caryn Christensen, PhD, and Ann S. Abbott, BS

Over the past decade, groups have become increasingly involved in making decisions in the medical arena. Case conferences, consultations, and morning rounds all involve clinical groups. In the policy domain, the development of practice guidelines and treatment algorithms is often the task of groups rather than individuals. The decisions produced by these interactions are seldom the result of simple democratic processes and are often driven by complex scripts for how one should proceed (either explicit rules or social norms). What is more, the groups themselves may often involve participants who vary widely in expertise, authority, and patient responsibility and may in part be designed to fulfill an educational function. Nevertheless, medical teams do have much in common with other professional decision-making groups. It is therefore important to examine the existing literature on group decision making and to explore its relevance to the domain of medicine.

Considerable research has focused upon the psychological processes employed when individuals make clinical decisions (Balla, 1985; Barrows, Freightner, Neufeld, & Norman, 1982; Elstein, Shulman, & Sprafka, 1978; Johnson, 1983; Miller, Pople & Meyers, 1982). Many of the classic biases and errors found in the psychological literature in judgment and decision making have been demonstrated with physicians and clinical materials. For example, in a classic study, McNeil, Pauker, Sox, and

We wish to express our grateful appreciation to Kathie Schmidt for her invaluable assistance with various aspects of this project. The authors would also like to thank LeKesha Whitworth for her assistance with library research and her insightful comments in response to previous drafts. Portions of this project were supported by Grant 1 R01 LM05481-01 from the National Library of Medicine, a Division of the National Institutes of Health, U.S. Public Health Service.

Tversky (1982) revealed that physicians would be more likely to recommend surgery when the outcomes were framed as potential gains rather than as potential losses (a 5% mortality rate is less appealing than a 95% survival rate). Other biases such as availability, hindsight, base rate neglect, and the influence of potential regret have all been investigated (Christensen, Elstein, Bernstein, & Balla, 1991). Our expanding knowledge of individual processes in medical decision making has not, however, brought with it equivalent gains in understanding group processes in medical decision making.

A major focus in the psychological literature on group decision making is whether the decisions produced by groups are superior to those produced by individuals and, by implication, whether it is worthwhile to invest in groups as a vehicle for making important decisions. The general consensus is that, on average, groups outperform individuals on such tasks, although group decisions frequently do not measure up either to the decisions made by their most capable individual members or to statistical aggregates of individual decisions (Einhorn, Hogarth, & Klempner, 1977; Hastie, 1986; Hill, 1987; Laughlin & Ellis, 1986; McGrath, 1984; Vollrath, Sheppard, Hinsz, & Davis, 1989). In other words, while groups tend to make better decisions than individuals, on average those decisions are often are not as good as they theoretically might be.

In the majority of previous studies, accuracy is gauged in comparison to some gold standard or agreed-upon correct solution (Hastie, 1986; Hastie & Rasinski, 1988). A gold standard applies to what Laughlin (Laughlin & Ellis, 1986) calls "intellective tasks" – tasks in which clear criteria exist for evaluating the quality of cognitive performance (vs. tasks in which there is no agreed-upon gold standard, making the assessment of accuracy more difficult). Medicine contains both types of tasks. In some realms, diagnostic and management decisions do have a gold standard of accuracy, either through a specific form of test or verification procedure (for diagnostic decisions) or through the revelations of events (when response to a treatment offers verification of a correct decision). Other tasks are judgmental and do not have any verifiably correct solution.

One recent overview of the literature comparing individual and group decision making suggests that there is no simple empirical answer to the question of whether groups are more or less accurate than individuals (Kerr, MacCoun, & Kramer, 1996). The authors focused on a specific list of bias phenomena (e.g., framing effects, preference reversals) and found that there was little consistency in the direction and magnitude of errors. The presence of error among teams depended jointly upon several factors, including (1) the size of the group, (2) the magnitude of individual bias, (3) the location of the bias, (4) the definition of the bias, (5) the normative ideal, and (6) the nature of the group process. Hence, the comparison of individuals and groups is quite complex, even when we limit ourselves to exploring the classical errors that are found in the literature on individual judgment and decision making. Further, the comparison may not be the most important issue when we move beyond basic research.

The strategy of comparing a group's decision-making performance to that of individuals may be inappropriate when applied to professional teams, especially in the field of medicine. Team-based decision making in a medical environment arises in large part out of the need to pool the diverse expertise of different physicians and other health care professionals in order to ensure that the actions of all involved are coordinated toward an appropriate and mutually agreeable goal. The need to train novice physicians in the art of clinical reasoning is also an important reason for group decision making in some settings. Therefore, instead of focusing upon individual versus group differences in decision-making performance, it may be more productive to explore the unique properties of team-based clinical decision making.

Few attempts have been made to study collaborative medical decision making. Some researchers have taken a relatively broad, almost anthropological view of medicine and have explored climate, roles, and interactions (Cicourel, 1990). Others have looked at narrowly defined tasks and have found, for instance, that a group of physicians may be more likely to continue heroic efforts in resuscitation than an individual physician (Knightengale & Miller, 1988). Still others have focused upon a specific event, such as rounds in a teaching hospital, and applied methods of discourse analysis in order to analyze discussions (Evans & Gadd, 1989). Systematic study of team medical decision making has been lacking. One place to begin such systematic study is by delineating the properties of the task environment.

Distribution of Information

One clear difference between individual and team-based decision making is that at the individual level all of the decision-making activity is carried out by one person, whereas in a team, portions of that work are often carried out by different people. To some degree, this offers teams the potential to consider a larger and more diverse sample of information than an individual decision maker. Different team members can attend to and analyze different aspects of a case using different tools and procedures. For example, the management of a critically ill patient with multiple medical problems may require input from several physicians in specialties ranging from internal medicine to psychiatry, as well as from such allied health care professionals as nurses and nutritionists. Due to their different roles and orientations, various individuals will naturally seek out and obtain different types of patient information. Moreover, different members of the medical team may have differential access to family members with distinct information. Finally, most physicians have been faced with situations in which there is significant variability in the patient's self-reports. To the extent that the diverse types of information obtained by team members are all relevant to the case, successful decision making requires that all of this information somehow be integrated.

One important mechanism for integrating case information is the patient's chart. The chart is intended to be a standard, fixed reference point for depositing and retrieving information that is relevant to the case. Unfortunately, there is wide variability in the amount and details of information cataloged, some of that information may not be fully understandable to all members of the decision-making team, and certain types of information (e.g., psychosocial informational patient desires or preferences, conflicting opinions of staff members) are not always included. Hence, patient charts may not offer a truly comprehensive record of all the information that has actually been acquired (Christoffel & Lowenthal, 1975; Ravitch et al., 1983). Group discussion, therefore, represents an integral mechanism for bringing together information.

A series of psychological studies have explored whether teams are competent in thoroughly discussing information during the decision-making process and bringing all pertinent information to light. For example, in one study (Larson, Foster-Fishman, & Keys, 1994), researchers asked groups of university students to study written descriptions of three hypothetical candidates running for student body president. Some of the candidate information was read by all students in a group (shared information), and some was read only by one student (unshared information). Although the students were told in advance that they were going to receive a mix of shared and unshared information, no one knew precisely which pieces of information were shared and unshared. Audiotape records revealed that, overall, groups discussed 44% of the information they shared but only 24% of the unshared information. Moreover, of the information that was mentioned, 41% of the shared information but only 30% of the unshared information was repeated.

The overreliance on shared information is clearly not an optimal use of group resources. It would actually be of greater help to discuss more of the unshared information. That is, discussing previously unshared information can add to the group's collective knowledge base, whereas discussing already shared information cannot. Given two pieces of information (one shared, one unshared) that are both important for making a correct decision, it seems more critical for a group to reveal the previously unshared information than it is for them to persevere with the information already available to everyone. Even without discussion, the shared information can be evaluated by all group members. Yet, despite the usefulness of discussing unshared information, it often receives less attention.

The tendency to discuss and repeat more shared than unshared information during group discussion can be traced in part to the statistical fact that when fewer people hold a given piece of problem-relevant information beforehand, there is simply a lower probability that that information will be mentioned (Stasser, 1988; Stasser & Titus, 1985). What occurs, therefore, during the group's discussion is similar to what would happen if a single individual were to draw random samples from multiple, partially redundant pools of information: he or she would oversample the redundant (shared) information and undersample the nonredundant (unshared) information. The tendency to mention more shared than unshared information during a group discussion can be expected to increase as (1) the group's size increases, (2) the overall amount of problem-relevant information increases, and (3) the percentage of shared (vs. unshared) information held in advance by individual group members increases. These postulates represent what Stasser has referred to as the "information sampling model" (Stasser 1988). Research evidence supports these predictions (Stasser, 1988, 1991; Stasser, Taylor, & Hanna, 1989; Stasser & Titus, 1985, 1987). Even under the most favorable conditions (i.e., small group size, low information load, and a small percentage of shared information), however, groups still tend to discuss disproportionately less of the previously unshared information. The value of unshared information in the decision-making process is highlighted in cases where a hidden profile exists. The term "hidden profile" refers to any situation in which the correct solution to a problem is obscured from team members because of the particular way in which problem-relevant information is initially distributed among them (Stasser, 1988; Stasser & Titus, 1985). As an example, consider a team of three physicians asked to evaluate two mutually exclusive diagnostic hypotheses for a particular patient. Imagine that a total of nine symptoms/findings are present, six implicating Disease X and three implicating Disease Y. If all nine pieces of information were known to the entire team, and if each were weighted equally in the overall evaluation, then the team should be more inclined to believe that the patient has Disease X than Disease Y (since more of the symptoms point to Disease X). Suppose, however, that prior to discussion, the information favoring Disease X is distributed such that two pieces are held by each team member, while all of the information favoring Disease Y is available to all team members. Thus, each member holds five pieces of information – two favoring Disease X and three favoring Disease Y. The profile that is apparent to each team member prior to group discussion – the manifest profile – favors Disease Y. On the other hand, the profile that would appear if all group members were to divulge all of their information favors Disease X. The hidden profile is likely to come to light only if there is a complete and open exchange of information among the team members. But the literature suggests that a complete exchange of information may not always take place.

Team Member Characteristics

In addition to the prediscussion distribution of information, teams are characterized by further diversity in the sense that individuals with very different backgrounds are often brought to work together. Clinical team members may differ in the amount and type of training they have received, as well as in demographic characteristics such as gender and sociocultural background.

Consider the potential impact of member status upon the exchange of information during group discussion. Most medical teams are composed of individuals who differ in the amounts of training they have had and/or the amounts of time they have spent in clinical settings. "Status" refers to one's rank, worth, or prestige within the group, as perceived both by oneself and by others. A physician's status is enhanced by having superior scientific training, more clinical experience, and more credentials of certification from professional associations (Bourdieu, 1981; Freidson, 1972). Status is often correlated with expertise, but cases do arise in which they are independent. Furthermore, in many working environments, high-status members must rely on lower-status members to obtain important case information. Therefore, status is no guarantee of decision-making effectiveness.

Still, there is substantial empirical evidence that high-status group members generally have more influence on the group and its decisions than do low-status group members (Davis, 1980; Penrod & Hastie, 1979, 1980). For instance, Maier and Hoffman (1960) found that groups spent much more of their time addressing the ideas of high-status members than they did exploring alternative problem solutions suggested by lower-status members. Similarly, in a study examining the influence of induced status, three-person decision-making groups first received feedback arranged to create the impression that one of their members had performed extremely well on an initial problem (past accomplishments also confer status) (Kirchler & Davis, 1986). Later, group decisions on two problems (a personnel-selection task and a resource-allocation task) were found to be highly influenced by the opinions of the high-status member.

Several investigations have also documented the specific communication patterns that evolve among group members who vary in status. In general, more communication is both initiated and received by high-status members than by low-status members, and the messages directed to high-status members tend to be more positive than those directed to low-status members (Bradly, 1978; Dean, Willis, & Hewitt, 1975; Fandt & Ferris, 1990; Shaw, 1981; Worcel, 1957). Furthermore, low-status group members more often accept the opinions and ideas of high-status members than vice versa, in part because they fear retribution and in part because they frequently are less confident in their own abilities (Costanzo, Reitan, & Shaw, 1968; Deutsch & Gerrard, 1955; Ross, Amabile, & Steinmetz, 1977; Rubin & Brown, 1975). In light of these patterns, we might expect that low-status members of a medical decision-making team will sometimes communicate less information during group discussions than will high-status members, and in general will have less influence on the team's decisions.

These patterns may not be problematic if high-status member(s) have direct access to all relevant case information. However, there are clinical situations in which the high-status team member (e.g., the attending physician) must rely upon less expert colleagues to supply at least a portion of the case information. For example, in teaching hospitals, attending physicians are held responsible for decisions about patient care, but it is often a novice physician who initially collects most of the case information. The faculty member eventually gets that information, in part by interrogating the novice. But as Cicourel (1990) has pointed out, because such interrogations often take place when time is at a premium, there is substantial variability in the amount of information that actually comes to light.

Because of this, the information management role of group leaders is crucial. Group leaders can encourage all members to share their opinions, regardless of whether or not their opinions are shared by other members of the group (Maier and Solem, 1952; Mucchi-Faina, Maass, and Volpato, 1991; Nemeth 1986; Nemeth and Wachtler, 1983; Peterson & Nemeth, 1996), or they can inform or even advocate their position before the group discusses all of the information (Flowers, 1977; Janis, 1982; Leana, 1985). The most successful leaders of team decision making may be those who serve a facilitory role in the group by encouraging all members to share both information and opinions and by reiterating information and opinions that have previously been discussed (Maier, 1967). Hence, status should be accompanied by behaviors that facilitate good decision making.

Several factors beyond status add complexity to the team decision-making environment. For instance, group dynamics in medicine, as in other professional arenas, has changed considerably in the last 50 years due to the influx of increasing numbers of women into the profession. A large body of older research in a variety of contexts indicates that women are often judged to be less competent than equally qualified men during problem solving and decision making (Lott, 1985; Wallston & O'Leary, 1981). In one study, Toder (1980) found that both female and male college students in mixed-gender groups evaluated female-authored articles less favorably than identical male-authored articles, whereas female subjects in all-female groups did not display gender discrimination. In another study, Nemeth, Endicott, and Wachtler (1976) found that even when men and women had the same amount of activity on a jury task, women were rated lower on such characteristics as leadership and influence on the group.

Others have found that not only are perceptions of members' behaviors influenced by the gender composition of the team, but also that women's ideas can be suppressed altogether in mixed-gender groups, particularly when women are in a distinct minority (Toder, 1980). This can be especially true when the women are considered to be of lower status than the men, for example, physicians and nurses (McMahan, Hoffman, & McGee, 1994; Stahelski & Tsukuda, 1990). Lamb and

Napodano (1984), studying physician–nurse practitioner collaboration in primary care settings, found that what few collaborative interactions did take place were initiated by the nurse practitioners.

Still, as increasing numbers of women become integrated into group decision tasks, group processes and perceptions may be changing. For instance, Hawkins (1995) examined group processes in mixed-gender groups of undergraduates working together over a 4-month period and found no significant gender differences in the production of task-relevant communication. In another study with a male-oriented task, Rogelberg and Rumery (1996) found that as the number of males on a mixed team increased, so did decision quality. However, the all-female teams outperformed the all-male teams, raising interesting issues of group dynamics.

Homogeneity, in terms of gender, may not always be clearly beneficial or harmful to the decision-making process. Group member homogeneity is one of the key factors that has been used to predict whether a group will be susceptible to groupthink (the tendency to go along with a powerful leader or majority opinion and not let dissenting opinions surface). Recent research indicates that homogeneous groups are generally more susceptible to groupthink than heterogeneous groups (Kroon, Van Kreveld, & Rabbie, 1992). Furthermore, one must consider whether a distinction in group processes may exist between groups created for temporary experimental purposes and real working groups of professionals.

Gender is not the only factor that impacts upon homogeneity in medical decision-making teams. Obviously a large proportion of foreign medical school graduates obtain postgraduate training and eventually practice in the United States. Similarly, growing numbers of African American and Latino practitioners continue to enter the mix. The great asset of diversity in bringing multiple perspectives and diverse information to team decision making also brings interpersonal complexity to the group interaction and must be understood.

Research on culturally diverse teams making nonmedical decisions has indicated that culturally mixed groups sometimes make decisions that are more conservative (less risky) than those of culturally homogeneous groups (Watson & Kumar, 1992). Other researchers have shown that cultural minorities may contribute less to decisions than nonminorities unless a system that creates constructive conflict is utilized (Kirchmeyer & Cohen, 1992). Clearly, each culture has its own norms about group processes, and it is difficult to predict how these norms will interact with any constellation of people. Still, the impact of cultural diversity in clinical teams cannot be ignored.

A Research Program in Team Medical Decision Making

The goal of our recent research program was to explore how thoroughly teams of physicians possessing some of the characteristics described earlier could discuss and integrate patient case information. Several studies were performed to address these issues (Christensen & Larson, 1993; Larson & Christensen, 1993; Larson, Christensen, Abbott, & Franz, 1996; Larson, Christensen, Franz, & Abbott, 1998). In most studies, three-person groups, each consisting of a third-year medical student, a first-year resident, and a third-year resident, were asked to diagnose hypothetical cases. Subjects first individually viewed patient cases presented via videotape. Information was distributed across the videotapes so that some of it was seen by all members of a team, while some was provided to only one team member (i.e., each team member was supplied with a "personalized" set of information).

Consider the following case description:

Jane Reynolds is a 45-year-old woman who presents at her doctor's office. The physician she is seeing today is covering for her regular doctor, who is away. Jane has a history of recurrent pneumonia and has not been feeling well. She thinks that she has the flu and is concerned about the possibility of having pneumonia again. Jane reports that she has been having trouble swallowing food and has had a cough, fever, and swollen lymph nodes. She also complains of being bothered by some sores in her mouth and a rash on her face. In addition, Jane mentions that she is suffering from joint pain, swelling, and stiffness, for which she has been taking a lot of aspirin. She has a history of arthritis, as does her mother. Jane's regular physician recently found that her white blood cell count was less than 4,000 and her antinuclear antibody was positive (she does not report this to the current physician). Jane mentioned to a medical student (on clerkship) on the way into the office that she is not looking forward to summer this year, as she loves outdoor activities but burns very easily in the sun.

Given the constellation of symptoms described, Jane is most likely to have lupus. This diagnosis, however, may not be immediately obvious to the physician that Jane is seeing since she is not aware of Jane's blood results or photosensitivity. The photosensitivity, in fact, is a factor that could easily be overlooked by many patients and physicians if they are not already considering particular diagnoses. The correct diagnosis of

Jane Reynolds's, case requires that information from numerous sources be combined.

This is one of two hypothetical clinical cases created for a study testing the effects of hidden profiles upon diagnostic decision making (Christensen, Larson, Abbott, & Franz, submitted). The diagnoses for the cases (lupus and Parkinson's disease) were chosen because they were moderately common and could include a variety of symptoms that would allow the consideration of other diagnoses. Cases were constructed by a general internist with the aid of Quick Medical Reference (QMR), one of the oldest and best-developed medical expert systems available, which at the time supported the diagnosis of more than 600 complex diseases in internal medicine (Camdat Corporation, 1994; Masarie & Miller, 1990). The information included in each case was selected such that, when the cases were considered together, the target diagnosis was ranked first by QMR (either lupus or Parkinson's disease). Hence, the gold standard for our studies was provided by a computerized expert system.

Multiple videotaped versions of each case were created, with slightly different versions to be viewed by the resident, intern, and medical student (versions A, B, and C). Each tape contained some information that was present in all tapes (shared information) and some information that appeared only in one tape (unshared information). In the "hidden profile" condition, information appeared in the three tapes such that any one tape would lead to the wrong diagnosis (according to QMR). To construct hidden profile cases, the most crucial pieces of diagnostic information were divided among the videotapes, making it impossible to generate a correct diagnosis without discussion. Tapes in the control condition also contained a mix of shared and unshared information; however, the critical information in this instance was shared (available in all tapes) so as to lead to a correct diagnosis without having to pool team members' information. Regardless of the particular distribution of information across tapes in any condition, each team collectively possessed a complete set of all available case information.

After individuals viewed their first tape, the team joined together and the resident was handed a "Team Diagnostic Report Form" that asked for the four most likely diagnoses and associated probabilities. The resident was told that as the senior member of the team, she/he would be responsible for the team's diagnosis. Teams were informed that their discussions would be videotaped. After the team discussion was completed, all persons were handed individual diagnostic forms, on which they listed their personal diagnostic decisions and associated probabilities, as well as factors that they considered important in generating their diagnoses.

Results revealed that the correct diagnosis was listed first more often by teams diagnosing control cases than by those diagnosing hidden profile cases. Overall, 17 of 24 hidden profile cases in this study were diagnosed correctly, while all of the control cases were correctly diagnosed. Further, in order to analyze the discussion of information, videotapes were coded by two raters who were unaware of the study hypotheses or of which information (cue set A, cue set B, cue set C) had been seen by each subject. "Shared information" was that which had been in all three videotapes prior to discussion, while "unshared information" had appeared in only one tape. As predicted, teams mentioned a larger percentage of their shared information (M = .67) than they did of their unshared information (M = .46).

Such suboptimal pooling may diminish the impact that unshared information has on the groups' final decision in comparison to the impact shared information will have. While there may be many clinical situations in which failure to utilize unshared information appropriately may not harm the quality of the diagnostic decision, some situations may arise in which the distribution of unshared information among members of a clinical team may be analogous to the hidden profile we created. In these situations, teams are vulnerable to making the same incorrect diagnoses that were made by the hidden profile teams in our study.

The results of a similar study utilizing clinical cases involving alcohol-induced hypoglycemia and kidney stones provided additional support for the information sampling model of group discussion (Larson et al., 1996). Again, teams of three (medical student, intern, resident) diagnosed cases after each team member viewed an interview containing some shared and some unshared information. A comparison of shared and unshared information revealed that a greater focus was placed on shared information. Not only was shared information more likely to be mentioned before unshared information, it also accounted for significantly more discussion time.

Additional analyses of the same study data allowed us to explore further the information management role that team leaders played in problem-solving and decision-making groups. Similarly to previous research indicating that group leaders have a high rate of participation in group discussion (Hastie & Pennington, 1991; Reynolds, 1984; Ruback,

Dabbs, & Hopper, 1984; Stein & Heller, 1979, 1983), an analysis of record-ings of group discussion revealed that team leaders were responsible for generating the largest amount of talk time and were more likely than other group members to repeat case information. This greater level of discussion participation may be indicative of a facilitory role taken on by the team leader. While team leaders continued to repeat shared and un-shared information that had been provided to them prior to discussion, they also repeated unshared information that was not known to them prior to discussion. By repeating all types of information during the discussion, the team leader essentially acts as the group's short-term memory, allowing more of the available information to be integrated into the decision-making process. In addition, by repeating unshared information, the leader can possibly offset the group's tendency to fo-cus on shared as opposed to unshared information. This interpretation is consistent with Maier's (1967) argument that information integration is an essential leadership role in problem-solving groups and is also in agreement with Larson and Christensen's (1993) functional analysis of group problem solving. While there are still significant problems with team decision making, these leaders were doing something very right.

Although we have learned a great deal about leader behavior and group processes in medical decision making, numerous characteristics of team members were difficult to study in our project. For example, in order to recruit teams of three decision makers varying in expertise who had to spend substantial time in our studies (a two- or three-hour ses-sion), we did not control the gender or sociocultural composition of our groups. More attention is needed to explore the influence of these factors. We would also like to study teams over a longer period of time to see if they can develop some understanding of members' roles that might al-low them to overcome some of the problems consistently demonstrated in uncovering unique information. If I am aware that a colleague is typically very attentive to a certain type of information (lab results, a clinical domain, etc.) and that colleague is cognizant of my areas of in-terest and my clinical strengths, we should all be better able to navigate the discussion of information.

Many other questions arise as we attempt to bridge the gap between psychological research and the actual clinical domain. For instance, much information in real-life encounters is neither totally shared (pos-sessed by all team members prior to discussion) nor totally unshared (possessed by only one member). One of the reasons that has been given in the psychological literature for groups' overreliance on shared information is that the credibility of unshared information is suspect. Because it is possessed by only one group member, there is no way of validating the information. Schittekatte and Van Hiel (1996) sought to rectify this situation by utilizing partially shared information (information available to two of four group members). In addition, they provided each subject with a sheet that highlighted which of their information was unshared or unique (mocking what happens with professionals who should be aware of what information is relevant for various members in light of subspecialty, previous training, or clinical role). Results indicated that although the teams still had an overall tendency to rely disproportionately on shared information, this tendency was reduced when partially shared information was used and when team members were made conscious of which information they uniquely held. Parks and Cowlin (1996) increased the influence of uniquely held information by making it demonstrable (having written descriptions of the problem available in some conditions which could be used to verify facts). When facts could not be verified, they needed to be supported by the majority of group members in order for significant discussion to take place.

The issue of group process becomes further complicated when one considers that medicine, like all work environments, now possesses not only interpersonal teams but also "technological teams" that must exchange information via computer terminals and other communication devices (fax, conference call, video display, etc.). Such teams will likely be influenced by some of the factors that impact face-to-face teams, but other factors may also apply. Dennis (1996) hypothesized that problems in revealing unique information would be reduced among teams that communicated via computer, since the technology provided anonymity (reducing status, etc.) and a means of recording all of the information that had been offered. However, the computerized groups in his study still relied heavily on previously shared information.

Clearly, there are many factors beyond those discussed in this chapter that impact upon team decision making in medicine. And as the clinical environment evolves (medically, demographically, technologically, etc.), issues will continue to change. Still, it appears that some of the problems that arise among nonmedical decision-making teams also apply to the clinical domain. As long as we continue routinely to rely upon groups to make important decisions, it is important to identify and limit their potential biases and errors. These efforts may allow us to someday declare that, in this important domain, two heads are, in fact, better than one.

References

Balla, J. (1985). *The diagnostic process*. New York: Cambridge University Press.

Barrows, H. S., Freightner, J. W., Neufeld, V. R., & Norman, G. R. (1982). The clinical reasoning of randomly selected physicians in general medicine. *Clinical and Investigative Medicine, 5*, 49–55.

Bourdieu, P. (1981). The specificity of the scientific field. In C. Lemert (Ed.), *French sociology* (pp. 257–292). New York: Columbia University Press.

Bradly, P. H. (1978). Power, status, and upward communication in small decision making groups. *Communication Monographs, 45*, 33–43.

Camdat Corporation (1994). Quick Medical Reference (QMR) Version 3.5 [computer program]. San Bruno, CA: Author.

Christensen, C., Elstein, A. S., Bernstein, L. M., & Balla, J. I. (1991). Formal decision supports in medical practice and education. *Teaching and Learning in Medicine, 3*, 62–70.

Christensen, C., & Larson, J. R., Jr. (1993). Collaborative medical decision making. *Medical Decision Making, 13*, 339–346.

Christensen, C., Larson, J. R., Jr., Abbott, A. S., Ardolindo, A., Franz, T. M., & Pfeiffer, C. (in press). Decision making of clinical teams: Communication patterns and diagnostic error. *Medical Decision Making*.

Christoffel, R., & Lowenthal, M. (1975). Evaluating the quality of ambulatory care: A review of emerging methods. *Medical Care, 15*, 877–884.

Cicourel, A. V. (1990). The integration of distributed knowledge in collaborative medical diagnosis. In J. Galegher, R. E. Kraut, & C. Edigdo (Eds.), *Intellectual teamwork: Social and technological foundations of cooperative work* (pp. 221–242). Hillsdale, NJ: Erlbaum.

Costanzo, P. R., Reitan, H. T., & Shaw, M. E. (1968). Conformity as a function of experimentally induced minority and majority competence. *Pychonomic Science, 10*, 329–330.

Davis, J. H. (1980). Group decision and procedural justice. In M. Fishbein (Ed.), *Progress in social psychology* (Vol. 1, pp. 157–229). Hillsdale, NJ: Erlbaum.

Dean, L. M., Willis, F. N., & Hewitt, J. (1975). Initial interaction distance among individuals equal and unequal in military rank. *Journal of Personality and Social Psychology, 32*, 294–299.

Dennis, A. R. (1996). Information exchange and use in small group decision making. *Small Group Research, 27*(4), 532–550.

Deutsch, M., & Gerrard, H. (1955). A study of normative and informational social influence on individual judgment. *Journal of Abnormal Social Psychology, 51*, 629–636.

Einhorn, H. J., Hogarth, R. M., & Klempner, E. (1977). Quality of group judgment. *Psychological Bulletin, 84*, 158–172.

Elstein, A. S., Shulman, L., & Sprafka, S. (1978). *Medical problem solving: An analysis of clinical reasoning*. Cambridge, MA: Harvard University Press.

Evans, D. A., & Gadd, C. S. (1989). Managing coherence and context in medical problem-solving discourse. In D. A. Evans & V. L. Patel (Eds.), *Cognitive science in medicine: Biomedical modeling* (pp. 211–252). Cambridge, MA: MIT Press.

Fandt, P. M., & Ferris, G. R. (1990). The management of information and impressions: When employees behave opportunistically. *Organizational Behavior and Human Decision Processes, 45*, 140–158.

Flowers, M. L. (1977). A laboratory test of some implications of Janis' groupthink hypothesis. *Journal of Personality and Social Psychology, 35*, 888–896.

Freidson, E. (1972). *Profession of medicine: A study of the sociology of applied knowledge.* New York: Atherton.

Hastie, R. (1986). Review essay: Experimental evidence on group accuracy. In B. Grofman & G. Guillermo (Eds.), *Information pooling and group decision making* (Vol. 2, pp. 129–157). Greenwich, CT: JAI Press.

Hastie, R., & Pennington, N. (1991). Cognitive and social processes in decision making. In L. B. Resnick, J. M. Levine, & S. D. Teasley (Eds.), *Perspectives on socially shared cognition* (pp. 308–327). Washington, DC: American Psychological Association.

Hastie, R., & Rasinski, K. A. (1988). The concept of accuracy in social judgment. In D. Bar-Tal & A. W. Kruglanski (Eds.), *The social psychology of knowledge* (pp. 193–208). New York: Cambridge University Press.

Hawkins, K. W. (1995). Effects of gender and communication content of leadership emergence in small task-oriented groups. *Small Group Research, 26(2),* 234–249.

Hill, G. W. (1987). Group versus individual performance: Are N+1 heads better than one? *Psychological Bulletin, 91,* 517–539.

Janis, I. L. (1982). *Victims of groupthink* (2nd ed.). Boston: Houghton Mifflin.

Johnson, P. E. (1983). What kind of expert should a system be? *Journal of Medicine and Philosophy, 8,* 77–97.

Kerr, N. L., MacCoun, R. J., & Kramer, G. P. (1996). Bias in judgment: Comparing individuals and groups. *Psychological Review, 103,* 687–719.

Kirchler, E., & Davis, J. H. (1986). The influence of status differences and task type on group consensus and member position change. *Journal of Personality and Social Psychology, 51,* 83–91.

Kirchmeyer, C., & Cohen, A. (1992). Multicultural groups: Their performance and reactions with constructive conflict. *Group and Organization Management, 17(2),* 153–170.

Knightengale, S., & Miller, D. (1988). *Group polarization in medical decision making.* Paper presented at the meeting of the Society for Medical Decision Making, Richmond, VA, November 1988.

Kroon, M. B., Van Kreveld, D., & Rabbie, J. M. (1992). Group versus individual decision making: Effects of accountability and gender on groupthink. *Small Group Research, 23(4),* 427–458.

Lamb, G. S., & Napodano, R. (1984). Physician–nurse practitioner interactions and participatory decision making with physicians. *American Journal of Public Health, 74,* 26–29.

Larson, J. E., Jr., & Christensen, C. (1993). Groups as problem solving units: Toward a new meaning of social cognition. *British Journal of Social Psychology, 32,* 5–30.

Larson, J. R., Jr., Christensen, C., Abbott, A. S., & Franz, T. (1996). Charting the flow of information in medical decision making teams. *Journal of Personality and Social Psychology, 71,* 315–330.

Larson, J. R., Jr., Christensen, C., Franz, T. M., & Abbott, A. S. (1998). Diagnosing groups: The pooling, management, and impact of shared and unshared case information in team-based medical decision making. *Journal of Personality and Social Psychology, 75,* 93–108.

Larson, J. R., Jr., Foster-Fishman, P. G., & Keys, C. B. (1994). Information sharing in decision-making groups. *Journal of Personality and Social Psychology, 67,* 446–461.

Laughlin, P. R., & Ellis, A. L. (1986). Demonstrability and social combination processes on mathematical intellective tasks. *Journal of Experimental Social Psychology, 22,* 17–189.

Leana, C. R. (1985). A partial test of Janis' groupthink model: Effects of group cohesiveness and leader behavior on defective decision making. *Journal of Management, 11,* 5–17.

Lott, B. L. (1985). The devaluation of women's competence: Effects of sex, marital status, and parental status. *Journal of Social Issues, 41,* 43–60.

Maier, N. R. F. (1967). Assets and liabilities in group problem solving: The need for an integrative function. *Psychological Review, 74,* 239–249.

Maier, N. R. F., & Hoffman, L. R. (1960). Quality of first and second solutions in group problem solving. *Psychological Monographs, 78,* 580.

Maier, N. R. F., & Solem, A. R. (1952). The contribution of a discussion leader to the quality of group thinking: The effective use of minority opinions. *Human Relations, 5,* 277–288.

Masarie, F. E., & Miller, R. A. (1990). QMR: A diagnostic decision-support program for internal medicine. *Group Practice Journal, 39,* 16–25.

McGrath, J. E. (1984). *Groups: Interaction and performance.* Englewood Cliffs, NJ: Prentice-Hall.

McMahan, E. M., Hoffman, K., & McGee, G. W. (1994). Physician–nurse relationships in clinical settings: A review and critique of the literature, 1966–1992. *Medical Care Review, 51,* 83–112.

McNeil, B. J., Parker, S. G., Sox, H. C., & Tversky, A. (1982). On the elicitation of preferences for alternative therapies. *New England Journal of Medicine, 306,* 1259–1262.

Miller, R. A., Pople, H. E., & Myers, J. D. (1982). Internist-I, an experimental computer-based diagnostic consultation for general internal medicine. *New England Journal of Medicine, 307,* 468–476.

Mucchi-Faina, A., Maass, A., & Volpato, C. (1991). Social influence: The case of originality. *European Journal of Social Psychology, 21,* 183–197.

Nemeth, C. J. (1986). Differential contributions of majority and minority influence. *Psychological Review, 93,* 1–10.

Nemeth, C., Endicott, J., & Wachtler, J. (1976). From the 50s to the 70s: Women in jury deliberations. *Sociometry, 39,* 293–304.

Nemeth, C. J., & Wachtler, J. (1983). Creative problem solving as a result of majority and minority influence. *European Journal of Social Psychology, 13,* 45–55.

Parks, C. D., & Cowlin, R. A. (1996). Acceptance of uncommon information into group discussion when that information is or is not demonstrable. *Organizational Behavior and Human Decision Making, 66,* 307–315.

Penrod, S., & Hastie, R. (1979). Models of jury decision making: A critical review. *Psychological Bulletin, 86,* 133–159.

Penrod, S., & Hastie, R. (1980). A computer simulation of jury decision making. *Psychological Review, 87,* 462–492.

Peterson, R. S., & Nemeth, C. J. (1996). Focus versus flexibility: Majority and minority influence can both improve performance. *Personality and Social Psychology Bulletin, 22,* 14–23.

Ravitch, M. M., Rovner, D. R., Jennett, P. A., Rothert, M. L., Holmes, M. M., Holzman, G. B., & Elstein, A. S. (1983). A chart audit study of the referral of obese patients to endocrinologists. *Medical Decison Making, 3,* 69–74.

Reynolds, P. D. (1984). Leaders never quit: Talking, silence, and influence in interpersonal groups. *Small Group Behavior, 15,* 404–413.

Rogelberg, S. G., & Rumery, S. M. (1996). Gender diversity, team decision quality, time on task, and interpersonal cohesion. *Small Group Research, 27*(1), 79–90.

Ross, L. D., Amabile, T. M., & Steinmetz, J. L. (1977). Social roles: Social control and biases in social perception. *Journal of Personality and Social Psychology, 28,* 69–76.

Ruback, R. B., Dabbs, J. M., & Hopper, C. H. (1984). The process of brainstorming: An analysis with individual and group vocal parameters. *Journal of Personality and Social Psychology, 47,* 558–567.

Rubin, J. Z., & Brown, B. R. (1975). *The social psychology of bargaining and negotiation.* New York: Academic Press.

Schittekatte, M., & Van Hiel, A. (1996). Effects of partially shared information and awareness of unshared information on information sampling. *Small Group Research, 27*(3), 431–449.

Shaw, M. E. (1981). *Group dynamics: The psychology of small group behavior.* New York: McGraw-Hill.

Stahelski, A. J., & Tsukuda, R. A. (1990). Predictors of cooperation in health care teams. *Small Group Research, 21,* 220–233.

Stasser, G. (1988). Computer simulation as a research tool: The DISCUSS model of group discussion. *Journal of Personality and Social Psychology, 24,* 393–422.

Stasser, G. (1991). *Facilitating the use of unshared information in decision making groups.* Paper presented at the 63rd annual meeting of the Midwestern Psychological Association, Chicago, May 1991.

Stasser, G., & Taylor, L. A., & Hanna, C. (1989). Information sampling in structured discussion among three- and six-person groups. *Journal of Personality and Social Psychology, 57,* 67–78.

Stasser, G., & Titus, W. (1985). Pooling of unshared information in group decision making: Biased information sampling during discussion. *Journal of Personality and Social Psychology, 48,* 1467–1478.

Stasser, G., & Titus, W. (1987). Effects of information load and percentage of shared information on the dissemination of unshared information during group discussion. *Journal of Personality and Social Psychology, 53,* 81–93.

Stein, R. T., & Heller, T. (1979). An empirical analysis of the correlations between leadership status and participation rates reported in the literature. *Journal of Personality and Social Psychology, 37,* 1993–2002.

Stein, R. T., & Heller, T. (1983). The relationship of participation rates to leadership status: A meta-analysis. In H. H. Blumberg, A. P. Hare, V. Kent, & M. F. Davies (Eds.), *Small groups and social interaction* (Vol. 1, pp. 401–408). Chichester, England: Wiley.

Toder, N. L. (1980). The effect of the sexual composition of groups on discrimination against women and sex role attitudes. *Psychology of Women Quarterly, 5,* 292–310.

Vollrath, D. A., Sheppard, B. H., Hinsz, V., & Davis, J. H. (1989). Memory performance by decision-making groups and individuals. *Organizational Behavior and Human Decision Processes, 43,* 289–300.

Wallston, B. S., & O' Leary, V. E. (1981). Sex makes a difference: Differential perceptions of women and men. In L. Wheeler (Ed.), *Review of personality and social psychology*, (Vol. 2, pp. 9–41). Beverly Hills, CA: Sage.

Watson, W. E., & Kumar, K. (1992). Differences in decision making regarding risk taking: A comparison of culturally diverse and culturally homogeneous task groups. *International Journal of Intercultural Relations, 16*(1), 53–65.

Worcel, P. (1957). Catharsis and relief of hostility. *Journal of Abnormal Social Psychology, 55*, 238–343.

Part IV

Applications

11 Assessing Patients' Preferences

Anne M. Stiggelbout, PhD

1. Introduction

In medical decision making, different attributes of treatment outcomes often have to be weighed. For instance, does the improved survival due to a new treatment outweigh the side effects of that treatment? Or do patients prefer a better quality of life to a longer survival, and will they therefore prefer a less toxic treatment? For such decisional purposes a valuation of the health outcomes is needed. In the clinical encounter, such a valuation is usually performed in an informal, implicit manner. The recent developments toward shared decision making have created a need for an explicit assessment of patient preferences for outcomes of treatment. Moreover, for the development of guidelines and for the formulation of health care policy, formal valuation of outcomes forms part of evidence-based medicine.

These valuations are obtained by utility assessment, a method of measuring the levels of subjective satisfaction, distress, or desirability that people associate with particular outcomes (Bush 1984). Utilities are defined as cardinal numbers that represent the strength of an individual's preference for particular outcomes when faced with uncertainty (Torrance and Feeny 1989). They are assigned to each outcome, or health state, on a scale that is established by assigning a value of 1 to the state of perfect health and 0 to death. In decision analysis the utilities of the possible outcomes of each treatment option are elicited and combined with the probabilities associated with these possible outcomes. Thus the expected utility of each treatment option is obtained, and the preferred treatment is the one with the highest expected utility (see Chapter 2, this volume). Quality-adjusted life years (QALYs) are obtained when the utilities are combined with the expected survival duration for each treatment outcome. QALYs express health status in terms of equivalents of "well years" of life and reflect the relative desirability of treatment outcomes with respect to quality of life and length of life. Utilities are used as the quality adjustment factor: life years in a health state are multiplied by the utility of that health state to obtain QALYs (see Chapter 3, this volume). For example, two years in a health state that is valued at only one half of perfect health, i.e., as having a utility of 0.5, are equivalent to 1 QALY ($2 \times 0.5 = 1$).

From the preceding discussion, it can be seen that the term *utility* is employed in two senses. First, it is used in the sense of a valuation of a health state, such as in "the utility for the health state angina is 0.8." This utility is the quality adjustment factor that is needed to calculate QALYs. Although some authors use utility scores in this sense as quality of life scores, utility is a concept essentially different from quality of life per se. Utilities reflect both the quality of life and the value of that quality of life to the patient (Guyatt et al. 1993). A second way in which the term *utility* is used is in an aggregate sense, such as in "the expected utility of treatment strategy. A is higher than that of strategy B," in which utility is used as an overall outcome measure of a decision analysis.

A distinction is usually made between utility, i.e., strength of preference under uncertainty, and value, i.e., strength of preference under certainty (Keeney and Raiffa 1976). In most medical decisions, outcomes may occur with a particular probability, and the decision problem is thus a problem of choice under uncertainty.

The rest of this chapter is primarily concerned with assessing patient preferences by the use of utility assessment, even though, for individual patient decision making, alternative methods have been developed. However, these methods, which are discussed at the end of the chapter, have not yet been extensively applied in practice and still need thorough evaluation. The chapter is organized as follows. In Section 2 a distinction is made between the different levels of health care decision making, a distinction that has implications for the methods to be used in preference assessment. Part of this section is devoted to health status classification systems, systems that are primarily used for assessing preferences of the general public but that nevertheless deserve mention in this chapter. Section 3, which pertains to the choice of the utility assessment method, discusses the methods most often used, the criteria for the selection of a method, and the conditions under which certain methods are more appropriate than others. Whether or not risk is involved in the decision at hand is such a condition that is of major importance for the choice of a method, and this issue is discussed in more detail in this section. Section 4 discusses scaling problems encountered in utility assessment, both at the upper end of the scale, where comorbidities play a role, and at the lower end, where states worse than death potentially exist. Section 5 is concerned with factors that may determine utilities, such as sociodemographics or quality of life. In Section 6, finally, nonutility-based preference methods are discussed. These methods have been developed for individual patient decision making as an alternative to utility-based methods. Utilities are notably used for group decision making. Why this is the case is explained in this section, and the alternative methods, the probability trade-off methods, are described. The chapter ends with a summary in Section 7.

2.   Levels of Decision Making in Health Care

Distinction of Three Levels and Its Consequences
for Preference Assessment

In health care, three levels of decision making are generally distinguished (Sutherland and Till 1993; Torrance 1986), which require different approaches to preference assessments. The first, the micro level, applies to individual patient decision making. A decision has to be made on the treatment for a particular patient, given his or her disease characteristics and sociodemographic and personal circumstances. The second, the meso level, pertains to guideline development at the level of patient groups or at the hospital level. At this level, decisions are made for defined groups of patients with the same disease. The third level is the societal or macro level, at which choices have to be made between programs when resources are limited. Sometimes a fourth level is distinguished, a meta level, at which choices have to be made between various fields of public expenditure, e.g., health care versus defense or versus education. The third and fourth levels address economic issues, but with growing budget constraints, the second and sometimes even the first level increasingly consider costs in addition to effectiveness.

The QALY concept is most appropriate for group-level analyses, either at the meso or at the macro level. In medical decision making at the micro level, patients' relative preferences for treatments are more often assessed than their preferences for health states, and for this purpose probability trade-off methods are used instead of utility assessment methods (Section 6). Another difference between the levels is the source of the utilities. In clinical decision making, patient preferences are needed because the purpose is to decide upon an optimal treatment policy for an individual patient or for groups of similar patients. Decision making at the societal level seeks to inform planning decisions and the relevant values are those of the general public (the ones who are to pay for the programs). This has been stressed in the recent consensus-based recommendations for cost-effectiveness analysis (Russell et al. 1996, Weinstein et al. 1996). However, the authors acknowledge that the general public should be well informed. In some instances, therefore, patients may be better proxies for a well-informed general public than is a representative sample of that public itself.

Health Status Classification Systems for Macro-Level Analyses

If preferences for health states are elicited from individuals currently in those states, the states need not be described to the individuals in any detail. They can simply be asked to rate their current health. At the macro level, preferences for health states are elicited from individuals not currently in those health states, and the task is therefore to impart a full and complete understanding of the health states to those individuals. This is not an easy task. Also, respondents usually need to value large numbers of health states in these types of studies. Therefore, another approach is generally used for societal decision making: relying on health status classification systems. Health status classification systems are customarily composed of two components: a descriptive system and a scoring formula. The descriptive system consists of a set of domains, or attributes (mobility, cognitive functioning, mood, etc.). A health state is described by indicating the appropriate level of functioning on each domain. For instance, in the EuroQol system, each domain is divided into three levels of severity corresponding to no problem, some problem, and extreme problem. When one level from each of the five domains (mobility, self-care, usual activities, pain/discomfort, and anxiety/depression) is combined, a total of 3^5, i.e., 243 health states are defined.

The scoring formula is used to calculate the utilities of the states thus defined by the descriptive system. The formula is generally based on utilities that have been obtained in part from direct measurement and in part from application of multiattribute utility theory or statistical inference to fill in values not measured directly. In both instances, only a limited number of valuations have been obtained from the surveyed population. Premeasured preferences from samples of the general public are available for these systems (Russell et al. 1996). It suffices to map the treatment outcomes onto the descriptive system, using information from patients undergoing the treatment, and to use the scoring formula with the premeasured values to obtain utilities from the general public.

Over the last two decades, a number of health status classification systems have been developed. These include the Rosser and Kind Index (developed in the United Kingdom; see Rosser and Kind 1978), the Quality of Well-being Scale (developed in the United States; see Kaplan and Anderson 1990), the Health Utilities Index (developed in Canada; see Torrance et al. 1995), and the EuroQoL (developed in Europe; see The EuroQoL Group 1990). Increasingly, the descriptive systems of such indexes are being used in clinical trials as well, to enable cost-utility analyses from a societal perspective, using the preference weights from the general public. As this chapter deals with assessment of patient preferences, we will not elaborate on these methods further but will refer the reader to the mentioned literature.

3. Selection of the Utility Assessment Method

Description of the Methods

The methods most often used to assess utilities in medical decision making are the Standard Gamble (SG), the Time Trade-off (TTO), and the Visual Analog Scale (VAS). These methods will be described in brief. In Chapter 3 (this volume) a more elaborate discussion of the application of SG and TTO is provided.

In the SG, subjects are asked to compare a sure outcome (the health state to be evaluated) with a gamble with probability p of the best possible outcome (perfect health) and $(1 - p)$ of the worst possible outcome (usually immediate death). The utility of the health state is then equal to the value of p at which a subject is indifferent between the health state for certain and the gamble.

In the TTO a subject is asked how much time x in a state of perfect health he or she considers equivalent to a period y in ill health (Torrance et al. 1972), or, framed in another way, how much time $y - x$ he or she would be willing to trade off to obtain better health. The TTO thus assesses the perfect health equivalent x. The simplest – and most frequently used – way to transform this perfect-health equivalent into a utility (ranging from 0 to 1) is to divide x by y.

VASs are rating scales that are simple and therefore often used to obtain valuations of health states. Subjects are asked to rate the health state by placing a mark on a 10 cm scale anchored by "perfect health" and "death" (or sometimes "best possible health" and "worst possible health"). The score is obtained by counting the number of millimeters from the "death" anchor to the mark and dividing by 100. It is a simple method that can be self-administered. The VAS does not reflect any trade-off that a patient may be willing to make in order to obtain better health in terms of neither risk nor life years.

As neither the TTO nor the VAS reflects the aspect of risk, or uncertainty, they do not elicit utilities in the strict sense (see Chapter 3 of this volume for the conditions under which the TTO leads to utilities).

Other methods of health state valuation have not gained widespread use in medical decision making. The most well known are the Willingness-to-Pay, the Magnitude Estimation and variations of the latter, the Equivalence Technique, and the Person Trade-Off method (for reviews, see Torrance 1986, Nord 1992, and Richardson 1995). A method that is enjoying renewed interest in the Willingness-to-Pay (WTP) method (Gafni 1991, O'Brien and Viramontes 1994, Johnson et al. 1997). This method has been developed in the context of cost–benefit analysis, a form of economic evaluation of health care programs in which health benefits are valued in monetary terms. The direct measurement of WTP uses survey methods to elicit stated dollar values for some nonmarket commodity, such as improved health. It does so by estimating individuals' maximum willingness to pay to secure implementation of a program. The method is similar to the SG in that it elicits what the person would be prepared to forgo from current consumption to achieve an expected health improvement. In the SG the value of a health state is measured in terms of what a person is prepared to forgo or trade off in terms of risk of death. Little empirical research has been done in which WTP is compared with other measures of health state preferences. O'Brien and Viramontes (1994) found some evidence for convergent validity with preferences measured by a standard gamble. The large variation that they saw in subjects' responses compromised its discriminant validity, however. They concluded that WTP holds conceptual promise but that more empirical research is needed before it can become recognized as a valid and reliable measurement tool.

Magnitude Estimation has been challenged on several grounds (Kaplan et al. 1995). The method is not based on any specific theory of measurement, and the meaning of the scores is not linked to any decision process. The method has not been thoroughly evaluated. The reports that have been published point to serious deficiencies (Kaplan et al. 1979). In the recent literature, the method is not used anymore. The Person Trade-Off is a recently developed method that directly seeks information similar to that required as the basis for policy decisions. It does not assess utilities for health states, but directly measures the social worth of alternative health care interventions (Richardson and Nord 1997). Basically it consists in asking subjects how many outcomes of one kind they consider equivalent in social value to x outcomes of another kind. It usually asks respondents to trade a lesser health benefit for a larger number of people against a larger benefit for a smaller number of people.

The PTO and the WTP do not assess health state utilities and have been used primarily for the purpose of making societal allocation decisions. For this reason, the rest of this chapter will focus on SG, TTO, and VAS only.

Rationale for the Selection of a Method

No clear consensus exists as to which instruments should be used. The SG, TTO, and VAS methods have all been recommended at some point in time or by some authors (Nord 1992). They have been widely used in decision analyses but seemingly arbitrarily.

Selection of an instrument should be based on considerations of its measurement properties. It should fulfill psychometric requirements with respect to feasibility, reliability, and validity. All three methods have been reported to be feasible, but the SG and the TTO only if individual interviews are performed. With respect to reliability, no method seems clearly superior to the others. Reliability of all three methods has been judged acceptable for decision making at the group level (Torrance 1986). Therefore, the choice predominantly rests on aspects of validity. No clear-cut answer has been given to the question of which instrument is most valid. The SG has been claimed to be the gold standard in terms of *criterion validity* because it obeys the axioms of von Neumann–Morgenstern utility theory. However, it has been shown to be subject to biases (Hershey et al. 1982, Llewellyn-Thomas et al. 1982, Schoemaker 1982) and framing effects (McNeil et al. 1982, Tversky and Kahneman 1981), which undermines its use as a gold standard. The TTO is considered to have the highest level of *content validity* because the question it poses is most closely associated with the sorts of health care choices that need to be made (Gerard et al. 1993, Nord 1992, Richardson 1995). In line with this argument, the question of whether or not risk should be captured by the analysis has repercussions for selection of the method. The most appropriate method with respect to content validity would be the SG if risk is involved; the TTO should be chosen if trade-offs between quality of life and length of life are involved and immediate risk is not a consideration. The VAS would then be appropriate only if neither risk nor trade-offs of quality of life and length of life are involved and the weighing of different dimensions of quality of life is required.

Finally, *convergent validity* of the methods has been repeatedly studied. Differences between SG, TTO, and VAS have been found in several studies (Torrance et al. 1995; for an overview, see Nord 1992). SG scores are usually higher than TTO scores, and these, again, are higher than VAS scores. These findings will be discussed next.

Differences between SG and TTO. These differences have mostly been explained by risk attitude. The TTO score is equivalent to utility only if the patient is risk neutral with respect to survival duration (see Chapter 3, this volume). In general, subjects are risk averse (McNeil et al. 1978, Miyamoto and Eraker 1985, Stiggelbout et al. 1994), and the TTO in that case overestimates the reduction in utility due to impaired health. In Chapter 3 of this volume, a way of adjusting TTO scores for risk attitude is discussed. As most people are risk averse, TTO scores will usually be adjusted upward and will become more similar to, or equal to, SG scores. It has indeed been found that differences between TTO and SG disappeared after such correction for the utility of life years (Stiggelbout et al. 1994). When such an adjustment, which is based on theoretical considerations, indeed leads to reconciliation of the methods, convergent validity of these methods is established.

Differences between VAS and SG/TTO. The VAS does not incorporate risk (unlike the SG) or a trade-off between quality of life and length of life (unlike the TTO). Given the fact that subjects tend to be risk averse and do not easily trade life years, this method leads to lower scores than the other two methods. A power model has been proposed by Torrance (1976) to transform mean VAS scores into mean TTO scores: $TTO = 1 - (1 - VAS)^{1.61}$. In a later study a similar parameter was proposed for a transformation from VAS into SG scores: $SG = 1 - (1 - VAS)^{2.27}$ (Torrance et al. 1996). The transformation applies only to averaged scores. At the individual level, too much unexplained variation in TTO scores or SG scores remains for the VAS to be a reasonable substitute. Stiggel-bout et al. (1996) found coefficients for the VAS–TTO transformation that were not significantly different from the coefficient proposed by Torrance. Bosch and Hunink (1996), however, reported significant differences between a TTO-transformed rating scale using Torrance's value of 1.61 and a directly measured TTO, although they did not estimate the parameter. The differences between the SG-transformed VAS and a directly measured SG were not statistically significant. Two other studies that have tried to replicate Torrance's model for averaged TTO scores have found coefficients that were significantly lower than his (Loomes 1988, Van Busschbach 1994). This may have been due to the use of anchors other than perfect health and death in the VAS in these studies. These studies used the same anchors (best and worst health) and found quite similar parameters.

No convincing theoretical explanation has been given for the existence of the power transformation. Therefore, the findings need to be replicated in other populations as well to strengthen our confidence in its use. The existence of a transformation that is stable across various populations and across various decision domains may have important implications for the feasibility of utility assessment. In that case, preferences can be elicited using a VAS, as the VAS can be self-administered, whereas interviews are needed for the administration of a TTO or an SG. Next, VAS scores can be transformed to SG or TTO utilities.

More on Risk: Effects and Implications

Two mechanisms may underlie risk aversion. Many people have a positive *time preference* or a decreasing marginal utility for time (meaning that they value earlier years higher than years later in the future). Calculating a TTO score by dividing x by y does not take the discounting of time into account and therefore underestimates the utility of the health state: the years that are traded are years at the end of the given life expectancy and thus are valued lower. This time preference effect should be distinguished from what has been called a *gambling effect* (Gafni and Torrance 1984). The SG involves a gamble with one's life, and most people are averse to this gamble. Therefore, the utility from the SG will be additionally higher than that from the TTO (the value of p at which one is indifferent will be inflated such that the risk of "immediate death," $1 - p$, is small). An even stronger gambling effect for the SG can be explained in terms of rank-dependent utility theory (see Chapter 3 of this volume for an elaboration). Wakker and Stiggelbout (1995) have argued that the SG as customarily used in medical decision making is biased due to this probability distortion, which leads to overly strong risk aversion and to an overestimation of the utility of a health state. If people underestimate the probability of obtaining perfect health in the SG or, equivalently, overestimate the probability of immediate death, the value of p will be inflated. Probability distortion will happen mainly at the upper and lower ends of the scale (large and small probabilities, i.e., very good and very poor health states, respectively). A solution is to use the weighting function proposed by prospect theory to calculate the utility corresponding to that probability (Tversky and Kahneman 1992).

In a study of lung cancer patients, McNeil et al. (1978) found a very strong risk aversion in seriously ill patients. They showed that the use of five-year survival rates, common in oncology, may lead to erroneous decisions in patients who are risk averse. Patients who value the years immediately following treatment more highly than later years may prefer conservative treatment to a surgical procedure that carries a risk of immediate death. Sutherland et al. (1982) and Stiggelbout et al. (1994) also predominantly found concave (risk-averse) utility curves in health professionals and cancer patients, respectively. Miyamoto and Eraker (1985) found patients hospitalized for angina to display widely varying risk attitudes. Some were extremely risk prone, others extremely risk averse, leading to an average risk coefficient that implied risk neutrality. Verhoef et al. (1994) found that most healthy women were risk seeking in the short term and risk averse in the long term (S-shaped utility curves). As risk attitude might vary with health, it is important to assess the risk attitude of patients, especially in situations where it might affect preferences for treatments. Cher et al. (1997) showed that incorporation of risk attitude in a Markov process model for benign prostatic hypertrophy affected the number of QALYs calculated by the model and thus the choice of the treatment strategy. Failure to consider attitudes toward risk may result in recommendations from decision models that do not make sense "at the bedside" (Asch and Hershey 1995; see also Chapter 12, this volume).

Little research has focused on methods for assessing risk attitude. In all the studies mentioned, certainty equivalents have been assessed using 50–50 standard gambles. This is a complex procedure, however, and is not easily applied in all clinical settings with all possible patient groups. Moreover, the SG is subject to biases, as discussed earlier. Alternative methods would be highly useful.

There has been discussion about whether risk can be ignored in decision making at the policy level. In practice, cost-effectiveness analyses are often performed without regard to risk attitude and without respect to variation in risk attitude among patients. The use of riskless utilities for group decision making has been defended with the argument that the purpose of group decision making is to decide upon the treatment that in the long run will provide the maximal amount of well-being (based on the statistical law of large numbers). Thus, from a hospital point of view, group policy making may be seen as a series of repeated decisions instead of a one-shot decision (Elstein and Chapman 1994). In making repetitive choices people act as expected value maximizers, whereas they seem to be risk averse in making unique choices. This would then argue for the use of riskless utilities for patients' actual health states for group policy making. However, a major argument against leaving out risk attitude is that in health care, unlike other societal fields, gains and losses in healthy years cannot be redistributed (Asch and Hershey 1995; Ben-Zion and Gafni 1983). Leaving out risk gives much greater relative weight to preventing or curing minor disabilities compared with major disabilities than do utilities (Torrance et al. 1995). It may therefore lead to anomalies in priority ranking of health care programs (Hadorn 1991).

Conclusions with Respect to the Choice of the Method

In choosing among the SG, TTO, and VAS methods, aspects of validity are of main concern, given the feasibility and acceptable reliability of all three. Since more valid results will be obtained if the method is meaningful to the respondent, content validity is an important criterion. Using this criterion, the SG would be appropriate if risk is involved, the TTO if trade-offs of quality and length of life are involved and risk is not, and the VAS if only qualitative trade-offs of different dimensions of quality of life are involved. On the basis of empirical findings, we conclude that the SG as customarily used in medical decision making is biased due to probability distortion. This distortion leads to overly strong risk aversion and to an overestimation of the utility of a health state. If the decision problem at hand involves a clear risk of an immediate bad outcome, the SG can be used to elicit the indifference probability, but then the weighting function proposed by prospect theory should be used to calculate the utility corresponding to that probability. If the problem involves a less pronounced risk of an immediate bad outcome, but trade-offs between near-term and long-term outcomes are at stake, the TTO is more appropriate, adjusted for risk attitude as described in Chapter 3 of this volume.

If trade-offs of length of life or risk of death are involved, the use of the VAS is unwarranted. Nevertheless, in practice it has been used in such situations, primarily for reasons of feasibility. A score obtained in this way will be an underestimate of the true utility (of the willingness of patients to live), and therefore the analysis will overestimate the benefit of alleviating the health problem under study. Therefore, in a situation in which a decision results in consequences with respect to life expectancy, one should transform the inconsequential VAS score into a utility (Nord 1991), even though the findings with respect to this transformation are not unambiguous.

Finally, a point can be made for the use of more than one method if it is feasible with respect to patient burden. By combining the information from a number of measures, one can increase the validity of the generalization of the results over that which would be obtained from employing only one measure.

4. Scaling Problems

Much attention has been devoted recently to issues of scaling (Fryback and Lawrence 1997a, Harris and Nease 1997, Nichols et al. 1996). Decision theory assumes that utilities range from 0 to 1, with "death" equal to 0 and "optimal health" or "excellent health" equal to 1. However, many applications place "absence of the disease under study" at the top of the scale rather than "perfect health." Because such studies do not account for comorbidity, they systematically overestimate the benefit of alleviating the index health condition relative to studies that consider "optimal health" as the best outcome. Thus, they underestimate the cost-effectiveness ratio of the treatments under consideration. To account for comorbidity, studies using the 0–1 "death–absence of disease" scale need to be rescaled to the 0–1 "death–perfect health" scale. This is achieved by multiplying the utility of the disease under study obtained on the former scale by the utility of the absence of the disease under study obtained on the latter scale. For example, if the utility of angina on the "death–absence of angina" scale is 0.7 and the utility of absence of angina on the "death–perfect health" scale is 0.87, the utility of angina on the "death–perfect health" scale is $0.7 \times 0.87 = 0.61$. Then the benefit from relieving angina (without relieving comorbidity) is not $0.3(1-0.7)$ but 0.26, which is the difference between 0.87 (no angina) and 0.61 (see Figure 11.1).

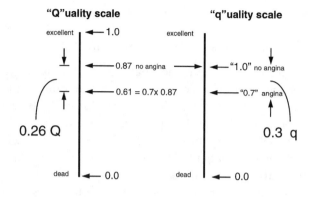

Figure 11.1. The relationship between the 0-1 dead–excellent health scale (left) and the 0-1 dead–absence of angina scale (right). Reprinted with permission from Fryback and Lawrence (1997a).

Other studies have used a scale ranging from ideal health to death but have subsequently assumed that elimination of the index condition results in ideal health, which is not the case if comorbidities are not relieved by the treatment. The more health in the absence of the index condition differs from "optimal health," the greater is the bias introduced by the failure to account for comorbidities. For comparisons across studies, analysts should explicitly consider the degree to which comorbidities affect patients' health states, i.e., assess health in the absence of the condition under consideration, on a scale from "ideal health" to "death."

Another complication may arise at the lower end of the scale because subjects have been found to consider some states worse than death (Dolan 1997, Patrick et al. 1994, Torrance et al. 1996). Patients themselves rarely state that their condition is worse than death, but healthy subjects with no experience with that condition sometimes do so. The difficulty with a scale with points worse than death is that there is no theoretical lower bound for this scale. The scores may give rise to skewed data, with subsequent difficulties in data analysis. Little has been written on this matter. The reason for this lack of attention may be that in many instances subjects will not have had the opportunity to assign negative utilities to states. To detect states worse than death, the existing methods need to incorporate modifications, which are generally not implemented.

5. Determinants of Preferences

Sociodemographics and Disease Experience

There is no compelling evidence that sociodemographic characteristics such as age, gender, socioeconomic status, marital status, race, or religion are associated with health state preferences. Froberg and Kane (1989), in their seminal series of papers, stated that this possibly was due to a power problem, since most of the studies until then had involved only small numbers of patients. However, since then, many large studies have been conducted, and no clear associations with sociodemographic characteristics have emerged. In general, the differences in valuations that are attributable to personal characteristics are trivial compared with the differences that are due to different elicitation methods and framing of the questions (see Froberg and Kane 1989 and Chapter 12, this volume).

Differences have been found in valuations assigned by patients with experience with the health state that is to be valued and by persons less familiar with the health state, such as health care workers or members of the general public. In general, patients with experience with the health state assign the highest values, members of the general public or patients without experience the lowest values, and health care professionals values between the two (Ashby et al. 1994, Boyd et al. 1990, O'Connor 1989, Rosser and Kind 1978, Sackett and Torrance 1978, and others). Several explanations for this phenomenon have been given. Having lived in a particular health state for some time, one may perceive it as more desirable than would someone who has not experienced it due to psychological processes such as coping and adaptation. Subjects unfamiliar with the condition appear to exaggerate its disutility. Furthermore, a patient truly facing a life-threatening illness may care more about risking a chance of immediate death (perceiving it as less hypothetical) than would someone who is not in immediate danger of dying and who thus would assign a higher utility on a standard gamble.

There is some indication that subjects who describe their current health as dysfunctional give higher valuations to all adverse health states (Kind 1995). This is in line with the finding that subjects in a health state generally rate that state higher than do subjects not in that state. Since the VAS was used in the study by Kind, adaptation seems the more likely one of the explanations given earlier rather than stronger risk aversion.

Quality of Life in the Health State to Be Valued

Many authors have assessed the relationship between descriptive (or psychometric) methods for the assessment of quality of life and preference-based (or valuation) methods. In 1993, Revicki and Kaplan published a review on this issue summarizing the evidence gathered up to that time. They concluded that preference-based methods and psychometric health status scores were only moderately correlated. Since then, other empirical studies have shown similar results. Correlations have been found to be poor to modest at most, and the dimensions of quality of life that have been found to correlate with valuations have varied from study to study. In some studies, values were more highly correlated with mental health; in other studies, with social functioning (see, e.g., Bosch and Hunink 1996, Chancellor et al. 1997, Chen et al. 1996, Nease et al. 1995, Nichol et al. 1996, Tsevat et al. 1993, 1996). To a large extent, this may be due to the statistical phenomenon that variation is required in the data for correlation to appear. In one study there will be more variation on the mental health dimension, in another on the social health dimension. But usually other explanations are given for the lack of correlation between descriptive and valuational scores. One is that more attributes may contribute to overall quality of life than those captured by the descriptive instrument. Moreover, risk and time are introduced in the valuation procedure, and may give rise to differences between description and valuation. The introduction of risk in the assessment may also cause ceiling effects in SG and TTO. When many health states cluster in the top end of the scale, little room is left for variation to be explained by the quality of life scores. And last, but not least, structures of preferences may differ across patients, which causes heterogeneity in the weights (importance) patients assign to health-status dimensions. It has indeed been shown that when heterogeneity is taken into account using latent class models, a larger proportion of the variation in evaluative scores is explained by the descriptive scores (Bult et al. 1996). More research is needed with respect to patient-specific weighting of dimensions of quality of life. Some descriptive instruments, such as the MACTAR (Tugwell et al. 1987) and the SEIQoL (Hickey et al. 1996), take patient importance ratings into account, but no link between these instruments and valuation methods has been provided. The main conclusion from the previous studies should be that essentially the two approaches measure distinct, though related, concepts and cannot be used interchangeably. Utilities reflect both the quality of life and the *value* of that quality of life to the patient.

A major reason why so many studies have been devoted to correlating quality of life scores and utilities has been the relative ease with which descriptive quality of life data are collected using self-administered questionnaires. Interviews are necessary for utility assessment in most settings. Therefore these measures are less likely to be included when budget constraints exist. Many studies are indeed available in which quality of life profiles and not utilities have been measured. For the purpose of cost-effectiveness analysis, it would be convenient if these data could be easily transformed into preferences.

One way to transform descriptive quality of life scores into preference-based scores is by mapping the quality of life data onto the descriptive system of a health status classification instrument. A health status classification system can be seen as a hybrid of the two approaches. It combines the descriptive approach, which is used to depict the health state, with a valuation of that health state. It should be borne in mind, though, that the valuations are not those of the patients who have provided the descriptive information, but those of a sample of the general public. The studies that have tried to map the quality of life data in this way have produced conflicting results. The findings of Coast (1992), using the Rosser Index, and those of Chancellor et al. (1997), using the EuroQoL, were disappointing. Gold et al. (1996) found more promising results using the Health Utilities Index.

Another way of obtaining valuations from quality of life profiles is by the use of prediction models. Fryback et al. (1997b) have developed a model to predict scores on the Quality of Well-being Scale, a preference-based instrument, from the SF36, a widely used generic quality of life instrument, using data from a large population-based study. This approach in fact consists of a double prediction, for the Quality of Well-being Scale is itself a health status classification system that links descriptive scores with preferences assessed in a large population-based sample through a scoring formula.

Predictions of utilities from quality of life scores are mainly used for macro-level (cost-effectiveness) analyses. The prediction of the utilities will never be perfect, but it may serve the purpose (see Fryback et al. 1997b for a discussion). In clinical decision making, where genuine patient preferences are needed, one needs to measure these preferences rather than infer them. Descriptive quality of life instruments should be used only to monitor population health, to estimate the burden of different conditions, and as endpoints in clinical trials. Valuations can be decisive in situations where one therapy or health care program is found to be superior in several aspects of health status but inferior in others, or when one program is superior with respect to life expectancy but inferior with respect to quality of life (Tsevat et al. 1996).

6.   Nonutility-Based Preference Methods

So far, this chapter has focused on utility assessment as a way of assessing patient valuations or preferences. This approach to obtaining preferences is used for the purpose of formal decision analysis (e.g., to calculate QALYs; see Chapter 3, this volume). Such a decision-analytic evaluation of a treatment involves assessing the utilities of the health states that result from that treatment and combining these utilities with the probabilities that these health states will occur. It is traditionally used when the purpose is to assess preferences for decisions at the group level, i.e., for guideline development or health care policy making. For individual patient decision making, several drawbacks of utility assessment have been observed, which have led to the development of alternative methods to assess preferences (Llewellyn-Thomas et al. 1996). First, utility assessment is cognitively complex, and subjects often do not behave according to expected utility theory. Moreover, the elicitation of utilities for transitory, nonchronic health states is more complicated than for chronic, stable states. Few authors have used utility assessment to evaluate the temporary states that a patient experiences when undergoing treatment (Jansen et al. 1998). Moreover, the methods are not sufficiently reliable for individual patient decision making.

For these reasons, new methods to assess patients' relative treatment preferences have been developed for individual patient decision making. These are the so-called probability trade-off methods. In these methods, patients' preferences for combined process-and-outcome paths are elicited in the following way. The patient is presented with two clinical options, for example, treatments A and B, which are described with respect to benefits and side effects and the chances thereof. The subject is asked to state a preference for a treatment. If treatment A is preferred, the interviewer systematically either increases the probability of benefit from treatment B or reduces the probability of benefit from treatment A (and vice versa if treatment B is preferred). The particular aspects of the treatments which are altered in this way, and the direction in which they are changed, are decided upon beforehand, according to the clinical characteristics of the problem and the nature of the research question (Llewellyn-Thomas 1997). For example, these may include the probability of side effects of treatment, risk of recurrence, or chance of survival. The relative strength of the preference for a treatment is assessed by determining the patient's willingness to accept the side effects of that treatment or forego the benefits of the alternative treatment. This general approach has been adapted specifically to a variety of treatment decisions. Examples are decisions about adjuvant chemotherapy in breast cancer (Levine et al. 1992) or ovarian cancer (Elit et al. 1996), benign prostatic hypertrophy (Llewellyn-Thomas et al. 1996), and radiotherapy for breast cancer (Llewellyn-Thomas et al. 1989, Whelan et al. 1995).

The resulting preference scores are specific to the original decision problem, and only the strength of the preference for treatment A relative to treatment B is obtained. The methods have not been developed within the realm of expected utility theory and have not been evaluated with respect to the assumptions of the theory. For formal decision analysis, they are therefore not suitable. However, for decision support they seem appropriate, as they are tailored to the clinical problem at hand and reflect the real-life situation more than does utility assessment. These methods have been employed "at the beside," using decision boards as visual aids (e.g., see Elit et al. 1996, Levine et al. 1992). The method seems a promising way to help patients who wish to engage in the decision-making process, i.e., to clarify and communicate their values. More research is needed to evaluate whether the method can indeed fulfill this function (Llewellyn-Thomas 1997).

It should be mentioned that, despite the noted disadvantages of utility assessment in decision making for individual patients, utility elicitation is nevertheless used in the clinical encounter. In this setting, the purpose of the elicitation is not to base decisions on absolute utility scores but to help patients clarify the values that are at stake in the decision problem. This application of utility assessment is described in detail in the next chapter.

7. Summary

Utility assessment is the most often used formal way to assess patient preferences in medical decision making. It is predominantly used for guideline development and policy making, i.e., for decision making for patient groups. For decisions for the individual patient, it can be useful to help a patient clarify his or her values. We have argued that in

selecting an instrument for utility assessment, the nature of the decision problem at hand determines to a large extent the choice of the
method used. The SG seems most appropriate in situations where risk
is involved, but as it generally leads to too strong risk aversion due to
probability distortion, a correction should be made. The TTO does not
include considerations of risk and is useful in situations with clear trade-
offs between quality of life and length of life. It can be accommodated
to include risk aversion. Risk is an important factor in many medical
decisions and should not be ignored. The VAS reflects neither risk nor
quality–length of life trade-offs and is therefore appropriate only in situations in which life expectancy is not an issue, e.g., when only different
domains of quality of life have to be weighed. Despite this feature, it
is used extensively for reasons of feasibility. The resulting scores, however, place too much weight on preventing or curing minor disabilities,
and transformation into a utility should therefore be performed. In designing utility assessment studies, careful attention must be paid to the
endpoints of the scale. If comparisons across studies are relevant, the
upper end should be optimal health, not absence of the disease under
study. In the case of comorbidity, the utility of absence of the disease under study will not be equal to 1. This needs to be taken into account if an
intervention eliminates only the disease under study, not the comorbidity as well. Otherwise, the analysis will overestimate the benefit of the
intervention.

At the other end of the scale, death is generally the lower endpoint.
If some states in the study are expected to be valued as worse than
death, the methods will need to be modified. Little is known about the
factors that determine the value that an individual assigns to a health
state. Sociodemographics explain little of the variation in preferences.
The only factor that has consistently been found to be associated with
preferences is disease experience. Experience with the health state that
is to be valued generally leads to higher utilities due to psychological
processes such as coping or adaptation.

Much research has been devoted to the association between descriptive quality of life profiles and the valuation of these profiles. The description of the quality of life in a particular health state turns out not
to be highly correlated with the valuation of that health state. Although
related, the two assessment methods do not capture the same construct.
If one nevertheless wishes to use descriptive quality of life data for
cost-effectiveness analysis, a solution may be to map the quality of life
scores onto a helath status classification system and use the preferences

from that system. The results of such procedures have so far been of ambiguous validity, though. Another approach would be to use prediction models based on large population-based data sets, such as that published by Fryback et al. (1997b).

Finally, an alternative to utility assessment has been discussed briefly: the probability trade-off technique, developed specifically for decision making at the level of the individual patient. This method results in a preference score of one treatment relative to another. It is not utility based and is therefore not suitable for formal decision analysis. The method still needs thorough evaluation. As the task resembles the real-life decision problem at hand, it may be more relevant to the patient than are the methods for utility assessment.

References

Asch DA, Hershey JC. Why some health policies don't make sense at the bedside. *Ann Intern Med* 1995;122:846–850

Ashby J, O'Hanlon M, Buxton MJ. The time trade-off technique: how do the valuations of breast cancer patients compare to those of other groups? *Qual Life Res* 1994;3:257–265

Ben-Zion U, Gafni A. Evaluation of public investment in health care. *J Health Econ* 1983;2:161–165

Bosch JL, Hunink MGM. The relationship between descriptive and valuational quality-of-life measures in patients with intermittent claudication. *Med Decis Making* 1996;16:217–225

Boyd NF, Sutherland HJ, Heasman KZ, Tritchler DL, Cummings BJ. Whose utilities for decision analysis? *Med Decis Making* 1990;10:58–67

Bult JR, Bosch JL, Hunink MGM. Heterogeneity in the relationship between the standard-gamble utility measure and health-status dimensions. *Med Decis Making* 1996;16:226–233

Bush JW. Relative preference versus relative frequencies in health-related quality of life evaluations. In: Wenger NK, Mattson ME, Furberg CD, Elinson J (eds): *Assessment of quality of life in clinical trials of cardiovascular therapies.* New York: Le Jacq, 1984, pp. 118–139.

Chancellor JVM, Coyle D, Drummond MF. Constructing health state preference values from descriptive quality of life outcomes: mission impossible? *Qual Life Res* 1997;6:159–168

Chen AY, Daley J, Thibault GE. Angina patients' ratings of current health and health without angina: associations with severity of angina and comorbidity. *Med Decis Making* 1996;16:169–177

Cher DJ, Miyamoto J, Lenert LA. Incorporating risk attitude into Markov-process decision models: importance for individual decision making. *Med Decis Making* 1997;17:340–350

Coast J. Reprocessing data to form QALYs. *BMJ* 1992;305:87–90

Dolan P. Modeling valuations for the EuroQol health states. *Med Care* 1997;35:1095–1108

Elit LM, Levine MN, Gafni A, Whelan TJ, Doig G, Streiner DL, Rosen B. Patients' preferences for therapy in advanced epithelial ovarian cancer: development, testing, and application of a bedside decision instrument. *Gynecol Oncol* 1996;62:329–335

Elstein AS, Chapman GB. Individual attitudes toward one-shot vs. sequential decisions: effects on acceptability of decision analysis. *Med Decis Making* 1994:14:430

Froberg DG, Kane RL. Methodology for measuring health state preferences – III: population and context effects. *J Clin Epidemiol* 1989;42:585–592

Fryback DG, Lawrence WF. Dollars may not buy as many QALYs as we think. A problem with defining quality-of-life adjustments. *Med Decis Making* 1997;17:276–284 (a)

Fryback DG, Lawrence WF, Martin PA, Klein R, Klein BEK. Predicting Quality of Well-being scores from the SF-36: results from the Beaver Dam Health Outcomes study. *Med Decis Making* 1997;17:1–9 (b)

Gafni A. Willingness-to-pay as a measure of benefits. Relevant questions in the context of public decision making about health care programs. *Med Care* 1991;29:1246–1252

Gafni A, Torrance GW. Risk attitude and time preference in health. *Manage Sci* 1984;4:440–51

Gerard K, Dobson M, Hall J. Framing and labelling effects in health descriptions: quality adjusted life years for treatment of breast cancer. *J Clin Epidemiol* 1993;46:77–84

Gold M, Franks P, Erickson P. Assessing the health of the nation. The predictive validity of a preference-based measure and self-rated health. *Med Care* 1996;34:163–177

Guyatt GH, Feeny DH, Patrick DL. Measuring health-related quality of life. *Ann Intern Med* 1993;118:622–629

Hadorn DC. Setting health care priorities in Oregon: cost-effectiveness meets the rule of rescue. *JAMA* 1991;265:2218–2225

Harris RA, Nease RF. The importance of patient preferences for comorbidities in cost-effectiveness analyses. *J Health Econ* 1997;16:113–119

Hershey JC, Kunreuther HC, Schoemaker PHJ. Sources of bias in assessment procedures for utility functions. *Manage Sci* 1982;28:936–953

Hickey AM, Bury G, O'Boyle CA, Bradley F, O'Kelly F, Shannon W. A new short form individual quality of life measure (SEIQoL-DW): application in a cohort of individuals with HIV/AIDS. *BMJ* 1996;313:29–33

Jansen SJT, Stiggelbout AM, Wakker PP, Vliet Vlieland TPM, Leer JWH, Nooy MA, Kievit J. Patient utilities for cancer treatments: a study on the chained procedure for the Standard Gamble and Time Trade-off. *Med Decis Making* 1998;18:391–399.

Johannesson M, Pliskin JS, Weinstein MC. A note on QALYs, time tradeoff, and discounting. *Med Decis Making* 1994;14:188–193

Johnson FR, Fries EE, Banzhaf HS. Valuing morbidity: an integration of the willingness-to-pay and health-status index literatures. *J Health Econ* 1997;16:641–665

Kaplan RM, Bush JW, Berry CC. Health status index. Category rating versus magnitude estimation for measuring levels of well-being. *Med Care* 1979;17:501–525

Kaplan RM, Anderson JP. The General Health Policy model: an integrated approach. In: Spilker B (ed): *Quality of life assessments in clinical trials*. New Haven: Raven Press, 1990, pp 131–149

Kaplan RM, Feeny D, Revicki DA. Methods for assessing relative importance in preference based outcome measures. *Qual Life Res* 1995;2:467–75

Keeney RL, Raiffa H. *Decisions with multiple objectives: preferences and value tradeoffs*. New York: Wiley, 1976

Kind P. The effect of past and present illness experience on the valuations of health states. *Med Care* 1995;33:AS255–AS263

Levine MN, Gafni A, Markham B, MacFarlane D. A bedside decision instrument to elicit a patient's preference concerning adjuvant chemotherapy for breast cancer. *Ann Intern Med*. 1992;117:53–58

Llewellyn-Thomas HA. Investigating patients' preferences for different treatment options. *Can J Nurs Res* 1997;29:45–64

Llewellyn-Thomas H, Sutherland HJ, Tibshirani R, Ciampi A, Till JE, Boyd NF. The measurement of patients' values in medicine. *Med Decis Making* 1982:2:449–462

Llewellyn-Thomas HA, Thiel EC, Clark RM, Patients versus surrogates: whose opinion counts on ethics review panels? *Clin Res* 1989;37:501–505

Llewellyn-Thomas HA, Williams JI, Levy L, Naylor CD. Using a trade-off technique to assess patients' treatment preferences for benign prostatic hyperplasia. *Med Decis Making* 1996;16:262–272

Loomes G. *Disparities between health state measures: an explanation and some implications*. York, Department of Economics, University of York, UK, 1988

McNeil BJ, Weichselbaum R, Pauker SG. Fallacy of the five year survival in lung cancer. *N Engl J Med* 1978;299:1397–1401

McNeil BJ, Pauker SG, Sox HC, Tversky A. On the elicitation of preferences for alternative therapies. *N Engl J Med* 1982:306:1259–1262

Miyamoto JM, Eraker SA. Parameter estimates for a QALY utility model. *Med Decis Making* 1985;5:191–213

Nease RF Jr, Kneeland T, O'Connor GT, Summer W, Lumpkins C, Shaw L, Pryor D, Sox HC. Variation in patient utilities for outcomes of the management of chronic stable angina. Implications for clinical practice guidelines. *JAMA* 1995;273:1185–1190

Nichol G, Llewellyn-Thomas HA, Thiel EC, Naylor CD. The relationship between cardiac functional capacity and patients' symptom-specific utilities for angina: some findings and methodologic lessons. *Med Decis Making* 1996;16:78–85

Nord E. The validity of a visual analogue scale in determining social utility weights for health states. *Int J Health Planning Manage* 1991;6:234–242

Nord E. Methods for quality adjustment of life years. *Soc Sci Med* 1992;34:559–569

O'Brien B, Viramontes JL. Willingness to pay: a valid and reliable measure of health state preference? *Med Decis Making* 1994;14:289–297

O'Connor A. Effects of framing and level of probability on patients' preferences for cancer chemotherapy. *J Clin Epidemiol* 1989;42:119–126

Patrick DL, Starks HE, Cain KC, Uhlmann RF, Pearlman RA. Measuring preferences for health states worse than death. *Med Decis Making* 1994;14:9–18

Revicki DA, Kaplan RM. Relationship between psychometric and utility-based approaches to the measurement of health-related quality of life. *Qual Life Res* 1993;2:477–487

Richardson J. Cost utility analysis: what should be measured: utility, value or healthy year equivalents? *Soc Sci Med* 1995;39:7–21

Richardson J, Nord E. The importance of perspective in the measurement of quality-adjusted life years. *Med Decis Making* 1997;17:33–41

Rosser R, Kind P. A scale of valuations of states of illness: is there a social consensus? *Int J Epidemiol* 1978;7:347–358

Russel LB, Gold MR, Siegel JE, Daniels N, Weinstein MC for the Panel on Cost-effectiveness in Health and Medicine. The role of cost-effectiveness analysis in health and medicine. *JAMA* 1996;276:1172–1177

Sackett DL, Torrance GW. The utility of different health states as perceived by the general public. *J Chronic Dis* 1978;31:697–704

Schoemaker PJH. The expected utility model: its variants, purposes, evidence and limitations. *J Econ Lit* 1982;2:529–563

Stiggelbout AM, Kiebert GM, Kievit J, Leer JWH, Stoter G, Haes JCJM de. Utility assessment in cancer patients: Adjustment of time trade-off scores for the utility of life years and comparison with standard gamble scores. *Med Decis Making* 1994;14:82–90

Stiggelbout AM, Eijkemans MJC, Kiebert GM, Kievit J, Leer JWH, De Haes JCJM. The "utility" of the Visual Analog Scale in medical decision making and technology assessment: is it an alternative to the Time Trade-Off? *Int J Technol Assess Health Care* 1996;12:291–298

Sutherland HJ, Llewellyn-Thomas H, Boyd NF, Till JE. Attitudes toward quality of survival. The concept of "maximal endurable time." *Med Decis Making* 1982;2:299–309

Sutherland HJ, Till JE. Quality of life assessments and levels of decision making: differentiating objectives. *Qual Life Res* 1993;2:297–303

The EuroQoL Group. EuroQol – a new facility for the measurement of health-related quality of life. *Health Policy* 1990;16:199–208

Torrance GW. Social preferences for health states: an empirical evaluation of three measurement techniques. *Socio-Econ Plan Sci* 1976;10:129–136

Torrance GW. Measurement of health state utilities for economic appraisal. A review. *J Health Econ* 1986;5:1–31

Torrance GW, Thomas WH, Sackett DL. A utility maximization model for evaluation of health care programs. *Health Services Res* 1972;7:118–133

Torrance GW, Feeny D. Utilities and quality-adjusted life years. *Int J Technol Assess Health Care* 1989;5:559–575

Torrance GW, Furlong WJ, Feeny DH, Boyle M. Multi-attribute preference functions. *Health Utilities Index PharmacoEcon* 1995;7:503–520

Torrance GW, Feeny DH, Furlong WJ, Barr RD, Zhang Y, Wang Q. Multiattribute utility function for a comprehensive health status classification system. Health Utilities Index Mark 2. *Med Care* 1996;34:702–722

Tsevat J, Goldman L, Soukup JR, Lamas GA, Connors KF, Chapin CC, Lee TH. Stability of time tradeoff utilities in survivors of myocardial infarction. *Med Decis Making* 1993;13:161–165

Tsevat J, Solzan JG, Kuntz KM, Ragland J, Currier JS, Sell RL, Weinstein MC. Health values of patients infected with human immunodeficiency virus. Relationship to mental health and physical functioning. *Med Care* 1996;34:44–57

Tugwell P, Bombardier C, Buchanan WW, Goldsmith CH, Grace E. The MACTAR patient preference disability questionnaire – an individualized functional priority approach for assessing improvement in physical disability in clinical trials in rheumatoid arthritis. *J Rheum* 1987;14:446–451

Tversky A, Kahneman D. The framing of decisions and the psychology of choice. *Science* 1981;211:453–458

Tversky A, Kahneman D. Advances in prospect theory: cumulative representation of uncertainty. *J Risk Uncert* 1992;5:297–323

Van Busschbach, J. *De validiteit van QALY's [The validity of QALY's]* Rotterdam: Sanders Instituut, 1994

Verhoef LCG, Haan AFJ de, Daal WAJ van. Risk attitude in gambles with years of life: empirical support for prospect theory. *Med Decis Making* 1994;14:194–200

Wakker P, Stiggelbout A. Explaining distortions in utility elicitation through the rank-dependent model for risky choices. *Med Decis Making* 1995;15:180–186

Weinstein MC, Siegel JE, Gold, MR, Kamlet MS, Russell LB for the Panel on Cost-Effectiveness in Health and Medicine. Recommendations of the Panel on Cost-Effectiveness in Health and Medicine. *JAMA* 1996;276:1253–1258

Whelan TJ, Levine MN, Gafni A, Lukka H, Mohide EA, Patel M, Streiner DL. Breast irradiation postlumpectomy: development and evaluation of a decision instrument. *J Clin Oncol* 1995;13:847–853

12   Applying Utility Assessment at the Bedside

Mary Kane Goldstein, MD, and Joel Tsevat, MD

Introduction

Most clinical decision making does not involve formal decision analysis (DA). In addition to being unfamiliar to most patients and physicians, DA is time-consuming and thereby costly. Some clinical decisions must be made urgently, without time for more than a quick explanation and a nod of assent. Other decisions are less urgent but less problematic: the physician is recommending the treatment that the patient anticipated and wanted, e.g., antibiotics for a urinary tract infection, and there is no need to employ special techniques to arrive at the decision to use antibiotics. But some medical decisions are fraught with uncertainty and leave both patients and physicians troubled about the best course of action when the alternatives all hold both the chance of improved outcomes and the risk of serious adverse effects. A decision may lead to an irrevocable action, e.g., a woman from a high-risk ovarian cancer family may decide to undergo surgical removal of the ovaries in the hope of preventing cancer. Other decisions include treatments that may continue for years and that may include substantial risk, e.g., a patient with chronic atrial fibrillation may decide to take anticoagulant drugs, with the attendant risk of bleeding, to reduce the risk of stroke. Still other decisions involve a trade-off of a higher short-term risk for the probability of a lower long-term risk, e.g., patients with some forms of coronary artery disease may have, on average, better survival with coronary artery bypass graft surgery than with medical therapy alone, but with a short-term risk of surgical complications. For such decisions,

Dr. Goldstein is supported by VA HSR&D and this work is supported in part by NIH R01 HS09042.

patients and physicians may choose to apply a (DA) approach to clarify alternatives and values.

Identifying the Decision Maker

An initial step in DA is identifying the decision maker. A decision may be defined as "an irrevocable allocation of valuable resources" (Howard & Matheson, 1983; Seiver & Holzman, 1989). The decision maker is the individual who has the authority to commit those resources.

Many published DAs in clinical medicine have taken the perspective of the clinician as decision maker (Hagen, 1992, Pauker & Kassirer, 1997, Richarson & Detsky, 1995). Other authors emphasize the patient as the decision maker because "each person, and only that person, has the right to make or to delegate decisions about risks to his life or well-being" (Howard, 1984). Biomedical ethics, by consensus, recognizes the right, also a legal right in the United States, of individuals to autonomy, or self-governance, that places final decision-making authority in the hands of the patient (Beauchamp & Childress, 1983). In this view, the clinician's input is one source of information for the patient's decision. Shared decision making is often viewed as an ideal (President's Commission for the Study of Ethical Problems in Medicine and Biomedical and Behavioral Research, 1982). In the model of shared decision making, the physician and the patient collaborate: the physician supplies expert medical knowledge to alert the patient to important medical considerations, while the patient, who is the expert on his/her own preferences, supplies the values that structure the decision (Brock & Wartman, 1990, Eddy, 1990; Emanuel & Emanuel, 1992). The patient then evaluates the alternatives and perhaps generates additional alternatives not present in the medical conceptualization of the issue (McConnell & Goldstein, 1999).

While considering the shared decision-making model reasonable as a rough guide to practice, Brock regards it as an ideal that is too simplistic and is subject to several challenges (Brock, 1993). He points out that it is difficult for physicians to provide patients with facts in a value-neutral way and, moreover, that it is not clear that the physician's role should be restricted in this way. Emanuel and Emanuel (1992) describe four models of the physician–patient relationship: informative, interpretive, deliberative, and paternalistic. They assert that the usual "fact–value division of labor" in shared decision making – with physicians providing facts and patients providing values – "embodies the informative model under a different label" rather than fostering mutual dialogue.

Keeney contrasts alternative-based decision making, in which the decision maker accepts the set of alternatives predetermined by someone else, with value-focused thinking, in which the decision maker generates the decision model starting from strategic objectives. Keeney asserts that "Values are more fundamental to a decision problem than are alternatives. . . . Alternatives are the means to achieve the more fundamental values" (Keeney, 1992, p. 3). The value assessment is not merely a process to assign utilities to predefined outcome states, but rather provides useful insight into all aspects of the decision process (Keeney, 1992, p. 157). Value-focused approaches with collaboration between the physician and patient in developing the decision model allow for truly shared decision making.

Individualizing the Decision Model

Individuals ostensibly facing the same decision, e.g., whether or not to obtain a genetic test, may generate very different decision models based on their personal values. APOE testing offers an example. APOE is a susceptibility gene that is associated with an increased risk of Alzheimer's disease when one or two ε4 alleles are inherited. APOE testing provides probabilistic information that is far from conclusive about whether or when the individual will develop Alzheimer's disease: at the population level the gene is associated with a risk of developing the disease, but its predictive value for individuals is limited (McConnell, Koenig, Greely, & Raffin, 1999). Holtzman and colleagues provide a detailed description of case studies of two individuals with a family history of Alzheimer's disease who are considering whether or not to undergo testing for APOE genotypes (Holtzman, Ozanne, Carone, Goldstein, Steinke, & Timbs, 1999). Working with a physician and a decision analyst, the individuals each generated a decision model. The two models included very different elements based on the personal values of the individual decision maker. For one individual, Kim, the DA process led to a major breakthrough in her thinking: She moved from a state of mind characterized by a perception that there was nothing she could do but wait for the onset of Alzheimer's disease to a new perception that she could use her experience as director of a child care center to structure her living environment in a way that would make it more suitable for someone with the disease. Once all her alternatives, uncertainties, and value trade-offs were integrated, it became apparent that the APOE test result would not affect her future plans or commitment of resources. For another individual, Sandra, the DA process revealed that a major consideration for her was balancing the allocation of her financial resources between a comfortable retirement and high-quality long-term care for Alzheimer's disease. For Sandra, the APOE test results could shift the probability distribution for Alzheimer's disease enough to make a difference in how she will allocate her resources. The DAs led to different choices about genetic testing for the two individuals. In both cases, while the test under consideration was a medical test, the determining factors in the decision were the impact that the test result might have on actions outside the medical realm.

Examples of Bedside Clinical Decisions Using Decision Analysis

The DA approach has been applied usefully in a number of clinical settings. Seiver and Holtzman (1989), in a report on medical decision making in the critical care setting, describe the purpose of DA as assisting the decision maker in achieving "clarity of action." Formal analysis of the decision reveals flaws that make the decision difficult: inconsistencies or lack of information. The process of building the decision model with the physician helps the patient, as a decision maker, develop insight into the problem. The steps of formulation, evaluation, and appraisal (interpretation of the formal recommendation) are followed by a feedback step of reassessing the decision model.

Here we describe several examples that illustrate the way DA, with its emphasis on patient preference, improves on decision rules that are solely medically based. The first example, prenatal testing, illustrates the limitations of a decision rule that uses a one-size-fits-all valuation of the outcomes and does not incorporate individual patient preference. The next example, a DA of the effects of prophylactic surgery on life expectancy for women with a genetic predisposition for cancer, shows how a DA based on published data can be a starting point for an individualized decision. The final example, treatment choices for prostate disease, illustrates the extent to which the optimal choice of therapy may be determined by how the patient values the quality-of-life outcomes.

Prenatal Testing for Down Syndrome

The risk of Down syndrome rises sharply after maternal age 35 years; however, since most pregnancies occur at younger ages, 80% of the cases occur in offspring of women younger than 35 years. Prenatal screening for this chromosomal disorder and for some other disorders is offered as part of routine prenatal care in the United States to women at high risk. Prenatal testing of amniotic fluid can identify a fetus with Down syndrome with greater than 99% sensitivity and specificity, but the procedure itself carries a risk of miscarriage. For some years, physicians' recommendations for prenatal testing of amniotic fluid for evidence of Down syndrome in the fetus were based on this decision rule: women who are at or above the age at which the risk of Down syndrome equals the risk of loss of the pregnancy from the procedure (i.e., age 35) should undergo the procedure. This decision rule assumes that all mothers, and other concerned parties such as fathers, equate the birth of a child with Down syndrome with the loss of a possibly normal fetus. However, many parents value those outcomes differently: some parents are willing to take on the responsibility of rearing a child with Down syndrome rather than risk the loss of the pregnancy, while other parents consider having a child with Down syndrome to be much worse than losing a normal fetus. A decision analytic approach allows incorporation of patient preference into the decision. It also allows for much more complex modeling as technology advances. For example, current decisions involve not only whether to have amniocentesis, but alternatively, whether to have chorionic villus sampling. Chorionic villus sampling can be done earlier in the pregnancy, but with less accuracy and perhaps greater procedural risk. A DA using previously published utilities identified patient preference characteristics that would favor amniocentesis over chorionic villus sampling (Heckerling & Verp, 1991). Kuppermann and coworkers have brought this study still closer to clinical reality by analyzing path-state preferences for varying sequences that reflect outcomes of concern to patients, such as undergoing the diagnostic test followed by miscarriage followed by inability to conceive again (Kuppermann, Shiboski, Feeny, Elkin, & Washington, 1997). The PANDA project at Stanford Medical Informatics includes data on six major diseases that can be diagnosed prenatally and considers four tests used in the diagnoses (Chajewska, Getoor, Norman, & Shahar, 1998; Norman, Shahar, Kuppermann & Gold, 1998).[1] Use of DA approaches to prenatal testing has greatly broadened the options available to the pregnant woman.

---

[1] See http://smi.web.stanford.edu/projects/panda/

Prophylactic Mastectomy and Oophorectomy in Women with
BRCA1 or BRCA2 Mutations

Women who carry mutations in the BRCA1 and BRCA2 genes have markedly increased risks of breast and ovarian cancer compared with the general U.S. population. An option for affected women who wish to reduce their risk of cancer is prophylactic mastectomy or oophorectomy (or both). The decision to undergo prophylactic surgery is intensely difficult for most women, given the possibility of profound effects on the woman's self-image. Moreover, the woman's level of risk from the mutation is uncertain, with estimates varying widely depending on the population surveyed, and the level of benefit from the surgery is uncertain since it does not provide complete protection against cancer. Schrag and associates developed a decision model to assist women facing this dilemma (Schrag, Kuntz, Garber, & Weeks, 1997). They calculated the effect of prophylactic surgery on life expectancy using various estimates of the risk of cancer and the efficacy of the procedure. Their analysis provides estimates of the risks and benefits of preventive strategies that "create a starting point for making these difficult decisions" (p. 1471). Physicians working in a shared decision-making mode with patients facing such decisions can use the model as the first iteration in the process of formulating and evaluating the patient's individual decision model. The model can be modified to reflect other outcomes of importance to the patient. The model presented by Schrag and associates explicitly omits utilities, thus allowing the individual to incorporate her own utilities. While incorporating population-based mean utility estimates is useful in decision models developed for public policy purposes, substituting other individuals' utilities in a model intended for a patient who wants to participate actively in decision making may not serve that patient well (Tsevat, Weeks, Guadagnoli, Tosteson, Mangione, Pliskin, Weinstein, & Cleary, 1994). Utility elicitation, specifically with the time trade-off method, has been shown to be feasible for use in clinical settings to elicit treatment preferences from women who may have a genetic predisposition to breast cancer (Unic, Stalmeier, Verhoef, & van Daal, 1998).

Benign Prostatic Hyperplasia and Prostate Cancer

Benign prostatic hyperplasia (BPH) can cause distressing symptoms. Treatment options include surgery, with an expected great improvement in symptoms that must be weighed against the small risks of operative death, incontinence, and erectile dysfunction. A DA for men with moderate symptoms suggested that patients' attitudes toward their symptoms and toward the prospect of postoperative sexual dysfunction should drive decision making regarding elective surgery (Barry, Mulley, Fowler, & Wennberg, 1988). Men facing the decision between surgery and watchful waiting were enthusiastic about an interactive videodisc-based shared decision-making program (Barry, Fowler, Mulley, Henderson, & Wennberg, 1995). Symptom frequency alone did not explain the patients' choices for or against surgery. For the subset of patients with frequent, moderate, or severe symptoms, the ratings of "bothersomeness" of symptoms and their attitudes toward the possibility of postoperative sexual dysfunction were the dominant predictors for choosing surgery (Barry et al., 1995, p. 779). Use of the shared decision-making program was associated with a shift toward watchful waiting and a reduction in surgery for treatment of BPH (Wagner, Barrett, Barry, Barlow, & Fowler, 1995).

Among men with prostate cancer, 60% present with tumors apparently localized to the prostate gland (Fleming, Wasson, Albertsen, Barry, & Wennberg, 1993). Localized prostate cancer presents a treatment dilemma: while prostate cancer is a deadly disease for some patients, there is no evidence that definitively supports the benefit of treatment over watchful waiting (Fleming et al., 1993). A DA model showed that radical prostatectomy and radiation therapy may benefit selected groups of patients, but that in most cases the choice of therapy is sensitive to the patient's preferences for various outcomes and to the discount rate (Fleming et al., 1993). The variability in individual patients' responses to the impact of prostatectomy on quality of life reinforces the importance of individualized decision making regarding radical prostatectomy (Fowler, Barry, Lu-Yao, Wasson, Roman, & Wennberg, 1995). Clinicians can assist men with localized prostate cancer in structuring an individualized decision, incorporating the man's preferences for the outcome health states. A self-administered paper-based instrument has been used successfully to assess patient utilities for health states associated with prostate cancer management (Albertsen, Nease, & Potosky, 1998).

Assessing Utilities

Utility elicitation techniques are discussed in detail in Chapter 11 of this volume. We focus here on utility assessment as it relates to bedside decision making.

Utility assessment has two major components: a thorough description of the possible outcomes for consideration by the decision maker and a rating or valuation of the outcomes by the decision maker.

Outcome State Descriptions

In medical decision analyses, descriptions of the outcome states consist primarily of health information. Typically, the patient has little familiarity with most or all of the possible outcome health states, so sufficient detail must be provided to allow the patient to imagine what life would be like in that state. Descriptions often include information in several different domains affecting health-related quality of life such as physical function, social function, and psychological state. More detailed information on the development of health state descriptions is available (Cadman & Goldsmith, 1986; Furlong, Feeny, Torrance, Barr, & Horsman, 1990; Patrick & Erickson, 1993; Torrance, 1982, 1986, 1987). The multiattribute utility function approach defines health states by combinations of attribute functional levels (Feeny, Furlong, Boyle, & Torrance, 1995; Furlong et al., 1990; Torrance, Boyle, & Horwood, 1982). Combinations of levels among attributes lead to a large number of possible health states. For public policy purposes, such health states can be used to estimate population means for utilities of hypothetical states. For individual decision making, the most relevant health states can be selected and described.

Preference assessment for health states with which a respondent has little personal experience have been criticized on the grounds that people have difficulty anticipating their future preferences, particularly with medical outcomes that are unfamiliar and thus difficult to envision (Redelmeier, Rozin, & Kahneman, 1993). However, patients facing difficult medical choices must somehow grapple with unfamiliar scenarios. While professional and patient educational materials often use pictorial or audiovisual approaches, traditional health state descriptions for utility elicitation have often been presented in the text-only format (Cadman and Goldsmith, 1986; Sackett and Torrance, 1978; Torrance, 1982; Torrance and Feeny, 1989). Early exceptions include audio representation to demonstrate the impact of voice quality (McNeil, Weichselbaum, & Pauker, 1981) and cartoon figures to augment descriptions of functional states (Hadorn, Hays, Uebersax, & Hauber, 1992). Graphics, slides, videotapes, and interactive videodiscs can be used to augment text descriptions of health states.

Utility Elicitation

Well-known techniques for rating and valuing health states include categorical scaling or rating scales (RS), the standard gamble (SG), and the time trade-off (TTO) (Froberg and Kane, 1989; Furlong et al., 1990). The ratings are performed on a scale that is conventionally anchored by best possible health (equal to 1) and worst possible health or death (equal to 0). Ratings are then comparable across a wide variety of diseases, treatments, and outcomes. Ratings for current health should account for morbid conditions other than the index condition being studied (Harris and Nease, 1997).

With the RS, respondents place each health state on a linear scale. This method is consistent with psychometric theory, but it does not directly incorporate utilities because no trade-off or risk is involved. Values assigned by RS techniques, compared with SG or TTO, have been consistently lower (Eddy, 1991; Llewellyn-Thomas, Sutherland, Tibshirani, Ciampi, Till, & Boyd, 1984; Nord, Richardson, & Mcarounas-Kirchmann, 1993; Revicki, 1992; Rutten-Van Molken, Bakker, Van Doorslaer, & Van Der Linden, 1995; Tsevat, Cook, Green, Matchar, Dawson, Broste, Wu, Phillips, Oye, & Goldman, 1995; Tsevat, Goldman, Lamas, Pfeffer, Chapin, Connors, & Lee, 1991; Tsevat, Solzan, Kuntz, Ragland, Currier, Sell, & Weinstein, 1996).

The SG is the method best grounded in von Neumann–Morgenstern utility theory (Kamlet, 1992; Patrick & Erickson, 1993; von Neumann & Morgenstern, 1944). It is, however, difficult for some individuals to understand because it requires a comparison of a probabilistic outcome with a certain outcome. Another approach is the time trade-off (Sackett and Torrance, 1978; Torrance, Thomas, & Sackett, 1972). The TTO is a question about how much life expectancy an individual would trade off to improve his or her quality of life. It attempts to present the respondent with a task that is simpler than the SG task while preserving an external metric (here, time) for comparison. Dolan and colleagues compared SG and TTO scores, with and without "props" (specially designed boards), reporting that both no-props variants might be susceptible to framing effects and that TTO props outperformed SG props (Dolan, Gudex, Kind, & Williams, 1996).

Utilities have been assessed by telephone interviews with patients undergoing total hip arthroplasty (Katz, Phillips, Fossel, & Liang, 1994) and with patients infected with human immunodeficiency virus (Tsevat et al., 1996).

Utilities and Health Status

Given that utility assessment can be difficult, it may be tempting to measure health status instead and then either use the health status score directly or impute a utility score from the health status score. Unfortunately, there are problems with both options. Like health ratings, health status measures do not conform to the axioms of expected utility theory and thus should not be incorporated directly into DAs or cost-effectiveness analyses. The second approach – trying to convert the patient's health status scores to utilities for his or her current state of health (as opposed to mapping health status onto someone else's utilities for that health state, the basis of multiattribute utility theory) – is complicated. Numerous studies have demonstrated that the relationship between one's current state of health and one's utility for that health state is at best modest (Bartman, Rosen, Bradham, Weissman, Hochberg, & Revicki, 1998; Bombardier, Ware, Russell, Larson, Chalmers, & Read, 1986; Bosch & Hunink, 1996; Bult, Hunink, Tsevat, & Weinstein, 1998; Chen, Daley, & Thibault, 1996; Churchill, Torrance, & Taylor, 1987; de Vries, Kuipers, & Hunink, 1998; Fowler, Cleary, Massagli, Weissman, & Epstein, 1995; Fryback, Dasbach, & Klein, 1993; Hornberger, Redelmeier, & Petersen, 1992; Llewellyn-Thomas, Sutherland, Tritchler, Lockwood, Till, & Ciampi, 1991; Llewellyn-Thomas, Thiel, & McGreal, 1992; Nease, Kneeland, O'Connor, Sumner, Lumpkins, Shaw, Pryor, & Sox, 1995; Nease, Tsai, Hynes, & Littenberg, 1996; Nichol, Llewellyn-Thomas, Thiel, & Naylor, 1996; Patrick, Mathias, Elkin, Fifer, & Buesching, 1998; Perez, McGee, Campbell, Christensen, & Williams, 1997; Revicki, 1992; Revicki, Wu, & Murray, 1995; Stigglebout, de Haes, Kiebert, Kievit, & Leer, 1996; Tsevat et al., 1991, 1995, 1996; Tsevat, Dawson, & Wu, 1998; Tsevat, Goldman, Soukup, Lamas, Connors, Chapin, & Lee, 1993). Working with a demographically homogeneous population, Fryback and colleagues were able to develop a quantitative link predicting a preference measure, the Quality of Well-Being Score, from a health status measure, the SF-36 (Fryback, Lawrence, Martin, Klein, & Klein, 1997). In more diverse populations, it may be necessary to adjust for socioeconomic status and race in order to achieve sufficient predictive power, as some (but not all) studies have found that utility ratings for health states of limited physical function differed significantly by race (Cykert, Joines, Kissling, & Hansen, 1999). Several studies of patient preferences for medical care for serious or terminal illness have shown differences by race, with African American patients requesting on average more life-sustaining treatments than their white counterparts (Caralis, Davis, Wright, & Marcial,

1993; Caralis & Hammond, 1992; Garrett, Harris, Norburn, Patrick, & Danis, 1993). Physicians' preferences for end-of-life treatment for themselves follow this same pattern, making it unlikely that low socioeconomic status or lack of familiarity with treatments account for the difference (Mebane, Oman, Kroonen, & Goldstein, 1999). The complex relationship of health status with health utility, and the interaction with age, race, gender, education, and income, is an area of active investigation.

Contingent Valuation

Utilities allow values to be assigned to health states without converting all goods to dollars and thus can be used in cost-effectiveness analysis, which estimates a cost per unit of health effect. Another method of quantifying the value of a nonmarket good is contingent valuation, in which individuals are asked how much they would pay for the good if a market for it existed. This method, also known as *willingness-to-pay* (*WTP*), was pioneered by Acton for valuation of mortality risks in a study of heart attack treatment (Acton, 1973). It has also been used to study the costs of treating hypertension (Johannesson & Jonsson, 1992; Johannesson, Jonsson, & Borgquist, 1991) and to understand how people value the benefits of treatments for infertility (Neumann & Johannesson, 1994). Contingent valuation can be used to estimate directly what an individual would be willing to pay for a certain change in morbidity and thus is particularly useful in cost–benefit analysis (Kenkel, Berger, & Blomquist, 1994). It has test–retest reliability comparable to that of other preference measures (O'Brien & Viramontes, 1994). However, contingent valuation does not provide directly for decision making based on health effects alone, without consideration of costs, and is not generally used in individual clinical decision making.

Computerized Support for Utility Assessment

Computers can simplify and standardize both the health state description and the utility elicitation components of the utility assessment process.

Automated Utility Elicitation

Software tools to automate elicitations were developed before tools for automating health state descriptions. One such elicitation tool is U-Titer, which supports TTO and RS techniques, using graphical aids for the assessment tasks. The clinician or investigator provides the respondents with a health state description, and then a trained interviewer uses the computer to conduct the utility elicitation. U-Titer has been used with more than 1,000 individuals for utility elicitation in clinical domains such as ischemic heart disease, psoriasis, breast cancer prevention, coronary artery bypass graft surgery, low back pain, osteoporosis prevention, mild hypertension, BpH, human immunodeficiency virus infection, and atrial fibrillation (Nease et al., 1996; Sumner, Nease, & Littenberg, 1991). Other software programs to support utility elicitation include UMaker (Pratt Medical Group, Boston) and Gambler (Gonzalez, Eckman, & Pauker, 1992). Computers offer the advantages of consistency from one presentation to the next and immediate data capture, which reduces data transmission errors. Computers can also be programmed easily to follow algorithms for varying the search procedures, for example, alternating the probabilities between high and low (*ping-pong* method), or presenting sequentially lower or higher probabilities (downward or upward titration). Computers can also easily store information such as tables of life expectancies and adjustments for comorbidities, and can be used to calculate an individual's life expectancy for the TTO based on data entered at the time the program is used. For research purposes, when large numbers of multiattribute health states must be valued by a group of people using a method that provides a subset of health states to each individual (the fractional factorial design), the computer can easily be programmed to select health states to present from a grid and to present the health states in random order.

Automated Health State Descriptions Combined with Utility Elicitation

Multimedia software, incorporating sound, pictures, video, and text, is particularly well suited to describe health states with which the respondent is unfamiliar. Multimedia software allows a more detailed description of the health states to be rated than does a paper-based method while preserving uniformity from one presentation to the next. Multimedia methods also allow for step-by-step education of the respondent about the utility elicitation technique, simplifying the SG and TTO. The software allows respondents to review previously described health states and to change their preference ratings after further thought. Multimedia software that conducts the entire interview essentially removes interviewer bias. Such programs allow the patient to spend as much time as he or she wishes with the material, so that health care professionals' time can be used for more focused questions and discussion.

Morss, Lenert, and colleagues developed an early version of a multimedia program describing health states and eliciting utilities (Morss & Lenert, 1992; Morss, Lenert, & Faustmann, 1993). Lenert, Goldstein, Garber, and colleagues developed and tested multimedia software for health states of functional dependency as described by the Activities of Daily Living (Goldstein, Michelson, Clark, & Lenert, 1993). Using a multimedia program describing health states related to Gaucher disease, these investigators and their colleagues showed that a multimedia presentation, compared with text descriptions, resulted in better recall and recognition of the health state descriptions (Goldstein, Clarke, Michelson, Garber, Bergen, & Lenert, 1994). In a survey of three groups of respondents – healthy subjects, patients with Gaucher disease, and patients with other chronic illnesses – they found that the respondents' self-rated current health state utility was an important determinant of utility values elicited for hypothetical health states (Clarke, Goldstein, Michelson, Garber, & Lenert, 1997). They also found that the computer could be used to study consistency in preferences across elicitation methods (Lenert, Morss, Goldstein, Bergen, Faustman, & Garber, 1997). Using software designed to compare the ping-pong method with a titration method, they showed that utility scores (values) are heavily influenced by the method of elicitation (Lenert, Cher, Goldstein, Bergen, & Garber, 1998). Cher and Lenert (1997) have developed a method for interactive use of Markov process decision models by patients and physicians at the bedside by using a method to determine efficiently which health state makes the largest contribution to the variance of the decision model, indicating which is the most informative utility to elicit next. Lenert and colleagues have recently developed a computer architecture for providing normative patient decision support over the World Wide Web (Scott, Cher, & Lenert, 1997).

Sanders and colleagues (Sanders, Hagerty, Sonnenberg, Hlatky, & Owens, 1999) have developed a 30-state Markov model that evaluates the cost-effectiveness of therapy with the implantable cardioverter defibrillator (ICD) or with amiodarone in patients at high risk for sudden cardiac death. The model is available on the World Wide Web. A Web user can change the input variables, evaluate the model, and view the results dynamically; thus, the model can be customized to the individual patient's situation. The model does not elicit utilities, but it allows the individual's utilities to be incorporated. The individual can then use the model to estimate the expected number of QALYs for each strategy.

Challenges and Limitations

Significant challenges remain in the clinical application of DA. One major factor is the time involved in developing an adequate decision model. Patients facing a major life decision are often willing to commit time and resources to the decision process, and physicians are accustomed to providing educational materials for patients to use at their leisure, but few physicians have the time or the skills to function as the decision analyst who works with the patient to build an individual decision model.

Another challenge is the difficulty many individuals experience in utility assessment. Some patients have religious or philosophical objections to concepts such as trading life for health or to gambling. Responses to health state descriptions are subject to framing effects: they may vary between first-person narratives and bullet points (Llewellyn-Thomas et al., 1984) and between descriptions that are framed positively or negatively (McNeil, Pauker, Sox, & Tversky, 1982; McNeil, Pauker, & Tversky, 1988). Multidimensional health state descriptions may tax the memory of the respondent. TTO requires that respondents perform the cognitively difficult task of trading off time rather than events, and it requires assumptions about the constant proportional trade-off of remaining life years (Loomes and McKenzie, 1989).

Paper-based methods involving props can be cumbersome, and computers are not universally available in clinical settings.

Despite these difficulties, DA is a powerful tool that can help physicians and patients in the collaborative process of decision making.

Conclusions

DA with a value-focused approach can lead to breakthroughs in individual thinking about problems. The approach can broaden the options under consideration. A decision model can structure complicated information in a way that makes it more manageable for the individual faced with a difficult choice. Paper-based methods of utility elicitation combined with the use of props can provide reliable utility estimates. Computers can provide support for complicated utility elicitation tasks and can be used to present multimedia health state descriptions.

References

Acton, J. J. P. (1973). *Evaluating Public Programs to Save Lives: The Case of Heart Attacks.* Santa Monica, CA: Rand Corporation.

Albertsen, P. C., Nease, R. F., & Potosky, A. L. (1998). Assessment of Patient Preferences among Men with Prostate Cancer. *Journal of Urology, 159,* 158–163.

Barry, M. J., Fowler, F. J., Jr., Mulley, A. G., Jr., Henderson, J. V., Jr., & Wennberg, J. E. (1995). Patient Reactions to a Program Designed to Facilitate Patient Participation in Treatment Decisions for Benign Prostatic Hyperplasia, *Medical Care, 33*(8), 771–782.

Barry, M. J., Mulley, A. G., Fowler, F. J., & Wennberg, J. W. (1998). Watchful Waiting vs. Immediate Transurethral Resection for Symptomatic Prostatism: The Importance of Patients' Preference. *Journal of the American Medical Association, 259*(20), 3010–3017.

Bartman, B., Rosen, M., Bradham, D., Weissman, J., Hochberg, M., & Revicki, D. (1998). Relationship between Health Status and Utility Measures in Older Claudicants. *Quality of Life Research, 7,* 67–73.

Beauchamp, T. L., & Childress, J. F. (1983). *Principles of Biomedical Ethics* (2nd ed.). New York: Oxford University Press.

Bombardier, C., Ware, J., Russell, I., Larson, M., Chalmers, A., & Read, J. (1986). Auranofin Therapy and Quality of Life in Patients with Rheumatoid Arthritis: Results of a Multicenter Trial. *American Journal of Medicine, 81,* 565–578.

Bosch, J., & Hunink, M. (1996). The Relationship between Descriptive and Valuational Quality-of-Life Measures in Patients with Intermittent Claudication. *Medical Decision Making, 16,* 217–225.

Brock, D. (1993). The Ideal of Shared Decision Making between Physicians and Patients. *Life and Death: Philosophical Essays in Biomedical Ethics.* New York: Cambridge University Press.

Brock, D., & Wartman, S. (1990). When Competent Patients Make Irrational Choices. *New England Journal of Medicine, 322,* 1595–1599.

Bult, J., Hunink, M., Tsevat, J., & Weinstein, M. (1998). Heterogeneity in the Relationship between the Time Tradeoff and Short Form-36 for HIV-Infected and Primary Care Patients. *Medical Care, 36,* 523–532.

Cadman, D., & Goldsmith, C. (1986). Construction of Social Value of Utility-Based Health Indices: The Usefulness of Factorial Experimental Design Plans. *Journal of Chronic Disease, 39*(8), 643–651.

Caralis, P. V., Davis, B., Wright, K., & Marcial, E. (1993). The Influence of Ethnicity and Race on Attitudes Toward Advance Directives, Life-Prolonging Treatments and Euthanasia. *Journal of Clinical Ethics, 4*(2), 155–165.

Caralis, P. V., & Hammond, J. (1992). Attitudes of Medical Students, House Staff, and Faculty Physicians Toward Euthanasia and Termination of Life-Sustaining Treatments. *Critical Care Medicine, 20,* 683–690.

Chajewska, U., Getoor, L., Norman, J., & Shahar, Y. (1998). *Utility Elicitation as a Classification Problem.* Paper presented at the Uncertainty in Artificial Intelligence: 14th Conference, San Francisco.

Chen, A., Daley, J., & Thibault, G. (1996). Angina Patients' Ratings of Current Health and Health without Angina: Associations with Severity of Angina and Comorbidity. *Medical Decision Making, 16,* 169–177.

Cher, D. J., & Lenert, L. A. (1997). Rapid Approximation of Confidence Intervals for

Markov Process Decision Models: Applications in Decision Support Systems. *Journal of the American Medical Informatics Association, 4*, 301–312.

Churchill, D., Torrance, D., & Taylor, D. E. A. (1987). Measurement of Quality of Life in End-Stage Renal Disease: The Time Tradeoff Approach. *Clinical and Investigative Medicine, 10*, 14–20.

Clarke, A. E., Goldstein, M. K., Michelson, D., Garber, A. M., & Lenert, L. A. (1997). The Effect of Assessment Method and Respondent Population on Utilities Elicited for Gaucher Disease. (Quality of Life Research, *6*(2), 169–184.

Cykert, S., Joines, J. D., Kissling, G., & Hansen, C. J. (1999). Racial Differences in Patients' Perceptions of Debilitated Health States. *Journal of General Internal Medicine, 14*, 217–222.

de Vries, S., Kuipers, W., & Hunink, M. (1998). Intermittent Claudication: Symptom Severity versus Health Values. *Journal of Vascular Surgery, 27*, 422–430.

Dolan, P., Gudex, C., Kind, P., & Williams, A. (1996). Valuing Health States: A Comparison of Methods. *Journal of Health Economics, 15*, 209–231.

Eddy, D. (1990). Anatomy of a Decision. *Journal of the American Medical Association, 263*, 441–443.

Eddy, D. M. (1991). Oregon's Methods. Did Cost-Effectiveness Analysis Fail? *Journal of the American Medical Association, 266*(15), 2135–1241.

Emanuel, E., & Emanuel, L. (1992). Four Models of the Physician–Patient Relationship. *Journal of the American Medical Association, 267*(16), 2221–2226.

Feeny, D., Furlong, W., Boyle, M., & Torrance, G. (1995). Multi-Attribute Health Status Classification System: Health Utilities Index. *PharmacoEconomics, 7*(6), 490–502.

Fleming, C., Wasson, J. H., Albertsen, P. C., Barry, M. J., & Wennberg, J. E. (1993). A Decision Analysis of Alternative Treatment Strategies for Clinically Localized Prostate Cancer. Prostate Patient Outcomes Research Team. *Journal of the American Medical Association, 269*(20), 2650–2658.

Fowler, F., Cleary, P., Massagli, M., Weissman, J., & Epstein, A. (1995). The Role of Reluctance to Give Up Life in the Measurement of the Values of Health States. *Medical Decision Making, 15*, 195–200.

Fowler, F. J., Jr., Barry, M. J., Lu-Yao, G., Wasson, J., Roman, A., & Wennberg, J. (1995). Effect of Radical Prostatectomy for Prostate Cancer on Patient Quality of Life: Results from a Medicare Survey. *Urology, 45*(6), 1007–1013; discussion 1013–1015.

Froberg, D. G., & Kane, R. L. (1989). Methodology for Measuring Health-State Preferences – I: Measurement Strategies. *Journal of Clinical Epidemiology, 42*(4), 345–354.

Fryback, D. G., Dasbach, E., & Klein, R. (1993). The Beaver Dam Health Outcomes Study: Initial Catalog of Health-State Quality Factors. *Medical Decision Making, 13*, 89–102.

Fryback, D. G., Lawrence, W. F., Martin, P. A., Klein, R., & Klein, B. E. (1997). Predicting Quality of Well-Being Scores from the SF-36: Results from the Beaver Dam Health Outcomes Study. *Medical Decision Making, 17*(1), 1–9.

Furlong, W., Feeny, D., Torrance, G., Barr, R., & Horsman, J. (1990). *Guide to Design and Development of Health-State Utility Instrumentation* (CHEPA Working Paper Series). Hamilton, Ontario: McMaster University.

Garrett, J. M., Harris, R. P., Norburn, J. K., Patrick, D. L., & Danis, M. (1993).

Life-Sustaining Treatments during Terminal Illness: Who Wants What? *Journal of General Internal Medicine, 8*, 361–368.

Goldstein, M. K., Clarke, A. E., Michelson, D., Garber, A. M., Bergen, M. R., & Lenert, L. A. (1994). Developing and Testing a Multimedia Presentation of a Health-State Description. *Medical Decision Making, 14*(4), 336–344.

Goldstein, M. K., Michelson, D., Clarke, A., & Lenert, L. (1993). A Multimedia Preference-Assessment Tool for Functional Outcomes. *Proceedings of the 17th Annual Symposium on Computer Applications in Medical Care*, 844–849.

Gonzalez, E., Eckman, M. H., & Pauker, S. G. (1992). "Gambler:" A Computer Workstation for Patient Utility Assessment. *Medical Decision Making, 12*, 350.

Hadorn, D. C., Hays, R. D., Uebersax, J., & Hauber, T. (1992). Improving Task Comprehension in the Measurement of Health State Preferences. A Trial of Informational Cartoon Figures and a Paired-Comparison Task. *Journal of Clinical Epidemiology, 45*(3), 233–243.

Hagen, M. D. (1992). Decision Analysis: A Review. *Family Medicine, 24*, 349–354.

Harris, R. A., & Nease, R. F. (1997). The Importance of Patient Preferences for Comorbidities in Cost-Effectiveness Analysis. *Journal of Health Economics, 16*, 113–119.

Heckerling, P. S., & Verp, M. S. (1991). Amniocentesis or Chorionic Villus Sampling for Prenatal Genetic Testing: A Decision Analysis. *Journal of Clinical Epidemiology, 44*(7), 657–670.

Holtzman, S., Ozanne, E., Carone, B., Goldstein, M., Steinke, G., & Timbs, J. (1999). Decision Analysis and Alzheimer Disease – Three Case Studies. *Genetic Testing, 3*(1), 71–83.

Hornberger, J., Redelmeier, D., & Petersen, J. (1992). Variability among Methods to Assess Patients' Well-Being and Consequent Effects on a Cost-Effectiveness Analysis. *Journal of Clinical Epidemiology, 45*, 505–512.

Howard, R. A. (1984). On Fates Comparable to Death. *Management Science. 30*(4), 547–573.

Howard, R. A., & Matheson, J. E. (Eds.). (1983). *Readings on the Principles and Applications of Decision Analysis*. Palo Alto, CA: Strategic Decisions Group.

Johannesson, M., & Jonsson, B. (1992). A Review of Cost-Effectiveness Analyses of Hypertension Treatment. *Pharmacoeconomics, 1*(4), 250–264.

Johannesson, M., Jonsson, B., & Borgquist, L. (1991). Willingness to Pay for Antihypertensive Therapy: Results of a Swedish Pilot Study. *Journal of Health Economics, 10*, 461–474.

Kamlet, M. S. (1992). *A Framework for Cost-Utility Analysis of Government Health Care Programs*. Washington, DC: Office of Disease Prevention and Health Promotion, Public Health Service, U.S. Department of Health and Human Services.

Katz, J. N., Phillips, C. B., Fossel, A. H., & Liang, M. H. (1994). Stability and Responsiveness of Utility Measures. *Medical Care, 32*(2), 183–188.

Keeney, R. L. (1992). *Value-Focused Thinking: A Path to Creative Decisionmaking*. Cambridge, MA: Harvard University Press.

Kenkel, D., Berger, M., & Blomquist, G. (1994). Contingent Valuation of Health. In G. Tolley, D. Kenkel, & R. Fabian (Eds.), *Valuing Health for Policy: An Economic Approach*. Chicago: University of Chicago Press.

Kuppermann, M., Shiboski, S., Feeny, D., Elkin, E. P., & Washington, A. E. (1997). Can Preference Scores for Discrete States Be Used to Derive Preference Scores for an Entire Path of Events? An Application to Prenatal Diagnosis. *Medical Decision Making, 17*(1), 42–55.

Lenert, L. A., Cher, D. J., Goldstein, M. K., Bergen, M. R., & Garber, A. (1998). The Effect of Search Procedures on Utility Elicitations. *Medical Decision Making, 18*, 76–83.

Lenert, L. A., Morss, S., Goldstein, M. K., Bergen, M. R., Faustman, W. O., & Garber, A. M. (1997). Measurement of the Validity of Utility Elicitations Performed by Computerized Interview. *Medical Care, 35*(9), 915–920.

Llewellyn-Thomas, H., Sutherland, H. J., Tibshirani, R., Ciampi, A., Till, J. E., & Boyd, N. F. (1984). Describing Health States: Methodologic Issues in Obtaining Values for Health States. *Medical Care, 22*, 543–552.

Llewellyn-Thomas, H. A., Sutherland, H. J., Tritchler, D. L., Lockwood, G. A., Till, J. E., & Ciampi, A. (1991). Benign and Malignant Breast Disease: The Relationship between Women's Health Status and Health Values. *Medical Decision Making, 11*, 180–188.

Llewellyn-Thomas, H. A., Thiel, E. C., & McGreal, M. J. (1992). Cancer Patients' Evaluations of Their Current Health States: The Influences of Expectations, Comparison, Actual Health Status, and Mood. *Medical Decision Making, 12*(2), 115–122.

Loomes, G., & McKenzie, L. (1989). The Use of QALYs in Health Care Decision Making. *Social Science and Medicine, 28*(4), 299–308.

McConnell, L., & Goldstein, M. (1999). The Application of Medical Decision Analysis to Genetic Testing: An Introduction. *Genetic Testing, 3*(1), 65–70.

McConnell, L., Koenig, B., Greely, H., Raffin, T., & Alzheimer's Disease Working Group of the Stanford Program in Genomics, Ethics, & Society. (1999). Genetic Testing and Alzheimer Disease: Has the Time Come? *Nature Medicine, 4*(7), 757–759.

McNeil, B. J., Pauker, S. G., Sox, H. C., & Tversky, A. (1982). On the Elicitation of Preferences for Alternative Therapies. *New England Journal of Medicine, 306*(21), 1259–1262.

McNeil, B. J., Pauker, S. G., & Tversky, A. (1988). On the Framing of Medical Decisions. In D. E. Bell, H. Raiffa, & A. Tversky (Eds.), *Decision Making: Descriptive, Normative, and Prescriptive Interactions* (pp. 562–568). Cambridge: Cambridge University Press.

McNeil, B. J., Weichselbaum, R., & Pauker, S. G. (1981). Speech and Survival: Tradeoffs between Quality and Quantity of Life in Laryngeal Cancer. *New England Journal of Medicine, 305*(17), 982–987.

Mebane, E. W., Oman, R. F., Kroonen, L. T., & Goldstein, M. K. (1999). The Influence of Physician Race, Age, and Gender on Physician Attitudes Toward Advanced Care Directives and Preferences for End-of-Life Decision Making. *Journal of the American Geriatrics Society, 47*, 579–591.

Morss, S. E., & Lenert, L. A. (1992). A Computerized Utility Assessment Tool for Evaluating the Side Effects of Antipsychotic Drugs. *Medical Decision Making, 12*(4), 350.

Morss, S. E., Lenert, L., & Faustmann, W. (1993). The Side Effects of Antipsychotic Drugs and Patients' Quality of Life: Patient Education and Preference Assessment with Computers and Multimedia. *Proceedings of the American Medical Informatics Association.*

Nease, R. F., Jr., Kneeland, T., O'Connor, G. T., Sumner, W., Lumpkins, C., Shaw,

L., Pryor, D., & Sox, H. C. (1995). Variation in Patient Utilities for Outcomes of the Management of Chronic Stable Angina. Implications for Clinical Practice Guidelines. Ischemic Heart Disease Patient Outcomes Research Team. *Journal of the American Medical Association, 273*(15), 1185–1190.

Nease, R. F., Jr., Tsai, R., Hynes, L., & Littenberg, B. (1996). Automated Utility Assessment of Global Health. *Quality of Life Research, 5,* 175–182.

Neumann, P., & Johannesson, M. (1994). The Willingness to Pay for In Vitro Fertilization: A Pilot Study Using Contingent Valuation. *Medical Care, 32,* 686–699.

Nichol, G., Llewellyn-Thomas, H. A., Thiel, E. C., & Naylor, C. D. (1996). The Relationship between Cardiac Functional Capacity and Patients' Symptom-Specific Utilities for Angina: Some Findings and Methodologic Lessons. *Medical Decision Making, 16*(1), 78–85.

Nord, E., Richardson, J., & Mcarounas-Kirchmann, K. (1993). Social Evaluation of Health Care versus Personal Evaluation of Health States. *International Journal of Technology Assessment in Health Care, 9*(4), 463–478.

Norman, J., Shahar, Y., Kuppermann, M., & Gold, B. (1998). *Decision-Theoretic Analysis of Prenatal Testing Strategies* (Technical Report SMI-98-0711). Stanford, CA: Stanford Medical Informatics, Stanford University.

O'Brien, B., & Viramontes, J. L. (1994). Willingness to Pay: A Valid and Reliable Measure of Health State Preference? *Medical Decision Making, 14*(3), 289–297.

Patrick, D., Mathias, S., Elkin, E., Fifer, S., & Buesching, D. (1998). Health State Preferences of Persons with Anxiety. *International Journal of Technology Assessment in Health Care, 14,* 357–371.

Patrick, D. L., & Erickson, P. (1993). *Health Status and Health Policy: Quality of Life in Health Care Evaluation and Resource Allocation.* New York: Oxford University Press.

Pauker, S. G., & Kassirer, J. P. (1987). Decision Analysis. *New England Journal of Medicine, 316*(5), 250–258.

Perez, D., McGee, R., Campbell, A., Christensen, E., & Williams, S. (1997). A Comparison of Time Tradeoff and Quality of Life Measures in Patients with Advanced Cancer. *Quality of Life Research, 6,* 133–138.

President's Commission for the Study of Ethical Problems in Medicine and Biomedical and Behavioral Research. (1982). *Making Health Care Decisions.* Washington, DC: U.S. Government Printing Office.

Redelmeier, D., Rozin, P., & Kahneman, D. (1993). Understanding Patients' Decisions: Cognitive and Emotional Perspectives. *Journal of the American Medical Association, 270*(1), 72–76.

Revicki, D. A. (1992). Relationship between Health Utility and Psychometric Health Status Measures. *Medical Care, 30*(5, Suppl), MS274–MS282.

Revicki, D. A., Wu, A., & Murray, M. (1995). Change in Clinical Status, Health Status, and Health Utility Outcomes in HIV-Infected Patients. *Medical Care, 33*(Suppl), AS173–AS182.

Richardson, W. S., & Detsky, A. S. (1995). Users' Guides to the Medical Literature: VII. How to Use a Clinical Decision Analysis. A. Are the Results of the Study Valid? *Journal of the American Medical Association, 273*(16), 1292–1295.

Rutten-Van Molken, M. P., Bakker, C. H., Van Doorslaer, E. K., & Van Der Linden, S. (1995). Methodological Issues of Patient Utility Measurement. *Medical Care, 33*(9), 922–937.

Sackett, D. L., & Torrance, G. W. (1978). The Utility of Different Health States as Perceived by the General Public. *Journal of Chronic Disease, 31*, 697–704.

Sanders, G. D., Hagerty, C. G., Sonnenberg, F. A., Hlatky, M. A., & Owens D. K. (1999). Distributed Decision Support for Guideline Development Using a Web-Based Interface: Prevention of Sudden Cardiac Death. *Medical Decision Making, 19*, 157–166.

Scharg, D., Kuntz, K. M., Garber, J. E., & Weeks, J. C. (1997). Decision Analysis – Effects of Prophylactic Mastectomy and Oophorectomy on Life Expectancy among Women with BRCA1 or BRCA2 Mutations. *New England Journal of Medicine, 336*(20), 1465–1471.

Scott, G. C., Cher, D. J., & Lenert, L. A. (1997). SecondOpinion: Interactive Web-Based Access to a Decision Model. *Proceedings of the AMIA Annual Fall Symposium*, 769–773.

Seiver, A., & Holtzman, S. (1989). Decision Analysis: A Framework for Critical Care Decision Assistance. *International Journal of Clinical Monitoring and Computing, 6*, 137–156.

Stigglebout, A., de Haes, J., Kiebert, G., Kievit, J., & Leer, J.-W. (1996). Tradeoffs between Quality and Quantity of Life: Development of the QQ Questionaire for Cancer Patients' Attitudes. *Medical Decision Making, 16*, 184–192.

Sumner, W., Nease, R., & Littenberg, B. (1991). U-titer: A Utility Assessment Tool. *Proceedings of the Annual Symposium on Computer Applications in Medical Care*, 701–705.

Torrance, G. W. (1982). Preferences for Health States: A Review of Measurement Methods. *Clinical and Economic Evaluation of Perinatal and Developmental Medicine, 20*, 37–45.

Torrance, G. W. (1986). Measurement of Health State Utilities for Economic Appraisal. *Journal of Health Economics, 5*, 1–30.

Torrance, G. (1987). Utility Approach to Measuring Health-Related Quality of Life. *Journal of Chronic Disease, 40*(6), 593–600.

Torrance, G. W., Boyle, M. H., & Horwood, S. P. (1982). Application of Multi-Attribute Utility Theory to Measure Social Preferences for Health States. *Operations Research, 30*(6), 1043–1069.

Torrance, G. W., & Feeny, D. (1989). Utilities and Quality-Adjusted Life Years. *International Journal of Technology Assessment in Health Care, 5*, 559–575.

Torrance, G. W., Thomas, W. H., & Sackett, D. L. (1972). A Utility Maximization Model for Evaluation of Health Care Programs. *Health Services Research, 7*(2), 118–133.

Tsevat, J., Cook, E. F., Green, M. L., Matchar, D. B., Dawson, N. V., Broste, S. K., Wu, A. W., Phillips, R. S., Oye, R. K., Goldman, L., & Investigators, S. (1995). Health Values of the Seriously Ill. *Annals of Internal Medicine, 122*(7), 514–520.

Tsevat, J., Dawson, N., & Wu, A. E. A. (1998). Health Values of Hospitalized Patients 80 Years or Older. *Journal of the American Medical Association, 279*, 371–375.

Tsevat, J., Goldman, L., Lamas, G. A., Pfeffer, M. A., Chapin, C. C., Connors, K. F., & Lee, T. H. (1991). Functional Status versus Utilities in Survivors of Myocardial Infarction. *Medical Care, 29*, 1153–1159.

Tsevat, J., Goldman, L., Soukup, J. R., Lamas, G. A., Connors, K. F., Chapin, C. C., & Lee, T. H. (1993). Stability of Time-Tradeoff Utilities in Survivors of Myocardial Infarction. *Medical Decision Making, 13*, 161–165.

Tsevat, J., Solzan, J. G., Kuntz, K. M., Ragland, J., Currier, J. S., Sell, R. L., & Weinstein, M. C. (1996). Health Values of Patients Infected with Human Immunodeficiency Virus: Relationship to Mental Health and Physical Functioning. *Medical Care, 34*(1), 44–57.

Tsevat, J., Weeks, J. C., Guadagnoli, E., Tosteson, A. N., Mangione, C. M., Pliskin, J. S., Weinstein, M. C., & Cleary, P. D. (1994). Using Health-Related Quality-of-Life Information: Clinical Encounters, Clinical Trials, and Health Policy. *Journal of General Internal Medicine, 9*(10), 576–582.

Unic, I., Stalmeier, P. F. M., Verhoef, L. C. G., & van Daal, W. A. J. (1998). Assessment of the Time-tradeoff Values for Prophylactic Mastectomy of Women with a Suspected Genetic Predisposition to Breast Cancer. *Medical Decision Making, 18*(3), 268–277.

von Neumann, J., & Morgenstern, O. (1944). *Theory of Games and Economic Behavior.* Princeton, NJ: Princeton University Press.

Wagner, E. H., Barrett, P., Barry, M. J., Barlow, W., & Fowler, F. J., Jr. (1995). The Effect of a Shared Decisionmaking Program on Rates of Surgery for Benign Prostatic Hyperplasia. Pilot Results. *Medical Care, 33*(8), 765–770.

13 Advances in Presenting Health Information to Patients

Holly Brügge Jimison, PhD, and Paul Phillip Sher, MD

Introduction

Health care delivery is undergoing dramatic changes. These trends include an emphasis on chronic disease management, evidence-based medicine, and the integration of psychosocial and community services with medical services. Additionally, consumers are demanding greater choice and involvement at all levels of health care. The availability of timely, relevant, and accurate health information for patients is now crucial to quality health care. Information technologies represent one of the potential "transforming" technologies to impact the delivery of health care and health information. Networks capable of merging audio, video, and text-based information into a multimedia product can provide a spectrum of new services to empower patients to become active participants in their medical decisions, as well as provide motivational methods to prevent illness, promote wellness, and provide consultation and self-care education. The information highway infrastructure, the Internet, and the World Wide Web can become the framework for a home health care delivery system that can be both cost effective and timely. This chapter focuses on how technology has been used to provide patients with health information, the principles of presentation methods, what is known about their effectiveness, and future trends.

Importance of Patient Involvement in Health Care and Medical Decisions

Accompanying the changes in health care delivery is a new consumerism and activism on the part of patients. Many patients now feel they have the right to understand their health care and to participate actively in decision making (Ende et al. 1989). One measure of this change is higher ratings of patient satisfaction linked to greater information exchange on the part of physicians (Devine 1992, Greenfield et al. 1985). Research indicates that access to health information enables patients to be more active participants in the treatment process, which can lead to better medical outcomes (Brody 1980, Greenfield et al. 1985, Korsch 1984, Mahler & Kulik 1990). Health education is an important aspect of doctor–patient communication. Patients report that they want to be informed about their medical condition (Ende et al. 1989, Waitzkin 1984), and the process of sharing information enhances the doctor–patient relationship. Patient involvement in medical care also involves the closely linked concepts of empowerment and self-efficacy. In general, empowerment can be thought of as the process that enables people to "own" their own lives and have control over their destiny (Deegan 1992, Wallerstein 1992). It is closely related to health outcomes in that powerlessness has been shown to be a broad-based risk factor for disease. Studies demonstrate that patients who feel in control in a medical situation have better outcomes than those who feel powerless (Casileth et al. 1980, Israel & Sherman 1990, Peterson & Stunkard 1989). Similarly, self-efficacy is a person's level of confidence that he or she can perform a specific task or health behavior in the future (Bandura 1977, Lorig et al. 1989). Several clinical studies have shown self-efficacy to be most predictive of improvements in patients' functional status (Cunningham et al. 1991, O'Leary 1985). Perceived self-efficacy has been shown to play a significant role in smoking cessation relapse rate, pain management, control of eating and weight, success of recovery from myocardial infarction, and adherence to preventive health programs (Allen et al. 1990, Maibach et al. 1996, Mullen et al. 1987, O'Leary et al. 1988, Strecher et al. 1986). However, it has been difficult to develop methods that reliably improve empowerment and self-efficacy in a variety of settings. Teaching goal-setting and problem-solving skills are examples of interventions that have had some success in improving self-efficacy. It is important for the developers of technology-based approaches to providing patients with health information to consider empowerment and self-efficacy during system design. The feeling of empowerment can be enhanced, for instance, by support groups, linked via their computers, that allow patients to feel connected to someone else with a similar medical problem. This has been demonstrated by the Comprehensive Health Enhancement and Support System (CHESS) in women with breast cancer and patients with acquired immunodeficiency syndrome (AIDS) (Gustafson et al. 1992, 1994, Pingree et al. 1993).

Addressing issues of patient compliance or, more appropriately, patients' adherence to their health care goals, is another important focus of health care information and shows the importance of bringing the patient into the health care decision-making loop. Patients cannot carry out treatments or recommendations that they do not understand or do not accept. Noncompliance is a serious and harmful aspect of health care. Some forms of noncompliance are failure to take medication as directed; failure to keep appointments; failure to follow a recommended diet; and failure to follow preventive health practices. The rate of noncompliance is alarmingly high. Various studies report noncompliance rates from 15% to 93% (Haynes & Taylor 1979, Ley 1982, Morrow et al. 1988, Stewart & Cluff 1972). Patient education interventions have been shown to reduce noncompliance (Leirer & Morrow 1988).

Finally, the paradigm shift from treating infectious disease toward the management of chronic disease and long-term care additionally requires more input from the patient and family members. For patients to be adequately informed for decision making regarding their medical care, it is important that they obtain information about the quality of life associated with the possible medical outcomes of these decisions. However, the reliable assessment of a patient's preferences and risk attitudes for clinical outcomes is probably the weakest link in clinical decision making. Information on patient preferences is important for tailoring information to patients and for providing decision support. Tailored information has been found to be more effective in providing consumer information (Skinner et al. 1994) and is preferred by patients (Jimison et al. 1992). The participation of informed patients in defining the quality of care and in the selection of treatment and preventive services may not only lead to greater patient satisfaction but also reduce the use of unnecessary services (Leaf 1993, Somers 1984). Recent efforts to explore the use of computers in health outcomes communication and in assessing patients' preferences for various health outcomes have started to address these issues (Goldstein et al. 1994, Jimison et al. 1992, Lenert et al. 1995).

Topics of Health Information for Patients

Health and wellness are important issues to Americans. The demand for more information comes from a variety of trends. Changing demographics, cost containment pressures, new approaches to disease management, greater consumer awareness and activism, and newly accessible technologies like computers and the Internet all produce demands for more and more health information. Surveys suggest that there is no typical health information consumer. Older people are better informed and tend to get information from multiple sources. Younger people are more likely to use new technologies such as the Internet. The disabled are much more likely to seek health information. Women are slightly better informed about health issues and are more likely to be consumers of health information. Socioeconomic factors such as education, income, language (non-English speaking), and cultural issues significantly affect information-seeking behavior. It is clear from survey results that a majority of consumers (60–80%) do have health-related questions. What does differ among various group studies is the sources of health information (Harris 1995). Patients and health care consumers desire a wide variety of information. The following sections provide an overview of the types of health information that patients are interested in accessing.

Wellness and Prevention (Nutrition/Diet, Exercise/Fitness, Emergency First Aid)

Health promotion, health risk appraisal, nutrition analysis, and fitness regimens are popular topics for consumers. Fitness and diet are two of the most common subjects in the popular press. Health risk appraisals are designed to help people understand health risks and to provide methods for reducing or eliminating risky behavior. Some of these programs are used by companies to target populations for health promotion and disease prevention.

Diseases, Screening, Symptom-Based Triage, Tests, and Treatments

Consumers are most often interested in information about specific health problems, the associated symptoms, and treatment information. Self-care is an important element of decision making for patients in that whenever a symptom or set of symptoms occurs, the patient needs to decide whether or not to seek professional medical care or manage the problem at home. In some cases, self-diagnosis or self-care is desired and patients look for information that will allow them to determine the etiology of the symptoms they are experiencing. Symptom-based triage is also being utilized by many health maintenance organizations (HMOs) through advice lines.

Informed Consent and Advance Directives

The goal of the informed consent process is to provide a mechanism for patients to participate in treatment decisions. This requires a thorough understanding of the benefits and possible risks before a patient undergoes treatment. The educational component of the informed consent process is often neglected, and patients frequently look elsewhere to get the necessary information for educated decision making. Similarly, educating patients about advanced life support while determining patient desires for end-of-life care is necessary for the appropriate use of advance directives.

Medical Histories, Home Medical Records, and Preparation for Office Visits

Consumers are more aware of the importance of maintaining their own medical records and medical history. This may expedite office visits with new health care providers. Maintaining up-to-date drug records avoids potential medication errors and adverse interactions. Effective physician–patient communication can be enhanced by utilizing these records along with written questions to prepare in advance for medical appointments.

Shared Decision Making (Decision-Making Assistance for Treatment Options)

Informed medical decision making is at the heart of consumers' information-seeking behavior. Relevant information about the benefits and risks of each alternative therapy are necessary for patients to participate in decision making. Information resources and individual preference elicitation, as well as information from patients who have already faced similar decisions, can be useful in preparing patients to be informed participants in medical care decision making.

Social Support and Communication with Other Patients

Some of the most useful information that consumers acquire comes from other patients with similar medical problems. This communication and information exchange is being fostered by support groups, which help patients cope with their specific diseases. These support groups are often organized by nonprofit societies in local communities. In addition to providing newsletters and face-to-face group meetings, such groups participate in bulletin board–style e-mail and in real-time chat groups on the Internet.

Choosing a Doctor, Hospital, Health Plan, Health Insurance, and Benefits

Consumers have become more quality and cost conscious in purchasing health insurance, including choosing among health plans, providers, and hospitals. Individual preferences based on a host of factors influence these decisions. The decision-making process requires comparative information on plan benefits and costs. Some information sources integrate quality data with the more traditional benefits.

Formats of Presentation

Consumers have a wide spectrum of choices for acquiring health information. They no longer depend entirely on their physician to get information about health and disease. The sources and format of health information extend from traditional paper-based systems to the latest communications technologies that utilize computers with CD-ROMs and Web access.

Brochures and Pamphlets

Paper brochures and pamphlets have always been available to provide information to consumers. Traditionally, these have been produced by government agencies and nonprofit organizations and are designed to educate the consumer on some aspect of health and wellness issues or to promote greater understanding of specific diseases. Similar paper-based materials are also being used by managed care organizations and individual physicians to provide information on such topics as medication instructions and surgical procedures. These patient education materials are designed as stand-alone products to be taken home by patients. The producers of such materials need to be sensitive to a wide variety of issues relating to the population being served. Cultural sensitivity, language, readability, and literacy demands are just a few of the issues that need to be understood if these materials are to be effective.

Media (Newspapers, Magazines, Television)

The news media (newspapers, magazines, and television) have played a traditional role in the dissemination of health care information to consumers. National and local newspapers and television news serve the public by providing regular health columns and programming and by reporting on the latest medical research. This role has expanded and changed with the rise of new media technology linked with the reconfiguration of the nation's health care delivery system. Television news and programming has devoted greater amounts of time to highlight and promote important health issues such as smoking, cancer (breast and prostate, in particular), and heart disease. Magazines have also addressed similar issues. Investigative reports in these media continue to provide consumers with information on all aspects of health and health care, including alternative or nontraditional therapies often not discussed by many physicians. The news media's continuing role should allow dissemination of health information at lower costs and with greater utility.

Telephone

The use of the telephone to provide health information has taken several forms. Phone services are available to provide prerecorded health information on a wide variety of health-related subjects. This service is usually purchased by hospitals or libraries for their customers. Each topic has a unique telephone extension, and consumers can call anytime and access specific information. One example of such a service is The Medical Information Line (Strategic Systems, Inc., Waltham, MA). Utilizing a touchtone menu, consumers can access prerecorded information on over 300 topics. The telephone has also been used to establish nurse/physician advice lines. These provide a less costly link between the consumer and the health care provider, and also function as a triage mechanism to determine which patients need to be seen by a health care professional and which ones can be treated with advice over the phone.

Videotape and Interactive Video

Videotape as a medium for training, education, and dissemination of health care information has been available for some time. Attempts to use this medium as a primary vehicle for patient information and education have not been entirely successful. Consumers rarely purchase these tapes. Some physicians use them in waiting rooms. Many are produced by medical vendors such as drug companies and don't always provide an unbiased perspective. Analog videodisk systems are widely used for interactive teaching programs. These devices can store video as well as still frames and offer rapid searching, freeze-frame, and slow motion features. Systems are available as stand-alones that do not require a separate computer, as well as more advanced models that link directly with a microcomputer for control. This technology has been used successfully for education and training. Interactive videodisk systems exist for shared decision making. The Foundation for Shared Decision Making developed several interactive videodisks, including one that helps men with enlarged prostates to participate more fully in deciding whether to have surgery (Kasper et al. 1992).

Computers and Telecommunication

Advances in computer technology and communications have provided consumers with access to enormous amounts of information. From their beginnings in the 1970s, personal computers have become a ubiquitous part of the workplace and of many homes. The power of today's systems has expanded access to information on a scale never before dreamed of. Technological developments influence the way information is stored and displayed. The trend today is to merge text, images, audio, video, graphics, and animation into an integrated program using multimedia authorware on multimedia platforms. The present trend in both computer and telecommunications hardware and software is to merge all communications technologies. The home television of the future will likely contain a built-in computer, fax machine, and telephone, and consumers will have the ability to communicate interactively to acquire health information and even consult with health care professionals. Systems in use today include home-based local storage (discs, CD-ROMs); large-scale reference systems and databases in libraries; software for print-on-demand patient education materials; kiosks in hospitals and clinics with education materials; and access to the Internet and World Wide Web, with their extensive resources covering health information, e-mail, newsgroups, chat rooms, bulletin boards, and communication with health care professionals. Another example of convergent technology is WebTV, consisting of a set-top box connected to the TV and a telephone line. In addition to purchasing the set-top box, consumers must pay a monthly Internet access fee, which includes e-mail service. Either the remote control or a separate keyboard allows the user to navigate the Internet. There is tremendous potential for this technology to provide health information to millions of households without personal computers.

Stand-alone computer systems in the form of kiosks with touch-screen displays and printing capabilities are also being used by hospitals and community service organizations to provide health information. One such system, Healthpoint, has been placed in post offices, libraries, pharmacies, bars, and health centers in a small town near Glasgow, Scotland. Usage is significantly greater than that of paper leaflets. In a telephone survey conducted five months after ten kiosks were located around the town, it was found that 17% of the population had used the system at least once. A commercial version is available that allows users to add new material (Jones et al. 1993).

Commercial Software for Patient Education

The number of commercial computer products supporting patients' health information needs is expanding so rapidly that it is difficult to maintain an updated inventory. The Informed Patient Decisions Group's *1996 Directory of Consumer Health Informatics* (Kieschnick et al. 1996) lists over 600 software products covering the spectrum of consumer health information needs, including such diverse areas as patient education, health promotion and prevention, nutrition and fitness, self-triage, maintaining health records, decision making, and health reference libraries. Many of these products are designed for patients unfamiliar with computers and for those with low reading skills. The newer systems typically have user interfaces that are much easier to understand and that make greater use of video and graphics. A number of products are available as general home health care references. These are designed as a single source of general health information similar to the home health references found with encyclopedias or as textbooks. The software is CD-ROM-based and has some type of search engine (for subject search), as well as the ability to print information. These products can be divided into those that are typically used by consumers at home with personal computers and the larger, more costly databases that are usually seen in health reference libraries.

Home references are health reference encyclopedias that, in most cases, were produced initially as textbooks and subsequently converted to electronic media. One such program for home use is the *Mayo Clinic Family Healthbook* (IVI Publishing, Eden Prairie, MN). Although mainly text, it also includes 75 videos, 600 photos and illustrations, and audio narration with information on over 1,000 medical conditions and 3,000 drugs. The program includes a Web browser and an automatic link to the Mayo Clinic site (http://www.mayo.ivi.com). Library reference databases are too costly for the average consumer. These databases combine information from journals, newspapers, and other media into a single source. One example, The Health Reference Center (Information Access Company, Foster City, CA) is a database with three years of medical information from periodicals, pamphlets, and reference books. Over 150 titles are indexed, with full text coverage of 100 titles, full text of over 500 medical information pamphlets, and indexing and full text of 5 leading medical reference books. The abstracts of technical articles are written in lay language. Recent versions also include patient education handouts from Clinical Reference Systems. This database can be accessed via the Web or CD-ROM.

A diverse collection of software products enumerate disease signs and symptoms, as well as explanations of diagnostic tests and treatment options. An example of such a program is the Complete Guide to Symptoms and Illness (Great Bear Technology, Morgan, CA), a resource with information on causes, diagnoses, treatments, complications, and outcomes of hundreds of medical problems. The software includes detailed multimedia-based material on more than 800 symptoms, over 500 illnesses, and 177 surgical procedures, as well as suggestions on how individuals can live longer and stay healthier. Specialized programs have been produced to cover high-interest topics, such as Breast Cancer Lighthouse (Gold Standard Media), a breast cancer resource that includes thirty minutes of audio quotes from fourteen breast cancer survivors. There are several drug reference programs designed to help consumers with information on prescription and nonprescription medications, including drug interactions and side effects. One such program is Mayo Clinic Family Pharmacist (IVI Publishing). The program enables users to obtain nontechnical information on over 8,000 brand name, generic, and over-the-counter drugs. The program also provides on-line access for answers to questions, such as why a drug is prescribed; dosage and usage information; adverse reactions; warnings; precautions; and possible interactions with other drugs, foods, and beverages. Most drug information systems allow the user to check for drug–drug interactions from a specific list of the patient's medications.

Patients and physicians often agree that the doctor is the most appropriate source of medical information (Beisecker & Beisecker 1990, Kreps 1990), but there can be misunderstandings when only oral information is provided (Kahn 1993a). Several options exist for supplementing physicians' advice. Written information that physicians give to patients has traditionally been provided in the form of one-page handouts or brochures on specific topics of interest. Kahn (1993b) reviewed programs for computer-generated patient handouts. Selected patient handouts are also available on the World Wide Web. Some examples of systems that provide tailored printouts of patient education and health promotion come from the work of Strecher and his colleagues on tailored messages for smoking cessation (Strecher et al. 1994), mammography (Skinner et al. 1994), and diet (Campbell et al. 1994). These are examples of systems with tailoring based on theoretical guidelines applying to patient education.

Programs are available to teach first aid and give home emergency medical advice. Although emergency medical information is available in the general home health references listed previously, some programs are designed specifically for this information. For example, First Aid Tutorial (Marketing Services Corporation of America, Brookfield, WI) presents basic first aid treatment for common medical emergencies including bleeding, shock, fractures, burns, and poisoning.

Self-care has an important element of decision making for patients in that whenever a symptom or set of symptoms occurs, the patient needs to decide whether to seek professional medical care or manage the problem at home. Several computer systems have targeted this need. The AMA Family Medical Guide uses flowcharts and branching algorithms to instruct patients on when to see a doctor and when to administer self-care. Prevention (preventive care, wellness, risk factors, nutrition) software can help in learning about disease risk, perform health evaluations, maintain medical records, estimate health care costs, and manage health expenses. Health risk appraisal systems use patient-specific information provided by the user to create a tailored summary of health risks. Computer programs can also help patients by organizing information and keeping a record of important issues that need to be addressed during an office visit. Preparing in advance for medical appointments can be important in effective physician–patient communication and shared decision making.

Internet and World Wide Web

In 1969, ARPANET, the first computer network, was established, linking mainframe computers at four geographically distant sites. Today, this rudimentary network has grown to become the vast interconnections of the Internet, with an estimated 50 million computer users. The exact number of sites and users is unclear and the statistics on use vary considerably, but they have shown a steady increase. The recent dramatic expansion of the Internet has been through the World Wide Web. The Web supports multimedia through a graphical interface that allows sophisticated text formatting, graphics, and embedded hypertext links to other locations on the Web and contains vast amounts of consumer health and medical information. Much of this information is posted by government agencies, medical foundations, universities, medical schools, individual physicians, health insurance companies, health care providers, individuals' personal Web pages, special interest support groups, and many health and medical-related companies (pharmaceutical companies, medical supply firms, etc.). At present, the World Wide Web is a democracy of free information exchange without regard for accuracy or objectivity. "Viewer beware" is the caveat for anyone looking for medical information on the Internet (Brown 1997). Some attempts have been made to rate and evaluate sites. Later on in this chapter we will discuss the issues surrounding the evaluation of health information quality. Major commercial on-line vendors (America Online, Compuserve, Prodigy) provide access to health information services including traditional reference materials and databases, as well as support groups and forum discussions of health-related topics. These services also provide forums, chat groups, and access to health-related newsgroups. Community health networks and on-line self-help networks are becoming more available to consumers, who are being transformed from passive receivers of health care into active participants.

There are many other Internet services: e-mail, mailing lists, the File Transfer Protocol (FTP), listservers, USENET (User's Network) newsgroups, Telnet, and Internet Relay Chat (IRC). Some of these services have wide application in consumer health informatics. E-mail and mailing lists allow patients to communicate with each other, as well as with some health care providers. Mailing lists allow groups of people to receive e-mail messages. Listservers are systems dedicated to a particular topic, with specialized software to maintain subscription lists and handle e-mail traffic. There are numerous health-related listservers. CANCERNET is a quick and easy way to obtain cancer information from the National Cancer Institute (NCI) using e-mail. CANCERNET offers information statements from the NCI's Physician Data Query (PDQ) database, fact sheets on various cancer topics from the NCI's Office of Cancer Communications, and citations and abstracts on selected topics from the CANCERLIT database. Selected information is also available in Spanish. For those without a computer, this information can be faxed via an automated fax system. USENET newsgroups provide a more informal approach to communications. There are many medical and health-related newsgroups among the over 4,800 newsgroups on the USENET. The activity varies, but all messages to the newsgroup are available to anyone who accesses the newsgroup. Many of these groups provide support to patients suffering from particular diseases. Patients find that communicating with other patients is very helpful and can actually improve health outcomes (Gustafson et al. 1992). Before newsgroups, bulletin board services (BBSs) were the main mechanism for group communication on specialized topics. There are 60,000 BBSs covering diverse subjects, including health care, special interest topics, and support groups. IRC is a multiuser chat computer protocol that allows the computer connection of users and provides a means for disease-oriented support group communication. Listservers, newsgroups, and BBSs all provide a mechanism for users to communicate with each other about any and all aspects of health care. Most of these resources are unmoderated, so all information needs to be verified. For chronic diseases, the newsgroups provide an important social function by allowing patients to share experiences about their disease, treatment, and prognosis. The entire function of some newsgroups is to provide such support.

Principles of Presentation and Interactivity

Interface Design

The technological demands for effective consumer health information and education are many and varied, especially when we include the need for video transmission and/or storage. The advances in computer hardware have been rapid, and many of the existing computer-based patient education products have not yet made use of the newer capabilities. However, the greatest barrier to effective computer-assisted patient education is a software issue – the design of the user interface. This is also the area that holds the most promise for improving patient education. The concept of the user interface encompasses the aspects of how humans interact with the information available in a computer system (screen display, interactivity, etc.). The user interface of computer-assisted patient education enables interactivity and tailoring to individual patients (Tibbles et al. 1992, Vargo 1991). Some of the basic potential advantages of a computer-based approach to patient education over traditional techniques are

> Consistent content and delivery
> Potentially more easily available than a health educator
> Potentially cost effective (compared to routine and consistent
> patient education by staff)
> Privacy of communication
> Active learning

In health education applications, interface designers have the challenge of addressing the disparate needs of the lay public. It is important to understand the user's capabilities and perspective. Some of the general interface design principles are the following:

- Give the user control – empower the user, allow exploration and browsing.
- Reduce the user's memory load – provide context and reminders, with minimal reliance on recall.
- Provide immediate feedback and the option of help at any point.
- Use familiar metaphors – windows and file folders are examples for most computers.
- Keep the interface consistent – for example, keep active buttons or menus in the same place on the screen throughout the interaction.
- Adapt to the user. For health education applications, there are several ways to tailor information:

> Self-paced instruction, with more detail if desired
> Ability to repeat, review, and receive coaching if responses are
> incorrect
> Tailor language, reading level, and medical experience to users'
> preferences

Tailoring based on health risk assessment
Provide automated, tailored record of patient understanding,
    knowledge, and confidence
Provide automated, tailored record of patient education

Tailoring Health Information for Patients

Patient education researchers and practitioners have long recognized the value of tailoring the presentation of material to individual patients in face-to-face encounters (Hewson 1993, Skinner et al. 1993). Patient educators routinely incorporate their knowledge of patient differences in adapting their patient interactions to accommodate variations in cultural backgrounds and health beliefs, as well as variations in language ability and medical background. Additionally, patient differences in medical condition require that clinicians modify their explanation of treatment options to an individual's level of risk and potential benefit. However, on a routine basis, patients are more likely to receive only a small amount of educational information from their physicians and perhaps a brochure to take home. To communicate patient education information, a brochure must be designed for the typical patient. The factors that physicians and health educators take into account with individual patients are difficult to replicate in a mass-produced brochure.

The early computer-based approaches to patient education did little to improve on brochures, but recent advances in authoring tools and computer hardware have led to the development of systems that have made progress toward emulating a sensitive and well-trained health educator with the ability to tailor the presentation of material to an individual's needs. Some examples of systems that provide tailored printouts of patient education and health promotion information are those of Strecher and his colleagues on smoking cessation (Strecher et al. 1994), mammography (Skinner et al. 1994), and diet (Campbell et al. 1994). These are examples of systems with tailoring based on theoretical guidelines applying to patient education. These systems assess information about the patient's perceived benefits and barriers associated with a health behavior (Health Belief Model: Becker 1974), the patient's readiness to change (Transtheoretical Model of Change: Prochaska & DiClemente 1983), and the patient's perceived causes of success or failure in undertaking a new health behavior (Attribution Theory: Weiner 1986). The contents of the resulting printed letters to patients then vary, depending on the results of these assessments. For example, smokers in the "precontemplative" stage (not thinking about quitting yet) would receive information only about the perceived risks of smoking-related disease and the perceived benefits of quitting (health improvement, cost savings, etc.). Information on potential barriers to quitting would not be addressed in this group. These researchers and developers have shown that the tailored printed material for patients is more effective than traditional generic materials in promoting positive health behavior change.

An alternative method for tailoring patient education materials is based on computer treatment decision models that use decision theory metrics to tailor patient education explanations and focus attention on variables that are most important to the individual patient (Jimison et al. 1992). These tailored patient education printouts were preferred to generic brochures by patients for applications in heart disease and benign prostatic hyperplasia.

Incorporating Patient Preferences

The concept of individual preferences is important for health communication applications that focus on decision making (Barry et al. 1995). Whereas patients need information about the quality of life associated with the medical outcomes of possible decisions, reliable assessment of individual preferences and risk attitudes for clinical outcomes are probably the weakest links in clinical decision making. Recent efforts to explore the use of computers in communication about health outcomes and in assessing patients' preferences for various health outcomes have started to address these issues (Barry et al. 1995, Goldstein et al. 1994, Jimison & Henrion 1992). Information on patient preferences is important for tailoring information to patients and for providing decision support. In addition to differences in preferences for health outcomes, patients differ in the degree to which they choose to be involved in decision making. Research confirms that age (younger), gender (females more than males), and education level (better educated) are strong predictors of the desire to be involved in medical decisions. There is also a greater desire to be involved in medical decisions that appear to require less medical expertise, such as knee injury as opposed to cancer (Thompson et al. 1993).

Evaluations of Health Information Systems

Although computers and multimedia techniques offer new capabilities and have the potential to enhance health information for patients, it is not clear that current implementations have been significantly more effective than traditional methods for health communication. The evaluation literature in this area is not large, and quite often the studies do not explicitly compare the technological intervention for health communication to other options. Studies of traditional health education materials generally show that videos and slides are more effective educationally than books and audiotapes (Alterman & Baughman 1991, Consoli et al. 1995, Funnell et al. 1992; Gillispie & Ellis 1993). Computer-based approaches offer interactivity, provide feedback in the learning process, and tailor information to the individual. Researchers evaluating computer-based tools for health communication have looked at effects on patient knowledge, attitudes, treatment selection, and health outcomes. With respect to patient knowledge, studies of computer-based health information systems have shown an increase in patient knowledge of treatment options with the use of computer tools (Chewning & Sleath 1996, Morgan 1993), and Barry et al. have shown the knowledge gains in benign prostatic hyperplasia to be greater with patient use of interactive video than with print material (Barry et al. 1995).

The studies of changes in patient attitudes with the use of computer-based health information tools have shown mixed results. Although some results show an increase in patient anxiety over the new information (approximately 40% of patients) (Shepperd & Fell 1995), the same studies show that most patients found the systems to be helpful and to improve the decision-making process. However, for evaluations specifically comparing brochures to an interactive decision aid, the increase in patient satisfaction was not statistically significant (Barry et al. 1995, Morgan 1993). There are few studies on the use of computer tools and self-efficacy or outcomes, but as an example, Chewning and Sleath's study of an interactive computer tool on contraceptive choice showed both an increase in self-efficacy and greater use of oral contraceptives after twelve months in low-income women less than twenty years of age (Chewning & Sleath 1996).

With all health information materials, care must be taken to ensure an evenhanded presentation of treatment alternatives and the description of potential outcomes. With video and multimedia techniques, it is especially important to ensure balanced presentations, as the power to persuade and possibly manipulate treatment decisions is even greater when patients identify with specific characters and personalities. However, one of the design goals of interactive treatment decision aids is to incorporate patient preferences for long-term health outcomes into the decisions, and in many cases, decisions made with patients' preferences will differ from routine medical practice. In evaluating decisions made by patients using interactive videos from the Foundation for Informed Decision Making, researchers found lower surgery rates for benign prostatic hyperplasia compared to those of patients who received no material (Wagner et al. 1995), but the surgery rates were not statistically significantly lower when compared to those of patients who received print material (Barry et al. 1995). For ischemic heart disease, revascularization surgery rates were also found to be lower for patients viewing interactive videodisks (Morgan 1993). With breast cancer treatment decisions, Chapman et al. found that video and multimedia presentations of information may have an increased effect on patients' decisions when compared with paper-based materials (Chapman et al. 1995). Overall, more research is needed to understand the potential impact of these systems on treatment decisions, especially when compared to more traditional methods of patient education.

Consumer Access to Health Information Via Technology

Each year Americans are swamped with new resources devoted to health, diet, wellness, and fitness. There are more than 40,000 producers of information. Publishers produce 1,000 new health books a year. National organizations provide brochures, pamphlets, and public information advertising in newspapers and on radio and television. There are 28,000 new audiovisual productions. Throughout the United States, hospitals have begun to provide health education. A total of 5,100 hospitals have health education programs, and many are beginning to build health resource libraries to be used by patients and family members. In our high schools, 9% of all credit hours are in health and physical education (Harris 1995). The new communication technologies (computers, CD-ROMs, and the Internet) are expanding information access at a dramatic pace, yet only 15% of U.S. households have access to the Internet or commercial on-line services, and the costs of owning a computer and getting on-line are a significant barrier to those who may need this information the most.

Internet Access

Currently, approximately 30 million U.S. adults use at least one application besides e-mail on the Internet. Another 3.6 million use e-mail alone. An additional 9.3 million have tried the Internet but are not current users. Presently, the top content areas of interest, in order of popularity, are news, hobbies, travel, entertainment, government/community, health/medicine, product information, sports, music, and games. When researchers asked about future activities that users intend to focus on, the top five areas were found to be on-line banking, adult education, health and medicine, personal investing, and travel. The health information areas that consumers are interested in accessing on the Internet include e-mail communication with their own doctor, fitness and stress management, disease information, injury treatment, prescription drug information, diet and food supplements, health support groups, health insurance, and child development (Brown 1996).

Barriers to the Access of Health Information

Cultural Aspects. Patients throughout the world, and even within the United States, come to the clinical encounter from widely disparate cultural backgrounds. Communication of information to the patient must take into account health care beliefs and quality-of-life priorities (Chachkes & Christ 1996, Kleinman et al. 1978). The framework for the Health Belief Model (Becker 1974) characterizes the factors associated with preventive health action on the part of a patient. These factors include perceptions about the personal benefits and barriers relating to a health action, as well as perceptions about the underlying personal health risk. A patient educator must be able to assess a patient's belief system and goals for change in order to be an effective advocate for the patient. For treatment planning, a clinician must also be able to accommodate varying patient backgrounds and values in developing shared treatment goals. Education, negotiation, and motivation are important components of the provision of quality medical care. They directly influence adherence to treatment goals, which in turn is critical for improved health outcomes (Bird & Cohen-Cole 1989; Lipkin 1987). Delbanco and Waitzkin both emphasize the importance of incorporating patient preferences on quality-of-life issues into medical decision making and the construction of treatment goals (Delbanco 1992, Waitzkin 1991). The need to tailor the clinical encounter based on patient preferences and background extends to patient education. Whereas it is difficult to account for these differences in the print and graphics media of commonly available patient education brochures, it is possible with computer tools to assess cultural backgrounds, beliefs, and preferences and to address these differences with varying user interfaces. Thus far, the more typical approach with existing computer tools and brochures is to target a specific audience with a specific product. In the future, we can expect that larger and more general systems will have user interfaces that adapt to a given user's personal and cultural preferences.

Language. A major barrier to effective patient–clinician communication, and even to basic clinical care, is that in many communities a large number of patients are not sufficiently fluent in English to either communicate or understand information about their basic medical needs. The use of translators in many languages and dialects during an office visit is labor intensive and expensive. Many hospitals and clinics use telephone operator services and three-way headsets to aid communication for short periods of time. However, it becomes more difficult to include patient education using these methods. In some areas, printed brochures are available in Spanish or other common languages. Yet, the inventory difficulties and expense associated with multiple versions of brochures can make a computer approach more attractive. Computer interfaces with easy access to similar information in multiple languages provide a useful solution to the translation problem. The basic data and program structures remain the same. There are also new software products to aid in translating English into other languages as a first pass to speed the new content development process.

Reading Level. A current challenge to educating patients is that only 28% of the American population has attended college and that approximately one out of five adult Americans is functionally illiterate, reading at or below the fifth-grade level (Doak et al. 1985). Currently, the most commonly used format for patient education is the brochure or pamphlet, making heavy use of text. However, most studies on the literacy of the general U.S. population show that approximately 20% are functionally illiterate (Hunter & Harman 1985) and that the reading comprehension of public clinic patients is about grade 6.5 (Davis et al. 1990). Most studies measuring the understanding of patient education materials have found that approximately 50% of the patients are unable to understand the written material (Doak et al. 1985, Holt et al. 1990, Vivian & Robertson 1980). Patient comprehension is a prerequisite to adherence to health care treatment goals, and the conventional techniques for patient education often fall short in this regard. Although guidelines for the development of patient education materials encourage the use of a reading level at or below the sixth or eighth grade, most materials are at far higher reading levels. Patient informed consent forms are often the most difficult to read, typically written at the college level. Studies of readability suggest that the existing forms for informed consent are often too complex and difficult for the average patient to understand (Baker & Taub 1983, Hopper et al. 1995, Jubelirer & Linton 1994, Meade & Howser 1992). Morrow and colleagues (1988) noted that consent forms are less comprehensible than the popular press and that research consent forms may be as difficult to read as medical journal articles. Many of the currently available written handouts for patients could be improved by presenting the content at a lower reading level. One of the advantages of the computer-based approach to patient education is that through the use of video clips, graphics, and audio, it is possible to provide educational materials without requiring the patient to read. Additionally, by assessing the user's approximate reading level or desired level of information complexity, it is possible for existing reading level metrics to limit the search of health databases to material at the appropriate level.

Level of Education and Medical Expertise. A variation of the readability problem has to do with the patient's ability to understand medical language. A highly educated patient may have very little medical background and be unfamiliar with much medical terminology. Conversely, a hospital or clinic employee with less formal education and lower reading ability could obtain a fairly high degree of understanding of medical terminology. Again, it is difficult to meet varying patient needs with a single brochure. Currently, most computer-based patient education products address this problem with built-in dictionaries with an automated word lookup feature to assist patients in reading text on medical topics. Recent work on tailoring the search for health information on the Internet includes developing user models that estimate a patient's level of education and medical experience (Pavel et al. 1996).

Not many of the currently available computer systems for health education are easy for all patients to use. Even searches on the World Wide Web require a certain degree of computer literacy. General consumer sophistication is increasing at the same time that computers are becoming easier for novices to use. However, it will be critical to ensure that developers incorporate culturally meaningful content and interfaces that address the needs of underserved populations. It will also be necessary to provide an information infrastructure that promotes equal access to information technology in order to strive for equal access to quality medical care.

Trends in Providing Health Information for Patients

Health care delivery is undergoing dramatic changes. Increasingly, our health care system is moving toward a managed care model. The objective of the health care reform is to emphasize quality while searching for ways to reduce future costs and spending. Under the new managed care environment, there has been a gradual shift in emphasis from treating illness to promoting health. This will require greater resources to provide effective patient education to improve outcomes and reduce costs. At the same time, demand or case management is being used to control utilization and maintain continuity of care for potentially high utilizers. HMOs are becoming aware of the marketing potential of patient education. Health plan members who were given convenient access to health education reported higher satisfaction. They also were more willing to utilize self-care for minor illnesses (Estabrook 1979).

In addition, traditional hospital-centered delivery systems are diminishing and new integrated continuum-of-care networks are emerging to take their place. The patient's home is a key element and may represent a low-cost alternative environment for monitoring, education, and therapy. Integrated communication networks will provide communication from patient to clinician and represent an ideal technology for the delivery of health services to the home. Treatment is moving out of hospitals to sites with lower-intensity services, as well as to nontraditional locations such as nursing homes with lower-skilled employees, assisted living and elder foster care facilities; retirement, senior, and community centers, and into the home with and without caregiver support. The Medicare budget for home health care has grown nine times in the past decade (Meyer & Gibbons 1997). The most common diseases being treated by home health caregivers are hypertension, congestive heart failure, coronary artery disease, obstructive lung disease, diabetes, osteoarthritis, and stroke. Telecommunication technologies may allow communication between caregivers and patients in the home or in other nontraditional sites. Computer networks serve as convenient and efficient tools for delivering medical services and information to patients at home (Brennan & Rippich 1994, Hekelman et al. 1994). It has been estimated that many medical problems that would normally result in a home visit do not necessarily need hands-on-care. Computers with an ancillary video camera are available that can also include monitoring devices such as a blood pressure cuff, pulse monitor, and stethoscope (Engstrom 1996). Although the equipment cost is high, cost savings over time can be significant. It is also anticipated that some of these functions may be possible utilizing a set-top box over a cable television without the need for a computer.

Current trends in medical care also include increased consumerism on the part of patients. They are more interested in participating in their medical care and treatment decisions, as well as in taking an active role in searching for their own health information. The direct patient use of the Internet and World Wide Web for seeking health information has skyrocketed, and all indications show that this growth in computer use will continue. One of the greatest difficulties will be to ensure the quality of the information obtained in this manner. All this points to a growing need for enhancing and coordinating efforts of health professionals in patient education and health communication.

Advances in communications and information processing technology will certainly change the way medicine is practiced, as well as the way patients receive information and interact with the medical care system. The future holds great promise for consumers to become empowered and active participants in their medical care decisions through increased and more effective access to health care information. The developers of commercial systems have advanced the field of consumer health informatics with many innovative systems. However, to achieve significant improvements in quality of care and health outcomes, researchers and system developers need to focus on applying the knowledge gained from previous work in health education to the design of new systems. The goals of research are to develop sound principles to inform the design of new systems for patient use and to measure the benefits derived from the use of those systems. This is a new and rapidly developing field, with significant innovations in the commercial sector. However, research in several areas is needed to significantly improve patients' health outcomes and to show the effectiveness of the systems to purchasers of health care. The criteria for evaluating computer-based diagnostic systems for patients are the same as the criteria for physician systems, namely, accuracy and effectiveness (Berner et al. 1994). However, the rapid deployment of these systems in an ever-changing medical care environment makes critical evaluation of consumer health information systems extremely difficult. Web sites change daily, and access to one system usually means increased access to many others. It is important to understand the potential effectiveness of investments in this area. Careful needs assessment before system development, usability testing during development, controlled clinical trials, and studies of use and outcomes in natural settings are all critical to our understanding of how best to provide health information and decision assistance to patients.

References

Allen, J.K., Becker, D.M., & Swank, R.T. (1990). Factors related to functional status after coronary artery bypass surgery. *Heart & Lung*, 19(4):337–43.

Alterman, A.I. & Baughman, T.G. (1991). Videotape versus computer interactive education in alcoholic and nonalcoholic controls. *Alcoholism*, 15(1): 39–44.

Baker, M.T. & Taub, H.A. (1983). Readability of informed consent forms for research in a Veterans Administration medical center. *Journal of the American Medical Association*, 250(19):2646–8.

Bandura, A. (1977). Self-efficacy towards a unifying theory of behavioral change. *Psychological Review*, 84(2):191–215.

Barry, M.J., Fowler, F.J., Mulley, A.G., Jr., Henerson, J, Jr., & Wennberg, J.E. (1995). Patient reactions to a program designed to facilitate patient participation in treatment decisions for benign prostatic hyperplasia. *Medical Care*, 33:771–82.

Becker, M.H. (1974). The health belief model and personal health behavior. *Health Education Monograph*, 2:324–473.

Beisecker, A.E. & Beisecker, T.D. (1990). Patient information-seeking behaviors when communicating with doctors. *Medical Care*, 28:19–28.

Berner, E.S., Webster, G.D., Shugerman, A.A., Jackson, J.R., Algina, J., Baker, A.L., Ball, E.V., Cobbs, C.G., Dennis, V.W., & Frenkel, E.P. (1994). Performance of four computer-based diagnostic systems. *New England Journal of Medicine*, 330(25):1792–5.

Bird, J. & Cohen-Cole, S.A. (1989). The three-function model of the medical interview. In M.S. Hale (Ed.), *Models of Teaching Consultation-Liaison Psychiatry* (pp. 65–88). Basel: Karger.

Brennan, P.F. & Ripich, S. (1994). Use of a home-care computer network by persons with AIDS. *International Journal of Technology Assessment in Health Care*, 10(2):258–72.

Brody, D.S. (1980). The patient's role in clinical decision making. *Annals of Internal Medicine*, 93:718–22.

Brown, M.S. (1996). Polish and glitz aside, Net resources fall short on the content yardstick. *Medicine on the Net*, 2(10):7–8.

Brown, M.S. (1997). Consumer health and medical information on the Internet: Supply and demand. FIND/SVD 1997 American Internet User Survey, URL-http://etrg.findsvp.com

Campbell, M.K., DeVellis, B.M., Strecher, V.J., Ammerman, A., De Vellis, R.F., & Sandler, R.S. (1994). The impact of message tailoring on dietary behavior change for disease prevention in primary care settings. *American Journal of Public Health*, 84(5):783–7.

Casileth, B.R., Zupkis, R.V., Sutton-Smith, K., & March, V. (1980). Information and participation preferences among cancer patients. *Annals of Internal Medicine*, 92:832–6.

Chachkes, E. & Christ, G. (1996). Cross cultural issues in patient education. *Patient Education and Counseling*, 27:13–21.

Chapman, G.B., Elstein, A.S., & Huges, K.K. (1995). Effects of patient education on decisions about breast cancer treatments: A preliminary report. *Medical Decision Making*, 15(3):231–9.

Chewning, B. & Sleath, B. (1996). Medication decision-making and management: A client-centered model. *Social Science and Medicine*, 42(3):389–98.

Consoli, S.M., Ben Said, M., Jean, J., Menard, J., Plouin, P.F., & Chatellier, G. (1995). Benefits of a computer-assisted education program for hypertensive patients compared with standard education tools. *Patient Education and Counseling*, 26:343–7.

Cunningham, A.J., Lockwood, G.A., & Cunningham, J.A. (1991). A relationship between perceived self-efficacy and quality of life in cancer patients. *Patient Education and Counseling*, 17(1):71–8.

Davis, T.C., Crouch, M.A., Long, S.W., Jackson, R.H., Bates, P., & George, R.B. (1990). The gap between patient reading comprehension and the readability of patient education materials. *Journal of Family Practice*, 31(5):533–8.

Deegan, P.E. (1992). The independent living movement and people with psychiatric disabilities: Taking back control over our own lives. *Psychosocial Rehabilitation Journal*, 15(3):3–19.

Delbanco, T.L. (1992). Enriching the doctor–patient relationship by inviting the patient's perspective. *Annals of Internal Medicine*, 116:414–18.

Devine, E. (1992). Effects of psychoeducational care for adult surgical patients: A meta-analysis of 191 studies. *Patient Education and Counseling*, 19:129–42.

Doak, C.C., Doak, L.G., & Root, J.H. (1985). *Teaching Patients with Low Literacy Skills*. Philadelphia: J.B. Lippincott.

Ende, J., Kazis L., Ash, A., & Moskowitz, M. (1989). Measuring patients' desire for autonomy: Decision making and information-seeking preferences among medical patients. *Journal of General Internal Medicine*, 4(1):23–30.

Engstrom, P. (1996). Telemedicine targets a rapid growth market: Home sweet home care. *Medicine on the Net*, 2(5):1–4.

Estabrook, B. (1979). Consumer impact of a cold self-care center in a prepaid ambulatory care setting. *Medical Care*, 17(1):1139–45.

Funnell, M.M., Donnelly, M.B., Anderson, R.M., Johnson, P.D., & Oh, M.S. (1992). Perceived effectiveness, cost, and availability of patient education methods and materials. *Diabetes Educator*, 18(2):139–45.

Gillespie, M.A. & Ellis, L.B.M. (1993). Computer-based patient education revisited. *Journal of Medical Systems*, 17:119–25.

Goldstein, M.K., Clarke, A.E., Michelson, D., Garber, A.M., Bergen, M.R., & Lenert, L.A. (1994). Developing and testing a multimedia presentation of a health-state description. *Medical Decision Making*, 14(4):336–44.

Greenfield, S., Kaplan, S., & Ware, J., Jr. (1985). Expanding patient involvement in care: Effects on patient outcomes. *Annals of Internal Medicine*, 102:520–8.

Gustafson, D.H., Bosworth, K., Hawkins, R.P., Boberg, E.W., & Bricker, E. (1992). CHESS: A computer-based support system for providing information, referrals, decision support and social support to people facing medical and other health-related crises. *Proceedings – the Annual Symposium on Computer*

Applications in Medical Care, 161–5. Bethesda, MD: American Medical Informatics Association.

Gustafson, D.H., Hawkins, R.P., Boberg, E.W., Bricker, E., Pingree, S., & Chan, C.L. (1994). The use and impact of a computer-based support system for people living with AIDS and HIV infection. *Proceedings – the Annual Symposium on Computer Applications in Medical Care*, 604–8. Bethesda, MD: American Medical Informatics Association.

Harris, J. (1995). *Summary Conference Report. National Assessment of Consumer Health Information Demand and Delivery*. Rancho Mirage, CA: Reference Point Foundation, Partnership for Networked Health Information for the Public, May 14–16.

Haynes, R. & Taylor, D. (1979). *Compliance in Health Care*. Baltimore: Johns Hopkins University Press.

Hekelman, F.P., Niles, S.A., & Brennan, P.F. (1994). Gerontologic home care: A prescription for distance continuing education. *Computers in Nursing*, 12(2):106–9.

Hewson, M.G. (1993). Patient education through teaching for conceptual change. *Journal of General Internal Medicine*, 8(7), 393–8.

Holt, G.A., Hollon, J.D., Hughes, S.E., & Coyle, R. (1990). OTC labels: Can consumers read and understand them? *American Pharmacy*, NS30:51–4.

Hopper, K.D., TenHave, T.R., & Hartzel, J. (1995). Informed consent forms for clinical and research imaging procedures: How much do patients understand? *American Journal of Roentgenology*, 164(2):493–6.

Hunter, C.S. & Harman, D. (1985). *Adult Illiteracy in the United States: A Report to the Ford Foundation*. New York: McGraw-Hill.

Israel, B.A. & Shurman, S.J. (1990). Social support, control and the stress process. In K. Glanz, F.M. Lewis, & B. Rimer (eds.), *Health Behavior and Health Education*, (pp. 187–215). San Francisco: Jossey-Bass.

Jimison, H.B., Fagan, L.M., Shachter, R.D., & Shortliffe, E.H. (1992). Patient-specific explanation in models of chronic disease. *Artificial Intelligence in Medicine*, 4(3):191–205.

Jimison, H.B. & Henrion, M. (1992). Hierarchical preference models for patients with chronic disease. *Medical Decision Making*, 7:351.

Jones, R., Naven, L., & Ashe, G. (1993). Use of a community-based touch screen public-access health information system. *Health Bulletin*, 51:34–42.

Jubelirer, S.J. & Linton, J.C. (1994). Reading versus comprehension: Implications for patient education and consent in an outpatient oncology clinic. *Journal of Cancer Education*, 9(1): 26–9.

Kahn, G. (1993a). Computer-based patient education: A progress report. MD *Computing*, 10:93–9.

Kahn, G. (1993b). Computer-generated patient handouts. *MD Computing*, 10:157–64.

Kasper, J.F., Mulley, A.F., Jr., & Wennberg, J.E. (1992). Developing shared decision making programs to improve the quality of health care. *Quality Review Bulletin*, 18:183–90.

Kieschnick, T., Adler, L.A., & Jimison, H.B. (1996). *1996 Health Informatics Directory*. Baltimore: Williams & Wilkins.

Kleinman, A., Eisenberg, L., & Good, B. (1978). Culture, illness, and care: Clinical lessons from anthropologic and cross-cultural research. *Annals of Internal Medicine*, 88:251–8.

Korsch, B.M. (1984). What do patients and parents want to know? What do they need to know? *Pediatrics*, 74:917–19.

Kreps, G.L. (1990). Communication and health education. In E.B. Ray, & L. Donohew (eds.), *Communication and Health: Systems and Applications*, (pp. 187–203). Hillsdale, NJ: Erlbaum.

Leaf, A. (1993). Preventive medicine for our ailing health care system. *Journal of the American Medical Association*, 269:66–8.

Leirer, V.O., & Morrow, D.G. (1988). Elder's nonadherence, its assessment, and computer assisted instruction for medication recall training. *Journal of the American Gerontology Society*, 36:877–84.

Lenert, L.A., Michelson, D., Flowers, C., & Bergen, M.R. (1995). IMPACT: An object-oriented graphical environment for construction of multimedia preference assessment instruments. *Proceedings of the 19th Annual Symposium on Computer Applications in Medical Care*. Philadelphia: Hanley & Belfus, 319–24.

Ley P. (1982). Satisfaction, compliance, and communication. *British Journal of Clinical Psychology*, 21:241–54.

Lipkin, M.J. (1987). The medical interview and related skills. In W.T. Branch & M.J. Lipkin (eds.), *Office Practice of Medicine* (pp. 1287–1306). Philadelphia: W.B. Saunders.

Lorig, K., Chastain, R.L., Ung, E., Shoor, S., & Holman, H.R. (1989). Development and evaluation of a scale to measure perceived self-efficacy in people with arthritis. *Arthritis and Rheumatism*, 32(1):437–44.

Mahler, H.I. & Kulik, J.A. (1990). Preferences for health care involvement, perceived control and surgical recovery: A prospective study. *Social Science and Medicine*, 31:743–51.

Maibach, E.W., Schieber, R.A., & Carroll, M.F. (1996). Self-efficacy in pediatric resuscitation: Implications for education and performance. *Pediatrics*, 97(1): 94–9.

Meade, C.D. & Howser, D.M. (1992). Consent forms: How to determine and improve their readability. *Oncology Nursing Forum*, 19(10):1523–8.

Meyer, G.S. & Gibbons, R.V. (1997). House calls to the elderly – A vanishing practice among physicians. *New England Journal of Medicine*, 337:1815–20.

Morgan, P.P. (1993). Illiteracy can have major impact on patients' understanding of health care information. *Canadian Medical Association Journal*, 148(7): 1196–7.

Morrow, D., Leirer, V., & Sheikh, J. (1988). Adherence and medication instructions: Review and recommendations. *Journal of the American Gerontology Society*, 36:1147–60.

Mullen, P.D., Laville, E.A., Biddle, A.K., & Lorig, K. (1987). Efficacy of psychoeducational interventions on pain, depression, and disability in people with arthritis: A meta-analysis. *Journal of Rheumatology*, 14(Suppl 15):33–9.

O'Leary, A. (1985). Self-efficacy and health. *Behaviour Research and Therapy*, 23(4):437–51.

O'Leary, A., Shoor, S., Lorig, K., & Holman, H.R. (1988). A cognitive-behavioral treatment for rheumatoid arthritis. *Health Psychology*, 7(6):527–44.

Pavel, M., Jimison, H.B., Anwar, J., Appleyard, R., & Sher, P.P. (1996). *User Models for Adaptive Searching of Patient Health Information on the Internet* (technical report). Portland: Oregon Graduate Institute.

Peterson, C. & Stunkard, A.J. (1989). Personal control and health promotion. *Social Science and Medicine*, 28:819–28.

Pingree, S., Hawkins, R.P., Gustafson, D.H., Boberg, E.W., Bricker, E., Wise, M., & Tillotson, T. (1993). Will HIV-positive people use an interactive computer system for information and support? A study of CHESS in two communities. *Proceedings – Annual Symposium on Computer Applications in Medical Care*, 22–6. Bethesda, MD: American Medical Information Association.

Prochaska, J.O. & DiClemente, C.C. (1983). Stages and processes of self-change of smoking: Toward an integrative model of change. *Journal of Consulting and Clinical Psychology*, 51:390–5.

Shepherd, C.D. & Fell, D. (1995). Marketing on the Internet. Innovative providers educate, inform and communicate through cyberspace. *Journal of Health Care Marketing*, 15(4):12–15.

Skinner, C.S., Siegfried, J.C., Kegler, M.C., & Strecher, V.J. (1993). The potential of computers in patient education. *Patient Education and Counseling*, 22(1):27–34.

Skinner, C.S., Strecher, V.J., & Hospers, H. (1994). Physicians' recommendations for mammography: Do tailored messages make a difference? *American Journal of Public Health*, 84(1):43–9.

Somers, A.R. (1984). Why not try preventing illness as a way of controlling Medicare costs? *New England Journal of Medicine*, 311:853–6.

Stewart, R.B. & Cluff, L.E. (1972). A review of medication errors and compliance in ambulant patients. *Clinical Pharmacology Therapy*, 13:463–8.

Strecher, V.J., DeVellis, B.M., Becker, M.H., & Rosenstock, I. M. (1986). The role of self-efficacy in achieving health behavior change. *Health Education Quarterly*, 13:73–91.

Strecher, V.J., Kreuter, M., Den Boer, D.J., Kobrin, S., Hospers, H.J., & Skinner, C.S. (1994). The effects of computer-tailored smoking cessation messages in family practice settings. *Journal of Family Practice*, 39(3), 262–70.

Thompson, S.C., Pitts, J.S., & Schwankovsky, L. (1993). Preferences for involvement in medical decision-making: Situational and demographic influences. *Patient Education and Counseling*, 22:133–40.

Tibbles, L., Lewis, C., Reisine, S., Rippey, R., & Donald, M. (1992). Computer assisted instruction for preoperative and postoperative patient education in joint replacement surgery. *Computers in Nursing*, 10(5):208–12.

Vargo, G. (1991). Computer assisted patient education in the ambulatory care setting. *Computers in Nursing*, 9(5):168–9.

Vivian, A.S. & Robertson, E.J. (1980). Readability of patient education materials. *Clinical Therapy*, 3:129–36.

Wagner, E.H., Barrett, P., Barry, M.J., Barlow, W., & Fowler, F.J., Jr. (1995). The effect of a shared decision making program on rates of surgery for benign prostatic hyperplasia. Pilot results. *Medical Care*, 33(8):765–70.

Waitzkin, H. (1984). Doctor–patient communication: Clinical implications of social scientific research. *Journal of the American Medical Association*, 252:2441–6.

Waitzkin, H. (1991). *The Politics of Medical Encounters: How Patients and Doctors Deal with Social Problems*. New Haven, CT: Yale University Press.

Wallerstein, N. (1992). Powerlessness, empowerment, and health: Implications for health promotion programs. *American Journal of Health Promotion*, 6(3):197–205.

Weiner, B. (1986). *An Attributional Theory of Motivation and Emotion*. New York: Springer-Verlag.

14   Computer-Assisted Clinical Decision Support

*Antoine Geissbuhler, MD, and Randolph
A. Miller, MD*

Introduction

It is possible to portray computer-based clinical decision support
systems (CDSS) expansively or strictly. A general definition would encompass any computer system that deals with clinical data or medical knowledge and would include electronic textbooks and laboratory reporting systems. A narrow definition would limit the scope of
CDSSs to knowledge-based systems that provide patient-specific advice. Which definition is more appropriate at the present time? One
way to answer this question is to examine the information needs of
physicians (Covell et al. 1985, Forsythe et al. 1992, Osheroff et al. 1991,
Timpka & Aborelius 1990). Osheroff et al. (1991) observed information needs expressed by physicians during patient case-oriented
teaching rounds in a university hospital. Of 337 requests concerning
patient care, 52% involved patient-specific information that could be
found in the patient record; 23% involved general knowledge that
could be found in a library, a textbook, or MEDLINE; and, 26%
involved synthesis of patient information and medical knowledge.
From this perspective, computer-based systems that provide patient-
specific information or access to general knowledge without patient-
specific advice, i.e., most electronic clinical information resources,
can play an important role in helping the clinical decision-making
process.

Some information needs are not expressed, as they are not recognized
by care providers (Williamson et al. 1989). Causes of such omissions include informational overload (McDonald 1976) and lack of knowledge.
Successful reminder- and alert-generating systems have been designed

to help focus the attention of clinicians on information that might otherwise be overlooked.

The potential of computer programs to assist physicians in making diagnoses for a specific patient has been recognized since the early days of computing (Ledley & Lusted 1959, Miller 1994). Clinical diagnostic decision-support systems use a variety of reasoning methodologies, such as Bayesian statistics, decision analysis, symbolic logic, or heuristic reasoning (Duda & Shortliffe 1983). These systems span a wide range of applications, from focused systems with narrow application domains (e.g., interpretation of electrocardiographic tracings of blood gas results) to general systems that can handle several hundred diagnoses and thousands of findings (Miller 1994). Similar methodologies have been used in the development of tools that provide therapy advice. A major concern for all systems is how to capture, store, and update clinical expertise.

To increase the usability and clinical utility of decision-support tools, efforts have been made to integrate them within comprehensive clinical information systems in order to limit the amount of data that clinican users must reenter across isolated systems. An important problem is the inertia that must be overcome to meet an information need. In the manual world, accessing information resources necessitates walking to a reference room or driving to a distant medical library and retrieving books from a shelf one at a time or, alternatively, locating and calling a clinical expert who can answer a clinical question authoritatively. These processes present a substantial impediment to rapidly answering clinical questions during practice. Biomedical informaticians wish to lower the "information acquisition threshold" by increasing the availability of CDSSs that make relevant clinical information "a mouse click away." Recent emphasis has been placed on optimally positioning CDSSs within the workflow of clinicians in order to increase their acceptance and provide just-in-time decision support (Cimino et al. 1995, Evans et al. 1998, Gardner et al. 1990, Geissbuhler & Miller 1996, Haynes et al. 1990, McDonald & Tierney 1992, Tierney et al. 1993).

This chapter describes illustrative examples of clinical information resources, attention-focusing tools, diagnostic decision-support systems and patient-management tools. It also addresses the issues of knowledge acquisition and representation. Finally, legal issues related to computer-based clinical decision support are discussed.

Information Resources

The Computer-Based Patient Record

The computer-based patient record (CPR) will become the main electronic source of patient-specific information relevant to patient care (Ball & Collen 1992, Dick & Steen 1991). Its advantages over the conventional paper-based record include better availability and readability. In 1991, after an 18-month study on improving patient records, the Institute of Medicine of the National Academy of Science recommended that health care practitioners should adopt the CPR as the standard for medical and all other records related to patient care. In the view of the Institute of Medicine Committee, the CPR is more than a digitized version of the conventional paper record; it provides broader functions to practitioners, is used actively in the process of patient care, and serves as a resource in the evaluation and management of patient care.

McDonald (Ball & Collen 1992) enumerates the information that physicians want most from the patient record: What drugs have been prescribed? What happened during the last hospitalization? As soon as they are produced, what are the laboratory test results? What was the patient's state during care by the previous physician? In addition, physicians want clear, well-organized displays of information, the ability to display trends and patterns, and the ability to select and organize subsets of information. The technology required to perform those tasks is currently available.

However, most of the obstacles in the implementation of a CPR are due to the difficulty of getting the data into it, in particular when the data are recorded by physicians (McDonald 1997). Free text information can be captured via dictation transcription, by systems that require input as structured text, and, as technology improves, potentially through voice recognition in the future. However, despite the progress in natural language processing techniques (Jain & Friedman 1997, Jain et al. 1996, Spyns 1996), most decision-support tools still require some form of structured, encoded data, preferably from the CPR. The capture of structured information requires the interaction with a computer program, either directly by the physician or by a transcriptionist. The advantages of capturing structured information directly from the physician are numerous. Transcription and interpretation errors are less likely to occur when data are collected at the source. Entry forms can be dynamically built based on previous information in order to optimize data capture.

Most relevant to decision support, captured information in a structured format facilitates implementation of intelligent tools that can provide immediate feedback as data are entered.

Despite these advantages, the implementation of direct data capture from physicians, and in particular order entry, remains a challenge (Sittig & Stead 1994). Various factors have contributed to difficulty and even failure in implementing such systems (Dambro et al. 1988, Massaro 1993, Spillane et al. 1990). Busy care providers are reluctant to use systems that slow their work and fail to provide obvious direct benefits (Dambro et al. 1988, Spillane et al. 1990). It has often been stated that 25% of the effort in implementing such systems is technology related and 75% is social engineering. Installation of major clinical systems engenders substantial sociocultural changes in the workplace. Such changes can cause major stress and disruptions throughout an institution (Massaro 1993). In institutions where comprehensive electronic medical record systems have been developed, direct physician order entry has often been reserved as one of the last projects to be implemented (McDonald et al. 1992).

General Medical Knowledge

Streamlined access to general medical knowledge – medical information that is neither patient nor institution specific – has the potential to fulfill important information needs (Osheroff et al. 1991, Forsythe et al. 1992). For example, the ability to perform literature searches using the MEDLINE bibliographic database in a clinical setting has been shown to improve decisions (Haynes et al. 1990) and to lower costs and lengths of stay (Klein et al. 1994). General medical knowledge is becoming increasingly available in electronic form, including bibliographic databases, digitized textbooks, full-text journals, and, more recently, multimedia documents. For example, MD Consult provides an interactive access over the World Wide Web (WWW) to dozens of textbooks and full-text journals from a consortium of publishers. It also provides access to practice guidelines, printable educational material for patients, and a drug information database. Digital libraries are enabling effective interaction with information distributed across computer networks (Schatz 1997).

Traditional electronic distribution mechanisms for general medical knowledge include static media such as CD-ROMs, which follow the publication paradigm of printed text, and dedicated online services, such as the MEDLARS bibliographic search engine of the National Library of Medicine. The development of computer networks, and in particular the Internet and the WWW, has provided a less structured environment that supports the widespread, multiauthored, multicentered distribution of hypertext multimedia documents and, more recently, software. This environment enables the unconstrained publication of information and services, including the distribution of medical knowledge that can be used in the medical decision-making process. As such, the WWW offers much promise in both the dissemination and the retrieval of medical information (Lowe et al. 1996). However, the unregulated nature of the WWW and the proliferation of Web sites makes it more difficult to retrieve valid peer-reviewed information or to assess content quality. Anyone can place any information, whether accurate or false, on the Web, and, consequently, many do. The majority of health-related information on the WWW is at best anecdotal and, unfortunately, inaccurate. This represents a significant concern if the information is to be used to make clinical decisions. Web sites of good reputation, similar to renowned textbook publishers or stringently reviewed journals, can be used as "anchors" for accessing information of reliable quality. The information on National Institutes of Health (NIH)-sponsored and academic medical school WWW sites is, as a rule, of reasonably high quality. The Health on the Net Foundation (HON) provides links to Web-based resources, selected based on a code of conduct approved by an international advisory board [www.hon.ch].

As an efficient, cross-platform, information distribution mechanism, the WWW (interface and paradigm) is becoming an important tool for integrating applications that provide access to medical information (Cimino et al. 1995). For example, the MINDscape interface developed at the University of Washington (Tarczy-Hornoch et al. 1997) provides integrated access to the medical record and to knowledge sources via the Web. The Web-based clinical information system at Columbia Presbyterian Medical Center provides links between its laboratory component and the DXplain diagnostic decision support system (Elhanan et al. 1996).

Local Medical Knowledge

All health-care delivery systems, whether for an individual practice or a large, multifacility institution, use a substantial amount of local knowledge (Covell et al. 1985, Forsythe et al. 1992). The local knowledge includes formalized policies and procedures and less structured – sometimes unwritten – operational rules. The latter form of information includes knowledge about how institutional systems actually work, how to apply the rules, and even how and when to break the formal rules (Forsythe et al. 1992). In a study of information needs in office practice, Covell et al. (1985) found that 17% of self-reported questions about the management of a patient required access to nonmedical information, e.g., "How do you arrange for home care for a patient?"

Third-party payers and regulatory agencies are exerting increased control over medical decisions. It is becoming critical for health care providers to develop, manage, and efficiently access local, regional, payer-specific, and national guidelines. For example, it is important for a practitioner to know which medications of a given therapeutic class are covered by the patient's health-care plan. As such, the formularies supported by individual health maintenance organizations and insurance providers change frequently. Health-care providers must implement processes to maintain and distribute this information.

In hospitals, each clinical department often has operational rules that influence the rest of the institution. For example, the operating hours of the radiology department, the turnaround time of a laboratory test, or the staffing levels of the pharmacy should be taken into account in planning diagnostic and therapeutic strategy. Departments, for their own use, often maintain local computerized spreadsheets or databases, such as reference values in the laboratory or algorithms for checking drug dosing and drug interactions in the pharmacy. With the development of integrated hospital information systems, this information should be shared with other departmental systems and made available at the point of decision making. For example, integrating the detection of drug interactions into a physician order entry system enables the generation of warnings at the time the ordering decision is made and therefore facilitates the correction of suboptimal decisions immediately at their source. One of the challenges of such integration is to respect the distributed nature of the expertise involved in building and maintaining knowledge bases while achieving efficient and unambiguous linkages across them. Strategies devised to achieve this goal include the development of a common institutional nomenclature such as the MED (Cimino et al. 1994) or VOSER (Rocha et al. 1994), the use of a standardized representation of rules such as the Arden syntax (Hripcsak et al. 1994, Pryor & Hripcsak 1993), the use of the Web technology as a mechanism for the distributed maintenance of linked documents (Geissbuhler & Grande 1997a), and the collaborative maintenance of knowledge in a central repository outside of departmental systems.

Clinical pathways provide another mechanism for sharing expertise (Ibarra et al. 1996, Koch & Smith 1995, Rietz et al. 1997). They serve as collaborative guidelines to identify and sequence the major interventions by care providers relevant to a particular patient problem. Designed to optimize the efficiency and quality of care delivery by reducing variance, clinical pathways provide a framework for care and reflect the collaboration required among many disciplines to treat patients. Clinical pathways are also used to generate customized flowcharts for the documentation of care and the tracking of variance. In general, pathways represent an institutional consensus and, as such, are expected to influence some aspects of the decision-making process of individual physicians. Computerized versions of clinical pathways are being implemented and integrated into clinical information systems, where they have the potential to influence the use and scheduling of resources, in particular by interacting with the order entry process (Gardner et al. 1990, Schriger et al. 1997, Tierney et al. 1993).

Attention-Focusing Tools

Computers can successfully extend the data processing capabilities of humans by monitoring clinical data and generating alerts or reminders in response to predefined rules. Reminders printed on encounter forms for ambulatory care (McDonald et al. 1977) significantly increase physicians' responses to clinical events that require attention (McDonald 1976) and increase compliance with guidelines (Lobach & Hammond 1997). The number of tests ordered decreases when physicians are presented with past test results (Tierney et al. 1987), the charges for diagnostic tests (Tierney et al. 1990), or an estimate of the probability that a given test will be abnormal (Tierney et al. 1988).

In the foregoing studies, the effect of reminders was independent of the physicians' level of training, and the rate of response to clinical events returned to baseline upon discontinuation of the reminders. These results support the notion that many medical errors are due to intrinsic limits in physicians' ability to process ongoing events, rather than to remediable flaws in their fund of knowledge (McDonald 1976, Miller 1956).

Real-time reminders are more effective than delayed feedback (Tierney et al. 1986). Reminders generated during the interaction of the physician with a charting system (Schriger et al. 1997), or an order entry system (Tierney et al. 1993), cause a decrease in the cost of care and an improvement of the compliance with guidelines. In hospitals, alerts can be generated in real time as a response to events such as abnormal test results. These systems (Gardner et al. 1992, Hripcsak et al. 1996, Rind et al. 1992, Tate et al. 1990) have been shown to improve the timeliness (Rind et al. 1992) and quality of patient care (Rind et al. 1994).

The event detection and notification system developed at the Brigham and Women's Hospital (Kuperman et al. 1996) provides a good example of a comprehensive approach. A monitoring process receives new data produced by various systems, such as laboratory resuts and orders for medications. Using rules from a knowledge base and previous information about the patient, the monitor determines if an alert should be generated. An "on-call" database reliably identifies the physician to notify, who is then automatically paged. If the alert is not viewed within 15 minutes by the physician, the nurse is notified by a visual cue on the nursing station monitor. Corrective actions suggested by the system can be ordered at the time of the acknowledgment of the notification.

Patient-Specific Consultations

Observations by Osheroff, Forsythe et al. (1991) suggest that the information retrieval resources and applications just described have the potential to meet three-quarters of physicians' information needs. In those applications, the role of the computer is to provide efficient retrieval and distribution of local and global information, with a limited understanding of the clinical context.

However, the potential of computers to help physicians reason about specific cases, to make diagnoses, or to manage therapy has been recognized since the 1950s (Ledley & Lusted 1959). Prototypes were developed by the 1960s, and working systems were available in the 1970s (Miller 1994). In 1979, Shortliffe et al. (1979) identified the following classes of diagnostic decision-support systems: clinical algorithms; clinical databanks that include analytical functions; mathematical pathophysiologic models; pattern-recognition systems; Bayesian statistical systems; decision-analytical systems; and symbolic reasoning or "expert" systems.

A clinical algorithm, or flowchart, is conceptually the simplest decision-making tool. It encodes the sequences of actions a good clinician would perform to solve a given problem using "discriminating questions" to distinguish among mutually exclusive alternatives (Bleich 1969). However, its use as a general mechanism for encoding decision-making knowledge is limited by its lack of scalability: as the problem domain becomes larger, the number of possible sequences of situations to be considered can grow exponentially as the number of combinations increases. Furthermore, this approach does not deal with the degree of uncertainty or incorrectness inherent in the nature of clinical data. Taking too many branches with uncertainty can leave one "out on a limb" with no way to recover when an earlier incorrect response is discovered. Nevertheless, programs using clinical algorithms have been successfully implemented in certain domains, especially those where detailed domain knowledge makes it possible to identify parameters useful for dividing diagnostic sets into nonintersecting subsets, such as acid-base and electrolyte disorders (Bleich 1972).

Databases of clinical data for selected groups of patients (e.g., the Duke Databank for Cardiovascular Disease [Rosati et al. 1975]) have been collected to measure the incidence of diseases, identify demographic factors, or measure therapeutic efficacy of specific interventions in defined populations. Statistical methods can be used to select a set of known cases similar to the case at hand and draw conclusions about diagnosis, therapy, or prognosis. For example, Selker et al. (1997) used clinical data from 13 major clinical trials and registries to create and validate predictive instruments regarding the utility of thrombolytic therapy for patients with acute myocardial infarction. The system can be incorporated into a computerized electrocardiograph machine and therefore placed in the critical workflow of clinicians who are evaluating patients with suspected acute myocardial infarction. Such predictive tools represent the distillation of a large volume of clinical experience into a convenient form that can be carried to the bedside and applied in a direct manner to a single patient. However, the risk inherent in this process of condensation is that subtle differences, such as rare occurrences, might be lost. Developers and users of evidence-based predictive tools should ask several questions (Miller 1997): How representative are the patients who were used in developing a given predictive tool? Which patients are likely to be misclassified and subjected to unnecessary interventions by a particular tool? How severe are the adverse effects that occur in patients receiving unnecessary interventions? The clinical significance of a computer-based decision-support tool resides in its ability to augment the native skills of the physician during clinical practice, not its function in isolation as an "omniscient oracle" (Miller 1996, Miller & Masarie 1990a).

Bayesian probability theory has provided a useful framework for the development of probabilistic decision-support systems. One of the first diagnostic decision-support systems to be utilized at widespread clinical sites was the system developed in the 1970s by de Dombal for the diagnosis of acute abdominal pain (de Dombal et al. 1972). Using sensitivity, specificity, and disease-prevalence data for various signs, symptoms, and test results, De Dombal's program calculated, using Bayes' theorem, the probability of seven possible explanations for acute abdominal pain (appendicitis, cholecystitis, small-bowel obstruction, pancreatitis, perforated peptic ulcer, diverticular disease, and nonspecific abdominal pain). Data were collected by physicians on structured forms and then entered into the computer. The program assumed that each patient had one of these seven conditions and provided a ranked list of the probability of each diagnosis. Another assumption, which keeps the statistical computations tractable, was that the findings used in the model were conditionally independent for all diagnoses. De Dombal's system has been shown to improve the diagnostic accuracy of surgical house officers and to improve patient care by lowering the rate of complications and unnecessary procedures due to incorrect diagnosis (Adams et al. 1986). It is interesting to note that the sole use of forms for collecting structured data, without the use of the computer, explained half of the improvement in diagnostic accuracy that accompanied the use of the system. The same authors also developed a set of educational programs (explanations of findings, case simulations) that further improved the performance of the physicians (de Dombal et al. 1991).

Nevertheless, the usability of a purely probabilistic approach to clinical decision making is limited (Aliferis & Miller 1995, Szolovits & Pauker 1978). The necessity of quantifying the a priori and conditional probabilities of diagnoses and their findings requires enormous amounts of data and is feasible only in well-constrained problem domains where enough epidemiological and clinical information is available – unless subjective probabilities are used. The assumptions that findings are conditionally independent, and that a set of diagnostic hypotheses can be constructed that is exhaustive and mutually exclusive, are generally incorrect. More complex probabilistic models have been developed to address some of these difficulties. These include Ben-Bassat's multi-membership Bayesian model (Ben-Bassat et al. 1980) and Bayesian belief networks (Herskovitz & Cooper 1991). Neural networks represent an entirely new approach to clinical decision support, although the weights learned by single hidden-layer networks may be analogous or identical to Bayesian probabilities.

Medical judgment, by the physician and by computer programs, must be based on both categorical and probabilistic reasoning (Szolovits & Pauker 1978), even if it has been demonstrated that humans are not good intuitive statisticians (Tversky & Kahneman 1974) and have limitations when dealing with multiple concurrent hypotheses (Miller 1956). The power of a problem solver depends both on its capacity to reason and on the expressiveness of its knowledge representation scheme. The prototypical CDDSs developed in the 1970s and early 1980s used a variety of problem-solving techniques and knowledge representations.

The MYCIN system (Shortliffe 1976), developed at Stanford University for the diagnosis and treatment of certain bacterial infections, implemented a clinical algorithm as a set of a few hundred concise rules and used a simple recursive algorithm, backward chaining, to apply each rule just when it was likely to yield information needed by another rule. The program could also provide explanations of its conclusions by tracing the rules that were used. This simple, uniform, modular representation of knowledge enabled the creation, modification, and removal of individual rules independently of each other. It also made possible the design of tools that reason about the knowledge in the rules and that could facilitate the acquisition and validation of new knowledge. A large number of rule-based diagnostic decision-support systems have been developed over the years. However, most rule-based diagnostic decision-support systems have been devoted to narrow application areas due to the extreme complexity of maintaining rule-based systems with more than a few thousand rules. Many of the data-driven warning and reminder systems incorporated into medical record systems use rules to identify conditions that trigger the reminders. Examples include the Regenstrief Medical Record System (CARE) developed by McDonald et al. (1976) and the HELP system developed by Warner, Pryor, Gardner, and colleagues (Kuperman et al. 1991, Pryor et al. 1983).

The CASNET/Glaucoma system (Weiss et al. 1978), developed at Rutgers University as a diagnostic and therapeutic program for glaucoma, represented its knowledge as a causal-associational network. It used causality as the fundamental notion in its reasoning scheme: any phenomenon had to have a causal pathway which could be traced back to an ultimate etiological factor. Knowledge was represented in two forms: a descriptive component consisting of observations and findings, pathophysiological states, disease states, and treatment plans; a normative component consisting of decision rules that state the inference of a pathophysiological state with some degree of confidence from an observed pattern of findings and the preference for a treatment with some degree of expectation of results from an observed pattern of findings. The likelihood of a node in the causal network was assessed based either on directly observable evidence, on expectation from known causally antecedent states, or by inference from known causally subsequent states. The CASNET formalism was generalized and extended in the EXPERT system (Weiss & Kulikowski 1979). The EXPERT system has been used extensively in developing systems that utilize criterion tables, including AI/Rheum (Lindberg et al. 1980), AI/Coag, and others.

The INTERNIST-1 system (Miller et al. 1982), developed at the University of Pittsburgh for diagnosis in general internal medicine, used an extensive knowledge base and heuristic programs that could construct and then resolve differential diagnoses. The building block for the knowledge base was the individual disease. For each of the 650 diagnoses entered into the system, a disease profile was constructed. The disease profile consisted of findings (historical items, symptoms, physical signs, and laboratory abnormalities) that have been reported to occur in association with the disease. Findings in each disease profile were associated with two variables: the evoking strength (equivalent to a positive predictive value) and the frequency (equivalent to a sensitivity level). As true quantitative information does not exist in the medical literature in most cases, the numbers used by INTERNIST-1 were judgmental in that they were compiled after a review of the available knowledge. Each finding was associated with a value that quantifies the importance of explaining the given finding in any patient. The knowledge base also detailed relations among diagnoses and among manifestations.

The development of QMR (Miller et al. 1986) as a successor to INTERNIST-1 illustrates an important philosophical change in the perceived role for CDSSs. The style of diagnostic consultation in INTERNIST-1 was a "Greek oracle" model. In this model, the physician, unable to solve a diagnostic problem, transferred all the relevant patient information to the expert system. The physician's subsequent role was that of a passive observer, answering yes or no to questions generated by INTERNIST-1. Ultimately, the program was supposed to provide the correct diagnoses and explain its reasoning.

There were fatal flaws in the Greek oracle model (Miller & Masarie 1990). A physician cannot convey his or her complete understanding of an involved case to a computer program. In addition, the physician who understands the patient as a person possesses the most important intellect to be employed during a consultation. The user should therefore control the process of computer-based consultation in the same manner that a pilot controls a complex aircraft in going from point A to point B. Encouraged by the critiquing model developed by Perry Miller and his colleagues (Miller 1984, 1986), recent CDSS developers have had as an objective to create a symbiotic system that takes advantage of the strengths of both the user's knowledge and the system's abilities.

However, despite the demonstration that CDSSs can be developed and function at an expert level, few have left the laboratory environment. One reason for the failure of CDSSs to reach widespread use is their lack of integration both within the workflow of physicians and within the architecture of clinical information systems. Textbooks are rarely taken from their shelves during a busy clinical practice. Similarly, physicians cannot be expected to access the various CDSSs available on "electronic shelves," as these are likely to present different user interfaces, and require the reentry of data – often already available in electronic form but encoded using a different nomenclature.

Current developments focus on integrating, in a coherent platform, all the aspects of information technology necessary to support and improve the delivery of care, including communication, logistical aspects of patient management, and clinical decision support. The prototypical example of a CDSS successfully integrated into a device is the automated analysis of recordings available on most modern electrocardiographs. An example of a CDSS successfully integrated into a hospital information system is the antibiotherapy management program developed by Classen, Pestotnik, Evans, and colleagues (Evans et al. 1998). This program, integrated into the workflow of physicians as an order entry system, uses patient-specific information from the hospital information system (the HELP system developed at LDS Hospital in Salt Lake City [Pryor et al. 1983]), epidemiological data derived from previous cases, and institutional and general knowledge to generate advice on the treatment of infections and the use of antiinfective agents. Issues addressed by the program include the review of radiological, pathological, and laboratory findings; the generation of alerts, suggestions, and interpretation regarding laboratory test results; alerts and suggestions regarding the dose, route, and duration of therapy; pharmacokinetic consultations; the detection of drug–drug and drug–laboratory test interactions; patient diagnoses and infections in the previous 5 years; antibiograms of the last 5 years; the cost of antiinfective agents; and monographs for antiinfective agents.

With the rapid growth of the body of medical knowledge, developers and users of CDSS are faced with the challenge of maintaining up-to-date knowledge bases. Signs and symptoms associated with diseases are relatively static but diagnostic tests evolve rapidly, with changes in their performance, invasivness, or cost. As the pathophysiological understanding of diseases improves, diagnostic entities are redefined. Developments in the area of medical therapy are even more rapid. This problem can be alleviated by distributing the process of maintaining the knowledge base. This implies that the models of knowledge representation can be shared and that methods are developed to link these knowledge bases. Giuse et al. (1993) has demonstrated that an appropriate consensus can be reached when multiple authors construct a knowledge base using carefully crafted common tools. Standards are being developed to facilitate the integration of distributed knowledge bases in clinical systems. Examples of standard nomenclatures include the Medical Subject Headings (MeSH) used to index literature references in MEDLINE and the GALEN compositional model of medical concepts (Rector & Nowlan 1994). The components of the UMLS project (Humphreys et al. 1998) provide translations across various nomenclatures and descriptions of information resources, thus enabling, for example, the automatic and intelligent creation of queries to various information sources. At a more technical level, emerging standards include protocols for data exchange such as the HL-7 message protocol, knowledge representation syntaxes such as the Arden syntax (Hripcsak et al. 1994, Pryor & Hripcsak 1993), and middleware technologies such as distributed object computing. High-level strategic frameworks such as the Integrated Advanced Information Management Systems (IAIMS) concept (Stead 1997) are being developed and implemented.

Ethical and Legal Issues Related to Computer-Based Clinical Decision Support

Goodman and Miller wrote: "Human values should govern research and practice in the health professions. Health informatics, like other health professions, involves issues of appropriate and inappropriate behavior; of honorable and disreputable actions; and of right and wrong. Students and practitioners of the health sciences, including informatics, share an important obligation to explore the moral underpinnings and ethical challenges related to their research and practice" (Miller & Goodman, 1998).

Of significance, "ethical and legal issues often overlap. Ethical considerations apply in attempts to determine what is good or meritorious, and which behaviors are desirable or morally correct in accordance with higher principles. Legal principles are generally derived from moral and ethical ones, but deal with the practical regulation of behaviors and activities" (Goodman & Miller, in press).

In a 1985 review of "Ethical and legal issues related to the use of computer programs in clinical medicine," Miller, Schaffner, and Meisel (1985) identified the following important ethical issues: when to use a clinical computer program; who should be qualified to use a clinical software program and for what purposes; what issues pertain to privacy and confidentiality; and how to approach problems of software validation and maintenance.

In response to these questions, Goodman and Miller (in press) identified a "set of principles for appropriate use of decision support systems":

1. A computer program should be used in clinical practice only after appropriate evaluation of its efficacy and documentation that it performs its intended task at an acceptable cost in time and money.
2. Users of most clinical systems should be health professionals who are qualified to address the question at hand on the basis of their licensure, clinical training, and experience. Software systems should be used to augment or supplement, not replace or supplant, such individuals' decision-making.
3. All uses of informatics tools, especially in patient care, should be preceded by adequate training and instruction, which should include the review of all available forms of previous product evaluations.

With respect to systems for clinical diagnosis, the "standard view" is that, while "human diagnosis is fraught with error, ... manual systems do not become outmoded simply because they may produce mistakes. ... Existing diagnostic decision support systems represent a promising new technology that ... is in its infancy.... For the remainder of this century and the beginning of the next, humans will be the primary purveyors of medical diagnosis. Perhaps, at appropriate times, they will be assisted by diagnostic decision support software" (Miller 1990b).

Miller and Gardner, representing a consortium of healthcare and information-related professional organizations, recommended that healthcare-providing institutions take responsibility for their own software environments in a manner that protects patients (Miller & Gardner 1997a, 1997b). It is difficult to establish the safety of individual clinical software programs for all potential users and uses; it is nearly impossible to establish the safety of large-scale systems containing dozens of individual, evolving, interacting applications that communicate over data networks. The consortium proposed four categories of risk to classify clinical software systems and four classes of monitoring that can be applied specifically based on the level of risk in a particular setting. Within this classification, stand-alone CDSSs can fall into different classes based on what level of advice they provide and how they provide it: B, excluded from regulation; C, simple registration and postmarket surveillance; and D, premarket approval and postmarket surveillance. For more details, refer to the table in Miller and Gardner (1997a, p. 844). The consortium recommended creation of local "Software Oversight Committees" to carry out the responsibility of patient protection at each institution of sufficient size. The complexity of local software environments is best understood, documented, monitored, and policed locally. The Food and Drug Administration (FDA) and other regulatory agencies have limited financial and personnel resources, general but not local expertise, and minimal day-to-day presence at the local level, so all but the most dangerous clinical software programs should be regulated on a local basis, with the FDA (or similar agencies) coordinating national-level surveillance activities and regulating high-risk clinical systems (Miller & Gardner 1997a, 1997b).

Certain advice-giving clinical programs may capture data from series of large, randomized controlled trials (RCTs) and use those data to make what appear to be sound, evidence-based recommendations. Yet, such programs still may have significant problems. Patients who exhibit (or mimic) the entry criteria for the clinical trials, but who have diagnoses

or conditions not seen or evaluated during the trials, may nevertheless be given (incorrect) treatment according to the RCT-derived guidelines (Miller 1997a). One mechanism to improve the safety of stand-
alone software systems is better product labeling (Geissbuhler & Miller
1997b). New clinical software labeling mechanisms could include both a
physical component (traditional label) and a "virtual" software component (such as a pointer to a WWW page that contains additional information on the product and is continually updated by the manufacturer).
Labels should document mechanisms utilized by a software package;
list and explain all terminology (clinical and other) used by the system;
explain how much training is required to use the system in various settings and how to obtain training; document where help can be obtained;
list intended/approved usages and their indications; state contraindi-
cations to use and known product limitations; provide version numbers
and dates for both programs and clinical data involved; document processes for building and maintenance of the biomedical knowledge base
underlying the program; give an expected duration of product validity
(including frequency of suggested updates); and provide records of previous evaluations and mechanisms for new problem/error reporting.

To date, few, if any, cases have been decided in courts involving stand-
alone clinical software systems (i.e., systems apart from hardware medical devices, such as cardiac pacemakers or radiation oncology devices).
Legal issues related to the use of clinical software programs revolve
around tort liability (Miller et al. 1985). In the United States, tort law
governs the sale and use of products and services ("items"). If the purchaser of an item is harmed through use or consumption of the item,
then, through tort liability, the purchaser may sue the manufacturer,
vendor, or service provider to recover damages.

Two major categories of tort liability are relevant to clinical software
programs: negligence and strict product liability. Negligence theory,
which applies more to services than to physical goods, states that a service provider must uphold the standards of the community in delivering
the service. Medical malpractice litigation falls under negligence theory.
It is important to understand that negligence theory allows for adverse
outcomes, so long as reasonable standards of practice are upheld. All 90-
year-old patients with bilateral pneumococcal lobar pneumonia do not
survive, even when diagnosed promptly and started immediately on appropriate antibiotics. Strict product liability, on the other hand, applies
independently of manufacturers' conduct. Strict liability applies only

to physical goods, not to services. Its purpose is more to compensate the injured than to punish errant vendors or manufacturers. If a product purchased by a user contains a defect (either due to manufacturing, transportation, or the sales process), and if that defect can be shown to be the direct cause of a user's injuries, then the manufacturer/vendor may be held liable under strict product liability, so long as the user was not appropriately warned of the defect (e.g., a label stating that metal ladders should not be brought into contact with electrical wires might relieve a manufacturer of some responsibility). It is not clear whether courts will treat clinical software programs as goods or services, so it is uncertain whether negligence or strict product liability will become the dominant legal principle applied. It is nearly certain that, as a minimum, the courts will apply negligence standards in legal cases involving "defective" clinical software systems. If strict product liability prevails, it could have a chilling effect on the entire clinical software industry because insurance rates would soar (or become unaffordable) and products would be expected to be free of defects (a standard not applied to human clinicians). Nevertheless, it is often difficult to demonstrate that clinical software products are defective (poor user training, failure of the user to interpret output properly, and failure of the user to override the system may be at fault).

A clinician who does not use a particular decision-support system may be sued for malpractice if his or her colleagues use such systems and it can be demonstrated that use of the system might have prevented the clinical mishap. On the other hand, a clinician user who believes the incorrect output of a clinical software program, and fails to override its advice, may also be found guilty of negligence, just as would be the case if the consultant were human. Both ways, only the lawyers win (not patients or clinicians). As stated previously, clinical systems should be used only if they improve the quality of performance (outcomes) at an acceptable cost in time and money.

A secondary legal question is the potential use of clinical "expert systems" as witnesses in malpractice litigation (Miller 1989). Two important criteria must be met before an individual can serve as an expert witness: he or she must possess "veracity" – the ability to be sworn to tell the truth (with penalties for not doing so) and the ability to be cross-examined (Frank 1988). At present, and for the foreseeable future, expert computer programs will not possess either quality and therefore cannot serve as witnesses in court.

Summary

The information needs of clinicians are extensive. They include patient-specific information, formal and informal knowledge, and which scope can be local to an institution or more general. Clinicians also need expert assistance to make decisions. Finally, some information needs are not recognized. CDSSs are playing an increasingly important role in satisfying these information needs.

Early CDSSs focused on the modeling and reproduction of expert knowledge and behavior. During the last two decades, the focus has shifted to the development of systems that extend, rather than replace, the capabilities of clinicians. CDSSs facilitate the access to electronic information resources such as electronic patient records, as well as local and general medical knowledge. They generate reminders and alerts about clinical events that require attention. Patient-specific consultations, for diagnostic or therapeutic assistance, are provided as interactive sessions driven by the clinician.

Recent work has focused on the integration of CDSSs on a coherent platform within the workflow of clinicians. Standards are emerging to facilitate the exchange of information and the collaborative development of knowledge bases.

The increasing availability and scope of CDSSs raises ethical and legal questions about their appropriate use, the maintenance of their quality over time, the liability of the developers and users of CDSSs, and the protection of the confidentiality of patient information.

Recommendations for the development, labeling, and use of CDSSs have been formulated. Regulatory agencies such as the FDA are considering national-level surveillance activities, and the role of institutional supervisory committees is being investigated.

References

Adams ID, Chan M, Clifford PC, Cooke WM, Dallos V, de Dombal FT, Edwards MH, Hancock DM, Hewett DJ, McIntyre N. Computer Aided Diagnosis of Acute Abdominal Pain: A Multicentre Study. *British Medical Journal.* 1986;293:800–805

Aliferis CF, Miller RA. On the Heuristic Nature of Medical Decision-Support Systems. *Methods of Information in Medicine.* 1995;34:5–14

Ball MJ, Collen MF, eds. 1992. *Aspects of the Computer-based Patient Record.* New York: Springer Verlag.

Ben-Bassat M, Carlson RW, Puri VK, Weil MH. A Hierarchical Modular Design for Treatment Protocols. *Methods of Information in Medicine.* 1980;19:93–98.

Bleich HL. Computer Evaluation of Acid-Base Disorders. *Journal of Clinical Investigation*. 1969;48:1689–1696

Bleich HL. Computer-Based Consultation: Electrolyte and Acid-Base Disorders. *American Journal of Medicine*. 1972;53:285

Cimino JJ, Clayton PD, Hripcsak G, Johnson SB. Knowledge-Based Approaches to the Maintenance of a Large Controlled Medical Terminology. *Journal of the American Medical Informatics Association*. 1994;1:35–50.

Cimino JJ, Socratous SA, Clayton PD. Internet as Clinical Information System: Application Development Using the World Wide Web. *Journal of the American Medical Informatics Association*. 1995;2:273–284

Covell DG, Unman GC, Manning PR. Information Needs in Office Practice: Are They Being Met? *Annals of Internal Medicine*. 1985;103:596–599

Dambro MR, Weiss BD, McClure CL, Vuturo AF. An Unsuccessful Experience with Computerized Medical Records in an Academic Medical Center. *Journal of Medical Education*. 1998;63:617–623

de Dombal FT, Leaper D, Staniland J, McCann AP, Horrocks JC. Computer-Aided Diagnosis of Acute Abdominal Pain. *British Medical Journal*. 1972;1:376–380

de Dombal FT, Dallos V, McAdam WAF. Can Computer Aided Teaching Packages Improve Clinical Care in Patients with Acute Abdominal Pain? *British Medical Journal*. 1991;302:1495–1497

Dick RS, Steen EB, eds. 1991. *The Computer-based Patient Record. An Essential Technology for Health Care*. Washington, DC: National Academy Press

Duda RO, Shortliffe EH. Expert Systems Research. *Science*. 1983;220:261–268

Elhanan G, Socratous SA, Cimino JJ. Integrating Dxplain into a Clinical Information System Using the World Wide Web. *Proceedings – AMIA Fall Symposium*. 1996:348–352

Evans RS, Pestotnik SL, Classen DC, Clemmer TP, Weaver LK, Orme JF, Jr., Lloyd JF, Burke JP. A Computer-Assisted Management Program for Antibiotics and Other Antiinfective Agents. *New England Journal of Medicine*. 1998;338:232–238

Forsythe DE, Buchanan BG, Osheroff JA, Miller RA. Expanding the Concept of Medical Information: An Observational Study of Physicians' Information Needs. *Computers and Biomedical Research*. 1992;25:181–200

Frank SJ. What AI Practitioners Should Know About the Law. Part One. *AI Magazine*. 1988;9:63–75

Gardner RM, Golubjatnikov OK, Laub RM, Jacobson JT, Evans RS. Computer-Critiqued Blood Ordering Using the HELP System. *Computers and Biomedical Research*. 1990;23:514–528

Gardner RM, Hawley WL, East TD, Oniki TA, Young WE. Real Time Data Acquisition: Experience with the Medical Information Bus (MIB). *Proceedings – Symposium on Computer Applications in Medical Care*. 1992;813–817

Geissbuhler A, Miller RA. A New Approach to the Implementation of Direct Care-Provider Order Entry. *Proceedings AMIA Fall Symposium*. 1996;689–693

Geissbuhler A, Grande JF. Embedding a Web-Broswer in an Order Entry System to Improve the Distributed Maintenance of Decision-Support Resources. *Proceedings AMIA Fall Symposium*. 1997a:939

Geissbuhler AJ, Miller RA. Desiderata for Product Labeling of Medical Expert Systems. *International Journal of Med Informatics*. 1997b;47:153–163

Giuse NB, Giuse DA, Miller RA, Bankowitz RA, Janosky JE, Davidoff F, Hillner BE, Hripcsak G, Luncoln MH, Middleton B. Evaluating Consensus Among Physicians in Medical Knowledge Base Construction. *Methods of Information in Medicine*. 1993;32:137–145

Haynes RB, McKibbon KA, Walker CJ, Ryan N, Fitzgerald D, Ramsden MF. Online Access to MEDLINE in Clinical Settings. A Study of Use and Usefulness. *Annals of Internal Medicine*. 1990;112:78–84

Herskovits EH, Cooper GF. Algorithms for Bayesian Belief-Network Precomputation. *Methods of Information in Medicine*. 1991;30:81–89

Hricpsak G, Ludemann P, Pryor TA, Wigertz OB, Clayton PD. Rationale for the Arden Syntax. *Computers & Biomedical Research*. 1994;27:291–324

Hripcsak G, Clayton PD, Jenders RA, Cimino JJ, Johnson SB. Design of a Clinical Event Monitor. *Computers & Biomedical Research*. 1996;29:194–221

Humphreys BL, Lindberg DAB, Schoolman HM, Barnett GO. The Unified Medical Language System: An Informatics Research Collaboration. *Journal of the American Medical Informatics Association*. 1998;5:1–11

Ibarra V, Titler MG, Reiter RC. Issues in the Development and Implementation of Clinical Pathways. *AACN Clinical Issues*. 1996;3:436–447

Jain NL, Knirsch CA, Friedman C, Hripcsak G. Identification of Suspected Tuberculosis Patients Based on Natural Language Processing of Chest Radiograph Reports. *Proceedings AMIA Fall Symposium*. 1996:542–546

Jain NL, Friedman C. Identification of Findings Suspicious for Breast Cancer Based on Natural Language Processing of Mammogram Reports. *Proceedings AMIA Annual Fall Symposium*. 1997:829–833

Klein MS, Ross FV, Adams DL, Gilbert CM. Effect on Online Literature Searching on Length of Stay and Patient Care Costs. *Academic Medicine*. 1994;69:489–495

Koch MO, Smith JA. Clinical Outcomes Associated with the Implementation of a Cost-efficient Programme for Radical Retropubic Prostatectomy. *British Journal of Urology*. 1995;76:28–33

Kuperman GJ, Gardner RM, Pryor TA. *HELP: A Dynamic Hospital Information System*. New York: Springer Verlag, 1991.

Kuperman GJ, Teich JM, Bates DB, Hiltz FL, Hurley JM, Lee RY, Paterno MD. Detecting Alerts, Notifying the Physician and Offering Action Items: A Comprehensive Alerting System. *Proceedings AMIA Annual Fall Symposium*. 1996:704–708

Ledley RS, Lusted LB. Reasoning Foundations of Medical Diagnosis. *Science*. 1959;130:9

Lindberg DAB, Sharp GC, Kingsland LC, et al. Computer Based Rheumatology Consultant. *Proceedings of MEDINFO 80*. Amsterdam, the Netherlands. 1980:1311–1315

Lobach DF, Hammond WE. Computerized Decision Support Based on a Clinical Practice Guideline Improves Compliance with Care Standards. *American Journal of Medicine*. 1997;102:89–98.

Lowe HJ, Lomax EC, Polonkey SE. The World Wide Web: A Review of an Emerging Internet-Based Technology for the Distribution of Biomedical Information. *Journal of the American Medical Informatics Association*. 1996;3:1–14

Massaro TA. Introducing Physician Order Entry at a Major Academic Medical Center: I. Impact on Organizational Culture and Behavior. *Academic Medicine*. 1993;68:20–25

McDonald CJ. Protocol-Based Computer Reminders, the Quality of Care and the Non-Perfectibility of Man. *New England Journal of Medicine.* 1976;295:1351–1355

McDonald CJ, Murray R, Jeris D. Computer-Based Record and Clinical Monitoring System for Ambulatory Care. *American Journal of Public Health.* 1977;67:240–245.

McDonald CJ, Tierney WM, Overhage JM, Martin DK, Wilson GA. The Regenstrief Medical Record System: 20 Years of Experience in Hospitals, Clinics, and Neighborhood Health Centers. *MD Computing.* 1992;9:206–217

McDonald CJ. The Barriers to Electronic Medical Record Systems and How to Overcome Them. *Journal of the American Medical Informatics Association.* 1997;4:213–221

Miller GA. The Magical Number Seven, Plus or Minus Two: Some Limits on Our Capacity for Processing Information. *Psychological Review.* 1956;63:81–97

Miller PL. A Critiquing Approach to Expert Computer Advice: ATTENDING. Boston: Pittman, 1984.

Miller PL. Critiquing: A Different Approach to Expert Computer Advice in Medicine. *Medicine et Informatique (London).* 1986;11:29–38

Miller RA, Pople HE, Myers JD. Internist-1, an Experimental Computer-Based Diagnostic Consultant for General Internal Medicine. *New England Journal of Medicine.* 1982;307:468–476

Miller RA, Goodman KW. Ethical challenges in the use of decision-support software in clinical practice. In Goodman KW (ed): *Ethics, Computing, and Medicine.* New York: Springer Verlag, 1998, 102–115.

Miller RA, Schaffner KF, Meisel A. Ethical and Legal Issues Related to the Use of Computer Programs in Clinical Medicine. *Annals of Internal Medicine.* 1985;102(4):529–536

Miller RA, Masarie FE, Myers JD. Quick Medical Reference (QMR) for Diagnostic Assistance. *MD Computing.* 1986;3:34–48

Miller RA. Legal Issues Related to Medical Decision Support Systems. *International Journal of Clinical Monitoring and Computing.* 1989;6:75–80

Miller RA, Masarie FE. The Demise of the Greek Oracle Model for Medical Diagnostic Systems. *Methods of Information in Medicine.* 1990a;29:1–2

Miller RA. Why the Standard View Is Standard: People, Not Machines, Understand Patients' Problems. *Journal of Medical Philosophy.* 1990b;15:581–591

Miller RA. Medical Diagnostic Decision Support Systems – Past, Present and Future: A Threaded Bibliography and Brief Commentary. *Journal of the American Medical Informatics Association.* 1994;1:8–27

Miller RA. Evaluating Evaluations of Medical Diagnostic Systems. *Journal of the American Medical Informatics Association.* 1996;3:429–431

Miller RA. Predictive Models for Primary Caregivers: Risky Business? *Annals of Internal Medicine.* 1997;127:565–567

Miller RA, Gardner RM. Summary Recommendations for Responsible Monitoring and Regulation of Clinical Software Systems. *Annals of Internal Medicine.* 1997a;127(9):842–845

Miller RA, Gardner RM. Recommendations for Responsible Monitoring and Regulation of Clinical Software Systems. *Journal of the American Medical Informatics Association.* 1997b;4(6):442–457

Osheroff JA, Forsythe DE, Buchanan BG, Bankowitz RA, Blumenfeld BH, Miller RA. Physicians' Information Needs: Analysis of Questions Posed during Clinical Teaching. *Annals of Internal Medicine.* 1991;114:576–581

Pryor RA, Gardner RM, Clayton PD, Warner HR. The HELP System. *Journal of Medical Systems.* 1983;7:87–102

Pryor TA, Hripcsak G. The Arden Syntax for Medical Logic Modules. International *Journal of Clinical Monitoring & Computing.* 1993;10:215–224

Rector AL, Nowlan WA. The Galen Project. *Computer Methods and Programs in Biomedicine.* 1994;45:75–78

Rietz C, Erickson S, Deshpande JK. Clinical Pathways and Case Management in Anesthesia Practice: New Tools and Systems for the Evolving Healthcare Environment. *AANA Journal.* 1997;65:460–467

Rind DM, Safran C, Phillips RS, Slack WV, Calkins DR, Delbanco TL, Bleich HL. The Effect of Computer-Based Reminders on the Management of Hospitalized Paitnets with Worsening Renal Function. *Proceedings of the Annual Symposium on Computer Applications in Medical Care.* 1992:28–32

Rind DM, Safran C, Phillips RS, Wang Q, Calkins DR, Delbanco TL, Bleich HL, Slack WV. Effect of Computer-Based Alerts on the Treatment and Outcomes of Hospitalized Patients. *Archives of Internal Medicine.* 1994;154:1511–1517

Rocha RA, Huff SM, Haug PJ, Warner HR. Designing a Controlled Medical Vocabulary Server: The VOSER Project. *Computers in Biomedical Research.* 1994;27:472–507

Rosati RA, McNeer JF, Starmer CF, Mittler BS, Morris JJ, Wallace AG. A New Information System for Medical Practice. *Archives of Internal Medicine.* 1975;135:1017–1024

Schatz BR. Information Retrieval in Digital Libraries: Bringing Search to the Net. *Science.* 1997;275:327–334.

Schriger DL, Baraff LJ, Rogers WH, Cretin S. Implementation of Clinical Guidelines Using a Computer Charting System; Effect on the Initial Care of Health Care Workers Exposed to Body Fluids. *Journal of the American Medical Association.* 1997;278:1585–1590.

Selker HP, Griffith JL, Beshansky JR, Schmid CH, Califf RM, D'Agostino RB, Laks MM, Lee KL, Maynard C, Selvester RH, Wagner GS, Weaver WD. Patient-Specific Predictions of Outcomes in Myocardial Infarction for Real-Time Emergency Use: A Thrombolytic Predictive Instrument. *Annals of Internal Medicine.* 1997;127:538–556

Shortliffe EH. *Computer-Based Medical Consultations: MYCIN. Artificial Intelligence Series.* New York: Elsevier Computer Science Library, 1976.

Shortliffe EH, Buchanan BG, Feigenbaum EA. Knowledge Engineering for Medical Decision-Making: A Review of Computer-Based Clinical Decision Aids. *Proceedings IEEE.* 1979;67:1207–1224

Sittig DF, Stead WW. Computer-Based Physician Order Entry: The State of the Art. *Journal of the American Medical Informatics Association.* 1994;1:108–123

Spillane MJ, McLaughlin MB, Ellis KK, Montgomery WL, Dziuban S. Direct Physician Order Entry and Integration: Potential Pitfalls. *Proceedings Annual Symposium on Computer Applications in Medical Care.* 1990:774–778

Spyns P. Natural Language Processing in Medicine: An Overview. *Methods of Information in Medicine.* 1996;35:285–301

Stead WW. The Evolution of the IAIMS: Lessons for the Next Decade. *Journal of the American Medical Informatics Association.* 1997;4:S4–S9

Szolovitz P, Pauker SG. Categorical and Probabilistic Reasoning in Medical Diagnosis. *Artificial Intelligence.* 1978;11:115–144

Tarczy-Hornoch P, Kwan-Gett TS, Fouche L, Hoath J, Fuller S, Ibrahim KN, Ketchell DS, LoGerfo JP, Goldberg Hl. Meeting Clinican Information Needs by Integrating Access to the Medical Record and Knowledge Resources via the Web. *Proceedings AMIA Fall Symposium.* 1997:809–813

Tate KE, Gardner RM, Weaver LK. A Computerized Laboratory Alerting System. *MD Computing.* 1990;5:296–301

Tierney WM, Hui SL, McDonald CJ. Delayed Feedback of Physician Performance versus Immediate Reminders to Perform Preventive Care; Effect on Physician Compliance. *Medical Care.* 1986;24:659–666

Tierney WM, McDonald CJ, Martin DK, Hui SL, Rogers MP. Computerized Display of Past Test Results; Effect on Outpatient Testing. *Annals of Internal Medicine.* 1987;107:569–574

Tierney WM, McDonald DJ, Hui SL, Martin DK. Computer Predictions of Abnormal Test Results; Effect on Outpatient Testing. *Journal of the American Medical Association.* 1988;259:1194–1198

Tierney WM, Miller ME, McDonald CJ. The Effect on Test Ordering of Informing Physicians of the Charges for Outpatient Diagnostic Tests. *New England Journal of Medicine.* 1990;322:1499–1504

Tierney WM, Miller ME, Overhage JM, McDonald CJ. Physician Inpatient Order Writing on Microcomputer Workstations; Effects on Resource Utilization. *Journal of the American Medical Association.* 1993;269:379–333.

Timpka T, Aborelius E. The GP's Dilemma: A Study of Knowledge Need and Use During Health Care Consultations. *Methods of Information in Medicine.* 1990;29:346–353

Tversky A, Kahneman D. Judgment under Uncertainty: Heuristics and Biases. *Science.* 1974;185:1124–1131

Weiss S, Kulikowski C, Amarel S, Safir A. A Model-Based Method for Computer-Aided Medical Decision-Making. *Artificial Intelligence.* 1978;11:145–172

Weiss S, Kulikowski C. EXPERT: A System for Developing Consultation Models. *Proceedings of the Sixth International Conference on Artificial Intelligence,* Tokyo, 1979.

Williamson JW, German PS, Weiss R, Skinner EA, Bowes F 3d. Health Science Information Management and Continuing Education of Physicians. A Survey of U.S. Primary Care Practitioners and their Opinion Leaders. *Annals of Internal Medicine.* 1989;110:151–160

15 Opportunities for Applying Psychological Theory to Improve Medical Decision Making: Two Case Histories

Robert M. Hamm, PhD, Dewey C. Scheid, MD, Wally R. Smith, MD, and Thomas G. Tape, MD

I. Introduction

Improving medical practice has been the ultimate goal of medical decision making research (Elstein, Shulman & Sprafka, 1978; Ledley & Lusted, 1959; Lusted, 1991; McNeil, Keeler & Adelstein, 1975; Schwartz, Gorry, Kassirer & Essig, 1973; Weinstein & Feinberg, 1980). It is a fundamental assumption that the decision theoretic framework must be useful, for its language – the likelihood that causes will produce effects, and the evaluation of the effects – captures the essence of what produces good in medical decisions. However, it is not easy to prove that decision theoretic ideas or techniques directly improve medical practice. Published in the medical literature, decision theoretic analyses may eventually influence medical practice through the activities of scholars, teachers, and practitioners of evidence-based medicine. Commissioned by policy-making bodies, cost-effectiveness analyses may influence policies governing what will be reimbursed, which in turn will govern physician behavior (Elixhauser, Halpern, Schmier & Luce, 1997; Power & Eisenberg, 1998). Not content with these long-term, indirect effects, researchers have made a number of attempts to directly influence

Acknowledgments are due to Neal Dawson, MD, Mary Jo Young, MD, Gretchen Chapman, PhD, Jim Cacy, PhD, and an anonymous reviewer for contributions and readings of early drafts of this chapter. Those who taught relevant Short Courses at meetings of the Society for Medical Decision Making, including those on the Basic (Al Connors, Jr., MD, and Gretchen Chapman, PhD) and Advanced (Andre Kushniruk, PhD, and Laura Militello, MA) Psychology of Medical Decision Making, on Information Mastery (Lorne Becker, MD, and David Slawson, MD), and on Changing Physician Behavior (Roy Poses, MD, William E. Tierney, MD., Caryn Christensen, PhD, and Louis F. Rossiter, PhD), helped make us aware of many important issues. Errors and omissions are our own.

physicians' medical practices through the application of decision theoretic concepts.

The analysis of medical decision making encompasses three approaches. The first is decision theoretic analysis: how can information be best used for accurate diagnosis and prognosis? What option has the highest expected utility? What option would use resources most cost effectively if applied universally? Second, there is the empirical analysis of medical practice: What decisions are actually made by individuals or institutions? When it is shown that physicians regularly don't make the choice with the highest expected utility, this is an opportunity for an intervention to seek improvement. Third, there is the psychological analysis of the decision maker: How is knowledge represented, information processed, and reasoning motivated? What strategies are used to make decisions? When it is shown that physician reasoning does not or cannot follow decision theory's rules, there is an opportunity for improvement. Attempts to apply the insights of the medical decision-making framework can build on any of these three forms of analysis.

The second section of this chapter will review the various efforts that have been made to apply decision theoretic ideas or research products in order to improve medical practice. Some of these attempts have succeeded, but there have been important failures. We will summarize the literature on projects that have applied decision analysis to individual patients, made evidence-based guidelines available to physicians, trained physicians to reason with analytical principles, provided decision-relevant information to physicians, or provided computerized decision aids. The third section will present two interventions in detail and analyze the reasons they did not accomplish their expected goals. The final section will present a descriptive metaphor: that physicians follow scripts when they make decisions about patients. We will argue that interventions will be more successful if they are based on a clear understanding of the scripts physicians currently use and if physicians are explicit about the alternative scripts that are proposed to improve their decision making.

II.   Attempts to Use Decision Theoretic Ideas to Improve Medical Decision Making

Create Decision Analyses

Researchers have attempted to involve physicians in decision analytic modeling. One approach is to construct a novel decision model for an individual patient's specific clinical situation. Structuring the tree, assessing probabilities, and assessing utilities is time-consuming and expensive (Zarin & Pauker, 1984), and is difficult to evaluate because one does not know what decision would have been made without the analysis.

Apply Decision Analyses

Alternatively, one can apply an existing decision analysis to the probabilities and values of the individual patient. Using existing trees eliminates the time and expense of constructing a decision analysis on the fly, in the middle of the business of patient care. When this was done to assist physicians in making a personal decision on whether to get hepatitis B vaccinations, it increased the vaccination rate (Clancy, Cebul & Williams, 1988). We have not found a published evaluation of whether applying existing decision analyses in this way improves patients' outcomes.

Apply Diagnostic Rules

The results of decision analytic research can be used to construct a prescription for how to handle a medical problem. In the form of rules or guidelines, these prescriptions can be made available to physicians in the hope that they will use them. An example of an analysis-based diagnostic rule applied to individual patients is an instrument for predicting acute ischemic heart disease. Physicians using this rule had 30% lower cardiac care unit (CCU) admission rates (Pozen, D'Agostino, Selker, Sytkowski & Hood, 1984), largely because it reduced their estimates of the probability of myocardial infarction (MI) for cases that have low probability (McNutt & Selker, 1988). Similarly, a paper-and-pencil scoring rule for sore throats caused physicians to reduce prescription of antibiotics when there was a low probability of streptococcal infection (McIsaac & Goel, 1998). Presumably such diagnostic rules are more accurate than physicians' unaided diagnostic reasoning, so physicians who use the rules make more appropriate decisions which benefit patients.

Analytically based rules have had some success in changing physicians' practices. The Ottawa Knee Rule, which suggests that radiography for knee injury is required only if patients demonstrate 1 or more of 5 findings related to age, function, or bone tenderness (Stiell et al., 1996), was taught to house staff and attending physicians in the emergency departments of two hospitals. Implementation led to a decrease in the use of knee radiography for adults, without patient dissatisfaction or missed fractures, and was associated with reduced waiting times and costs (Stiell et al., 1997).

However, demonstrated efficacy of diagnostic rules does not lead to wide acceptance. For example, beginning in the early 1970s, a group of investigators developed and tested a computer-based clinical decision support system designed to improve the diagnosis of abdominal pain (de Dombal, Leaper, Staniland, McCann & Horrocks, 1972). A multicenter trial, conducted at 8 institutions in the 1980s, showed computer-aided diagnosis of abdominal pain to be more accurate than unaided physicians (Adams et al., 1996). It reduced unnecessary admissions, negative laparotomy rates, and perforated appendix rates and thus substantially reduced medical costs. Despite a measure of success over a 25-year period that would almost certainly ensure widespread adoption of a new biomedical technology, the system remains a research curiosity. Why? As would be expected, application in new populations and new settings, along with attempts to generalize to include more causes of abdominal pain, challenged the diagnostic accuracy of the system (Sutton, 1989). More important, however, may be the realization that the program's requirement for structured data input actually trained novice clinicians to collect data, improving their unaided diagnostic accuracy to a level comparable to that of computer-aided diagnosis (Wellwood, Johannessen & Spiegelhalter, 1992). Paradoxically, use of the system decreased after it was demonstrated that the benefit could be due to the computer program's training rather than its decision rules.

Apply Decision Analysis-Based or Evidence-Based Guidelines

Decision analytic reviews of the evidence can be used to produce general guidelines for how to handle patients with a disease. This was the intent of the guidelines developed by the Agency for Health Care Policy and Research (e.g., McCormick, Cummings & Kovner, 1997). Although many published guidelines are based on experts' opinions, guidelines based on meta-analytic evidence reviews (Cook, Greengold, Ellrodt & Weingarten, 1997), organized with a decision tree and possibly evaluated for cost effectiveness (Berg, 1996), qualify as products of decision theoretic analysis.

Despite some successes, several problems still remain with this approach. Published guidelines have had only limited effects on physicians.

For example, simply widely publishing and endorsing a consensus statement on appropriateness of cesarean sections didn't move Canadian physicians' actual practice toward compliance, even though physicians' opinions about best practice were congruent with the consensus statement (Lomas et al., 1989). Although health maintenance organization (HMO) physicians in the United States were familiar with and hopeful about the role of guidelines for improving patient care, these attitudes did not always correlate with implementation of prevention guidelines into their clinical practices (Weingarten et al., 1995). Similarly, 69% of surveyed U.S. family physicians reported a positive attitude about practice guidelines, but only 44% reported using any guidelines (Wolff, Bower, Marbella & Casanova, 1998). Among younger physicians, more thought that guidelines could be useful tools. Most preferred guidelines that could be modified (87%) and that were no longer than two pages. Only 27% of respondents knew where to locate a guideline on a particular topic (Wolff et al., 1998).

Guidelines that have been disseminated and heeded may be applied unevenly, with unequal outcomes. This has been shown for guidelines on hypertension (Fahey & Peters, 1997) and depression (Callahan, Dittus & Tierney, 1996). Guidelines, when applied, may not always have positive effects on patient outcomes. Canadian researchers recently assessed the evidence for the effectiveness of clinical practice guidelines in improving patient outcomes in primary care. Of 91 trials identified through the search, 13 met the criteria for inclusion in the critical appraisal. The most common conditions studied were hypertension (7 studies), asthma (2 studies), and cigarette smoking (2 studies). Four of the studies followed nationally developed guidelines, and 9 used locally developed guidelines. Six studies involved computerized or automated reminder systems, whereas the others relied on small-group workshops and education sessions. Only 5 of the 13 trials (38%) produced statistically significant improvements in patient outcomes (Worrall, Freake & Chaulk, 1997). Interventions that compare physicians' own performance to the guideline may be more effective than those that simply present information about the guideline (Wensing, van der Weijden & Grol, 1998).

The use of guidelines may not be cost effective. A guideline for low back pain proved not to be cost effective in practice (Suarez-Almazor, Belseck, Russell & Mackel, 1997), which may account for its low rate of use (Freeborn, Shye, Mullooly, Eraker & Romeo, 1997). Additionally, guidelines that utilize the decision theoretic approach to maximize cost effectiveness for individual patients often do not maximize cost effectiveness for populations of patients (Granata & Hillman, 1998).

Train Physicians in Decision Theoretic Reasoning

Another approach for improving medical decision making is to train physicians to make decisions consistent with decision theory's prescriptions for reasoning. To avoid common reasoning errors, physicians' judgments can be debiased and their consciousness can be raised about heuristic strategies (Hansen & Helgeson 1996; see Chapter 7, this volume). Although education in decision analytic principles generally helps people reason in accord with the principles (Nisbett, Fong, Lehman & Cheng, 1987), it has not directly been tested whether physicians trained in general decision theoretic or statistical principles make better medical decisions. Despite the low rate of explicit statistical training in medical schools (Klatzky, Geiwitz & Fischer, 1994), it has been observed that medical school increased students' statistical knowledge (Nisbett et al., 1987), perhaps due to exposure to examples of statistical reasoning (Fong, Krantz & Nisbett, 1986). Training in the related skill of critical appraisal of the medical literature improved medical students' knowledge but did not improve residents' knowledge or their use of the literature (Norman and Shannon, 1998).

Train Physicians to Judge the Concepts Required by Decision Theoretic Analyses

If physicians could better assess the information that decision analyses require, perhaps they would make better decisions. A large body of work has focused on developing techniques for improving individuals' judgments of probability. Although outcome utilities are as relevant as event probabilities to a physician's decision, we are not aware of any studies that have assessed the effect of increasing the accuracy of physicians' utility assessment.

Many attempts to improve physicians' judgment have been based on feedback techniques developed from multiple cue probability learning (MCPL) experiments. Although these experiments originally focused on judgment accuracy (e.g., correct diagnoses), probability is intrinsic in the language with which accuracy is assessed, and MCPL techniques have come to be used to increase the accuracy of probability judgments. The MCPL paradigm, developed in the 1950s by judgment psychologists, uses an artificial judgment task to study learning in a laboratory setting. In a series of trials, a subject estimates the value of an unknown target variable based on the values of several cues and is provided with information about the correct answer. The target variable is usually a weighted linear combination of the cue values. To make the task more realistic (i.e., unpredictable), a random error is often added to the target variable. Thus, even when the subject fully understands the underlying relationship between the cues and the target variable, he or she cannot be completely accurate. The theory underlying MCPL experiments is the Brunswik lens model of perception, in which judgment about an intangible variable is mediated through a number of observable cues that are probabilistically related to the variable (Cooksey, 1996; Doherty & Kurz, 1996).

The learning in MCPL experiments occurs through repetitive practice with various types of feedback about one's performance. Several generalizations emerge from MCPL experiments (Doherty & Balzer, 1988). First, simply supplying the correct answer after each trial (outcome feedback) seldom leads to efficient learning. The mathematical complexity of the tasks combined with the random error term causes frustration in subjects who try to deduce a precise prediction rule from outcome feedback data. Second, a novel type of feedback called *cognitive feedback* proved remarkably effective in promoting efficient learning. Cognitive feedback involves showing subjects their inferred cue-weighting pattern in comparison to the "correct" weighting pattern. Cue weights are computed by linear regression predicting subjects' estimates from the cue values. Subjects typically complete a block of trials, receive their computed cue weights, and are advised to try to make their cue weights match the correct weights during the subsequent block of trials. Usually only two or three rounds of cognitive feedback are needed to achieve mastery of even complex prediction tasks. More recently, task information has been recognized as a major part of cognitive feedback (Balzer, Doherty & O'Connor, 1989). That is, simply telling a subject the underlying weighting scheme of an MCPL task yields most of the benefit of cognitive feedback; subjects need not be shown their own weighting scheme in order to improve.

Beginning in the 1970s, investigators began to apply MCPL principles to analyze physicians' judgment in both real and hypothetical medical situations. Examples include diagnosis of gastric ulcer (Slovic, Rorer & Hoffman, 1971), pulmonary embolism (Wigton, Hoellerich & Patil, 1986), streptococcal pharyngitis (Poses et al., 1992), acute otitis media (Gonzalez-Vallejo, Sorum, Stewart, Chessare & Mumpower, 1998), and urinary tract infection (Wigton, Patil & Hoellerich, 1986); assessment of depression severity (Fisch, Hammond, Joyce & O'Reilly, 1981), cardiac risk (Tape, Kripal & Wigton, 1992), and rheumatoid arthritis severity (Kirwan, Chaput de Saintonge, Joyce & Currey, 1983; Kirwan & Currey, 1984). Wigton has reviewed the methodology and its application to medical research (Wigton, 1988, 1996). Many studies used a clinical prediction rule as the standard of excellence for assessing physician judgment. The weights of the variables in the prediction rule substitute for the "correct" cue weights in the MCPL paradigm. Based on the observation that subjects in MCPL experiments had increasing difficulty as the random error term was made larger, a new type of feedback called *probability feedback* was introduced. Instead of providing the correct answer – the actual patient outcome – as the outcome feedback method would do, the probability feedback method provides a calculated probability of that outcome using the appropriate clinical prediction rule. Probability feedback trains physicians to perform in a similar manner to a clinical prediction rule without explicitly learning the rule. In some studies (Tape et al., 1992; Tape, Steele & Wigton, 1995), probability feedback improved physicians' judgments more than cognitive feedback did.

As an application of the probability judgment training techniques developed in the MCPL research, a recent study sought to increase physicians' use of mammography for breast cancer screening to recommended levels by training physicians to combine available information to make risk-based judgments of patients' need for mammography (Saver, Taylor, Treadwell & Cole, 1997). However, this did not increase the rate at which physicians ordered mammography for their patients (T. Taylor, personal communication, January 28, 1998). A similar study, which trained physicians to judge diagnostic probabilities for strep throat more accurately, had no effect on rate of antibiotics prescribing (see Section III).

Present Decision-Relevant Information in a More Accessible Form

Another approach assumes that physicians would know how to use information if they had it and changes the system to improve access to information in a variety of ways. Some researchers have emphasized the need to reformat decision-relevant information so that physicians can utilize it more easily. To allow students' knowledge base to contain information applicable to individual patients, Klayman and Brown (1993) have proposed that textbooks should present disease–symptom association information in the form of a list of diseases associated with a symptom rather than a list of symptoms associated with a disease (see also problem-based learning, as in Neufeld & Barrows, 1974). Gigerenzer and Hoffrage have advocated presenting information about diagnostic test characteristics in terms of absolute frequencies rather than conditional probabilities (Gigerenzer, 1996; Gigerenzer & Hoffrage, 1995). Although physicians find these easier to understand, the absolute frequences have to be calculated anew whenever the base rate changes. Those promoting physician awareness of the evidence for treatments teach strategies for reading journals that focus on discovering decision-relevant information (Slawson, Shaughnessy & Bennett, 1994; Slawson, Shaughnessy, Ebell & Barry, 1997).

Provide Decision-Relevant Information

Giving the physician tools for accessing information that is relevant to a decision analytic strategy assumes that the physician did not already know this information and trusts that the physician can use it. For example, providing the probability of drug efficacy and of side effects helped physicians rank drug options more appropriately for hypothetical case vignettes (Carter, Butler, Rogers & Holloway, 1993). However, risk estimates and triage recommendations for patients with acute chest pain, provided to physicians in the emergency department by stapling the algorithm to the progress note form, did not reduce the admission rate for patients with a low probability of heart attack (Lee et al., 1995). A study which provided accurate prognostic probabilities and patient preferences to physicians dealing with end-of-life decisions did not produce the expected improvements (see our second case history, presented later).

Use Computers to Support Physician Decision Making

Computers can offer three general types of clinical decision support. (1) Information management tools (hospital information systems, bibliographic retrieval systems, computer patient record systems, and searchable digitized medical libraries) help the clinician access pertinent knowledge. (2) Tools for focusing clinicians' attention on specific data (clinical laboratory alerts, reminders, drug interaction detectors, and feedback systems that compare actual care with care rules) can remind clinicians of options or events they should consider. (3) Tools that apply analytic knowledge for specific patients include computer-aided diagnosis (Shortliffe, 1987), prediction of outcomes such as hospital survival (Knaus et al., 1991), and drug dosage calculation. While hundreds of studies of clinical decision support systems have been published, recent critical appraisals of the literature found only 68 controlled trials that studied clinicians and measured either performance or patient outcomes. Nine of 15 studies of computer-aided drug dosing, 1 of 5 studies of computer-aided diagnosis, 14 of 19 studies of preventive service reminder systems, and 19 of 26 studies of other computerized decision support systems showed improvements in performance. Only 6 of 14 studies that measured patient outcomes reported improvements (Hunt, Haynes, Hanna & Smith, 1998; Johnston, Langton, Haynes & Mathieu, 1994). Another review of 98 randomized clinical trials of computerized information services found that 76% evaluated aspects of the process of care (Balas et al., 1996). Many of the interventions were considered successful: provider prompt/reminder (19/19), computer-assisted treatment planner (15/19), provider feedback (13/19), computerized medical record and information access (14/19), prediction (5/6), and computer-aided diagnosis (2/4).

We hope this brief survey of avenues for applying decision theoretic ideas to medical practice may stimulate readers' interest in figuring out how to make each of these approaches work. Each avenue is complex and could benefit from a review that analyzes what elements and conditions allow for an effective intervention. The purpose of this chapter, however, is to critique two examples of unsuccessful attempts to improve medical decision making (in Section III), to evaluate the psychological theories assumed, and to offer alternatives. We present these "case histories" because retelling their stories can clarify why the interventions failed and why that failure was surprising: "what were we thinking?" Each of these projects was a natural extension of what was generally known about decision theory, decision psychology, and even the sociology and organizational theory of decision making. Someone designing an intervention today might take the same approach. Our criticisms are not necessarily new; the studies' authors themselves acknowledge most of what we say. We review these studies for physicians and psychologists interested in applying decision theory to improve medicine in the hope that the case histories will help people see the kind of theory needed to support attempts to change medical practices and the kind of research that needs to be done.

III.   Case Histories: Examples of Disappointing Attempts to Improve Medical Decision Making

Case History 1: Intervention to Reduce Overprescription of Antibiotics

Poses, Cebul, and Wigton (1995) attempted to improve physicians' management of patients with sore throats. Physicians at their clinics were prescribing antibiotics to more than 35% of pharyngitis patients, though fewer than 10% of sore throats are caused by streptococcus, which is the most common cause of sore throat that can be treated with antibiotics. Although it is often said that physicians give antibiotics for colds because patients want them, in fact physicians do not know when their patients with viral upper respiratory infections want antibiotics, getting antibiotics does not satisfy the patients more (Hamm, Hicks & Bemben, 1996a), and antibiotics do not improve their outcomes (Hamm, Hicks & Bemben, 1996b). Presumably prescribing antibiotics for viral sore throats is equally ineffective. It is considered inappropriate to prescribe unnecessary antibiotics because of their cost, because individual patients can have adverse reactions, and because organisms develop resistance when exposed to antibiotics. In an attempt to reduce this rate of antibiotic prescription, Poses et al. (1995) trained physicians to judge the probability of streptococcal pharyngitis more accurately.

This improvement strategy was based on the premise that physicians who make more accurate judgments about the likelihood of disease will make more accurate diagnoses and, in turn, select treatments that will lead to the best possible outcomes (see McNutt & Selker, 1988). The researchers assumed that physicians' decisions on how to treat are made using a process similar to the threshold strategy for treating proposed by Pauker and Kassirer (1980). They selected their method of training to make accurate probability judgments based on a series of research projects studying physicians' judgments.

Threshold Strategy. The threshold strategy for treating (Pauker & Kassirer, 1980) suggests that physicians should make a probability judgment about the likelihood of a diagnosis and then make a decision about treatment based on whether the judged probability exceeds a threshold for action. For example, a physician examining a patient with a sore throat must decide whether to prescribe antibiotics. The appropriateness of antibiotics depends on whether streptococcal infection is present. The threshold strategy recommends that antibiotics be given if the probability of streptococcal infection is greater than a treatment threshold probability (Cebul & Poses, 1986; McDonald, 1996), which is in turn a function of the benefits and harms of treating people who have, or don't have, a streptococcal infection.

Pauker and Kassirer's (1980) prescriptive threshold strategy has taken on a descriptive role. It has been proposed as a model for how physicians actually make decisions. For example, a 1988 textbook asserts, "In practice, the treatment threshold probability is often chosen intuitively" (Sox, Blatt, Higgins & Marton, 1988, pp. 243–245). This descriptive threshold model assumes that the physician judges the probability of streptococcal infection and, if it exceeds the threshold for treatment, prescribes antibiotics. If the judged probability is less than the treatment threshold, the physician then decides whether the probability is greater than the test threshold for doing a diagnostic test for streptococcal infection.

Probability Judgments. Although physicians seldom make explicit probability judgments in day-to-day practice, it is assumed that they make an implicit assessment of probability. Physicians' quantitative estimates in research studies have been shown to be highly correlated with their management decisions (Christensen-Szalanski & Bushyhead, 1981; Eisenberg, Schumacher, Davidson & Kaufman, 1984; Poses, Cebul, Collins & Fager, 1985; Tierney et al., 1986). Formal methods have been developed to derive judgment thresholds from clinicians' decisions (Eisenberg & Hershey, 1983). Results from these types of studies, along with the theoretical framework of the threshold model, have spawned research in assessing and improving physicians' judgment (reviewed in Section II).

Studies which formally assess the quality of physician judgment have used measures of both discrimination and calibration (Poses, Cebul & Centor, 1988; see Chapter 8, this volume). Discrimination measures the ability to distinguish those with a condition of interest from those without the condition. Calibration measures the degree to which

judged probabilities of the condition match actual frequencies of occurrence. Studies of judgment in a variety of fields, including medicine,
have shown surprisingly poor discrimination and calibration among
subjects considered to be experts (Hammond, 1996).

Studies of clinical judgment with cognitive feedback, reviewed in
Section II, demonstrated tremendous variation among physicians in
their weighting of the various clinical cues available to them in a given
judgment task. Physicians' initial discrimination and calibration scores
tended to be quite low, but they improved substantially with feedback.
Such findings provided encouragement that judgment analysis could be
a powerful technique for improving patient care. However, it had not
yet been shown that improved judgment translated into better medical
care.

Study Details. To bridge this gap, Poses et al. (1995) did a study to see
whether improving physicians' judgment improved actual clinical decisions. This controlled study compared the streptococcal pharyngitis
judgments and decisions of physicians in an intervention practice and a
control practice. The intervention consisted of a computer teaching program, periodic disease prevalence reports, and a state-of-the-art lecture
on diagnosis and management of pharyngitis. The control physicians
received only the lecture. The computer program presented cases of
pharyngitis with both probability feedback and cognitive feedback. The
investigators examined physicians' subsequent decisions on whether to
prescribe antibiotics for patients in their practices.

The control group physicians' judgment accuracy and rate of antibiotic use did not change significantly after the lecture. The intervention improved both the calibration and the discrimination of physicians'
judgments of whether hypothetical patients had streptococcal pharyngitis. The average probability estimate of streptococcal infection dropped
from 31% before to 11% after the intervention (and approached the true
disease prevalence of 5.4%). Discrimination, measured by the area under
the receiver operator characteristic (ROC) curve, increased from 0.68 to
0.74. Thus, as with other judgment and feedback trials, the intervention
improved physicians' judgment.

However, the intervention did not reduce physicians' overprescription of antibiotics. The data showed a statistically nonsignificant trend
in the opposite direction: physicians wrote prescriptions for 34.5% of
patients with pharyngitis before the intervention and for 40.0% of

patients after the intervention. The inferred threshold for antibiotic prescribing[1] dropped from 45.7% to 12.7%. The surprising failure to improve decisions on antibiotic use in physicians whose judgment had been improved led to the amusing title of this paper: "You can lead a horse to water" (Poses et al., 1995).

When a theory is applied to practice but does not produce the expected result, one must ask: "Is the theory wrong or did we not operationalize it well? Should we try again, with better control? Or must we seek a more adequate theoretical framework?" It was assumed that decisions are suboptimal because judgments are suboptimal. Judgments were improved, yet performance did not improve. The disconnection between judgment and decisions in this study raises important questions. Does the probability threshold model of decision making apply here? Were the physicians' decisions related in any way to their knowledge of the probability of streptococcal infection?

In accounting for the results, the authors of this study theorized that physicians usually make judgments on an ordinal categorical scale such as "not sick," "mildly sick," and so on. Since they do not explicitly make numerical probability judgments, the computer teaching and feedback exercises may have seemed unrelated to actual decision making, for which they continued to use their preintervention judgment process. The authors conclude: "Trying to teach physicians to quantitate uncertainty may be futile unless we also teach them what quantitated uncertainty means and how to incorporate it into their decision processes" (Poses et al., 1995, p. 73). An alternative explanation could be that when the physicians learned to recalibrate their probability judgments, they also recalibrated their antibiotic threshold judgments, so the net effect was no change in antibiotic prescription rate. Both of these explanations preserve the treatment threshold model as the theory of how physicians decide whether to treat sore throats with antibiotics. Another possibility, however, is that physicians do not actually follow any sort of strategy in which treatment is based on the probability that the patient has a streptococcal infection.

The results cannot be explained by any theory that says that the physicians paid attention to their patients' utilities, as decision theory would prescribe. In any form of subjective expected utility theory,

---

[1] This is the stochastic threshold, at which there is a 50% chance of prescribing antibiotics for the patient, calculated for the group of physicians.

judged utilities would be multiplied by probabilities. Since the physicians received no training relevant to utilities, their judgment of the utilities would be unchanged. Hence, when multiplied by the lower, recalibrated probabilities, there should have been a difference – the subjectively expected utility of treating with antibiotics should have been less. A utility account for the physician's decision making could explain the lack of change only if the physicians made no use at all of the probability information, which would be a poor normative strategy.

The failure of one study to link improved probability judgments to improved decisions does not prove that judgment feedback techniques are useless. However, it does underscore the need to formally evaluate methods intended to improve judgment in the context of real medical decisions – not just case vignettes. Clearly, much more research is needed in three areas: (1) accurate description of physicians' decision-making processes; (2) evaluation of alternative strategies for improving judgment; and (3) research on these issues in a variety of clinical problems to ensure that any effective methods can be considered broadly applicable. Much of the research to date has been guided by theories of how decisions *should* be made rather than how decisions *actually* are made. Such theory-driven interventions may fail if they teach physicians skills that are irrelevant to their decision-making processes. Understanding more about how physicians make decisions can help us design better interventions to improve their decisions.

An element of an effective approach is suggested by a recent study (McIsaac & Goel, 1998), which showed that an explicit decision support tool, a scoring rule, can reduce antibiotic prescriptions for sore throat. Physicians were asked to mark symptoms on a paper questionnaire, count them, and circle which of three categories the patient fell into. Next to the category was the action recommended by a no-test/test/treat decision rule. Each participating physician used the questionnaire with one patient. The control questionnaire asked the same questions but did not show the scoring rule. This intervention reduced the rate of antibiotics (though at $p < .10$, not $p < .05$), especially for patients with a low probability of streptococcal pharyngitis. Although this study provides significant information about strategies that may work, it does not demonstrate any lasting effect of the intervention. Indirectly, it contributes to an understanding of how physicians actually make decisions to use antibiotics, for it is consistent with the theory that they follow rules, and the more available the rule, the more likely it is to be followed (Anderson, 1993). If additional research were to prove that 1 exposure (or 30) to this rule led to an enduring change[2] in the antibiotic prescription strategy for sore throat, this would be strong support for some form of rule-based pattern or script theory (see Section IV). The implication might be that practice in following a rule or script, rather than practice in making accurate probability judgments, would be the more direct route to a change in physician behavior.

Case History 2: Intervention to Reduce Futile End-of-Life Care

Our second example of a well-justified but unsuccessful effort to improve medical practice using decision theoretic concepts is the Study to Understand Prognoses and Preferences for Outcomes and Risks of Treatment (SUPPORT). It included a randomized prospective trial of an intervention aimed at improving thinking and decision making about seriously ill hospitalized patients (Hofmann et al., 1997; The SUPPORT Principal Investigators, 1995). It provided information pertinent to decision making – the patient's survival probability and preferences regarding treatment and outcomes – and left the decision making to the physician. It used a computer model to increase physicians' knowledge of prognostic probabilities, and explicitly elicited the patient's preferences and communicated them to the physician.

The Problem of Futile End-of-Life Care. The SUPPORT intervention addressed the problem that many resources are used ineffectively in futile care at the end of life, even when the patient has expressed a preference that this not happen. What are the barriers to letting patients die comfortably, without useless interventions? How might the decision process be changed to avoid some futile care?

Observation of end-of-life decision making for more than 4,000 patients at multiple sites in Phase I of the SUPPORT study showed that physicians were not very aware of patients' preferences concerning end-of-life decision making. Patients who died spent a median of 8 days comatose, being mechanically ventilated, or in an intensive care unit (ICU). A do not resuscitate (DNR) order was written for 79% of those who died, but 46% of those orders were written less than 2 days before death, which is often too late to make much difference (The SUPPORT Principal

---

[2] One exposure learning has been demonstrated with everyday decision making (Ahn, Brewer & Mooney, 1992) and, although the interpretation is controversial, with medical decision making (Green & Mehr, 1997).

Investigators, 1995). Patient surrogates (family members or others) reported after the patients died that 50% of the patients had been in pain for at least half of their waking hours (The SUPPORT Principal Investigators, 1995).

Intervention. An intervention designed to improve communication and decision making for seriously ill patients was implemented in a randomized controlled trial. To increase the accuracy of the physician's prediction of whether patients would survive, a state-of-the-art predictive model (Knaus et al., 1995), developed for the study, was applied to each patient, and its results were provided to the physician. This computer program estimated the probability that the patient would survive to 2 months and to 6 months, the prognosis for outcome if cardiopulmonary resuscitation (CPR) were needed, and the probability of severe disability. It was applied to current information for the patient on days 2, 4, 8, 15, and 26 after the patient was enrolled in the study (The SUPPORT Principal Investigators, 1995). The model's report for each patient was given to the physician and placed in the medical record, where every physician and nurse could read it. It was expected that clarifying the patient's prognosis would let the physician know whether CPR would help the patient through a crisis rather than prolong dying.

To increase the physicians' knowledge of the patient's preferences with regard to CPR, the patient and surrogates were interviewed concerning their beliefs about the prognosis, the patient's quality of life, preferences about CPR, desire for information from the physician, the existence of any advance directives, and the degree of the patient's pain. The questions called for categorical responses regarding trade-offs such as living with unavoidable suffering versus dying (N. Dawson, personal communication, March 27, 1998). The report summarizing this interview was provided to the physician and put in the medical record. It was expected that with this information, the physician would be able to make decisions consistent with the patient's preferences. The third component of this intervention was the addition of a skilled nurse to the care team to facilitate communication between patient, surrogates, physicians, and staff.

Results. The intervention had almost no effect. Comparisons were made between more than 2,500 intervention patients and 2,200 controls, randomized by hospital service (16 intervention services, 11 control

services), after adjustments.[3] The intervention had a marginally significant effect on the proportion of patients whose doctor understood the patient's preferences when interviewed 10 days after patient enrollment[4]
(22% more; 95% confidence interval [CI] -0.01 to .49). But this increased
understanding did not make physicians write DNR orders earlier for
those patients who died, nor did it decrease the number of days they
spent being sustained in undesirable states by intensive treatment (in a
coma, in an ICU, or being ventilated mechanically). In fact, the proportion of dying patients who were reported to have been in pain most of
the time increased 15% (95% CI 0 to .33). The median resource use, not
counting the cost of the study nurse or the prognostic model, increased
5% (95% CI -0.01 to 0.12).

Assumptions. The expectation that the SUPPORT intervention would
reduce the amount of intensive end-of-life care was based on several
assumptions (Table 15.1), some of which were critiqued when the results were published (Lo, 1995; The SUPPORT Principal Investigators,
1995). With respect to our theme, the study assumed that if it provided
physicians with information that decision theory says is relevant for
decision making (survival probabilities with and without CPR and patient preferences), they would use it. However, the study did not seek
to verify this assumption: perhaps the typical physician's end-of-life
decision-making strategy makes no use of such information.

The intervention may not have provided enough information for a
decision theoretic strategy to use. In expecting that an accurate estimate
of the patient's survival probability could help physicians make better end-of-life decisions, the SUPPORT study implicitly assumed that
physicians use a strategy which pays attention to the probability of
survival. They also assumed that physicians' strategies take account
of patient preferences for the process of dying. We infer that the designers had in mind some form of subjective expected utility strategy
which would take account of the probability of survival and also its utility. Because end-of-life decision making involves a potential reversal,
from "going all out" to "letting go," a decision theoretic strategy can be

---

[3] Comparisons are adjusted with respect to a model that includes baseline (Phase I) characteristics of the specialty group, the hospital, and their interaction (specialty group
within hospital), as well as measured patient characteristics.

[4] Physicians' understanding of patients' preferences may have increased with time, as
the study nurse continued to be active after the interview.

Table 15.1. *Assumptions Made by the SUPPORT Intervention About the Decision Process in End-of-Life Decision Making*

Assumptions about the role of prognostic probabilities in the physician's decision strategy

  Physicians understand and use the prognostic information provided.

  The prognostic model provided new information that could change the physicians' decisions.

  Physicians use a decision strategy that attends to prognostic probability.

Assumptions about the patient's preferences

  Patients have meaningful, stable preferences about end-of-life care.

  All patients want less intervention.

  Discussion promotes a preference for withholding intervention.

  There is enough time for the patient to formulate and express preferences and for the physician to interpret the patient's answers.

Assumptions about the role of patient preferences in the physician's decision strategy

  Knowing the patient's preferences can improve the physician's decision making.

  It is effective to communicate patient preferences to the physician by a paper report and by the nurse.

Assumptions about the physician's decision-making process

  The physician has a strategy for dealing with end-of-life decisions that can use the information provided.

  The patient, family, nursing staff, and physician want to make plans about end-of-life decisions.

  The physician will seek opportunities to consider withholding or withdrawing life support.

  End-of-life decisions are handled by individual physicians, so it is sufficient to focus the intervention on the physician.

---

simplified to a threshold strategy: below a particular probability of survival, the physician will cease to make life support efforts. Since the probability of the patient's death is uncertain, providing an accurate estimate of a low survival probability would allow the physician to see that the probability is below the threshold and stop intensive interventions. The patient's preferences would affect the location of the threshold. The patient who wants everything done would have a lower threshold probability for withdrawing life support than the patient who does not want futile care.

The information provided by the SUPPORT study was not enough to tell a physician following a decision theoretic strategy, such as subjective expected utility or, more specifically, a probability threshold strategy, what to do. The threshold strategy, for example, assumes that the physician has different probability thresholds for different patients. For the physician to be able to adjust the threshold to respect a patient's preferences, the patient would either have to indicate a threshold probability below which to withhold resuscitation or provide an assessment of how he or she would evaluate the relevant outcomes, from which the threshold could be deduced.[5] But the SUPPORT questionnaire did not elicit the patient's survival probability threshold or the numerical evaluations of the utilities of the relevant outcomes that would be required for the physician to deduce a threshold. Therefore, even a physician with a computerized decision model could not deduce from the information provided what the appropriate survival probability threshold for the patient would be. Hence the precise survival probability the study provided could not affect the end-of-life decision making unless the physician already had a threshold probability in mind for this patient, based perhaps on experience with similar patients.

The most important assumption of the SUPPORT study, however, may be the assumption that the physician will use decision theory–relevant information if it is made available. On the contrary, we expect that even if precise numerical measurements of the patient's utilities had been included in the patient preference report, the intervention would not have changed physicians' end-of-life decision making. Without explicit training, physicians do not know how to apply a subjective expected utility strategy to numerical probability and utility information. Even those familiar with the concepts may require tools to apply them (Winterfeld & Edwards, 1986). Physicians could be trained to use such a strategy, but the SUPPORT study did not train them (and the training would be difficult). Any attempt to change physicians' end-of-life decision making needs to consider the processes by which they make these decisions.

IV. Physicians' Scripts: Framework for Understanding Decision-Making Processes

Our review of two unsuccessful attempts to improve physicians' decision making through decision theoretic means has shown a common theme. Each study assumed that physicians use a rational decision

---

[5] The formula for deducing the treatment threshold from utility judgments is illustrated in the bgphthut.x14 calculator spreadsheet, which can be downloaded from http://www.fammed.ouhsc.edu/robhamm/cdmcalc.htm.

strategy. The streptococcal pharyngitis study stated that this was a probability threshold strategy. The end-of-life study was not explicit about the form of the strategy; either a subjective expected utility model or a probability threshold model would apply. The interventions sought to improve the information such a strategy would need. The negative results suggest that this assumption was wrong: perhaps physicians do not apply a rational decision strategy to such information. What do they do then? Understanding how physicians think is essential for changing their behavior. We now offer a metaphor from cognitive psychology, the *script*, which we believe can provide an alternative framework for understanding and improving physicians' decision making process.

Strategy versus Script

We must distinguish between (1) a statement of a decision-making strategy and (2) the decision-making process that actually goes on in the physician's mind. The threshold strategy we have been discussing is a statement of a decision strategy. As such, someone could propose it as a prescription for what to do (Pauker & Kassirer, 1980), and someone else could argue that it is not a good prescription. The script, on the other hand, is a statement describing how the physician makes the decision. Someone could propose that physicians have a script that carries out a threshold strategy; others could argue either that the script fails to carry out the strategy or that it does something completely different.

A physician following a script recognizes and understands the clinical situation, considers responses for that sort of situation that are stored in memory, makes decisions and plans, and then carries them out. For our purposes, it does not matter whether we call this *script use* (Abernathy & Hamm, 1994; Chapter 4 of Abernathy & Hamm, 1995; Schmidt, Norman & Boshuizen, 1990), *recognition primed decision making* (Klein, 1993), *case-based reasoning* (Riesbeck & Schank, 1989), or *rule-based reasoning* (Anderson, 1990, 1993).[6] The point is that for physicians to follow a particular explicit strategy, such as to withhold life support below a survival probability threshold, they would have to learn a script, recognize its applicability to a specific clinical situation, decide to use it, and exercise control in following it. Elements of the script's

---

[6] The term *heuristic strategy* is similar (Kahneman, Slovic & Tversky, 1982), but it is usually applied to phenomena on a smaller scale (McDonald, 1996), and it has connotations of error (Cohen, 1993) that could distract from our theme.

knowledge structure would include a representation of what can be expected in the clinical situation, the features by which the situation can be recognized, the actions that can be done in the situation, and the efficacy of those actions in attaining the pertinent goals. Physicians may not be fully aware of the scripts they use or of the strategies that are embodied in their scripts, particularly when their knowledge has been developed through extensive experience (Abernathy & Hamm, 1995).

If a physician's behavior is controlled by such a script, there are two approaches for changing it. One is to work with the physician's script as it is and to change the inputs, expecting different outputs according to the nature of the script. That in effect was the approach of the SUPPORT study: provide better inputs (survival probability estimates and patient preference statements) and expect the output (decision the physician made concerning withholding or withdrawing life support) to be better. Another example would be to change the rewards available for a familiar action. The other approach is to try to change the physician's script. Explicitly aiming to change the rules of a person's script has proven very useful in improving people's behavior in other domains. For example, computer tutors have been developed for training high school and remedial college students in geometry and algebra (Koedinger, Anderson, Hadley & Mark, 1995). The programs make models of the individual student's problem-solving scripts (sets of rules that they apply in particular situations) and then identify incorrect rules the student uses which need to be changed. To help the student change, the tutor provides explicit statements of both the correct rule and the student's wrong rule, and provides practice so that the student can learn to use the correct rule automatically in the appropriate situation. Analogously, a framework which describes physicians' end-of-life decision-making scripts explicitly, as a set of rules that guide them in what to do in a given situation, may be helpful for figuring out physicians' behavior and for working with them to change the behavior.

Physician Scripts

The idea that physicians recognize situations and follow well-learned scripts for dealing with familiar problems offers a way to understand what happened in the SUPPORT study and why its assumptions about physicians' decision strategy may not be correct. A physician's knowledge base can be considered a collection of scripts that show what to do in different types of situations (Abernathy & Hamm, 1995; McDonald,

1996; Riesbeck & Schank, 1989; Schmidt et al., 1990). The script is activated through a pattern recognition process. When several patterns are activated, deciding which to follow is accomplished through a "conflict resolution" process (Lesgold, 1988). We might consider the conflict between scripts to be a form of competition in which the winner – the best fit – controls the physician's behavior. The recognition and selection processes are affected by past reinforcement as well as by anticipation of future reinforcement. Additionally, the recognition and selection processes are fallible, so the physician can consider at any time whether another script might be better (though this is most likely when the current script does not "fit").

Scripts are learned through explicit study, implicit modeling, practice, and review (Abernathy & Hamm, 1994, 1995). Practice and experience allow the development of more efficient mental representations (Anderson, 1993; Lesgold, 1984; Schmidt et al., 1990). At intermediate stages in learning medicine, the student or physician will have some scripts that are very well developed, others that are known just in outline form, and others that may not be known at all. Development of a particular script depends on how much experience one has had with that kind of situation, how much explicit attention has been paid to the script, and the script's success when used. The more developed a script is, the more variants it has (Riesbeck & Schank, 1989) and hence the more likely it can match a particular clinical situation.

The physician who knows a patient may die will not necessarily use an "end-of-life" script. That script may not be developed enough to be activated or may not be strong enough to prevail against competing scripts. The nearness of death may simply increase the intensity with which the physician applies an available script for taking care of illness, or the desperation of the search for just the right solution within one's large collection of life-preserving scripts, rather than causing a transition to an end-of-life script.

How Can Physicians' Behavior Be Changed?

From the perspective of applying psychology to improve medical decision making, we suggest that the attempts to change end-of-life care (The SUPPORT Principal Investigators, 1995) and the management of sore throats (Poses et al., 1995) should have explicitly considered the scripts physicians use when making decisions. Neither study explicitly aimed to teach the physicians scripts that carry out better decision strategies or to increase their use of scripts that they already know but have not been using. To change physicians' behavior, it is necessary to understand and change the cognitive representations (scripts, cases, or rules) that organize their knowledge of what is, what to do, and what outcomes to expect. An attempt to improve script-mediated physician behavior needs to be based on an explicit understanding of such scripts and a theory of how they can be changed. In this section, we will sketch how this approach could be applied to the problem of end-of-life decisions.

Proposal for How to Change Physicians' Scripts

Based on the theory that physician behavior depends on learned scripts, we propose that the following five steps are needed to ensure the success of an attempt to improve medical decision making in a particular setting.

1. Discover the physicians' particular decision-making scripts, and understand how their use is rewarded and how they compete with each other in this context.
2. Analyze the scripts and the situation to see how the unsatisfactory outcomes are produced. How would the script and/or the situation need to be different in order to lead to better outcomes?
3. Develop new scripts and/or new ways for the system to work so that a physician using those scripts in this situation would make satisfactory decisions.
4. Test to verify that the redesigned scripts and situations can work.
5. Implement a change by explicitly training all relevant people to use the new scripts, along with needed system changes.

It may be possible to change medical practices without explicitly attending to all these steps. But following the steps would either accomplish the desired change or else make it evident long before the implementation stage that it was not going to work. We now review what would be involved in systematically applying this approach to end-of-life decision making.

1. *Study existing end-of-life decision-making scripts, the motivations for their use, and script conflict resolution processes.* As a starting point for

proposing alternative scripts, research is needed to discover the variety of end-of-life scripts physicians actually have and why they use these scripts. This might be approached through some form of cognitive task analysis (Klein, 1993; Kushniruk, Patel & Fleiszer, 1995; Patel, Kaufman & Arocha, 1995). Physicians could be studied while thinking aloud as they work or respond to hypothetical cases. Comparisons could be made between experts and novices (Abernathy & Hamm, 1994) or between physicians known to handle end-of-life issues aggressively or conservatively. The scope of this research should include discovering the approaches physicians use for handling conflict between several of their own scripts that apply to the situation, as well as conflicts between physicians who have different scripts.

2. *Analyze and critique the existing scripts in context.* The goal of this analysis would be to understand why the scripts physicians currently use do not produce the desired decisions. The analysis may involve formal modeling of the scripts (e.g., stating them as rules). The analysis must take account of the situation in which the script is applied (Gruppen, 1997), for it may be impossible to follow a script if the situation does not support it by providing the conditions necessary for it to be carried out or by rewarding its use. In fact, some analyses have found the source of poor medical outcomes to be in the system rather than in the individuals (Moray, 1994; Vincent & Knox, 1997). The analysis would need to identify not only the weaknesses but also the strengths of the physicians' current scripts and the system's procedures and rewards.

The analysis could be theoretical, comparing how the physicians' scripts actually function with an account of how end-of-life decision making should be done. It could also be empirical, comparing the scripts of physicians who handle end-of-life decisions differently. For example, it might be found that the scripts of physicians who use intensive intervention in the last days of life less frequently are more complicated or have the character of a *metascript* (that is, they refer to the existence of other scripts). The contrasted physicians' scripts might differ in content, such as whether they explicitly include early discussion of death with the patient and family (Lynn, Harrell, Cohn, Wagner & Connors, 1997), or marshall support from the staff, or include steps to provide the family with time to process grief, guilt, and regret.

3. *Design better scripts.* We assume that the best way to improve end-of-life decision making is explicitly to teach physicians to follow a script that addresses how to support the end-of-life process. The desired script must produce satisfactory decisions when used under the conditions in

which physicians actually must make such decisions. If such a script cannot be found (in use by some physicians), then it will be necessary to design one. The previous analysis would identify elements to be used in the design process. Such a redesign cannot be adequate unless a script that produces the desired decisions can win the competition with other scripts and control behavior in this clinical situation. The physician must find the script rewarding to use. Because of the important role of the context, it may be necessary to redesign the script and the situation simultaneously.

At this point, of course, we do not know the best script. Logically, it should include methods for gathering information about the patient's preferences and about the prognosis. It should promote the widely held value that there is a good way to die, which is prevented by futile attempts to prolong life. It should have some sort of decision rule, which may or may not involve strategies we have discussed such as (1) evaluating the expected utility of the options (continue or cease life support), (2) comparing the current prognosis to the patient's threshold, or (3) comparing the patient to a set of prototypical cases and doing what was done in those cases. If a decision rule that requires information about the patient's preferences or prognosis were recommended, then it would be necessary to plan to modify the system in which the physician practices so that survival probability and patient utility information was available.

New scripts would need to be worked out for each actor, not just the doctor. For example, if physicians are going to be trained to pay attention to nurses' information, then nurses must also be trained to produce good information. Therefore, the analysis would need to identify all the people who control the decision, and the design phase would need to ensure that they all had scripts that, when working together, would produce the desired decisions. Recent efforts that emphasized considering the whole system have met with success (Berwick, 1996; Berwick, Godfrey & Roessner, 1990). Although these projects did not explicitly address individuals' decision-making scripts, the organizational change process provided an opportunity for existing scripts to be analyzed in detail and new scripts to be learned.

4. *Test the feasibility of the redesigned script*. It is essential that work be done to verify that it is possible for physicians to learn and apply any proposed script in multiple real-world contexts. Can the typical individual learn the script? Can the script prevail against the competitors? Can it be applied in various contexts, such as hospitals, hospices, and nursing

homes? Can required new procedures be implemented in the system? Can use of the new script and the new procedures be sustained over time? These feasibility tests would be similar in scale to the "Plan-Do-Study-Act cycles" advocated for quality improvement efforts (Berwick, 1998). Measurements used in such a test should include observations to verify that the desired scripts are being learned and are chosen over their competitors, as well as observations on whether physicians who learn the scripts change their behavior as expected. If the scripts cannot be learned, if physicians and others cannot be motivated to follow them, or if they have no effect, it would be risky to proceed with a large-scale implementation (Lo, 1995).

5. *Implement the script through training in its use.* Once a workable script has been identified, implementation requires a feasible organizational change program to train all the relevant people in an institution to use it. It is essential to have hospital leaders actively support such a program (Blumenthal, 1993); those institutions with a good working relationship between doctors and administrators tend to adopt new guidelines successfully (Sonnad & Matuszewski, 1996). The program would need not only to teach the target script, but also to provide sufficient practice so that the script can gain control of behavior in the face of conflicting scripts. The goal of this training would be to ensure that the new script will come quickly to mind, that the physicians can follow it accurately and confidently, and that they will be able to use it in a variety of situations in the face of competing scripts.

There are a variety of techniques for instructing in the content of scripts and for motivating their use. Successful training would not require the learner or the trainer to know the technical psychological vocabulary ("we are learning a new script"). One approach is to couch the information in the form of stories or narratives (Ryan-Wenger & Lee, 1997; Smith, Hamrick & Anspaugh, 1981), particularly narratives that reflect the contexts of practice (Gruppen, 1997). In a computerized simulation for teaching students about ethical decision making, on a CD-ROM (Martin, Reese, Brown & Baros-Johnson, 1997), the case on end-of-life decision making has an example of explicitly teaching a script. The consultant recommends a sequence of steps a doctor could take in the conversation with the wife of a dying man, with justifications for each step and things to do in case of contingencies. Lo (1995) offered many useful suggestions for organizational change that would affect clinicians' scripts. These include: have case management meetings regarding individual patients; recognize clinicians who provide outstanding end-of-life care; have respected senior physicians give conferences on how to discuss the prognosis with patients, elicit their concerns and preferences for care, and negotiate a mutually acceptable plan of care; have a physician noted for communication skills accompany other physicians when they discuss life-sustaining interventions with patients; and give individual feedback to physicians on their performance (Lo, 1995).

Guidelines (algorithms, flowcharts, or practice patterns) are a tool frequently used in communicating the content of a recommended medical practice. However, as we showed earlier, promulgating complete sets of explicit rules has often not changed behavior as much as expected (Wolff et al., 1998). Training people to use a script requires more than giving them paper copies of the specification of the strategy. Steps must be taken to ensure that people learn it, to support them in the practice necessary to master it (Gemson et al., 1995), and to reward their use of the script on an ongoing basis (Harris, Fry, Jarman & Woodman, 1985).

It may seem excessive to train medical practitioners (Howard, Gaba, Fish, Yang & Sarnquist, 1992) with an approach as elaborate as that used to train airline pilots (Helmreich & Wilhelm, 1991) and military units (Cannon-Bowers, Tannenbaum, Salas & Volpe, 1995). Our society cannot afford this degree of deliberateness for all desired changes in medical practices. Some changes don't seem to need such a deliberate approach (Green & Mehr, 1997). It might be possible to shortcut the process yet accomplish desired changes. For example, possibly the formal description of existing scripts could be skipped. Perhaps the strategy of a physician who is judged to have good results could be adopted, avoiding a full analysis to identify the best strategy. The small-scale testing approach (Berwick, 1998) could be applied, and changes could be adopted in subsets of an organization with the hope that, if successful, others will adopt them later. But if a nonoptimal behavior resists change interventions designed using a more intuitive approach, we would recommend the approach outlined previously, based on the psychological model of how the physician behaves that we have summarized as the script metaphor.

V. Conclusion

We hope this review of attempts to use decision theoretic ideas to improve physicians' decision-making behavior has given psychologists and physicians ideas for research projects and intervention approaches.

There have been relatively few direct tests of whether decision theory–relevant information can improve medical decision making. While some attempts have been unsuccessful, the possible approaches have not been exhausted.

We presented two unsuccessful attempts to improve physicians' decision making by providing more accurate probability information. These studies assumed that physicians keep track of a probability for their patient (that the patient has streptococcal pharyngitis in the first example; that the patient will die in the second), compare it to a threshold probability, and act if the patient's probability exceeds that threshold. The threshold theory may be a good prescription, but evidently it was a poor description.

It would be an error to conclude from these studies that it is futile to support physicians' use of a decision theoretic strategy, such as the probability threshold strategy or a subjective expected utility strategy. Our interpretation of these studies, on the contrary, suggests that the interventions were not decision theoretic enough. Although some information that a decision theoretic strategy could use was provided, the studies did not ensure that the physicians knew how to apply such a strategy to the information. Additionally, the information in one study was not sufficient for any particular decision theoretic decision rule (neither subjective expected utility nor threshold) to recommend a decision. Adding information without an organizing principle only creates confusion. It would have been possible, however, to provide the organizing principle, in the form of a strategy for utilizing the information provided, or a tool which applies the strategy to the information for the physician. This perspective leads to the conclusion that if only the decision theoretic improvement had been better, then physicians would have used it.

While we have proposed that physicians faced with sore throats or end-of-life decisions seldom use scripts that overtly follow a threshold strategy, the question of what they actually do is obviously a matter for research to determine. Those who would improve medical decision making must take account of the complex scripts which guide physicians' decision making. This has important implications for any attempt to improve medical decision making, whether or not it be through the application of decision theoretic concepts. While it seems axiomatic to suggest that changing behavior requires changing scripts, the art and science of changing physicians' scripts have not yet been developed.

References

Abernathy, C. M., & Hamm, R. M. (1994). *Surgical Scripts.* Philadelphia: Hanley and Belfus.

Abernathy, C. M., & Hamm, R. M. (1995). *Surgical Intuition.* Philadelphia: Hanley and Belfus.

Adams, I. D., Chan, M., Clifford, P. C., Cooke, W. M., Dallos, V., de Dombal, F. T., Edwards, M. H., Hancock, D. M., Hewett, D. J., McIntyre, N., Somerville, P. G., Spiegelhalter, D. J., Wellwood, J., & Wilson, D. H. (1996). Computer aided diagnosis of acute abdominal pain: A multicentre study. *Br Med J, 293,* 800–804.

Ahn, W.-K., Brewer, W. F., & Mooney, R. J. (1992). Schema acquisition from a single example. *J Exp Psychol, 18,* 391–412.

Anderson, J. R. (1990). *Cognitive Psychology and Its Implications* (2nd ed.). New York: W. H. Freeman.

Anderson, J. R. (1993). *Rules of the Mind.* Hillsdale, NJ: Erlbaum.

Balas, E. A., Austin, S. M., Mitchell, J. A., Ewigman, B. G., Bopp, K. D., & Brown, G. D. (1996). The clinical value of computerized information services: A review of 98 randomized clinical trials. *Arch Fam Med, 5,* 271–278.

Balzer, W. K., Doherty, M. E., & O'Connor, R. O. (1989). The effects of cognitive feedback on performance. *Psychol Bull, 106,* 410–433.

Berg, A. O. (1996). Clinical practice guideline panels: Personal experience. *J Am Board Fam Pract, 9,* 366–370.

Berwick, D. M. (1996). A primer on leading the improvement of systems. *BMJ, 312,* 619–622.

Berwick, D. M. (1998). Developing and testing changes in delivery of care. *Ann Intern Med, 128,* 651–656.

Berwick, D. M., Godfrey, A. B., & Roessner, J. (1990). *Curing Health Care: New Strategies for Quality Improvement.* San Francisco: Jossey-Bass.

Blumenthal, D. (1993). Total quality management and physicians' clinical decisions. *JAMA, 269,* 2775–2778.

Callahan, C. M., Dittus, R. S., & Tierney, W. M. (1996). Primary care physicians' medical decision making for late-life depression. *J Gen Intern Med, 11,* 218–225.

Cannon-Bowers, J. A., Tannenbaum, S. I., Salas, E., & Volpe, C. E. (1995). Defining team competencies and establishing team training requirements. In R. Guzzo & E. Salas (Eds.), *Team Effectiveness and Decision Making in Organizations* (pp. 333–380). San Francisco: Jossey Bass.

Carter, B. L., Butler, C. D., Rogers, J. C., & Holloway, R. L. (1993). Evaluation of physician decision making with the use of prior probabilities and a decision-analysis model. *Arch Fam Med, 2,* 529–534.

Cebul, R. D., & Poses, R. M. (1986). The comparative cost-effectiveness of statistical decision rules and experienced physicians in pharyngitis management. *JAMA, 256,* 3353–3357.

Christensen-Szalanski, J. J. J., & Bushyhead, J. B. (1981). Physicians' use of probabilistic information in a real clinical setting. *J Exp Psychol, 7,* 928–935.

Clancy, C. M., Cebul, R. D., & Williams, S. V. (1988). Guiding individual decisions: A randomized, controlled trial of decision analysis. *Am J Med, 84,* 283–288.

Cohen, M. S. (1993). Three paradigms for viewing decision biases. In G. A. Klein,

J. Orasanu, R. Calderwood, & C. E. Zsambok (Eds.), *Decision Making in Action: Models and Methods* (pp. 36–50). Norwood, NJ: Ablex Publishing Corporation.

Cook, D. J., Greengold, N. L., Ellrodt, A. G., & Weingarten, S. R. (1997). The relation between systematic reviews and practice guidelines. *Ann Intern Med, 127*, 210–216.

Cooksey, R. W. (1996). *Judgment Analysis: Theory, Methods, and Applications.* San Diego, CA: Academic Press.

de Dombal, F. T., Leaper, D. J., Staniland, J. R., McCann, A. P., & Horrocks, J. C. (1972). Computer-aided diagnosis of acute abdominal pain. *BMJ, 2*, 9–13.

Doherty, M. E., & Balzer, W. K. (1988). Cognitive feedback. In B. Bremer & C. R. B. Joyce (Eds.), *Human Judgment: The SJT View* (pp. 163–197). Amsterdam: North Holland Elsevier.

Doherty, M. E., & Kurz, E. M. (1996). Social judgment theory. *Thinking and Reasoning, 2*, 109–140.

Eisenberg, J. M., & Hershey, J. C. (1983). Derived thresholds – determining the diagnostic probabilities at which clinician initiate testing and treatment. *Med Decis Making, 3*, 135–168.

Eisenberg, J. M., Schumacher, H. R., Davidson, P. K., & Kaufman, L. (1984). Usefulness of synovial fluid analysis in the evaluation of joint effusions: Use of threshold analysis and likelihood ratios to assess a diagnostic test. *Arch Intern Med, 144*, 715–719.

Elixhauser, A., Halpern, M., Schmier, J., & Luce, B. R. (1997). Health care CBA and CEA from 1991 to 1996: An updated bibliography. *Med Care, 36*, MS1–MS9.

Elstein, A. S., Shulman, L. S., & Sprafka, S. A. (1978). *Medical Problem Solving: An Analysis of Clinical Reasoning.* Cambridge, MA: Harvard University Press.

Fahey, T., & Peters, T. J. (1997). Clinical guidelines and the management of hypertension: A between-practice and guideline comparison. *Br J Gen Pract, 47*, 729–730.

Fisch, H.-U., Hammond, K. R., Joyce, C. R. B., & O'Reilly, M. (1981). An experimental study of the clinical judgment of general physicians in evaluating and prescribing for depression. *Br J Psychiatry, 138*, 100–109.

Fong, G. T., Krantz, D. H., & Nisbett, R. E. (1986). The effects of statistical training on thinking about everyday problems. *Cogn Psychol, 18*, 253–292.

Freeborn, D. K., Shye, D., Mullooly, J. P., Eraker, S., & Romeo, J. (1997). Primary care physicians' use of lumbar spine imaging tests: Effects of guidelines and practice pattern feedback. *J Gen Intern Med, 12*, 619–625.

Gemson, D. H., Ashford, A. R., Dickey, L. L., Raymore, S. H., Roberts, J. W., Ehrlich, M. H., Foster, B. G., Ganz, M. L., Moon-Howard, J., Field, L. S., Bennett, B. A., Elinson, J., & Francis, C. K. (1995). Putting prevention into practice: Impact of a multifaceted physician education program on preventive services in the inner city. *Arch Intern Med, 155*, 2210–2216.

Gigerenzer, G. (1996). The psychology of good judgment: Frequency formats and simple algorithms. *Med Decis Making, 16*, 273–280.

Gigerenzer, G., & Hoffrage, U. (1995). How to improve Bayesian reasoning without instruction: Frequency formats. *Psychol Rev, 102*, 684–704.

Gonzalez-Vallejo, C., Sorum, P. C., Stewart, T. R., Chessare, J. B., & Mumpower, J. L. (1998). Physicians' diagnostic judgments and treatment decisions for acute otitis media in children. *Med Decis Making, 18*, 149–162.

Granata, A. V., & Hillman, A. L. (1998). Competing practice guidelines: Using cost-effectiveness analysis to make optimal decisions. *Ann Intern Med, 128,* 56–63.

Green, L. A., & Mehr, D. R. (1997). What alters physicians' decisions to admit to the coronary care unit? *J Fam Pract, 45,* 219–226.

Gruppen, L. D. (1997). Implications of cognitive research for ambulatory care education. *Academic Med, 72,* 117–120.

Hamm, R. M., Hicks, R. J., & Bemben, D. A. (1996a). Antibiotics and respiratory infections: Are patients more satisfied when expectations are met? *J Fam Pract, 43,* 56–62.

Hamm, R. M., Hicks, R. J., & Bemben, D. A. (1996b). Antibiotics and respiratory infections: Do antibiotic prescriptions improve outcomes? *J Oklahoma State Med Assoc, 89,* 267–274.

Hammond, K. R. (1996). *Human Judgment and Social Policy: Irreducible Uncertainty, Inevitable Error, Unavoidable Injustice.* New York: Oxford University Press.

Hansen, D. E., & Helgeson, J. G. (1996). The effects of statistical training on choice heuristics in choice under uncertainty. *J Behav Decis Making, 9,* 41–57.

Harris, C. M., Fry, J., Jarman, B., & Woodman, W. (1985). Prescribing – a case for prolonged treatment. *J R Coll Gen Pract, 35,* 284–287.

Helmreich, R. L., & Wilhelm, J. A. (1991). Outcomes of crew resource management training. *Int J Aviat Psychol, 1,* 287–300.

Hofmann, J. C., Wenger, N. S., Davis, R. B., Teno, J., Connors, A. F., Jr., Desbiens, N., Lynn, J., Phillips, R. S., & the SUPPORT Investigators. (1997). Patient preferences for communication with physicians about end-of-life decisions. *Ann Intern Med, 127,* 1–12.

Howard, S. K., Gaba, D. M., Fish, K. J., Yang, G., & Sarnquist, F. H. (1992). Anesthesia crisis resource management training: Teaching anesthesiologists to handle critical incidents. *Aviat, Space, Environ Med, 63,* 763–770.

Hunt, D. L., Haynes, R. B., Hanna, S. E., & Smith, K. (1998). Effects of computer-based clinical decision support systems on physician performance and patient outcomes: A systematic review. *JAMA, 280,* 1339–1346.

Johnston, M. E., Langton, K. B., Haynes, R. B., & Mathieu, A. (1994). Effects of computer-based clinical decision support systems on clinician performance and patient outcome: A critical appraisal of research. *Ann Intern Med, 120,* 135–142.

Kahneman, D., Slovic, P., & Tversky, A. (Eds.). (1982). *Judgment under Uncertainty: Heuristics and Biases.* New York: Cambridge University Press.

Kirwan, J. R., Chaput de Saintonge, D. M., Joyce, C. R. B., & Currey, H. L. F. (1983). Clinical judgment analysis: Practical application in rheumatoid arthritis. *Br J Rheumatol, 22,* 18–23.

Kirwan, J. R., & Currey, H. L. F. (1984). Clinical judgment in rheumatoid arthritis: IV. Rheumatologists' assessments of disease remain stable over long periods. *Ann Rheum Dis, 43,* 695–697.

Klatzky, R. L., Geiwitz, J., & Fischer, S. C. (1994). Using statistics in clinical practice: A gap between training and application. In M. S. Bogner (Ed.), *Human Error in Medicine* (pp. 123–140). Hillsdale, NJ: Erlbaum.

Klayman, J., & Brown, K. (1993). Debias the environment instead of the judge: An alternative approach to reducing error in diagnostic (and other) judgment. *Cognition, 49,* 97–122.

Klein, G. A. (1993). A recognition-primed decision (RPD) model of rapid decision making. In G. A. Klein, J. Orasanu, R. Calderwood, & C. E. Zsambok (Eds.), *Decision Making in Action: Models and Methods* (pp. 138–147). Norwood, NJ: Ablex.

Knaus, W. A., Harrell, F. E., Jr., Lynn, J., Goldman, L., Phillips, R. S., Connors, A. F. Jr., Dawson, N. V., Fulkerson, W. J., Jr., Califf, R. M., Desbiens, N., & the SUPPORT Investigators. (1995). The SUPPORT prognostic model: Objective estimates of survival for seriously ill hospitalized adults. *Ann Intern Med, 122,* 191–203.

Knaus, W. A., Wagner, D. P., Draper, E. A., Zimmerman, J. E., Bergner, M., Bastos, P. G., Sirio, C. A., Murphy, D. J., Lotring, T., Damiano, A., & Harrell, F. E., Jr. (1991). The APACHE III prognostic system: Risk prediction of hospital mortality for critically ill hospitalized adults. *Chest, 100,* 1619–1636.

Koedinger, K. R., Anderson, J. R., Hadley, W. H., & Mark, M. A. (1995). *Intelligent tutoring goes to school in the big city.* Paper presented at the 7th World Conference on Artificial Intelligence in Education, Washington, DC.

Kushniruk, A., Patel, V., & Fleiszer, D. (1995). *Analysis of medical decision making: A cognitive perspective on medical informatics.* Paper presented at the Annual Symposium on Computer Applications in Medical Care.

Ledley, R. S., & Lusted, L. B. (1959). Reasoning foundations of medical diagnosis. *Science, 130,* 9–21.

Lee, T. H., Pearson, S. D., Johnson, P. A., Garcia, T. B., Weisberg, M. C., Guadagnoli, E., Cook, E. F., & Goldman, L. (1995). Failure of information as an intervention to modify clinical management: A time-series trial in patients with acute chest pain. *Ann Intern Med, 122,* 434–437.

Lesgold, A. M. (1984). Human skill in a computerized society: Complex skills and their acquisition. *Behav Res Methods, Instruments, Computers, 16,* 79–87.

Lesgold, A. M. (1988). Problem solving. In R. J. Sternberg & E. E. Smith (Eds.), *The Psychology of Human Thought* (pp. 188–213). New York: Cambridge University Press.

Lo, B. (1995). Improving care near the end of life: Why is it so hard? *JAMA, 274,* 1634–1636.

Lomas, J., Anderson, G. M., Domnick-Pierre, K., Vayda, E., Enkin, M. W., & Hannah, W. J. (1989). Do practice guidelines guide practice? The effect of a consensus statement on the practice of physicians. *N Engl J Med, 321,* 1306–1311.

Lusted, L. B. (1991). The clearing "haze": A view from my window. *Med Decis Making, 11,* 76–87.

Lynn, J., Harrell, F., Jr., Cohn, F., Wagner, D., & Connors, A. F., Jr. (1997). Prognoses of seriously ill hospitalized patients on the days before death: Implications for patient care and public policy. *New Horizons, 5*(1), 56–61.

Martin, R., Reese, A. C., Brown, E. M., & Baros-Johnson, J. (1997). *The Doctor's Dilemma: Essentials of Medical Ethics* (CD-ROM). Tampa, FL: Gold Standard Multimedia.

McCormick, K. A., Cummings, M. A., & Kovner, C. (1997). The role of the Agency for Health Care Policy and Research (AHCPR) in improving outcomes of care. *Nurs Clin North Am, 32,* 521–542.

McDonald, C. J. (1996). Medical heuristics: The silent adjudicators of clinical practice. *Ann Intern Med, 124*(1 Pt 1'), 56–62.

McIsaac, W. J., & Goel, V. (1998). Effect of an explicit decision-support tool on decisions to prescribe antibiotics for sore throat. *Med Decis Making, 18,* 220–228.

McNeil, B. J., Keeler, E., & Adelstein, S. J. (1975). Primer on certain elements of medical decision making. *N Engl J Med, 293,* 211–215.

McNutt, R. A., & Selker, H. P. (1988). How did the acute ischemic heart disease predictive instrument reduce unnecessary coronary care unit admissions? *Med Decis Making, 8,* 90–94.

Moray, N. (1994). Error reduction as a systems problem. In M. S. Bogner (Ed.), *Human Error in Medicine* (pp. 67–91). Hillsdale, NJ: Erlbaum.

Neufeld, V. R., & Barrows, H. S. (1974). The "McMaster Philosophy": An approach to medical education. *J Med Educ, 49,* 1040–1050.

Nisbett, R. E., Fong, G. T., Lehman, D. R., & Cheng, P. W. (1987). Teaching reasoning. *Science, 238,* 625–631.

Norman, G. R., & Shannon, S. I. (1998). Effectiveness of instruction in critical appraisal (evidence-based medicine) skills: A critical appraisal. *Can Med Assoc J, 158,* 177–181.

Patel, V. L., Kaufman, D. R., & Arocha, J. F. (1995). Steering through the murky waters of a scientific conflict: Situated and symbolic models of clinical cognition. *Artif Intell Med, 7*(5), 418–438.

Pauker, S. G., & Kassirer, J. P. (1980). The threshold approach to clinical decision making. *N Engl J Med, 302,* 1109–1117.

Poses, R. M., Cebul, R. D., & Centor, R. M. (1988). Evaluating physicians' probabilistic judgments. *Med Decis Making, 8,* 233–240.

Poses, R. M., Cebul, R. D., Collins, M., & Fager, S. S. (1985). The accuracy of experienced physicians' probability estimates for patients with sore throats. *JAMA, 254,* 925–929.

Poses, R. M., Cebul, R. D., & Wigton, R. S. (1995). You can lead a horse to water: Improving physicians' knowledge of probabilities may not affect their decisions. *Med Decis Making, 15,* 65–75.

Poses, R. M., Cebul, R. D., Wigton, R. S., Centor, R. M., Collins, M., & Fleischli, G. (1992). Controlled trial using computerized feedback to improve physicians' diagnostic judgments. *Academic Med, 67,* 345–347.

Power, E. J., & Eisenberg, J. M. (1998). Are we ready to use cost-effectiveness analysis in health care decision-making? A health services research challenge for clinicians, patients, health care systems, and public policy. *Med Care, 36,* MS10–MS17.

Pozen, M. W., D'Agostino, R. B., Selker, H. P., Sytkowski, P. A., & Hood, W. B. (1984). A predictive instrument to improve coronary-care-unit admission practices in acute ischemic heart disease: A prospective multicenter clinical trial. *N Engl J Med, 310*(20), 1273–1278.

Riesbeck, C. K., & Schank, R. C. (1989). *Inside Case-Based Reasoning.* Hillsdale, NJ: Erlbaum.

Ryan-Wenger, N. A., & Lee, J. E. M. (1997). The clinical reasoning case study: A powerful teaching tool. *Nurse Pract, 22*(5), 66–70.

Saver, B. G., Taylor, T. R., Treadwell, J. R., & Cole, W. G. (1997). Do physicians do as they say? The case of mammography. *Arch Fam Med, 6,* 543–548.

Schmidt, H. G., Norman, G. R., & Boshuizen, H. P. A. (1990). A cognitive perspective on medical expertise: Theory and implications. *Academic Med, 65,* 611–621.

Schwartz, W. B., Gorry, G. A., Kassirer, J. P., & Essig, A. (1973). Decision analysis and clinical judgment. *Am J Med, 55*, 459–472.

Shortliffe, E. H. (1987). Computer programs to support clinical decision making. *JAMA, 258*, 61–66.

Slawson, D. C., Shaughnessy, A. F., & Bennett, J. H. (1994). Becoming a medical information master: Feeling good about not knowing everything. *Fam Pract, 38*(5), 505–513.

Slawson, D. C., Shaughnessy, A. F., Ebell, M. H., & Barry, H. C. (1997). Mastering medical information and the role of POEMs – patient-oriented evidence that matters. *J Fam Pract, 45*, 195–196.

Slovic, P., Rorer, L. G., & Hoffman, P. J. (1971). Analyzing the use of diagnostic signs. *Invest Radiol, 6*, 18–26.

Smith, D. L., Hamrick, M. H., & Anspaugh, D. J. (1981). Decision story strategy: A practical approach for teaching decision making. *J School Health, 51*, 637–640.

Sonnad, S. S., & Matuszewski, K. A. (1996). *Technology Assessment – Case Study: Implementing Radiopaque Contrast Media Guidelines*. Oak Brook, IL: Clinical Practice Advancement Center, University Health System Consortium Services Corporation.

Sox, H. C., Jr., Blatt, M. A., Higgins, M. C., & Marton, K. I. (1988). *Medical Decision Making*. Boston: Butterworths.

Stiell, I. G., Greenberg, G. H., Wells, G. A., McDowell, I., Cwinn, A. A., Smith, N. A., Cacciotti, T. F., & Sivilotti, M. L. (1996). Prospective validation of a decision rule for the use of radiography in acute knee injuries. *JAMA, 275*, 611–615.

Stiell, I. G., Wells, G. A., Hoag, R. H., Sivilotti, M. L. A., Cacciotti, T. F., Verbeek, P. R., Greenway, K. T., McDowell, I., Cwinn, A. A., Greenberg, G. H., Nichol, G., & Michael, J. A. (1997). Implementation of the Ottawa Knee Rule for the use of radiography in acute knee injuries. *JAMA, 278*, 2075–2079.

Suarez-Almazor, M. E., Belseck, E., Russell, A. S., & Mackel, J. V. (1997). Use of lumbar radiographs for the early diagnosis of low back pain: Proposed guidelines would increase utilization. *JAMA, 277*, 1782–1786.

Sutton, G. C. (1989). Computer-aided diagnosis: A review. *Br J Surg, 76*, 82–85.

Tape, T. G., Kripal, J., & Wigton, R. S. (1992). Comparing methods of learning clinical prediction from case simulations. *Med Decis Making, 12*, 213–221.

Tape, T. G., Steele, D., & Wigton, R. S. (1995). Learning to differentiate bacterial from viral meningitis: A non-linear judgment task with case simulations and feedback. *Med Decis Making, 15*, 419.

The SUPPORT Principal Investigators. (1995). A controlled trial to improve care for seriously ill hospitalized patients: The Study to Understand Prognoses and Preferences for Outcomes and Risks of Treatments (SUPPORT). *JAMA, 274*, 1591–1598.

Tierney, W. M., Fitzgerald, J., McHenry, R., Roth, B. J., Psaty, B., Stump, D. L., & Anderson, F. K. (1986). Physicians' estimates of the probability of myocardial infarction in emergency room patients with chest pain. *Med Decis Making, 6*, 12–17.

Vincent, C., & Knox, E. (1997). Clinical risk modification, quality, and patient safety: Interrelationships, problems, and future potential. *Best Practices Benchmarking Healthcare, 2*, 221–226.

Weingarten, S., Stone, E., Hayward, R., Tunis, S., Pelter, M., Huang, H., &

Kristopaitis. R. (1995). The adoption of preventive care practice guidelines by primary care physicians: Do actions match intentions? *J Gen Intern Med, 10*, 138–144.

Weinstein, M. C., & Feinberg, H. V. (1980). *Clinical Decision Analysis.* Philadelphia: W. B. Saunders.

Wellwood, J., Johannessen, S., & Spiegelhalter, D. J. (1992). How does computer-aided diagnosis improve the management of acute abdominal pain? *Ann R Coll Surg Engl, 74*, 40–46.

Wensing, M., van der Weijden, T., & Grol, R. (1998). Implementing guidelines and innovations in general practice: Which interventions are effective? *Br J Gen Pract, 48*, 991–997.

Wigton, R. S. (1988). Use of linear models to analyze physicians' decisions. *Medi Decis Making, 8*, 241–252.

Wigton, R. S. (1996). Social judgment theory and medical judgment. *Thinking Reasoning, 2*, 175–190.

Wigton, R. S., Hoellerich, V. L., & Patil, K. D. (1986). How physicians use clinical information in diagnosing pulmonary embolism: An application of conjoint analysis. *Med Decis Making, 6*, 2–11.

Wigton, R. S., Patil, K. D., & Hoellerich, V. L. (1986). The effect of feedback in learning clinical diagnosis. *J Med Educ, 61*, 816–822.

Winterfeld, D. V., & Edwards, W. (1986). *Decision Analysis and Behavioral Research.* New York: Cambridge University Press.

Wolff, M., Bower, D. J., Marbella, A. M., & Casanova, J. E. (1998). U.S. family physicians' experiences with practice guidelines. *Fam Med, 30*, 117–121.

Worrall, G., Freake, D., & Chaulk, P. (1997). The effects of clinical practice guidelines on patient outcomes in primary care: A systematic review. *Can Med Assoc J, 156*, 1705–1712.

Zarin, D. A., & Pauker, S. G. (1984). Decision analysis as a basis for medical decision making: The tree of Hippocrates. *J Med Philos, 9*, 181–213.

Index

Abdellaoui, M., 93
abdominal pain, and computer-aided diagnosis, 389
abortion, and prenatal testing, 260
absorbing state, and Markov processes, 44
accuracy analysis: baseline assumptions, 213–14; combining of predictions, 241; decomposition studies, 231–5; definitions of terms, 243–7; formulas and symbols, 247–9; lens model analysis, 235–7, 242; measures of, 214–26, 242; methodological issues, 226–8; overview of, 211–14; potential modifiers of, 237–41; studies of physicians, 228–31
Acton, J. J. P., 323
adaptation, and health states, 302
adjusted normalized discrimination index (ANDI), 225
administrative and billing systems, and cost-effectiveness analysis, 172
advanced directives: bioethics, 256; patient education, 338
adverse reactions, and clinical drug trials, 118
African Americans, and utility ratings for health states, 322
age, and decisions to withdraw life support, 262–3
Agency for Health Care Policy and Research, 389
aggregated approach, to lens model analyses, 236
AIDS (acquired immunodeficiency syndrome): patient empowerment, 336; progression of and level of CD4 cells,

52–4; rate of progression from HIV infection to, 41, 50
AI/Rheum system, 373
alcohol-induced hypoglycemia, 278
Alzheimer's disease, 315–16
AMA Family Medical Guide, 344
anesthesiology, 187, 202
angina, and patient preferences, 298, 300, 301f
antibiotherapy management program, 374–5
antibiotics: cost-effectiveness analysis, 171–2; decision tree and prescription of, 25; intervention to reduce overprescription of, 396–401
anticoagulant therapy, and atrial fibrillation, 13–14, 151–6
APACHE II model, 241
APOE testing, 315–16
Arden syntax, 375
Arkes, H. R., 185–6, 188, 194–5, 205
ARPANET (computer network), 345
artificial intelligence, 15
artificial judges, 213
Asch, David A., 177, 262
Ascher, W., 153–4
Asian flu, 189
association-based decision errors, 205
asymmetric funnel plots, 127–8
atrial fibrillation (AF), and anticoagulant therapy, 13–14, 151–6
attention-focusing tools, and computer-assisted clinical decision support, 368–9
attraction effect, and choice options, 194

423